Germany Rediscovers America

FRIEDRICH SCHOENEMANN, THE FATHER OF *Amerikakunde*,
AMERICAN STUDIES IN GERMANY

Germany
Rediscovers America

Earl R. Beck

1968

Florida State University Press
Tallahassee, Florida

A Florida State University Press Book

CONTENTS

PREFACE

"WAD SOME POWER the giftie gie us, to see oursels as ithers see us." The old familiar lines of Robert Burns express a frequent longing of Americans. We want to know what others think of us. Many historical studies have been written based on the travel literature of foreign observers. We Americans, who are not always sure ourselves of what makes us tick, of the real character of our civilization and way of life, have been vitally interested in the views of observers from abroad. Much of the literature of the period prior to 1914, however, reflected the growing pains of a civilization in flux, of a way of life still in process of formation. Too little attention has been given to the views of those travelers who, in the period after the First World War, visited this country in full awareness that they were observing a new colossus, a new world power, a new civilization whose universal impact was inescapable.

Of all those who came in the great flood of travelers crossing the ocean after peace had lifted the bars to wartime travel, none were more predisposed to be critical than the Germans. Few of them could suppress their inward hatred for an enemy who had shocked Germans with an unexpected intrusion into a war which, they felt, did not really concern America and in which most Germans still regarded their cause as a just one. This hatred had been heated by press reports of the harsh wartime treatment of Americans of German origin. It was not abated by the circumstances surrounding the Treaty of Versailles, for Germans believed that Americans had betrayed promises of a mild and just peace.

But the hatred of Americans was accompanied by an unwilling respect. There was no doubt in the minds of German travelers that America had been the decisive factor in the defeat of German arms. They came to see the marvels of American *technik* which

ix

had made this possible, the wonders displayed by the world's first "Economic Miracle" (*Wirtschaftswunder*). They came to see the nation which they now regarded as first among the world's great powers.

Those who came were predominantly members of the German intelligentsia. They bore with them the rigidity of a traditional *Weltanschauung*, an ideological approach to life, an approach which made it difficult for them to understand or sympathize with a society dominated by pragmatism. They bore with them many preconceptions and *cliché* points of view. Some of them were travelers who never left home, who paced the traffic-burdened streets of American cities with distaste, who sought in America vestiges of German language groups and German culture and shuddered at the pitiful remnants they found. Many found confirmation of the opinions they had already formed—that America was a "cultureless," "soulless," materialist nation which had nothing really worthwhile to offer the world except the pursuit of the almighty dollar.

Those who found more in America, who discovered not only material but also spiritual values, were in a distinct minority. One of the most puzzling aspects of the Weimar period is the predominance of virulently anti-American literature in the midst of a strong current of "Americanization" in Germany! Clearly the criticisms of the intelligentsia did not convince the masses. In spite of a "bad press" the impact of America on Germany during the Weimar years was a profound one. It was temporarily eclipsed during the Nazi regime only to be restored and reinforced in the post-World War II era.

Today Germany is without doubt "Americanized." German streets differ little from American streets—there is the same bustle of traffic, the same shrill whistle of the policeman, the same shortage of parking places. Germans have their own skyscrapers, their own version of the search for the almighty dollar and the material comforts which accompany it. But little conversation is required to discover that "Americanism" in other forms is still subject to many of the reservations which accompanied it during the Weimar period. For Germans the literature of those days still retains some validity—it represented the first really close view of the United States by their fellow countrymen—it was indeed a kind of "rediscovery" of America. There have, of course, been additions and reinterpretations, especially since World War II. A much larger volume of studies by American authors has been translated into German. There remains, however, a need for fundamental reevaluation.

Yet the accomplishment of this reevaluation poses many problems. Who can rule accurately upon the validity of judgments relating to American national characteristics, cultural accomplishments, or way of life? An individual American cannot claim this right any more than can an individual German. His view of his own country is too limited, too narrow, too personal to allow him to profess competence for this task.

The author has, as a consequence, not sought to set forth a quantitative accounting of the accuracy of the "America books" of the Weimar period and of Bonn. Rather, he has sought, upon a highly subjective basis and with recognition of his own shortcomings, to weave from the myriad-colored threads of these accounts a tapestry of the American civilization seen by these German travelers.

It is clear from the contents of this book that some of these travelers have made a much more favorable impression on the author than have others. The author believes that some travelers are possessed of the ability to achieve a much higher degree of empathy for new scenes and new institutions than are others. He believes that some travelers are much more flexible in their habits and ways of thought than are others. The most essential qualification of a good traveler and observer is self-criticism. He who recognizes his own shortcomings and those of his own nation is best able to assess the strengths and weaknesses of others.

All in all the Germans of the Weimar period had available an unusually extensive selection of materials relating to the United States, but it required study rather than desultory reading for a German of that period to derive from them a reasonably accurate picture of life in this country. There was in Germany a small but dedicated group of scholars who were aware of this fact. They were the pathfinders of a new branch of knowledge, American studies or *Amerikakunde* as it was called. Their work was still in its primitive beginnings when Hitler came to power. It has been immensely strengthened in the post-World War II period but has not yet reached its full maturity. The author hopes that this book may underscore the significance of their work, that it may give Ameri-

cans an indication of the importance of providing for foreign
visitors an opportunity of knowing more than the superficialities
of American civilization, and that it may also suggest to readers
the dangers of overestimating the importance of personal observations of countries and ways of life unfamiliar to the observer.

The definition of "Germany" as used in the title of this book
is subject to debate. The author has used the term in its broadest
sense. Thus he has included a number of works published in
Austria and Switzerland as well as in Germany itself. All of these
contributed to the discussion of American civilization taking place
within Germany during the Weimar period. Some of these, such as
the study of American Protestantism by the Swiss theologian Adolf
Keller, were more widely known than the books written by the
Germans of the Reich itself. Since the basic objective of this volume
has been to sketch the image of the United States displayed to
German readers, a strictly national definition of the word "Germany" would have resulted in distortion.

The author owes myriad debts for assistance in his work on
this volume. The Research Council of the Florida State University provided continuing support for labors stretching from 1959 to
1966, including a research trip to Europe during the summer of
1961 and the provision of a research assistant for the academic
years 1964-65 and 1965-66. To Charles R. Kampfschulte, who filled
this position conscientiously and efficiently, a very large debt of
gratitude must be acknowledged. The work in Europe was aided
by the library staffs at the Zentralbibliothek in Zürich, particularly
Drs. Isler and Bopp; at the Schweizerische Sozialarchiv, particularly
Dr. E. Steinemann; at the Westdeutsche Bibliothek at Marburg,
particularly Dr. Kramm, Fräulein Präel, and Fräulein Rünger;
at the University library at Marburg, the Ernst Reuter Haus in
Berlin, the University library and State Library in Hamburg, and
the State Library in Bremen. Helpful suggestions were provided by
Drs. Ernst Fraenkel, Emil Dovifat, and Karl Dietrich Bracher.
Zürich library work was lightened by the hospitality of Dr. Walter
Deuchler and his family and the natural attractions of Hamburg
were enhanced by the warmth and friendliness of the parents and
uncle of my good friend Elke Frank.

A special debt is owed to the continuing patience and helpfulness of the librarians at Florida State University, particularly
to N. Orwin Rush, Reno Bupp, and to Misses Florence Bethea,

Frances L. Munson, Peggy M. Sutor, Carolyn Dapo, and Mrs. Madeline Hoffman.

My colleagues Weymouth T. Jordan and Donald D. Horward were kind enough to read the manuscript in its entirety. The former's recent Fulbright assignment at Erlangen and the latter's keen feeling for style and organization made their comments of very great value. I am also grateful for the critical reading of the manuscript by Thomas D. Clark, whose work in the area of travel literature has been of outstanding significance, for the many helpful suggestions of James Preu, the editor of the Florida State University Press, and for the proofing of the galleys by my colleague Wallace Reichelt.

The author wishes also to acknowledge and express his gratitude for the following copyright clearances: to the *History of Education Quarterly* for permission to use portions of his article, "The German Discovery of American Education," which appeared in March, 1965; to *The Historian* for permission to use portions of his article, "Friedrich Schönemann, German Americanist," published in May, 1964; to Dr. William M. Brewer and *The Journal of Negro History* for permission to use portions of his article, "German Views of Negro Life in the United States, 1919-1933," published in January, 1963; to George Allen & Unwin, Ltd., for clearance for quotations from Moritz J. Bonn's *The American Adventure*; to Felix Meiner Verlagsbuchhandlung, Hamburg, for quotations from Kuno Francke's *Deutsche Arbeit in Amerika; Erinnerungen*; to Harper & Row, Publishers, Incorporated, for quotations from Count Hermann Keyserling's *America Set Free*; to C. Bertelsmann Verlag for quotations from Hermann Werdermann's *Das religiöse Angesicht Amerikas: Einzeleindrücke und Charakterzüge*; to J. C. B. Mohr Verlag for quotations from Adolf Keller's *Dynamis, Formen und Kräfte des amerikanischen Protestantismus* and Charlotte Lütkens' *Staat und Gesellschaft in Amerika. Zur Soziologie des amerikanischen Kapitalismus*; to Amalthea Verlag for quotations from Emil Müller-Sturmheim's *Ohne Amerika geht es nicht* and Ernst Prosinagg's *Das Antlitz Amerikas. 3 Jahre diplomatische Mission in den U.S.A.*; to W. Kohlhammer G. m. b. H. for quotations from Golo Mann's *Vom Geist Amerikas; eine Einführung in amerikanisches Denken und Handeln im zwanzigsten Jahrhundert*; to S. Fischer Verlag G. m. b. H., Frankfurt/Main, for quotations from Moritz J. Bonn's *Geld und Geist*;

vom Wesen und Werden der amerikanischen Welt and his *"Pros-perity"; Wunderglaube und Wirklichkeit im amerikanischen Wirt-schaftsleben*; Carl Brinkmann's *Demokratie und Erziehung in Amerika*; Heinrich Hauser's *Feldwege nach Chicago*; Manfred Hausmann's *Kleine Liebe zu Amerika. Ein junger Mann schlendert durch die Staaten*; Julius Hirsch's *Das amerikanische Wirtschafts-wunder*; Arthur Holitscher's *Wiedersehn mit Amerika; Die Ver-wandlung der U.S.A.* and his *Amerika Heute und Morgen; Reise-erlebnisse*; and Alfred Kerr's *New York und London, Stätten des Geschicks. Zwanzig Kapitel nach dem Weltkrieg*; to Hawthorn Books, Inc., Publishers, for quotations from Herbert von Borch's *The Unfinished Society*; to Deutsche Verlags-Anstalt G. m. b. H. for quotations from Ernst Jäckh's *Amerika und Wir. Amerikanisch-deutsches Ideenbündnis*, 1929, 1951; from Emil Kimpen's *Die Ausbreitungspolitik der Vereinigten Staaten*; and from Friedrich Schönemann's *Die Vereinigten Staaten von Amerika*; to Verlagshaus Frankfurt Societäts-Drückerei for quotations from Arthur Feiler's *Amerika-Europa. Erfahrungen einer Reise*; to Paul Zsolnay Verlag and Frau Dr. Anna Wyler-Salten for quotations from Felix Salten's *5 Minuten Amerika*; to Verlag Ullstein G. m. b. H. for quotations from Alice Salomon's *Kultur im Werden*; to B. G. Teubner Ver-lagsgesellschaft for quotations from Walther Fischer's *Amerika-nische Prosa. Vom Bürgerkrieg bis auf die Gegenwart (1863-1922)* [Teubner wishes me to state that it expressly retains copyright privileges and permissions with respect to this book]; and to C. Grote'sche Verlagsbuchhandlung for quotations from Gustav Frens-sen's *Briefe aus Amerika*.

Last, but far from least, to a long suffering family who have accepted willingly the many kinds of sacrifices which this work has entailed, my deepest gratitude and love.

Earl R. Beck

Spring, 1967

Chapter I

DISAPPOINTMENT AND DISILLUSION

German Views of the United States before the First World War: "Our America": In 1936 Colin Ross published a book in Germany which he entitled *Unser Amerika,* "Our America." Ross was a famous traveler who had become one of Hitler's principal sources of geographical information.[1] But by the time he published this particular volume, the implications of its title were ridiculous. The German element in the United States was no longer tied in sentiment and loyalty to the land of their origins. However, Ross was merely perpetuating a misconception which dated back to the years prior to World War I. For on the eve of that conflict Germans did, indeed, regard the United States as "Our America." This pleasant feeling of complacency persisted into the early years of the war itself.

In retrospect there was much naïveté and a good deal of provincialism among Germans on the eve of the First World War. The generation which followed that of Bismark was profoundly stirred by the great achievements of unification and the equally great achievements in industrial expansion which followed. There was pride in the strength of the new nation. And even more there was pride in Germany's intellectual accomplishments, a belief in Germany's cultural preeminence. Actually, it was Bismarck's not-too-cultured pragmatism and the businessman's materialism which had raised Germany to the position of a first-rate power. It was something of a self-deception on the part of German intellectuals that they made German *Kultur* the symbol of the new nationalism, that they described their country as "the land of Goethe and Schiller," not as "the land of the Saar, the Ruhr, and the Prussian

[1]See my article, "Colin Ross in South America, 1919-1920," *The Americas,* XVII, No. 1, 53-63 (July, 1960).

1

grenadier." One can only conclude that most German writers turned their eyes away from the mushrooming chimneys and smoky factory towns along the Rhine, that they ignored or sought to ignore the unpleasant accompaniments of modernization and industrialization.

Politically they were similarly uncritical. The great mass of Germans were not dissatisfied with things as they were, did not feel themselves politically oppressed, did not believe there was any design for imperialism in the military preparations made by the State. They did fear a French war of revenge; they did believe in a Slavic menace to Teutonic ideals; and they did believe that England was greatly distressed by Germany's economic competition. There was a broadly held, strongly entrenched sense of complacent self-satisfaction, an unquestioning assumption of the superiority of things German, and a deep-seated fear of a multiplicity of envious neighbors.

As a consequence, Germans were not capable of an objective appraisal of the world outside Germany. They were, to be sure, greatly fascinated by things distant and different. German travelers had touched upon the remotest parts of the world, often with notebooks in hand to record careful observations of things seen. And, indeed, Germans had excelled in their presentation of sociological and anthropological views of remote islands in the Pacific and of backward countries around the world. They had not excelled in their analyses of highly civilized countries, even those close at hand. They were poor psychologists, and they viewed the world about them exclusively from a German frame of reference.

This was true also of their view of the United States. Here a whole line of untested assumptions prevailed. Most prominent was an exaggerated impression of the role of German-Americans in the life of the nation. It was natural that German travelers prior to the First World War should find the status and life of their erstwhile countrymen of greatest interest. It was also natural that their discovery that many German-Americans maintained their adherence to the cultural strengths of the homeland—to a love for German literature and music—led them to ignore the minimal political significance of the group, which had proved less cohesive and aggressive than the Irish-Americans, for example. They were disappointed that German speech rapidly gave way to English, but they were confident that in time German culture would gain superiority over less worthy cultural backgrounds.[2] Then, too, Germans had found an immense lure in the stories of cowboys and Indians, in the romantic but unrealistic West conjured up by the prolific writings of the popular novelist, Karl May.[3] This intensified their impression that the United States still remained a "colonial" area, still largely a backward wilderness region. Some travelers, of course, in the period before the First World War began to savor the strength of an economic giant, to find in America a parallel of the same rapid industrialization taking place in Imperial Germany. Those who did so found American businessmen professing admiration for the Kaiser's leadership and expressing a kind of brotherly spirit in arms which belied critical notes in the "jingo" press.[4] It was little wonder that some Germans even contemplated the possibility of a "Teutonic" alliance of England, Germany, and the United States.[5]

On the whole, therefore, German views of the United States remained roseate, complacent, somewhat patronizing. The events of the First World War were to underscore the superficiality of these views, the gross ignorance of the Germans in respect to the new giant across the Atlantic.

2. *The Shock of the American Entry into the First World War*: The First World War brought many kinds of disappointments and disillusionments to the Germans. The thundering roar of the "guns of August" had begun in an atmosphere of light-hearted optimism, with the expectation of a "fresh and merry" war to be over within a few weeks. The weeks dragged into months and the

[2]This, substantially, is the burden of Karl Lamprecht's *Americana: Reiseeindrücke, Betrachtungen, Geschichtliche Gesamtansicht* (Freiburg i. B., 1906), 146-47. Similar, Hugo Münsterberg, *Aus Deutsch-Amerika* (Berlin, 1909), 145.

[3]See Joseph Wechsberg, "Winnetou of Der Wild West," *Saturday Review*, XLV, No. 42 (October 20, 1962), 52, 60-61; same, *The American West*, I, No. 3 (Summer, 1964), 32-39.

[4]Ludwig Max Goldberger, *Das Land der unbegrenzten Möglichkeiten; Beobachtungen über das Wirtschaftsleben der Vereinigten Staaten von Amerika* (Leipzig, 1903), 267, 289-290.

[5]See comment in Sigmund Skard, *American Studies in Europe, Their History and Present Organization* (Philadelphia [c. 1958]), I, 253. Hugo Münsterberg in his book *Aus Deutsch-Amerika*, 236-237, proclaimed that the visit to the United States of Prince Henry had wiped out all doubts of friendship between the two peoples and established the basis for the closest of co-operation. Postwar critics were to challenge the significance of the visit.

months into years, and the sense of frustration on the battle front
found echo in the mood of discontent at home. Strikes in munitions factories, the "turnip winter," weariness with *Ersatz* sapped
the strength of domestic morale. It was to a Germany already
battle weary that the news came of the American declaration of
war on April 2, 1917.

The event itself was not entirely a surprise. German newspapers had followed the course of submarine warfare. The public
had been informed of American protests against its employment.
A year before the declaration Friedrich Naumann had warned his
countrymen that the United States was moving into an era of imperialism and that Wilson was maneuvering the country to enter
into what would be labeled "an unselfish war for the rights of
mankind." German newspapers, Naumann declared, were not
taking this situation seriously enough and were misleading the
German people in glossing over the significance of American participation in the war, if it should come.[6]

But still the actual fact brought shocked anger and dismay.
Perhaps the historian Erich Brandenburg best expressed the general mood when he wrote:

> The attitude of the United States during the World War
> has evoked our deep surprise from the very beginning. For
> years Germany had been concerned for the friendship of the
> United States. . . ; many thought they saw in the United
> States our future ally—be it against England or against the
> yellow race. We had the greatest respect for the accomplish-
> ments of the American people and hoped so greatly that this
> feeling would find an echo on the other side of the ocean
> since a considerable part of the inhabitants of the United
> States is of German descent and even today speaks German.[7]

3. Woodrow Wilson—"der grosse Teufel": After their initial
shock, German writers of the war years settled down to the normal
routine of throwing brickbats at the enemy. For most of them

[6]"Die amerikanische Neutralität," in *Die Hilfe*, XXII (1916), quoted in
Ernst Fraenkel, *Amerika im Spiegel des deutschen politischen Denkens. Aeusserungen deutscher Staatsmänner und Staatsdenker über Staat und Gesellschaft
in den Vereinigten Staaten von Amerika* (Köln und Opladen [c. 1959]),
234-235.

[7]"Die Vereinigten Staaten und Europa," *Deutsche Rundschau*, CLXXII,
21 (July, 1917); similar, "Zerstörte deutsche Illusionen über Amerika," *Neue
Preussische Zeitung*, July 3, 1918.

the easy explanation of America's entry was a personal one. Woodrow Wilson had planned it from the first, hoodwinked a gullible and unsophisticated people, and led them into a war they didn't want. The unrestricted submarine warfare had only provided a needed excuse. Other motives had outweighed that of shocked morality.[8]

Dr. Georg Barthelme, the only accredited German correspondent to remain in the United States after the declaration of war, returned to Germany late in 1917 to publish virulent pieces from his "American Sketchbook." He emphatically supported the position that the war was an unpopular one: "It was *Wilson*, who wanted it, *Wilson* who brought it to pass, *Wilson* who declared war, *Wilson* who is responsible for it."—"by far and away the larger part of the country cringes in dog-like submission. It knows there is no real reason for war or hope for victory."[9]

Barthelme reflected the general tenor of the German press. Roosevelt and Wilson were joined as "Deutschenfresser"—"German-eaters."[10] The charge of personal responsibility was bolstered by reports of the measures adopted by the American government for war-time dictatorship. "Thus, the entire war which the United States conducts against Germany," charged the *Weser Zeitung*, "so far as the American people is concerned, those who bleed for it, pay for it, and may well also sacrifice their lives for it, is built upon false pictures. False is the idol of democracy for which it supposedly fights, since the people had, as the course of the outbreak of the war demonstrated, no influence upon their fate."[11] The able journalist, C. A. Bratter, grasped a phrase from Nicholas Long-

[8]*E.g.*, Otto Hoetzsch, "Der Krieg und die grosse Politik," *Neue Preussische Zeitung*, September 2, 1917; Major K. Hosse, "Amerikas Bedeutung für die militärische Lage," *Weser Zeitung*, October 14, 1917; "Amerika und der U-Bootkrieg," *Neue Preussische Zeitung*, June 16, 1918. Moritz Bonn had, of course, provided more reasonable explanations. See page 25.

[9]*Kölnische Zeitung*, VII, February 2, 1918; I, January 13, 1918. Similar, "Wie in Amerika gegen die Deutschen gearbeitet wird," *Neue Preussische Zeitung*, April 8, 1918; Albrecht Penck, *U. S.-Amerika, Gedanken und Erinnerungen eines Austausch-Professors* (Stuttgart, 1917), 152-153. "Viendre" in the *Berliner Tageblatt*, July 5, 1918, added that Wilson's personality declined constantly during the war—"The longer the war lasts, the more the destructive means which he set in motion in behalf of his mission for the welfare of the world become an end in themselves."

[10]*Neue Preussische Zeitung*, April 8, 1918.

[11]"Deutschland und Amerika, 1917/1918," February 2, 1918.

worth's speech in the House of Representatives to label Wilson the "Mikado of America," and noted that even the consideration of the assignment of such overwhelming powers to the President as those involved in the Overman Act (Bratter evidently had not learned of its later passage) "shows that only the outward form of American political life is democratic not its content."[12]

The motives attributed to Wilson's actions were varied. Prominent, of course, was his inherent Puritanism, his Anglophilia, his defense of Anglo-Saxon traditions.[13] The strength of his support of England, thought one historically minded observer, was intensified by his gratitude as a Southerner for English help during the Civil War![14] Economic motives—the desire to avoid a depression, the hope of acquiring the potash deposits of Alsace-Lorraine— were alleged.[15] Now and then jealousy of German culture was charged[16] and not infrequently Jewish machinations against Germany.[17]

4. The "Failure" and "Sorrows" of the German-Americans: German anger at the "unwarranted intrusion" of the United States into European affairs became more emotional with reports of

[12]*Weser Zeitung*, June 19, 1918.

[13]*E.g.*, *Kölnische Volkszeitung*, September 22, 1917. Perhaps the fullest exposition of this theme was set forth in Moritz J. Bonn's book, *Musste es sein?* (3. völlig umgearbeitete und stark erweiterte Ausgabe von "Amerika als Feind." *Fehler und Forderungen*. *Schriftenreihe zur Neugestaltung deutscher Politik*, Herausgegeben von Palatinus, 7. Heft. München, 1919). After detailing the lines of cultural influence in the United States and the part of the "New England Brahmans" in setting the cultural pattern, Bonn ended by stating, "America is still today culturally a colony, whose motherland predominantly, although not exclusively, was England." (12)

[14]Georg Barthelme, "Aus meinem amerikanischen Skizzenbuch," VIII, *Kölnische Zeitung*, February 6, 1918.

[15]Dr. W. Roth, "Das elsässische Kali ein amerikanisches Kriegsziel," *Vossische Zeitung*, November 23, 1917; Georg Münch, "Amerika als Feind Europas," *ibid.*, September 22, 1918. A Professor K. Dove later attributed American interest in the war to the desire to establish itself in Africa and to eliminate the competition of cotton production in Togo and of other raw materials from the rest of that continent. "Die amerikanische Gefahr," *Hamburger Fremdenblatt*, September 20, 1918.

[16]Adolf Hepner, "Amerikanische Zeitgeschichte," *Kölnische Zeitung*, December 20, 1917.

[17]Georg Kuh, *Das wahre Amerika* (*Flugschriften für Oesterreich-Ungarns Erwachen*, 36. Heft. Wien, 1918), 26.

German-Americans being whipped "for the women and children of Belgium" or painted with the Stars and Stripes to enhance their patriotism.[18]

With the declaration of war there had come a sharp pang of disappointment at the weakness of German-Americans, who ought to have prevented such an occurrence. This *Versagen,* this disgraceful failure of German-Americans, initiated a line of criticism in which some homeland Germans almost disavowed their American compatriots. Indeed, the pages of the *Kreuzzeitung* in Berlin suggested that since the phrase "German loyalty" (*Deutsche Treue*) no longer had meaning to them, all German-American organizations should eliminate the "German" in their titles, its presence there as much an embarrassment to homeland Germans as to the German-Americans themselves![19]

For many others, however, the wartime travail of their erstwhile countrymen underscored the tensions under which they had been living and clearly disclosed the falsity of America's democratic pretensions. Bismark, complained one commentator, had told the German-Americans to be loyal to their new country, but now Americans were proceeding on the motto that "the only good German is a dead German."[20] America, wrote another, was being "Russified"—its cultural level was lower than that of the dark land of the tsars.[21] The impression of lawlessness across the Atlantic, "the right of murder" in the United States, was heightened by de-

[18]"Die Sicherheit von Leib und Leben unter der amerikanischen Demokratie (Das Mordrecht in den Vereinigten Staaten)," *Neue Preussische Zeitung,* August 8, 1918; "Die Verfolgung der Deutsch-Amerikaner," *ibid.,* September 22, 1918; "Amerikanische 'Kulturtaten,'" *Weser Zeitung,* June 14, 1918; "Der Mobgeist in Amerika," *Vossische Zeitung,* September 7, 1918.

[19]Quoted in Wilhelm Müller, *Die Deutschamerikaner und der Krieg* (Wiesbaden, 1921), 5; see also Erich Brandenburg's indirect criticisms, "Die Vereinigten Staaten und Europa," *Deutsche Rundschau,* CLXXII, 26-27 (July, 1917); *cf.* "Zerstörte deutsche Illusionen über Amerika," *Neue Preussische Zeitung,* July 3, 1918. The critical attitude became even more exaggerated after the war—see, *e.g.,* Georg von Skal, "Deutsch-Amerika von Heute," *Hamburger Fremdenblatt,* November 1, 1919.

[20]"Viendre," "Amerika im Krieg: die Deutschamerikaner und ihre Leiden," *Berliner Tageblatt,* July 23, 1918.

[21]*Weser Zeitung,* June 22, 1918. Wilson's connection with these acts of terrorism was frequently alleged: "No one has so quickly converted a democracy into an autocracy as Wilson," charged the *Neue Preussische Zeitung,* June 25, 1918.

tailed summaries of lynchings in the South with graphic descriptions of the sufferings of the victims.[22] "In no case will Germany seek its political examples and dogmas in America," concluded one critic.[23] And another proclaimed that the treatment of German-Americans gave the lie to American protestations that they were fighting against the "system of Prussian militarism," not the German people.[24]

This was the *Götterdämmerung* of German life in America. In anger, one German wrote, "the 24 to 25 million people of German descent who live here (in the United States) have served only as 'cultural fertilizer' for the building of a hostile people and state."[25] But another was moved more by pity than by anger:

> The German population of America bears the woes of weakness. It suffers and succumbs. And in this lies the great tragedy which clutches at our heart, the course of fate which we are not able to turn. But come what may, one thing we know, that the Germans over there fall like heroes on ships at sea or in the trenches, with "Deutschland, Deutschland über alles" on their lips and in their hearts.[26]

5. *The Crusade of the Star-Spangled Banner*: In the midst of these wartime efforts to stir emotions grown dull with years of fighting, there is often a genuine note of questioning—how could Americans really believe the charges against Germans, the propaganda of the Entente? One easy explanation was that hostility toward Germany had appeared long before the World War—had indeed existed since the time of the Spanish-American War.[27] For years, wrote a

[22]Felix Baumann, "Richter Lynch: Amerikanische Sittenbilder," *Weser Zeitung*, October 20, 1918; "Amerikanische Menschlichkeit," *Kölnische Zeitung*, June 26, 1918; Anon., *Im Schatten amerikanischer Demokratie und Freiheit* (Charlottenburg [1918]), 61-65.

[23]"Das undemokratische und unsoziale Amerika," *Kölnische Volkszeitung*, September 22, 1917.

[24]"Wie man in Amerika Krieg führt," *Kölnische Zeitung*, July 18, 1918.

[25]J. Hoffmann, "Amerikas Stellung zu dem Ausgang des Krieges," *Neue Preussische Zeitung*, January 26, 1919. Expressed in very similar language by Adolf Hitler in his "Second Book," *Hitler's Secret Book* (New York [c. 1961]), 91.

[26]Georg Barthelme, *Aus meinem amerikanischen Skizzenbuch* (Köln, 1918) [originally serialized in various German newspapers], 84.

[27]E.g., Archivrat Dr. J. Lulvés, "Ein Urteil über Nordamerika aus dem Jahre 1902," *Neue Preussische Zeitung*, September 29, 1918.

former exchange professor, Americans had referred to the Germans as "damned dutch" and had increasingly grown away from their original sympathies for the land of thinkers and poets as this land also became more powerful economically and militarily.[28] Some Germans blamed the American attitude on ignorance. A Bremen merchant cited a geography textbook used in Savannah, Georgia, which read:

> Germany is a country in Europe which is covered the most of the year with ice and snow; the inhabitants live in huts and travel around in reindeer sleds. In the southern part of the country grows some wine and wheat. What else they need to sustain life must be imported from the United States.[29]

Only gradually did some Germans come to realize that Americans could find in obscure publications, "the hasty productions of excited beer bench politicians in the homeland," some ground for their feelings. As for Belgium, the "astonishing lack of knowledge and naivete" of Americans plus their civilian mentality had made it impossible for them to realize "that war can be hard and must be hard even for the civilian populations" concerned.[30]

There was, of course, much singing in the dark at the outset. The American help would not really be significant. "Will the U.S. raise an 'army of millions?'" asked an infantry captain in the *Kölnische Zeitung*, and answered the query, "not at all."[31] German writers emphasized the lack of military preparation of the United States, predicted that it would require two years to raise and equip an effective army, let alone get it through the U-boat lines.[32] Even von Hindenburg, reported one writer later, had expected that American help to the Entente would not be of significance until

[28]Penck, *U. S.-Amerika*, 140-145. German anti-Semites charged that the association of German-Americans with Jews had provided a background for the wartime hostility which they encountered. "Erklärungen für die Entstehung der deutschfeindlichen Stellung in Amerika," *Kölnische Volkszeitung*, September 9, 1918.

[29]The accompanying portrait showed Samoyed huts. Obviously, said the writer, the textbook author had picked up some materials from a German encyclopedia without noticing that they did not apply to Germany itself! *Weser Zeitung*, October 4, 1918.

[30]Bonn, *Musste es sein?*, 20-23.

[31]December 21, 1917.

[32]"Amerikanische Kriegsgefahr," *Weser Zeitung*, April 4, 1918; "Bilder von der amerikanischen Heimatfront," *Neue Preussische Zeitung*, April 21, 1918.

six to twelve months after the entry into the war.[33] In German eyes the "war of the businessman" was not to be feared; Uncle Sam could not serve as "Ersatzmann" for Russia.[34] And, above all, the spirit was not there. Things in America had to be done "auf kaltem Wege," by illegal means. The time of enchantment was over—for America it was now "a gray, professorial war."[35]

This somewhat forced optimism dissipated rapidly in the face of news from the battlefront. Some writers, although preserving the optimism necessary to pass official censors, began to hint at the size of America's contributions, to reopen the debate on the use of the U-boat, to wonder, "Did it really have to be?"—that the United States had been brought into the war.[36] There began also to be a realization that the American public supported the war effort. Eugen Rosenstock assured his readers that the "Crusade of the Star Spangled Banner" was a real one. It was a crusade against the Kaiser with the legends of German militarism associated with his name and against the Sultan:

> What, then, is the dogma for which America fights? It is this: *Man himself is good!* But tyrants falsify and distort his nature. Human nature creates of itself peace and freedom, the brotherhood of nations and justice. But princes prevent this natural development.[37]

[33]Adolf Hepner, "Deutschlands Amerika-Kenntnis," *Sozialistische Monats-hefte*, 1919, 342-344. Hepner was another of the voices criticizing the widespread ignorance of America in Germany. From twenty-six years experience in the United States, he related, he had sought during the war to contradict this assumption that America was militarily weak.

[34]"Der Krieg der Geschäftsleute," *Neue Preussische Zeitung*, July 14, 1918; J. Hoffmann, "Onkel Sam als Ersatzmann für Russland," *ibid.*, January 2, 1918.

[35]"Viendre," "Amerika im Kriege," *Berliner Tageblatt*, May 30, 1918.

[36]Persius [C. L. Lothar], Kapitän zur See, "Amerika ein Jahr im Krieg," *Berliner Tageblatt*, April 4, 1918. The title *Musste es sein?* was given the third edition of Moritz Bonn's wartime book, *Amerika als Feind* [see fn. 13, above]. Writing in 1922, Hermann von Giehrl strongly stressed the surprise Germans had felt at the rapid movement of men and supplies to Europe and at the actual materialization of the "army of the million" which had been promised. *Das amerikanische Expeditions-korps in Europa 1917/18* (Berlin, 1922), 43.

[37]*Hochland*, XVI, subvol. I, 113-122 (November, 1918)—obviously written just prior to the armistice. Leo Schwering in an article, "Was erstrebt Nordamerika?," *Deutsche Arbeit*, III (1918), 439-446, also wrote that Wilson was supported by the masses, that Americans took the war in "bitter Ernst," and felt for the first time a really genuine national spirit.

Rosenstock, of course, did not make these statements in the assumption that they were true, but he and other writers began to realize that Germany confronted a new and vigorous opponent, determined to press the war to the finish. They attributed this, of course, to propaganda, to that which an outstanding Americanist in the postwar period labeled the work of the "Wahnsinnsmacher," "the producers of madness." The degree of this "madness" was attested by the role of a five-year-old boy as one of America's four-minute speakers—he also discussed democracy with the President. "Naturally, such a baby could only turn up in America where one loves the grotesque," commented a German observer.[38]

As for the battlefront, commentators also began to realize that Americans were doing better than expected. They attributed this to the use of regular army troops and predicted hopefully that untrained forces would not show up so well.[39] One writer felt it necessary to assure his readers that the American was "no superman," especially in the military field.[40]

In spite of such hints that American activities on the Western front were becoming increasingly effective, however, the news of October and November, 1918, fell upon Germany with all the impact of an ice-cold shower. There was never any doubt in German minds who had been responsible for their defeat—it was the Americans.[41] This impression of strength, of technical accomplishment, of sudden preeminence in the military field which the Germans had considered their own preserve created a passionate desire for clarification and provided the basis for the strange dichotomy which characterized German attitudes towards the United States in the years that followed—a warring between admiration for the material accomplishments of America and a deep revulsion in re-

[38]J. Hoffman, "Die lärmende amerikanische Heimatfront," *Neue Preussische Zeitung*, August 20, 1918; Friedrich Schönemann, " 'Wahnsinnsmacher,' Amerikanische Kriegsliteratur," *Vossische Zeitung*, February 26, 1921.

[39]"Amerikanische Kriegstaumel und Verfolgungssucht," *Kölnische Volkszeitung*, August 29, 1918.

[40]"Die amerikanische Gefahr," *Kölnische Zeitung*, August 20, 1918.

[41]*E.g.*, Karl Scheffler, "The Star-Spangled Banner," *Vossische Zeitung*, February 21, 1919—"I will not go into sentimentalities. America has beaten us. It alone. It has worn down our armed forces with the fullness of its war materials and has subdued our population with hunger. This is bitter, but it can, at least, be factually discussed." *Cf.* Giehrl's later judgment, *Das amerikanische Expeditions-korps*, 51.

gard to the cultural accompaniments of these achievements. The wartime psychology faded somewhat in the years that followed but significant remnants survived for the second world conflict.

6. Germans and the Wilsonian Peace: Meanwhile, in those days of uncertainty, of the "November Revolution" which created the Weimar Republic, of the hardships of the post-armistice blockade, of the unrest, disappointment, and disillusion bound up with the outcomes of a lost war, Germans began hopefully to look to America for some lessening of their burdens. It is a little surprising after the wartime calumny directed against him to see Germans now reposing their hopes in Wilson. There were, of course, plenty of prophets of doom who warned that these hopes would prove fruitless. Wilson, asserted Georg Münch, really wanted to put Germany and the Central Powers back into the conditions existing after the Thirty Years War.[42] J. Hoffmann, who had long served as "America expert" for the *Neue Preussische Zeitung*, pointed out that the tone of Wilson's notes revealed no change in his hostility to Germany and added that even if there were good will for Germany in America, little could be expected when the peace treaty was made—"He who has lived in America will have experienced how far away what happens in Europe seems to one living on the Ohio or the Mississippi. One has the feeling that these are occurrences on a strange planet." There was, warned Hoffmann, no real ground for the "completely ineradicable optimism" holding the fort in Germany.[43] The *Berliner Tageblatt's* "Viendre" agreed that there was need for caution in respect to America's role— "America wishes, after it got into this war contrary to all its expectations, to hasten back to its old calm." But, Viendre added, one thing was certain. The war had brought an end to the "monumental simplicity of American thinking." With new dangers—Russia and Japan—in the offing and with the course of negotiations developing as it was, America was turning a sharper eye on the realities of the situation in Europe—this was "not a disagreeable thought" to Germans, he added.[44]

[42]"Amerika als Feind Europas," *Vossische Zeitung*, September 22, 1918.

[43]"Zur Charakteristik der Wilsonischen Politik," *Neue Preussische Zeitung*, October 20, 1918; "Die amerikanische Psyche," *ibid*., December 29, 1918; "Die Stellung Amerikas bei den Friedensverhandlungen," *ibid*., April 6, 1918.

[44]"Stimmung in Amerika," April 29, 1919.

In the months of peace negotiations which followed Germans were, however, once again disappointed, and Wilson received again the label of a deceiver. In German eyes there was complete logic in their hatred of Wilson—he had talked neutrality and led America into a war against them; he had talked of a peace without victory and assisted in drafting the punitive Treaty of Versailles. It was to be the unusually perceptive observer who offered any defense of America's wartime president in post-war Germany.[45]

But the United States Senate did, at least, refuse to ratify the Treaty of Versailles. Germans received this news with approval—it was a sign that "the clever, factual, passionless business-man's spirit" of the Americans had begun to free itself from "English hatred and French fear" and to understand that Germany's aid in the reconstruction of the world's economy would be needed.[46]

Other signs of an American attitude more sympathetic to Germany also began to appear. The American Commission for Aid to European Children visited Germany and began to assist in dealing with the problem of German children left weakened by the rigorous wartime blockade.[47] Americans, not all of German descent, contributed to funds to assist in recovery.[48] The United States seemed to be realizing the economic plight of Germany and the need for a more rational handling of peace problems. Even J. Hoffmann, the critical columnist of the ultra-conservative *Neue Preussische Zeitung*, began to descry the beginning of more sensible American viewpoints in respect to the financial treatment of Ger-

[45]One of the first real defenses was by a physicist!—Dr. Friedrich Dessauer, "Wie Amerika in den Krieg kam," *Vossische Zeitung*, December 6, 1921— "Wilson was no scoundrel. He failed when it came to turning into reality the thoughts he sincerely held. But no matter how much we may doubt him and the justice, greatness, and honorable character of our enemies, we would be, without his influence, even more in misery (than we are)."

[46]"Amerika lehnt den Frieden von Versailles ab," *Weser Zeitung*, November 19, 1919. Dr. Friedrich Glaser added, "But the criticism which was brought against the Versailles Peace Treaty (in the United States Senate) justifies the expectation that Germany can at least count on a certain amount of nonpartisan feeling in America in respect to the questions coming up in regard to the execution of the treaty, such as is nowhere else, at least not in Western Europe, to be found." "Amerika nach dem Weltkrieg," *Berliner Tageblatt*, August 22, 1919.

[47]*Der Welt-Spiegel*, April 27, 1919; February 20, August 22, 1921.

[48]J. Hoffmann, "Das Wiedererwachen des amerikanischen Deutschtums," *Neue Preussische Zeitung*, October 29, 1921.

many.[49] The Americaphobe Georg von Skal warned his readers never again to expect friendship in the United States, but suggested that America's business sense would bring better treatment.[50] And although some German commentators found the eventual separate peace signed with the United States only the outcome of "cat-brawls and flea-snapping" across the Atlantic and of a desire to seize German property,[51] saner observers pointed out that German private property was not confiscated but only retained and that for the first time Germany had been dealt with across the conference table as an equal.[52]

7. *Unbekanntes Amerika*: Germans had come to the end of the First World War, however, with great bitterness about America's role of action both in the war and in the negotiations for peace. It was a new and unknown America which loomed up before them—a "totally different country," as C. A. Bratter labeled it.[53] Their attitude towards it combined respect for its technical accomplishments—it had won the war—with hostility towards its institutions and way of life. There was a tremendous curiosity, unfortunately not accompanied very frequently by a real willingness to reconsider preconceptions.

At home there were a few scattered impressions to be gained of Americans from "America on the Rhine" at Koblenz. Unlike the situation after World War II, however, when America came to Germany personified by her occupation troops, the small occupation forces after World War I made little impact on the German scene. German newspaper observers were largely hostile to what the Koblenzers called the American "cockroaches." Part of this feeling was undoubtedly justified. Regulations prohibiting friendly intercourse with Germans were firmly observed. A drunken American lieutenant who tried to kiss a German girl lost

[49]"Amerikanische Empfindungen gegenüber Deutschland," *Neue Preussische Zeitung*, February 9, 1921.

[50]"Die deutsch-amerikanische Verständigung," *Weser Zeitung*, December 9, 1919.

[51]"Der Krieg um den Frieden," *Kölnische Zeitung*, June 13, 1921.

[52]Dr. Max Jordan, "Die deutsch-amerikanische Friedensbesprechungen vor dem Abschluss," *Berliner Tageblatt*, August 22, 1921; "Die Bedeutung des Friedenschlusses," *ibid.*, August 26, 1921.

[53]"Das ganz andere Land"—title of first chapter of his wartime book, *Amerika, von Washington bis Wilson* (Berlin, 1917).

his rank as a consequence. Possession by Germans of American cigarettes, foodstuffs, or equipment was severely punished, even if the Americans themselves had given away or sold the articles concerned. One German who found an American cigarette lying on a table and lit it had to pay a thousand marks for the pleasure of his smoke.

In the midst of postwar shortages in Germany the provisioning of American soldiers seemed fantastically extravagant. One newspaperman described it with malicious jealousy—

> Even the common soldier lives like a first class passenger on an ocean steamer. He receives meat twice or even three times a day, and that not in a thin soup of vegetables and potatoes from which he first has to seek it out before he can eat it, but rather in good bourgeois fashion served up with gravy. If he has satiated himself with countless beef-steaks and after that slurped down his real-bean coffee with milk and sugar, then there is available to him—and, of course, especially to the officers—daily a pound of the finest chocolate or canned confectionery at a price of 4 marks. The most regular use of this pleasant arrangement is made, especially since the common soldier daily receives eight marks and a lieutenant forty marks pay for his life of leisure. But woe to the soldier who from his excess either gives or sells something, and three times woe to the [German] civilian who takes it or receives it.[54]

A later observer, however, found that some of the American hostility to the Germans had melted—they appreciated good German housekeeping, unknown to them at home, loved to play baseball with children, and helped Germans with food and other needed things when they could avoid the MP's. Koblenz had become, however, by this time the promised land of the "Schieber," the black-marketeer, and this illegal trade threatened ruin to the morality of the whole community. Other dangers to morality existed also. The flapper dress of the French girls who haunted the streets was being imitated by the German *Backfisch*. However, admitted the newspaperman somewhat wonderingly, the American soldier was more likely to mope homesickly in his room with the picture of the girl "back home" than to seek German companion-

[54]Dr. Erich Wolf, "Bei den Amerikanern am Rhein," *Berliner Tageblatt*, March 19, 1919.

ship.[55] The departure of American troops from Koblenz brought surprisingly few "Fräuleins" to see them off.[56]

Nor were the reports of ex-prisoners-of-war and internees very revealing. Some of them undoubtedly suffered hardship—Karl Hentzschel, a German soldier imprisoned first in military prison at Fort Bliss and later as a civilian internee at Fort Douglas, related an odyssey of cold, poor food, and brutal treatment.[57] Dr. Ludwig Darmstädter, a prisoner-of-war at Villingen, fared much better—he reported good food, comfortable quarters, and provisions for entertainment.[58]

As a consequence, America still seemed mysterious, remote, and enigmatic. Not in search of a mecca but in search of answers to burning questions, a flood of Germans began to cross the Atlantic in the early twenties. As one of them later wrote, each of the travelers felt somewhat like a new Columbus as he came to see this "unknown America."[59] But the efforts of these new explorers faced many obstacles. They left a Germany involved in the pangs of its first experiment in democracy, a Germany enmeshed in almost hopeless economic problems, a Germany embittered by defeat but unshaken in its conviction of moral, intellectual, and cultural superiority. They came to an America still highly motivated by wartime prejudices, an America plagued by postwar economic dislocations, an America deprived by prohibition of the relaxation of alcohol but not that of sex and dance. It was not America at its best which the Germans of the 1920's saw, and they were not really inclined to make careful and objective evaluations. A part of the tragedy of Weimar in Germany lies in the tragedies of Harding and the vagaries of the jazz age in America.

[55]Dr. Reinhold Zenz, "Aus dem amerikanischen Deutschland," *Weser Zeitung*, September 18, 19, 20, 22, 1919.

[56]Picture, *Welt-Spiegel*, December 18, 1921. On the other hand, Erich von Salzmann, who visited America in 1921, found former servicemen who had stayed in Germany acting as miniature propaganda chiefs for Germany! "Moden und Methoden," *Vossische Zeitung*, February 11, 1923.

[57]"Aus amerikanischer Gefangenschaft," Berlin *Tägliche Rundschau*, August 23, 26, 28, 1919.

[58]"Im amerikanischen Kriegsgefangenenlager," *Vossische Zeitung*, October 29, 1918.

[59]Professor Georg Swarzenski, "Europäisches Amerika," *Frankfurter Zeitung*, January 30, 1927.

Chapter II

THE FLOOD OF "STUDY TRIPS"

ure of the Unknown: *Amerikakunde*, "knowledge about America," was, proclaimed Friedrich Schönemann in 1921, a "contemporary necessity."[1] Schönemann had just returned from a war-long stay at Harvard. His interest in America was partially scholarly, partially propagandist in inspiration. His advice about the study of American life and institutions was most largely addressed to German intellectuals.

But, by the time he wrote, hundreds of Germans were already on their way across the Atlantic. They came possessed by the urge to see for themselves the strange and alien civilization of the New World. The First World War had made it clear that the United States was not to be understood in the calm, complacent terms which had been used prior to the war. America was different— the lure of the unknown reached into myriad homes. It brought a constant influx of curious visitors who were to produce a veritable flood of literature, a whole category of publications— the "America books."

One of the travelers in a review of later writings on the subject underscored in striking language the significance of this literature:

> The flood of books about America mirrors one of the most important facts in the spiritual life of today. The victory [of the United States] in the World War has for the first time presented that great land to European eyes as an actual personality with a new and individual way of life. The time is past for the quick jest, the high-spirited disregard, the enforced but depreciatory recognition. The young nation has placed its feet too firmly on the paths of world history and has become the world's leader. Other nations draw back in fear; they listen; they are astounded. A great riddle is to be

[1] *Amerikakunde. Eine zeitgemässe Forderung* (Berlin, 1921).

17

solved; the leading power in the external relationships of the area of Western culture demands understanding. The door to a new chapter of world history has been opened. America stands on the threshhold.[2]

The "America books," sometimes ponderous but more often slim and modest volumes, reflected varied experiences and diverse backgrounds. One item they had in common. Almost universally their authors considered that they had been engaged in a "Studienreise," a "study trip." Perhaps it was part of the German mentality to wish to assert a serious purpose in that which was often a simple sight-seeing expedition. For many of these visits to the United States represented casual and disorganized views of the country. The travelers seldom defined in advance the objectives of their study, plotted out the means by which these might be attained, and then sought to evaluate scientifically the results of their observations. From the most random samplings, sometimes liberally padded by reading in the newspapers [in spite of violent complaint against the American form of this medium], these travelers emerged with sweeping generalizations of fact and interpretation.

It is easy, of course, to criticize the superficiality of these accounts. Yet it must be recognized that such criticisms can be made of almost every travel narrative written. Everyone who visits a foreign land carries with him myriad, often unrealized, preconceptions. Colin Ross once wrote that prior to his travels he sought to hold his mind free from these advance conclusions: that he carefully avoided the reading of newspapers from or books about the countries he was to visit.[3] The wisdom of this procedure is, of course, dubious and no matter how vigorously it were carried out, it would not free one from the backgrounds of family upbringing and educational training, from the well-formed patterns of mental attitudes and ways of life. How vividly these things influence one's concept of a strange, new country can be seen dramatically in Ludwig Lewisohn's powerful account of his early experiences in the United States.[4]

[2]Eugen Kuhnemann, "Vier Schlesier über Amerika," *Schlesische Monatshefte*, IV, 502-507 (November, 1927).

[3]*World in the Balance; an Analysis of World Problems after Twenty Years' Travel About the World* (London, 1930), xiii.

[4]*Up Stream: an American Chronicle* (New York [c. 1922]).

2. Travelers Who Never Left Home: Those who came to the United States in the 1920's were from many walks of life. But the vocal visitors, the authors of "America books" and articles, were predominantly from the intellectual classes. College professors and secondary school teachers led the list, followed most closely by journalists and free-lance writers. There was a goodly sampling of the views of political leaders, art experts, clergymen, labor leaders, and businessmen. Far less frequent were the writings of simple farmers or ordinary laborers. Only one traveler blatantly described himself as a "bum," although there were several who referred to themselves as adventurers![5]

Thus the image of America carried back to Germany by these vocal visitors was profoundly shaped by the frame of reference they carried with them—their own image of their homeland. This was the very group which had been most strongly molded by the culture of the nineteenth century. By the nature of their intellectual training, their mental flexibility, their ability to adjust to new and unfamiliar situations had been reduced, their willingness to reconsider and revise standards of evaluation largely atrophied. They were confronted by a mental challenge that was insurmountable. They saw a complex and diverse civilization in which many approaches to life were totally foreign to their experience. Too frequently the repulsion engendered by that which was new and different threw them off balance and led them to write more from an emotional approach than from an intellectual one.

What was really needed, suggested one intellectual who came on a fellowship which allowed him time to see and to understand, was patience and the willingness to pursue a "feeling-in" process. Otherwise the contrasts between America and Germany were so great that the writings of the frustrated visitors became "seismographs of spiritual cataclysms."[6] Friedrich Schönemann later stated that nowhere in the world, certainly not in England or France, had so much "half-knowledge" about America been printed as in Germany. "Most of our America literature," he wrote, "is neither

[5]Heinz Otto, *Mein "Bummelleben" in Amerika. Die Beichte eines Toren* (Hamburg, 1925); Oskar Kollbrunner, *Treibholz. Irrgänge eines Amerikafahrers* (Frauenfeld, 1926); Karl H. Meyer (Karl Ey), *Mit 100 Mark nach U. S. A.; ein deutsches Schicksal in Amerika* (Berlin [1930]); *cf.* the popular pre-war adventure story of Erwin Carlé (Rosen), *Der deutsche Lausbub in Amerika, Erinnerungen und Eindrücke von Erwin Rosen* (3 vols. Stuttgart [c. 1911-1913]).

[6]Wilhelm Röpke in *Hamburg-Amerika Post*, I, No. 9 (1929), 281.

a compliment for our thoroughness and historical sense nor even for our willingness to see the world as it actually is."[7]

It may, indeed, be suggested that many of those who crossed the Atlantic and trekked three thousand miles across the American continent never really left home. They knew what they expected to see before they arrived in America; they saw what they expected to see (only usually worse than they had anticipated); and they went back home to share with their countrymen the results of their "research."

These "inner-directed" individuals often judged America poorly because they knew their homeland poorly. Men of the nineteenth century, they remained wedded to the culture of the prewar era and continued to equate that halcyon age of cultural greatness with aristocratic conceptions of government and society. By instinct they were hostile to democracy. By training they were strongly inclined toward the metaphysical and theoretical rather than the material and the pragmatic. By virtue of the narrowness of the life of the German intellectual they were frequently ignorant of the full scope of life at home, hence easily shocked when they saw a broad section of society in America. Frequently they were to characterize as "American" trends and traits and approaches to life which could have been amply found in Germany itself.

3. "Pattern" and Non-"Pattern" Tourists: The majority of these visitors followed a "pattern" with individual variations here and there. That pattern involved direct-line moves from one urban center to another—typically, New York (the skyscrapers), to Detroit (Henry Ford), to Chicago (slaughter houses and Sears Roebuck), to Salt Lake City (the Mormons) , and San Francisco (Chinatown), or vice versa. They all talked about America's Puritan traditions, but few of them visited New England. They glibly discussed the patriarchal society of the South—but they didn't see it. Their view of the wheatlands of the Midwest was gained from a train clipping along at fifty miles an hour. Many of them did visit Los Angeles (Hollywood), but only a handful saw the great lumbering operations of the Northwest.

Most conspicuously absent from the average visits was any real sampling of rural America. Niagara Falls, Grand Canyon, Yellow-

[7]*Die Vereinigten Staaten von Amerika* (Stuttgart, 1932), I, xiii.

stone National Park, etc. of course attracted their share of visitors. But the little country towns which lay between the great cities and which were in the twenties much more significant than now were seldom seen by German travelers. Infrequent also were German visits to American homes, to the suburban areas lying around the city "bustle" which so much impressed these visitors. As a consequence they missed much of the more relaxed aspects of America—they seldom saw Americans mowing their yards in the evening, watching baseball games in the neighborhood play-grounds, or having picnics in the park. They did not see Americans talking across backyard fences or sitting quietly on their front porches. For most of these visitors America was a land of honking automobiles, bustling shop-girls, over-strained businessmen, and blatant materialism. Little wonder that the books which emerged from the "pattern" travels also paraded a "pattern" of stale clichés.

Since the non-"pattern" tourists usually produced more original and more penetrating views of American life, often from less extensive visits, it is of some value to note how they differed from their countrymen. One very frequent difference was that these travelers came to the United States with a more serious purpose than casual observation. Many of them had a mission—the raising of funds for German relief, attendance at an international convention, visits to members of a particular religious denomination, for example. Many of them were engaging in genuine "study-trips"— to learn how concrete roads were built, to study social welfare activities, to observe medical or dental procedures, to investigate labor conditions and the conduct of business by American labor unions, or to study American education. The "mission" which brought these visitors to America took them out of the routine of casual contacts, gave them the opportunity for more than desultory conversations with Americans, and frequently gave them a chance to visit in the homes of those who were their American counterparts.

Some of the non-"pattern" tourists differed from the "pattern" tourists only in their willingness to observe more cautiously and less positively, in their ability to establish rapport with those they met, in their more scientific attitude toward personal observations— the recognition that personal samplings were extremely fallible and that value judgments must be based upon more than German or even European standards. These qualities were, however, not broadly represented among the German travelers of the Weimar period—they are, indeed, unusual among travelers of any place and time!

4. *"Specialists," Good and Bad*: There were, of course, considerable numbers of Germans whose interest in America was more than passing and ephemeral. The development of *Amerikakunde*, of a more scientific and comprehensive knowledge of American life and civilization, became the objective of a narrow but devoted group of scholars. Some of these were travelers who added to their personal experiences a careful study of various aspects of American life. Others appear to have written on the United States without having visited it. In many cases it is difficult to determine whether the writer of an "America book" or an "America article" in a periodical relied on personal observation or abstract research. But the writings of those who sought to be experts on the United States were an important part of the America literature of the period competing for public attention with the travel accounts of the dilettantes.

It is difficult to judge the influence of the work of these specialists. The best of them, because of the specialized nature of their interests, wrote for restricted audiences. It cannot be doubted that much of the more superficial writing circulated more widely than did the profound. And even the best "experts" passed through periods of greater and lesser objectivity. The impact of their work was probably not yet fully felt when the Nazi era supervened, but they established the foundations for the post-World War II flowering of American studies in Germany.[8]

The pathfinder for these new studies, "the father of *Amerikakunde*," was Friedrich Schönemann. Schönemann was twenty-five when he first came to the United States in 1911.[9] Originally

[8]The monumental study of Sigmund Skard, *American Studies in Europe: Their History and Present Organization* (Philadelphia [c. 1958]) has traced the growing significance of this subject in the curriculum of European universities. See pages 208-357 for his discussion of its influence in Germany. The more interpretative monograph by Skard, *The American Myth and the European Mind: American Studies in Europe, 1776-1960* (Philadelphia [c. 1961] has also been of value to this study—see particularly Chapter 3, "America at Europe's Crossroads (1918-1945)," 59-82.

[9]For a detailed account of Schönemann's life and work see my article, "Friedrich Schönemann, German Americanist," *The Historian*, XXVI, No. 3, 381-404 (May, 1964).

a specialist in German literature, Schönemann put nine years of teaching in the United States to good use, reading broadly in American literature and history. His initial experiences in this country were restricted to the east coast, where he taught at Hunter College, Wesleyan University, and Harvard. He spent the years of the First World War at the latter institution, returning to Germany in August, 1920.

The war had impressed Schönemann with Germany's need for a better understanding of the United States. He became an Americanist with the ardent mission of popularizing and propagandizing American studies. His first "America book," entitled *Amerikakunde. Eine zeitgemässe Forderung* (*American Studies. A Contemporary Necessity*), was a clarion call for attention to this field.[10] Throughout his academic career, first at the University of Münster in Westphalia and later at the University of Berlin, Schönemann sought to reach the general public as well as a scholarly audience. As a consequence, both he and his subject field were regarded with reservations by his colleagues. Schönemann did not acquire a full professorship until early in the Nazi era.[11]

Meanwhile, Schönemann had engaged in a broad range of publications, capped in 1932 by a two-volume general work on the United States. A second visit in 1929 had broadened his acquaintance with this country.[12] Schönemann in his writings combined caustic criticism of American "willingness to be led about by the nose" and of American vacillation with an ardent defense of the sense of unity, the dedication to democracy, and the beginnings of cultural achievement he had found in the United States. He also sought to convince his countrymen that Europe

[10]Published in Bremen, 1921. The propagandist note was underscored in the review of the book by Herman George Scheffauer, "Amerikakunde," *Gartenlaube*, 1921, No. 22, 456-457.

[11]Professor Martin Weinbaum, who was associated with Schönemann in Berlin, and Schönemann's second wife have both emphasized the great odds against which Schönemann struggled in seeking to advance his field of work. The promotion to full professor had been approved before the Nazi period, but Schönemann, in spite of party membership, waited three years to obtain it. See details in article cited in *fn.* 9.

[12]See description, Toni Harten-Hoencke (first Mrs. Schönemann), "Eine Vortragsreise durch Nordamerika nach dem Kriege," *Tägliche Rundschau* (Berlin), Nov. 24, 1930.

and America were by no means so widely separated spiritually as many European critics assumed.[13]

Perhaps nearest to Schönemann in his contributions to the development of American studies during this period was Walther Fischer, the outstanding Weimar expert on American literature. Fischer stayed much closer to his field of specialization than did Schönemann and obtained a somewhat greater degree of respect for his scholarly endeavors.

Fischer's doctoral work was completed at the University of Pennsylvania, where he also served until 1914 as an instructor in French.[14] Like Schönemann he turned from this initial specialty to American studies, although he taught and published within the broader framework of English literature and English philology. During the Weimar years he progressed through the academic ranks at Würzburg and Dresden to arrive at a full professorship at the University of Giessen.

Fischer's major contributions to German Americana were two volumes on the history of American literature, a discussion of "American English" in the standard German handbook on the United States, and a group of essays on the problems of American studies.[15] It is doubtful that his works became well known to the general public. Among scholars they obtained respect, and it was natural that Fischer should become editor of the German *Jahrbuch für Amerikastudien* (*Yearbook for American Studies*) after the Second World War.[16]

[13]On American credulousness, *Die Kunst der Massenbeeinflussung in den Vereinigten Staaten von Amerika* (Stuttgart, 1924), 58. Defensive articles, "Strömungen des amerikanischen Lebens," *Süddeutsche Monatshefte*, XXVII (1929), 655, 659; "Der Amerikanismus in deutscher Auffassung," *Literarische Handweiser*, LXIV (1927/1928), No. 3, 161-166; "Das Amerika von Heute," *ibid.*, LXVII (1930/1931), No. 3, 453-460. *Cf. Die Vereinigten Staaten von Amerika* (Stuttgart, 1932), I, 114-115.

[14]Biographical details here and following from *Wer Ist's*, various dates, and Horst Oppel, "Walther Fischer zum Gedächtnis," *Die neueren Sprachen*, n.s. X (1961), 143-145.

[15]*Amerikanische Prosa. Vom Bürgerkrieg bis auf die Gegenwart* (1863-1922) (Leipzig, 1926); *Geschichte der nordamerikanischen Literatur* (Leipzig, 1928); *Hauptfrage der Amerikakunde. Studien und Aufsätze* (Bielefeld, 1928); with A. Haushofer, E. Hylla, *et al., Handbuch der Amerikakunde* (Frankfurt a. M., 1931); "Amerikakunde und die deutsche Schule," *Neue Jahrbücher für Wissenschaft*, V (1929), 54-64.

[16]See Skard, *American Studies*, I, 273 and Oppel, see *fn.* 14.

Two other German scholars wrote extensively on the United States although their teaching fields were not American Studies. Moritz J. Bonn, the economist, like Schönemann and Fischer, taught in a number of American universities until forced by the entry of the United States into the First World War to return to Germany in 1917.[17]

A trilogy of wartime books by Bonn explained and in part apologized for the American participation.[18] During the immediate postwar period Bonn was heavily involved in work with Germany's reparations problems, but in 1925 he returned to the subject of the United States, initiating another series of volumes seeking to explain American "prosperity" and to warn against the possibilities of depression.[19] His *magnum opus, Die Kultur der Vereinigten Staaten von Amerika* (*The Culture of the United States of America*) was the only major study of the United States by a German author to be translated into English.[20] Sane and sober, it, like Schönemann's volumes, provided a combination of criticism and apology. But its emphasis was much more heavily on politics and economics and it made little pretense of real scholarship.[21]

The fourth "America expert" of the Weimar period remained predominantly a specialist on German philosophy and the literature of Goethe and Schiller. This was Eugen Kühnemann, who taught at Harvard in the prewar period and during that time wrote a biography of its president, Charles W. Eliot.[22] In 1912-1913 he was the first Carl Schurz Professor at the University of Wisconsin.

[17]Bonn has related the story of his life in the delightful memoirs, *Wandering Scholar* (New York [c. 1948]).

[18]*Amerika als Feind* (*Die Staaten und der Krieg*, hrsgbn. von Palatinus, Heft 1. München und Berlin [1917?]); *Was will Wilson?* (*Fehler und Forderungen. Schriftenfolge zur Neugestaltung deutscher Politik*, hrsg. von Palatinus, 6. Heft. München [1918?]); *Musste es sein?* (*Fehler und Forderungen*, hrsg, von Palatinus, 7. Heft. München, 1919).

[19]*Amerika und sein Problem* (München, 1925); *Geld und Geist. Vom Wesen und Werden der amerikanischen Welt* (Berlin [1927]); *Die Kultur der Vereinigten Staaten von Amerika* (Berlin, 1930); *"Prosperity," Wunderglaube und Wirklichkeit im amerikanischen Wirtschaftsleben* (Berlin, 1931).

[20]*The American Adventure; a Study of Bourgeois Civilization* (New York [c. 1934]).

[21]Bonn disclaimed pretenses of scholarship. See *Wandering Scholar*, 3.

[22]*Charles W. Eliot, President of Harvard University* (*May 19, 1869-May 19, 1909*) (Boston, 1909). For biographical details see Kühnemann's

During the war itself he gathered funds in the United States for the rehabilitation of East Prussian territory overrun by the Russians and sought to reach German-Americans with a defense of the German position. The failure of these latter efforts resulted in a bitterness reflected in his wartime writings on the United States.[23] But by 1927 Kühnemann, who had returned to his professorship in philosophy at the University of Breslau, was again writing sympathetically about America and Americans. The close of the Weimar period saw the publication of an enthusiastic life of George Washington set in the framework of an appreciative sketch of the later course of American history and of a travel account relating the experiences of 17,297 miles of lecture journeys in the United States.[24]

Kühnemann's view of America was sympathetic, his judgments were perceptive; but he never brought to the study of American life and civilization the serious scholarship of Schönemann and Fischer, he never taught courses in American studies *per se*, and he never produced a major contribution to German literature on the United States. His major field remained German philosophy—*Amerikakunde* was essentially a bypath.

Besides these four men whose work in the field of American studies may be counted most outstanding, there was a considerable group of individuals who made significant but less comprehensive contributions to the new specialty. Some of them wrote little but taught courses dealing with aspects of American life and history. Others wrote on particular aspects of the American scene. But the number of those who devoted themselves enthusiastically and whole-heartedly to this new subject field was remarkably small.

A number of German historians produced volumes on the history of the United States, although none of them appear to have made it an exclusive specialty. Able general accounts were written by Paul Darmstädter, Professor of History at the University of Göttingen, by Carl Brinkmann at the University of Tübin-

---

memoirs, *Mit unbefangener Stirn. Mein Lebensbuch* (Heilbronn, 1937) and the brief sketch by "P. K.," "Erinnerungen an Eugen Kühnemann," *Breslauer Nachrichten*, II (1950), No. 18, 14.

23*Deutschland, Amerika, und der Krieg* (Chicago, 1915); *Deutschland und Amerika: Briefe an einen deutsch-amerikanischen Freund* (München, 1918).

24*Georg Washington, sein Leben und Werk* (Bremen, 1932); *Amerikafahrt, 1932* (Breslau, 1933).

gen, Konrad Haebler, director of the State Library in Berlin, and Friedrich Luckwaldt of the Technical University of Berlin.[25] None of these were marked, however, by real genius. The contributions of German historians on specialized themes and in the field of biography were somewhat more impressive.[26]

Sociological studies of some merit were published. In this classification may be placed the study by Carl Brinkmann, *Demokratie und Erziehung in Amerika* (*Democracy and Education in America*), the title of which is misleading. Brinkmann, in turn historian, national economist, sociologist, and political scientist, was in this volume the sociologist setting forth a thoughtful and sympathetic interpretation of American life and thought.[27] Charlotte Lütkens, who held no formal chair of sociology during this period, produced a critical but trenchant sociological interpreta-

[25] See bibliography. Apparently no translations of the standard survey histories of the United States were available. James Truslow Adams' *Epic of America* was published in translation in 1933. Harold Faulkner's *American Economic History* appeared in translation in 1929. Even James Bryce's *American Commonwealth* was not translated into German until 1924.

[26] Worthy of note are C. A. Bratter's *Amerikanische Industriemagnaten* (Berlin [c. 1927]); Hermann Lufft's *Samuel Gompers: Arbeiterschaft und Volksgemeinschaft in den Vereinigten Staaten von Amerika* (Berlin, 1928); Graf Albrecht von Montgelas' *Abraham Lincoln, Präsident der Vereinigten Staaten von Amerika* (Wien und Leipzig [c. 1925]); Gustav Adolf Rein's *Die drei grossen Amerikaner: Hamilton, Jefferson, Washington. Auszüge aus ihren Werken* . . . (Berlin, 1923) and his *Die historische Forschung über die Ursprünge der Verfassung der Vereinigten Staaten von Amerika* (München und Berlin, 1920?). Georg Friederici continued his work on the American Indians with his *Hilfswörterbuch für den Amerikanisten; Lehnwörter aus Indianersprachen und Erklärungen altertümlicher Ausdrücke, deutsch-spanisch-englisch* (Halle, 1926) and added a monograph on the colonial period, *Das puritanische Neu-England. Ein Beitrag zur Entwicklungsgeschichte der nordamerikanischen Union* (*Studien über Amerika und Spanien*, hrsg. von Karl Sapper *et al.*, völkerkundlich-historische Reihe, 1. Heft. Haale an der Saale, 1924). Käthe Spiegel wrote on the *Kulturgeschichtliche Grundlagen der amerikanischen Revolution* (München und Berlin, 1931) and Otto Vossler of the University of Leipzig provided a trenchant volume on *Die amerikanischen Revolutionsideale in ihrem Verhältnis zu den europäischen untersucht an Thomas Jefferson* (Beiheft 17 der *Historischen Zeitschrift*. München und Berlin, 1929). The only major study of the post Civil War period of American history was Emil Kimpen's *Die Ausbreitungspolitik der Vereinigten Staaten* (Stuttgart, 1923).

[27] (Berlin, 1927). Brinkmann's *Geschichte der Vereinigten Staaten* was published in 1924. He also published an article defending American spirituality, "Geistiges aus Amerika," *Die neue Rundschau*, XXVII, subvol. II (1926), 241-252.

tion of American capitalism.[28] And Andreas Walther, Professor of Sociology at Göttingen (later Hamburg), summarized for German scholars the accomplishments of American sociological study.[29]

Studies of American religion were relatively numerous and of good quality. Honors must be divided among the Swiss Professor of Theology at Zürich, Adolf Keller; Hermann Werdermann, Professor of Religion in Berlin; Hermann Sasse, Professor at Erlangen; and Karl Bornhausen, who taught religion at Marburg and Breslau.[30]

In respect to American business and industrial methods there was a plethora of volumes, a number of them worthy of praise. Julius Hirsch, former State Secretary in the Reich Economics Ministry, wrote the most widely known volume, which first used the term "Economic Miracle" for the United States.[31] Friedrich Aeroboe, an expert on land utilization in Breslau before he became rector of the University of Berlin, wrote on economics and culture in the United States.[32] Friedrich von Göttl-Ottlilienfeld, Professor of Theoretical National Economics and Director of the Political Science Statistics Seminar at the University of Berlin, wrote somewhat pompously on "Fordism."[33]

Still other aspects of American life received attention from German scholars. Emil Dovifat of the University of Berlin wrote a thorough and careful study of American journalism.[34] Erich Hylla, Professor of International Pedagogical Research at Frankfurt on the Main, produced the most significant book on the American educational system. Probably the best geographical treatise was that written by Kurt Hassert, Professor of Geography at the Technische Hochschule in Dresden.[35] German writing on the political system of the United States was disappointing. Bonn and

[28]Staat und Gesellschaft in Amerika. Zur Soziologie des amerikanischen Kapitalismus (Tübingen, 1929).

[29]Soziologie und Sozialwissenschaften in Amerika und ihre Bedeutung für die Pädagogik (Karlsruhe, 1927).

[30]See bibliography and discussion in Chapter X.

[31]Das amerikanische Wirtschaftswunder (Berlin, 1926).

[32]Wirtschaft und Kultur in den Vereinigten Staaten von Nord-Amerika (Berlin, 1930).

[33]Fordismus: ueber Industrie und technische Vernunft (Jena, 1926).

[34]Der amerikanische Journalismus, mit einer Darstellung der journalistischen Berufsbildung (Stuttgart, 1927).

[35]By Hylla, Die Schule der Demokratie; ein Aufriss des Bildungswesens

Schönemann provided worthwhile summaries, but the only significant scholarly study was that by Fritz Linn on the American presidency.[36]

There was, then, during the Weimar period a small grouping of scholarly volumes relating to America. But their leavening effect on the more superficial Americana of the day was insufficient. Too few Germans knew of the work of the sober and factual-minded scholars. Undoubtedly many more of them were acquainted with the writings of four men whose "America books" are subject to reservations as respects both the thoroughness of their research and the sincerity of their authors.

The first of these was the free-lance writer Arthur Holitscher. Holitscher produced four books on the United States. His first volume, a simple travel account, antedated the First World War but ran through new editions well into the postwar period.[37] Meanwhile, Holitscher had added an interpretative wartime propaganda piece, and in 1923 he refurbished his original book under a new title emphasizing "Life, Work, and Literature" in the United States.[38] After a second visit he published in 1930 a somewhat more mature travel study than that which he had written previously.[39] Holitscher clearly relied on travel and conversation rather than research. He was responsible for some astounding errors of fact and chose always to emphasize the dramatic. He served his German audience a diet planned to suit its tastes.

The last observation is even more true of the writings of Adolf Halfeld, who had taken a doctoral degree in political science at Hamburg before entering a career predominantly journalist in nature. From 1924 to 1929 he was the New York correspondent of the *Hamburger Fremdenblatt* and the *Münchener Neueste Nachrichten*. It was during the course of this stay in America that he published his book *Amerika und der Amerikanismus. Kritische*

---

der Vereinigten Staaten (Langensalza [1928]); Hassert, *Die Vereinigten Staaten von Amerika als politische und wirtschaftliche Weltmacht geographisch betrachtet* (Tübingen, 1922).

[36]*Die staatsrechtliche Stellung der Präsident der Vereinigten Staaten von Amerika* (Bonn, 1928).

[37]*Amerika heute und morgen. Reiseerlebnisse* (Berlin, 1912). The eleventh edition appeared in 1919.

[38]*Das amerikanische Gesicht* (Berlin, 1916); *Amerika, Leben, Arbeit und Dichtung* (Berlin, 1923).

[39]*Wiedersehn mit Amerika. Die Verwandlung der U.S.A.* (Berlin, 1930).

Betrachtungen eines Deutschen und Europäers (*America and Americanism. Critical Observations of a German and a European*). On its cover the volume carried the note that it was "das Gegenstück zu Henry Ford," "the answer to Henry Ford," and promised its readers, "He who has read this book is strengthened against preaching Americanism."[40]

Halfeld stated in very literary German in boldly drawn pictures all of the critical clichés denying American political, cultural, and social achievements. The page and chapter headings were slogan-like: "Chains on the spirit," "cultural feminism," "the omnipotence of the idea of success," "college militarism," etc. Clearly the author was directing himself to the prejudices and antagonisms of the Germans. If popularity and favorable reviews are an index, he succeeded.[41]

Two other would-be savants who wrote extensively on America while living in Germany were not Germans by birth. One was, indeed, an American by birth but both spiritually and physically an expatriate. This was Herman Scheffauer, who began his campaign of vilification against his own country shortly after the war, directing virulent denunciations against Woodrow Wilson for his treatment of the Germans.[42] In 1923 he published the book which became one of the most widely known volumes on the United States, *Das Land Gottes. Das Gesicht des neuen Amerikas* (*The Land of God. The Face of the New America*).[43] In its completely negative evaluation of American life and achievements it was in close accord with the volume by Halfeld. Scheffauer published another book in 1925 dealing with the literature of protest against the "spiritual America" of the day.[44] His career of anti-American invective was cut short in 1927 when Scheffauer, estranged from his wife, an English poetess, shot his secretary, the daughter of a Russian general, and then slashed his own wrists.[45]

---

[40] (Jena, 1927).

[41] For an example of the reviews, see Albert Lorenz, "Amerikanismus: Betrachtungen zu dem Werk Halfelds 'Amerika und der Amerikanismus,'" *Der Volkserzieher*, 1928, Beilag, "Der Bücherfreund," 1.

[42] *The German Prison-House. How to Convert it into a Torture Chamber and a Charnel; Suggestions to President Wilson* (Leipzig, 1920); *Blood Money; Woodrow Wilson and the Nobel Peace Prize* (Hamburg [1921]).

[43] (Hannover, 1923).

[44] *Das geistige Amerika von Heute* (Berlin, 1925).

[45] *New York Times*, October 8, 1927, 4:2; October 9, 1927, II, 2:1.

The fourth of the quasi-experts was by birth an Estonian nobleman. Graf Hermann Keyserling was the scion of a prominent Livonian family with a long tradition of intellectual accomplishment. After study in Geneva, Dorpat, Heidelberg, and Vienna, he obtained a doctoral degree in geology in 1920 and a year later published two books relating to that field.

Geology, however, failed to satisfy the inner urges of Keyserling's spirit. After his initial work in that field, Keyserling read Houston Stewart Chamberlain's *Foundations of the Nineteenth Century*, conceived a tremendous admiration for the Teutonic-minded Englishman, and was able to meet and work with him in Vienna. He also began his foreign travels, culminating in a trip around the world, 1911-1912. During the First World War he was declared unfit for military service and spent the fighting years on his estates at Raykull. Land expropriation laws deprived him of his family possessions in 1918, and in 1920 he moved to Darmstadt, where he established his "School of Wisdom." By this time he had also marked out his claim to be a philosopher by a number of publications and later asserted that he had at one time been recommended for an appointment to the faculty of the University of Berlin.[46]

In 1925 Keyserling published a lengthy and rambling "Travel Diary" containing the marks of the intuitive-psychological approach to the understanding of nations which became his motif. Keyserling believed that through the resolution of the internal stresses of his own personality he had discovered a formula of general application. Understanding and recognizing the woes of the *id* released the tensions of the individual and, in the same fashion, if a nation recognized its strengths and weaknesses, it too would be "set free" from many of its problems.[47]

By the time of his travel diary Keyserling had already begun to consider himself an expert on America. A thin and wandering chapter was devoted to his transcontinental trip from San Francisco to New York. His interpretative comments on America were expanded in his *Das Spektrum Europas* (*The Spectrum of Europe*),

[46]For life see *Kölnische Zeitung*, July 19, 1930; sketch, "My Life and My Work," in *The World in the Making* [*Die neuentstehende Welt*] (New York [c. 1927]), 3-88.

[47]See *The Travel Diary of a Philosopher* [translation of *Das Reisetagebuch eines Philosophen*], 2 vols. (New York [c. 1925]).

which probably became his best known volume.[48] In it Keyserling sought to set forth the national character of each of the major states of Europe. Although not really original, the various essays were indeed provocative, styled in vivid form, and close enough to the mark to win acclaim. The book underscores Keyserling's continued adherence to the traditions of the Balt and the aristocrat. It is not surprising to find him labeling the Germans the most creative people of Europe and stressing the role of the "grand seigneur" as typified particularly by the Hungarian nobility. What is surprising is to find him picturing trenchantly the introspectiveness of the German, the essential inwardness of the Teutonic scholar, and then asserting in contradiction to this thesis that the Germans should serve as the mirror of Europe and stressing their ability to understand other peoples.

All of this indicates that Keyserling, far from being a really perceptive observer of America, was actually merely a typical viewer of the New World scene, accepting most of the clichés concerning it and forming judgments within an emotional framework—scarcely veiled fears of Americanization and hostility to democratic institutions—and writing his major study in English under a title, *America Set Free*, which mirrored his belief that *He* had the answers to the real problems of all nations including this childlike one beyond the Atlantic.[49] Presumably the most important of these answers was that America must set herself free from Puritan restraints and from her naïve pride in her accomplishments. Once she recognized her weaknesses, the groundwork would be laid for progress. These suggestions were not particularly profound and not so different from the conclusions of many Germans of lesser reputation. Americans then and later have questioned Keyserling's stature as an expert on the United States.[50]

Americans are much more likely to find a revelation of understanding in some of the less serious studies of their country than in the volumes produced by some of the experts. Alfred Kerr, the

---

[48] (Heidelberg [c. 1929]).

[49] (New York and London, 1929).

[50] It would appear that in his later life Keyserling concentrated most heavily upon the development of the personality of the individual, a subject in respect to which some of his writings were undoubtedly significant contributions. See *Graf Hermann Keyserling. Ein Gedächtnisbuch* hrsg. von Keyserling Archiv (Innsbruck, 1948).

poet, awakens chords of delight because the spirit of his writing is so essentially American—he likes fast elevators, the bustle of traffic, tall buildings, creative activity—and Americans![51] For the same reason Manfred Hausmann's *Kleine Liebe zu Amerika* (*Little Love Song to America*) stirs happy feelings, although it presents little more than snapshots of the passing scene.[52] Of the serious works produced during the period, Schönemann's volumes, Kühnemann's travel book of 1932, and Bonn's general work on America share a place of prominence with Arthur Feiler's *Amerika-Europa*,[53] Anton Erkelenz' *Amerika von Heute* (*America of Today*),[54] and Arthur Rundt's *Amerika ist Anders* (*America is Different*).[55] Their authors were men of significance. Feiler was then the chief economic editor of the *Frankfurter Zeitung* and a member of the socialization committee of the German Economic Council. Erkelenz was the chairman of the German Democratic Party and Rundt a journalist. These men wrote with a willingness to see, to praise as well as to criticize, to portray rather than simply to win an audience. The vividness and validity of their observations are reflected in many of the later chapters of this book.

But of all the America books of the twenties none produces a kindlier impression than that of Hermann Werdermann on American religious life.[56] Werdermann spent a year in the midtwenties at Eden Theological Seminary in St. Louis. He taught American students, he attended American churches, he observed all that came before him. When he returned to Germany, he wrote his book, but began it with an apology:

> When one makes a journey to America, one is soon possessed by the desire to let others share the infinite [variety of] new impressions which one has acquired. But after being

---

[51]See *New York und London. Stätten des Geschicks. Zwanzig Kapitel nach dem Weltkrieg* (8. und 9. Auflage, Berlin, 1929); *Yankee-Land. Eine Reise* (Berlin, 1925).

[52]*Kleine Liebe zu Amerika. Ein junger Mann schlendert durch die Staaten* (7.-11. Auflage, Berlin, 1931).

[53]*Amerika-Europa. Erfahrungen einer Reise* (Frankfurt a. M., 1926).

[54]*Amerika von Heute. Briefe von einer Reise* (Berlin-Charlottenburg, 1927).

[55] (Berlin-Charlottenburg, 1926).

[56]*Das religiöse Angesicht Amerikas; Einzeleindrücke und Charakterzüge* (Gütersloh, 1926). Quotations here and later with permission of C. Bertelsmann Verlag.

over there half a year one becomes again doubtful of this
decision to set down impressions in literary form for the
benefit of others. There is too much which has stormed over
the observer, and it is too heterogeneous, and, as a living
thing, it makes every formula ridiculous, turns to dust every
rendition into words. When one has most observantly gazed
into "the face of America," then one believes many times
that he has seen it rightly and grasped its meaning, but in
the next moment that same clear insight becomes a riddle
which defies every solution, like a sphinx before which one
is silent. But this riddle-like character, this changing quality,
is indeed a fundamental characteristic of the picture of
America. . . .[57]

Unlike Keyserling, Werdermann read everything he could get
his hands on about America, measuring it against his own impressions. Travel books, he suggested, set forth three levels of accomplishment: the first involved acquaintance with the novel, which
might evoke simply surprise or enthusiasm. A closer acquaintance
often involved disappointment as the traveler became disturbed by
unfamiliar patterns of life and thought. The third stage, familiar-
ity, also brought understanding.[58]

Werdermann, like Schönemann, found most German books
about America disappointing. There was too much holding to one's
own standpoint, too little real meeting of the mind or of the soul—
"Truth and love have been so seldom bound together."[59]

In the chapters which follow, the emphasis is primarily upon
the impressions of the United States set forth by those who traveled
in the country and returned to write about their experiences. The
image of America which they provided should have been subject
to the correction of sober-minded scholars who knew America well
and were capable of providing perspective upon ways of life and
habits of thought quite different from those in Germany. But in
Weimar Germany the number of men like Werdermann who preserved the canons of cautious scholarship in evaluating a strange
new world was too small. And the number of those who have
joined together truth and love in their studies of the United States
is probably even yet too small.

57Ibid., 5.
58Ibid., 8.
59Ibid., 9.

Chapter III

THE AMERICAN LANDSCAPE

*I*t *Begins with New York*: The orientation of the new German visitor to the United States began almost universally in New York City. The view of its massive skyline from the arriving steamer occasioned mixed emotions. Sometimes the traveler found the city beautiful when covered with softening mists and the haze of distance. More frequently even on the steamer and certainly when he began to venture through the traffic-laden streets between the mountainous buildings, the average German was horrified. The noise, the bustle, the impersonality, the evidence of crass materialism, and the lack of attention to form and beauty repelled him. Some visitors came in time to see in these gigantic buildings a new kind of beauty. But most of them experienced an initial shock from which they never quite recovered. Here in New York they were confronted with a symbol of a new age, perhaps even more—Colin Ross, one of Germany's professional travelers, found that New York "includes within itself all the cities of the world and beyond this, the most absurd, fantastic, and unlikely [things] which exist."[1]

Some of the travelers lingered on in the great city assuming that it reflected the high points of American life. Felix Salten of *Bambi* fame suggested that New York revealed the quest of the American for change:

> Nowhere in the world have I found a great city whose raging development can be seen so quickly and clearly from the appearance of the streets. Here there exists no yesterday; today flits quickly by; and everything drives for tomorrow and the day after tomorrow; everything pushes toward the future.[2]

[1]*Fahrten- und Abenteuerbuch* (Berlin, 1930), 127.

[2] *5 Minuten Amerika* (Wien, 1931), 23-24. Quotations with permission of Paul Zsolnay Verlag and Frau Dr. Anna Wyler-Salten.

For some Germans the city also underscored the pressure of America on man's soul. Of the skyscrapers of New York Gerhard Venzmer wrote:

> And as they grasp there for the heavens, these stone-clad symbols of the American spirit, they lurch with invisible fists raised against the stranger and implant within his soul in that first meeting the seed-corn of the ways of thought from which they sprang. For under the gigantic mass effect the first person singular disappears and one feels himself unwillingly pulled into the brew, a lonely atom in a giant, flooding wave.[3]

"These tall buildings of Manhattan," he added, "are the face of America carved in stone."[4]

But Venzmer sought to portray New York "without its makeup." Very different was the impression of Alfred Kerr, the poet, who from his first visit to New York in 1914 had found "Beauty, beauty, beauty." And, he had added, "A new love lives in my heart; her name is 'New York.' "[5]

For Kerr was different from many of his countrymen— "But I love trains which hurry, basins which fill themselves, and elevators which go."[6] In three books his descriptions of New York are a panegyric on prosperity and success, on the beauty of American skyscrapers and the practicality and human qualities of those who worked within them, on the glitter of Broadway and the variety of artistic and musical accomplishments displayed there. New York, he proclaimed, was "a music city of high rank."[7] It was also "a European theater city. Of course in process of formation."[8] Although three-fourths of its theater accomplishments were the product of "old tricks," a fourth represented a new art. It was an error to think, as did the average European, "that on the stage there are only cheap effects, sensation, firecrackers, and a search for excitement."[9]

Again and again, Kerr stressed, "I speak of these things [of

[3]*New York ohne Schminke* (Hamburg [1930]), 48.

[4]*Ibid.*, 35.

[5]*New York und London*, 96. Quotations with permission of S. Fischer Verlag G.m.b. H, Frankfurt/Main.

[6]*Ibid.*, 98.

[7]*Ibid.*, 89.

[8]*Ibid.*, 76.

[9]*Ibid.*, 75.

New York] with love—for it is untrue that only 'civilization' lies behind them. Rather it is true that culture and fantasy also peer between them. A banquet for the artist. And for the thinker: because the power of the machine replaces that of man."[10]

Kerr was not alone in his favorable judgments. Another literary traveler, Erich von Salzmann, who had last visited New York in 1914, found in 1921 that the city had become beautiful—the buildings showing a new "enlightenment" with clarity and simplicity of lines, and advertising reduced to a not unappealing, more dignified electrical version. New York, said Salzmann, had become thoroughly American—it was the metropolitan city of the morrow: "North America has become . . . a world concept in itself. And New York is its living symbol."[11]

And Franz Westermann, an engineer, found that the tempo and activity "set the nerves of the observer into vibrant motion and stirred his blood to more rapid circulation." He could understand, after seeing it himself, why a friend had told him: "He who has lived and worked in New York for a few years no longer feels comfortable in older parts of the world and is drawn back here again in spite of his intentions to seek escape from this city."[12]

Louis Schulthess also learned to know and like New York, "the heart and head of the land," and Goethe expert Waldemar Oehlke found the city beautiful most particularly because it made no effort to be anything but what it was.[13]

2. Quer Durch: Most German travelers, however, after a few days in New York moved on in a rush to complete a transcontinental journey. "Quer durch"—"straight across"—was the slogan, for this carried with it the impression of an all-encompassing visit and helped to establish the traveler as a new-made expert on America. The fabulous expanse, from Berlin to middle Africa, as Kerr expressed it, constituted a tremendous lure.[14]

The quest for distance, however, reduced the degree of

[10]*Ibid.*, 30.

[11]"Die Grossstadt von Morgen," *Vossische Zeitung*, February 5, 1921.

[12]*Amerika, wie ich es sah. Reiseskizzen eines Ingenieurs* (Halberstadt, 1925), 11-12.

[13]Schulthess, *Durch den amerikanischen Kontinent* (Augsburg, 1920), 149-150; Oehlke, *In Ostasien und Nordamerika als Deutscher Professor. Reisebericht 1920-1926* (Darmstadt, 1927), 142.

[14]*Yankee-land*, 11.

sampling involved. Usually the visitor, as noted above, hopped from one city to another, judging the countryside between by the landscape whizzing by the window of his railroad coach.

The consequence was that cities dominated the accounts, and the German visitors sought to characterize them and to classify them. Most frequently visited, as might be expected, were Chicago, Washington, Detroit, San Francisco, and Los Angeles. Salt Lake City was a popular midway stop between Chicago and San Francisco. New Orleans was usually chosen if the journey dipped southward; Boston for New England. Visits to small cities and rural areas were infrequent.

As a result German impressions of the various sections of the United States were often derived at second hand. Again the stereotype dominated discussions. Few sought from first hand observation to check *a priori* assumptions against what actually existed.

3. Puritan New England—Bypassed but Significant: Perhaps the most neglected section of the country was New England. Its formative influence upon the American way of life was recited by almost every traveler. But very few visited the area. To do so, of course, placed a serious obstacle in the path of plans for transcontinental travel. Money and time negated the side trip from New York City north and east before starting the long journey westward.

Aside from those Germans, such as Schönemann, who learned something of New England from teaching experiences at Harvard, there were few who could speak of the region from the standpoint of personal observation. One of these few was Annalise Schmidt, whose book on *The American Man: on the character of America and of the American* (*Der amerikanische Mensch: vom Wesen Amerikas und des Amerikaners*) appeared in 1920. Miss Schmidt had spent an icy winter in a little village in Vermont a year before the war. The sunshine which accompanied the cold mitigated the climate, she found, but nothing dispelled the coldness of character of the people:

> A Vermont farmer looks like a nervous, perpetually troubled, underfed city dweller. The women are thin, hateful, sexless figures. The children with few exceptions are sickly and painfully wise beyond their years. When one takes a walk and they pass by in their sleighs or little wagons, one

never meets a friendly glance. The expression of great vexa-
tion, of superficial meditation, seems fixed on the men's
freshly-shaved, sectarian faces. It appears that they never
embrace all of their fellow men with sympathy. . . . They have
nothing of the suppleness, sturdiness, and fullness of daily
existence which make our farmers part of their soil. . . .
Ideas without sun seem to fill their thought world.[15]

And, as noted below, Miss Schmidt dealt most harshly with Puritanism and with its little white churches "too cold for God himself."[16]

Alfred Kerr, on his part, visited the United States twice before
deciding that he could not leave the third time without visiting
Boston. With New Orleans he placed Boston as the only other
city of the United States preserving a sense of earlier history. As
for New England:

New England—is this what one calls the whole region? Indeed, there is hidden here much of the spiritual in the
things of the intellect.
Indeed, there is to be found in this cold northern state of
Massachusetts a special kind of man. Close-lipped; con-
scientious; dry.[17]

And Kerr left the region with obvious relief to return to New
York—"the noisy, turbulent, insolent, ingenious, incomparable
city."[18]

Theodor Devaranne, an evangelical pastor who visited as a
representative of the foreign mission work of the church back home,
was more favorably impressed. Architectural styles, he found, were
superior to those elsewhere and there was a certain sense of nobility in the ease and grace of living displayed by the older
families.[19]

4. The "Feudal" South: To a considerable degree the South shared
the disadvantage of New England in that it involved for German
visitors an interruption or diversion from the normal quest for

[15]Der amerikanische Mensch. Vom Wesen Amerikas und des Amerikaners
(Berlin, 1920), 9, 66.
[16]Ibid., 9-11.
[17]Yankee-land, 194-195.
[18]Ibid., 198.
[19]Amerika, du hasts nicht besser! Reisebriefe aus Amerika (Heidelberg,
1929), 58-60.

"Quer durch," the transcontinental tour. As a consequence, it, too, often received cliché treatment in German accounts.

However, where New England labored under the handicap of preconceived hostility, the South found initial sympathy. It was a "feudal" region, its institutions reflecting those familiar back home. Moritz Bonn, although noting that the majority of settlers in the South were small farmers, added that these little people preserved the marks of feudalism:

> They have preserved down to the present day the outward marks of their unadulterated English origin: golden hair, blue eyes, sharply-cut features of almost aristocratic stamp. In their poverty-stricken surroundings they have maintained the mentality of the aristocrat, with their outlook proper to a feudalism founded on negro slavery.[20]

And he added that the upper classes, in spite of earlier contributions to American life, were now responsible for economic backwardness:

> Their upper classes succeeded in creating an atmosphere of restfulness, well-being and contentment—closely related to the French ideal of *bien-etre*—which at times indeed even extended to their slaves; they cultivated an attitude of retrospection, which their own sons and daughters, as well as the offspring of their poor kinsfolk in the mountain valleys, find it hard to abandon even today.[21]

Arthur Holitscher made very similar comments linking "a pretense of nobility" (*Adelsdünkel*) to what he erroneously called the "Republicans of the Southern States"![22] And Dr. Paul Rohrbach added for the South the term "Cavalier culture" and remarked that what he read of that area reminded him of those relationships which had existed previously in Pomerania or East Prussia or in his Baltic homeland of Livonia with the pride in family relationship to the n'th degree. Elsewhere in America, however, Rohrbach found everywhere evidence of standardization and leveling and the South no longer counted in the country as a whole.[23]

20*The American Adventure*, 31. Quotations with permission of G. Allen & Unwin, Ltd., London.

21*Ibid.*, 170.

22*Wiedersehn mit Amerika. Die Verwandlung der U. S. A.* (Berlin, 1930), 116.

23"Ein Blick in Amerikas Zukunft," *Kölnische Zeitung*, June 11, 1924.

A less pessimistic view of the New South was presented by a Swiss observer, L. Korr. He wrote that just on the other side of the federal capital the traveler notes that the land, the people, and the surroundings have suddenly changed:

> The people are different; they seem to think differently, to feel differently, and to work differently. The stranger feels involuntarily that the life and joy-giving sun burns more brightly and has given men a different tempo of life.[24]

But then he added that the third generation of Southerners since the Civil War was now beginning to put aside its resentments, to take on industries, and employ the capital, energy, and creative power of the North. Electricity, iron and steel works, tobacco, cotton-seed oil, furniture and rayon factories now found their home in this section. Its potentialities, he suggested, were still not fully exploited—coal, iron, marble, granite, copper, manganese, zinc, phosphate, earth for porcelain ware, and nut trees were there, and "an agricultural land blessed by God" where crops could be raised all year round. Cotton production had, he related, shifted predominantly to Texas, "a state larger than all of Germany." All in all, he stated in summary,

> The old romantic South has disappeared. Its swan song is still heard but only in the plays and comedies of the New York stage. The industrial wave moving irresistibly forward and the efforts toward rationalization can no longer be held back. The Southern states are seeking with all their might to lure more capital from the North. But whether the South will be happier thereby, whether racial hatred, poverty, and illiteracy will disappear and the standard of living be raised, that is another question.[25]

Friedrich Schönemann also stressed the existence of a New South. Once cotton had been king, he wrote, and like European kings he [King Cotton] had accumulated more and more land for himself and ruthlessly despoiled it. He had enslaved the majority of his subjects for the benefit of a small ruling class and had thereby created wealth and a temporarily glittering civilization. But King Cotton had also involved his realm in a fearful war between brothers, the outcome of which was total collapse. Today he still exercised power although there were internal divisions between

[24]"Der erwachende Süden," *Neue Zürcher Zeitung*, March 20, 1930.
[25]*Ibid.*

those things associated with his dynasty and the new world growing up around it.[26]

The New South, as Schönemann saw it, was being erected upon the realization that many conceptions of the Old South had been excessively romantic. But he expressed the hope that the section would retain some of its earlier character:

> In the interest of American culture it is to be hoped that the South will build itself up on the basis of its best tradition, so that with all the political and economic progress, it does not become simply a new (southern) version of Yankeedom, but much more preferably that it creates from its sense for the form of life and its joy in the grace of living, from its greater lightness of heart and its cheerfulness something like an American art of living. In this still revolution of the spirit the New South becomes perhaps the most interesting part of the United States of today.[27]

Most of the comments reproduced above, however, derived more largely from study than from observation. Few travelers saw a real cross-section of the area. For those who did dip into the region, Florida, New Orleans, and Texas held the greatest interest. Most other areas were seen as the travelers passed rapidly through them on their way to somewhere else.

The primary position of Florida in the travel accounts is not surprising. Some of the visitors came in the midst of the "boom" of land speculation, some shortly afterwards as values precipitately declined. Some came as scientists to explore an untouched primitive world. Some came as sea voyagers, where ease of access explained the visit.

While Leo Fall's operetta, "Roses from Florida," opened in Cologne,[28] Joseph Ponten, a well-known German writer, reveled in the Florida Sunshine in 1929 and read the news of foot-deep snow on the Riviera and frozen canals in Venice! For Florida, he suggested, climate was what gold had once been for Alaska:

> It is the Spain of the United States; it lies like Spain between two seas, the ocean and an inland sea. It produces like Spain the southern fruits. In the winter it is warmed not only by

[26]*Die Vereinigten Staaten*, II, 318. Quotations with permission of Deutsche Verlags-Anstalt, Stuttgart.

[27]*Ibid.*, 324.

[28]*Kölnische Zeitung*, August 31, 1929.

the sun but by the . . . Gulf Stream, which passes by visibly blue near the coast, and in summer it is cooled by a steady sea-breeze.

In comparison with the rest of the United States, he added, which had approximately the climate of the milder parts of Siberia, "the Land of Sunshine" was a term which had real meaning.[29]

Ponten described the boom and its collapse, the creation of "the city of wonder," Miami, out of nothing, the formation of suburbs with gates proclaiming the names of their founders:

> In the wilderness of the palmetto groves the "suburbs" stretch outwards. Each has one or more decorated city gates on which the name of the founder of the city is often proudly set forth. For here in America one is neither very fearful nor reticent with the use of his own name. Here and there on the system of streets which are built up alphabetically stands a dwelling house, erected by the city founder to attract the hoped for would-be-home-owners, and often the house is empty and waiting. And in these [houses] every kind of "taste" is served. There are, indeed, beautiful houses, villas, and country homes, especially beautiful because of their gardens filled with the finest tropical flowers, cared for by Negro gardeners. This land in which there is still much to be learned about construction escapes only in its business houses and factories a quite sentimental and often romantically colored eclecticism. There are country houses in the style of a secluded Spanish monastery or of a coldly noble Tuscan villa; but one can also choose Venetian, Turkish, Indian, Chinese, and old-Christian-Byzantine. Southern architecture builds [excessive] daintiness—little towers, little balconies, little courts, little fountains—but in spite of all the showiness the cool shaded courts have a pleasant effect in this land of sun. The little fountain sprays and the people rock in their rocking chairs in the February heat. A canary marks time inside.[30]

Ponten's half-cynical, half-admiring description continued as he noted the presence of a moneyed aristocracy and of eccentricities in houses and living styles. But, in the end, he acknowledged the great future of Miami:

> "The magic city"—the courage to use such a description is a part of the excessive, somewhat childish and even cheap

[29]"Aus den Vereinigten Staaten," *ibid.*, August 11, 1929. Egon Erwin Kisch also compared Florida with Spain— . . . *beehrt sich darzubieten: Paradies-Amerika* (Berlin, 1930), 88 ff.

[30]*Ibid.*

American optimism. And still, in spite of all the deception of speculation and bombast, the optimists are right: there is sound thought in the idea that one day this whole land will be the winter garden of the industrial and commercial North; for the natural wealth of the land will continue to rise, the welfare of the people will develop fabulously, and even the worker will take his winter vacation in the South. Then all plans will take on reality here and you will not have to be Alexander, who founded a dozen Alexandrias in Middle Asia, to have cities named after you—if you can raise the money, if you have plans, if you are on good terms with lady fortune and if you can afford to bide your time. Above all "the magic city" is a name which is actually spoken here with affection and is used as an official co-name for the city of Miami—one sees it on the shields of the autos which are at home here—the most effective form of advertising, and its enchantment will imprint itself on the spirits of those in the wintry North and have the intended effect upon them.[31]

Economics Professor Bruno Dietrich echoed Ponten's predictions of Florida's future: *"For the most immediate future Florida is without doubt a typical example of unlimited economic opportunities and therewith of the most modern feature in the economic configuration of the U.S.A."*[32] And Annie and Raoul Francé, who visited Florida chiefly for scientific purposes—to study the formation of lignite in the swamps of the Everglades—found the state a land of a fabulous future: ". . . everything grows here, as if this were the Garden of Eden, as the land is often named, and it is no exaggeration when a serious work of economics says in respect to the Everglades that they are a portion of the earth which will one day feed not only all of Florida but a goodly portion of the earth itself."[33]

There were those visitors, of course, who were repelled by the artificial character of Florida's east coast. Heinrich Hauser be-

[31]*Ibid.*

[32]*U. S. A. Das heutige Gesicht* (Breslau, 1926), 133. Italics Dietrich's.

[33]Raoul Heinrich Francé, *Lebender Braunkohlenwald. Eine Reise durch die heutige Urwelt* (Stuttgart, 1932), 40. Quotation with permission of Frau Annie Francé-Harrar (Raoul's wife), who called Florida the "land of excess" and also described it in glowing tones in her *Florida. Das Land des Überflusses* (Berlin-Schöneberg [c. 1931]). Another natural scientist, the paleobiologist of the University of Vienna, Othenio Abel, devoted several sections of his book, *Amerikafahrt. Beobachtungen und Studien eines Naturforschers auf einer Reise nach Nordamerika und Westindien* (Jena, 1926) to the mangrove swamps and hammocks of southern Florida—56-96; 162-183.

gan his wanderings in Florida, but found it "Wannsee and Luna Park [German amusement parks] exaggerated into monstrousness"— "an artificial paradise," "a theatrical review which has become permanent."[34] And sea captain Carl Kircheiss, in spite of a friendly reception in Miami, called it "the Sin-Babel of the U.S.A." declaring it existed only "by the brutal will to survive."[35] And Felix Baumann, who published several volumes on the darker side of American life, related that the center of bordel life in America had moved to Jacksonville and the "American riviera," the Atlantic coast, and in even more exaggerated form to Tampa, the "Monte Carlo of America."[36]

Many of these travelers went from Florida into other parts of the South. Josef Ponten, for example, passed from Florida proper across the panhandle (which reminded him of the *Caprivizipfel* in Africa) into the Gulf Coast and Mississippi Delta region. With disappointment he found remnants of German settlements—"Lac des Allemands" and "Robertcove"—losing their German character and noted the omnipresent Negro workers in cotton fields and tobacco plantations—"they say it goes as well for them as they could wish."[37]

Manfred Hausmann passed in his happy-go-lucky travels through the swamps and forests of South Carolina and Georgia into the "paradise" of Florida, Daytona Beach, enjoyed the vistas of the Keys from his train window, made the friendship of a police sergeant in the "magic city" of Miami, "thumbed" his way to Palm Beach, eavesdropped on an evening "concert" on the porch of colored workers at the Dude Farm, "studied" false geography in a sight-seeing bus in Jacksonville ("The St. Johns was the only river in the world which flowed North!"), learned the glories of the Civil War in Atlanta, and passed through Chattanooga and across the Mississippi on his way northward.[38]

[34]*Feldwege nach Chicago* (Berlin, 1931), 18.

[35]*Meine Weltumsegelung mit dem Fischkutter Hamburg* (Leipzig, 1942 [originally published in Berlin, 1928]), 208.

[36]*Aus dunklen Häuser Amerikas. Chicago die Stadt der Verworfenen. Sittengeschichte aus den Vereinigten Staaten* (Stuttgart, 1920), 68-9.

[37]"In deutschen Dörfern am Mississippi," *Kölnische Zeitung*, August 18, 1929. Ponten did not publish these accounts until 1937, when they appeared under a title emphasizing the later portions of his journey, *Besinnliche Fahrten im Wilden Westen* (Leipzig, 1937).

[38]*Kleine Liebe, passim.*

Many German visitors, of course, registered their interest in New Orleans, although the portraits of that city were never so sharply drawn as those of New York and Chicago. Although Kerr found with dismay that a cold winter had taken its toll of some of the palm trees, he found New Orleans "alluring," but believed that the French flavor of the city, like the frost-damaged palm trees, showed evidence of decline.[39]

Rudolph Hensel sweltered in the heat but admired the broad avenues and the remnants of French and Spanish architecture, and noted with pleasure that German elements retained proper German names and manners.[40]

Lajos Steiner felt much at home here, where "the heavy blood of the Anglo-Saxon is mixed with the lighter of the Latin" and where old and new were combined.[41]

And Heinrich Hauser found it "the first American city that I know in which work, sport, and amusement are properly weighed against one another: Americanism softened by southern climate."[42] But for Hauser the high spot of New Orleans was his view of the Creole girls on an excursion boat:

> The Creole girls with long, waving, colored dresses, look like flowers. Like very proud tulips moved by the wind. They are tall, like slender palms next to the mostly shorter men. Their faces are long ovals, dark and encased deeply in flat, black hair. Their teeth are very white, their lips are very red. They dance in the manner of 1880: with their bosoms they lean against their partners. Their long, narrow rumps describe an elegant curve toward the rear and end there in two pleasing, round hills. Somewhere from this point downward the legs are hung; they move as if dangling, not at all as though they are a part of the women. It is unbelievable, but it is wonderfully beautiful. Only women who are so unbelievably developed could achieve this mad posture. The few American girls who are here do not begin to come up to them.[43]

Hauser visited other parts of the Mississippi South also—

[39]*Yankee-land*, 31-34.

[40]*Die neue Welt. Ein Amerikabuch* (Dresden, 1929), 124-128.

[41]*Unter Palmen, Bohrtürmen, Wolkenkratzern. Eindrücke aus Nord- und Latein-Amerika* (Stuttgart, 1931), 88-89.

[42]*Feldwege nach Chicago*, 43. Quotations with permission of S. Fischer Verlag G.m.b.H., Frankfurt/Main.

[43]*Ibid.*, 45-46.

Natchez with its flowers, Arkansas City with "Negro children, black swine, snarling dogs, cows with bells, rusty tractors, plows, mules, and broken down Ford trucks," and on up the Mississippi with Negro girls in the harbor towns singing, "Come in, come in, darling," to Memphis.[44]

Texas also received a considerable share of German attention, largely because entry through the Gulf ports of Houston and Galveston gave an easy way onwards to "the Wild West." German visitors marveled at the size and developing business of these port cities—Houston already America's third largest harbor, "the city of tomorrow and the day after tomorrow."[45] Heinrich Hauser was also impressed with the people:

> Wonderfully beautiful girls, dark, like the advertisements on the peach cans, their movements free as if they are accustomed to wide, open places. A highly developed race, the men often really gigantic. Open jackets. Suits of good material and splendidly sloppy. Impressive at first glance: old women with white hair, but their skin has the freshness of young girls and their movements are athletic. They laugh and show blinding teeth. They are women who have lived a free and happy life.[46]

But Texas also displayed all the evils of segregation and all the harshness of law enforcement, with its chain gang prison labor. Kurt Faber, a self-described "greenhorn," visited its jails twice, described the exploitation of prison labor, and found that in Texas "the color line leads even into the hospitals, yes, even into the grave."[47]

In all of the above, the cities more properly considered purely "Southern" appear much neglected. Atlanta, Savannah, Columbia, etc., were not very frequently visited. The Baroness Ilse von Rechenberg described the back country of Georgia as she and her family saw it while moving from a farm in Maryland to a new home in Florida. They found Savannah "a wonderfully pretty, typical southern city," but the swamps, the heat, the Bible verses on the roadsides, the absence of good places to eat made them

[44]*Ibid.*, 65-96.

[45]*5 Minuten Amerika*, 60-61.

[46]*Feldwege nach Chicago*, 20.

[47]*Rund um die Erde. Irrfahrten und Abenteuer eines Grünhorns* (Berlin, 1924), 67-131; quotation, 72.

happy to leave Georgia and get into Florida.[48] Not even Savannah gained the praise of Egon Kisch, who found that its Negro quarter cast shadows on the title of his book *Paradise America*, the appearance of the children there, he said, scarcely equalled that of the beggars of North Africa.[49]

The fullest account of a visit to Georgia was that set forth by Felix Salten, the author of the *Bambi* books. "Here in the state of Georgia," he wrote, "is a southern garden. The same trees, the same flowers as we have. Only more splendid, coming to ecstasy under the hot kisses of a tender sun."[50] He admired the "villas" of Atlanta, the city park larger than that of Schönbrunn castle at home, and found the city much happier than those of the North:

> The city of Atlanta is filled with merriment, with lovable, hospitable people eager to be of service. Much more than in the North one is patted on the back and shoulders with a friendly smile, and much more vigorously. One is often taken by the arm and supported as if he were feeble or a baby. Really charming.

But he found that these "people without nerves" let things slide—nothing in his hotel room worked properly, not the bath, nor the water faucets, nor the doors, nor the service—only the radio which blared noisily in the hall. And most disturbing of all were the racial bars which excluded even the "whitest" Negroes from social intercourse with the Whites. Salten ignored warnings not to go to the Negro university there and, if he did so, not to shake hands with the students or professors. (The man who gave him the advice had a Negro servant and a Negro chauffeur whom he treated almost as personal friends.) He attended chapel, presided over by the woman president "out of whose eyes the goodness shines," and listened to a choral program ("lights transformed into sound") in which the lark-like voice which dominated the singing belonged to the darkest and least appealing of the choir members. He talked about "the problem" with the professors there but found

[48]"D. v. R." (Dorothee von Rechenberg), "Wie man in Amerika Farmer wird. Ungeschminkte Bilder aus dem Leben eines deutschen Ehepaares," Berlin *Tägliche Rundschau*, December 28-31, 1927; April 21-25, 1928. The author has told the story of the Rechenbergs more completely in the "Vista" section of the Sunday *Tallahassee Democrat*, May 9, 1965.

[49]*Paradies-Amerika*, 84.

[50]*5 Minuten Amerika*, 63. The visit to Georgia is described 53-58; 63-74. Quotations with permission of Paul Zsolnay Verlag and Dr. Anna Wyler-Salten.

himself "painfully embarrassed" by the color bars of the South. Perhaps he summarized best the overriding view of most Germans when he wrote, "Here is the South with its fulness, with its glow and with its neglect of things, with its pleasantness and with its danger, with its good and with its barbarous instincts, with its sun and with its deep shadows."[51]

5. *The "Valley of Democracy"*: The broad area between the Appalachians and the Rockies was, for German visitors, the heart of American life, the "valley of democracy." The nation's center of gravity, they believed, had moved from New England into this broad area sheltered by two mountain ranges and two oceans.[52]

Annalise Schmidt, who reacted so violently against the chill of New England, found things much different beyond the Appalachians:

> There between the Alleghenies and the Rocky Mountains, in the plains of the great rivers and lakes, is the home of the true American. His most appealing qualities are generosity and a somewhat easy-going good will, concern, and perceptive understanding towards his family, his friends, his surroundings. Art, for this true American, is somewhat distant and unknown. . . . In his sensitivity for all that is vital and powerful he is a heathen, but at the same time by temperament a mystic. But he is educated as a Puritan. In most [Americans] these contrary elements dwell side by side.[53]

In very similar tone Ludwig Müller, a school superintendent in Wuppertal-Barmen, wrote:

> Here [between the Appalachians and the Rockies] dwells perhaps the purest type of American. In the mixing of peoples which takes place here in the Middle West a type of man has developed cautious and mistrustful of European connections, Puritanically severe even in those circles which would indignantly reject this religious label although they are still held fast by its grim power, millions who find self-reliance within the vast reaches of their land and know themselves protected between two mountain ranges and two oceans.[54]

[51]*Ibid.*, 62.

[52]E.g., Carl Baumann. "Zum Wesen des Amerikanismus," *Zofingia, Zentralblatt des Zofingvereins*, LXXI, 220-237 (1931), 237.

[53]*Der amerikanische Mensch*, 91.

[54]In Walther Fischer and others, *Handbuch der Amerikakunde*, 102.

Many of the visitors were familiar with the Turner thesis of the formative influence of the frontier on American life and paid due respect to the democratization of life and government which had been a part of the westward push. Few, however, made any discrimination between the "Middle West" as Americans know it and the area beyond.

Almost all of them visited Niagara Falls with proper expressions of respect. But once beyond the Appalachians, the travelers turned to the business world—to the industrial cities, Detroit,[55] Duluth,[56] on occasion River Rouge (for the new Ford plant),[57] but above all Chicago! Chicago was to Germans the symbol of the Middle West. "It is," suggested one writer,

> not only for decades the gate to the immeasurable prairie but also the economic, political, and in growing measure the spiritual center of the Middle West, where conservatism and democracy, quiet patience and deepest passion, Puritan religiosity and an increasingly stronger freedom of thought are united in a truly American contrasting effect. Here one believes in the separateness of the United States, is sceptical in respect to any foreign propaganda, partially because of the experience of the war and postwar years, and wishes just to exist and to be left alone.[58]

But many Germans were critical. Dr. Bernhard Goldschmidt found the contrasts of light and shadow, of wealth and poverty, too great—the city was depressing.[59] Westermann considered it the most disagreeable city of his visit—New York by contrast a very clean city![60] Engineer Gottfried Huldschiner labeled it "a horrible monstrosity of a city."[61] And Felix Salten mingled small praise with large doses of criticism, contrasting the "happy, harmless industriousness of its people" with "the insane criminal chronicle of its bootlegger band" and adding:

> The good is present in the humanity, citizenship, patience, industry, and prosperity [of its people]. The fullness [of life]

[55]See Westermann, *Amerika, wie ich es sah,* 18-27.

[56]Dietrich, *U. S. A., das heutige Gesicht,* 87-92.

[57]E.g., Georg Kühne, *Von Mensch und Motor, Farm und Wolkenkratzer. Reiseskizzen eines deutschen Ingenieurs* (Leipzig, 1926), 42-46.

[58]Ludwig Müller in *Handbuch der Amerikakunde,* 102.

[59]*Von New York bis Frisco. Ein deutsches Reisetagebuch* (Berlin, 1925), 72-74.

[60]*Amerika, wie ich es sah,* 38-39.

[61]"Vom Golden Gate zum Hudson," *Vossische Zeitung,* August 10, 1923.

is there in gigantic paradisiac proportions. But all this is continually shattered by much too corrupt officials. . . .[62]

If New York had its lover and advocate in Alfred Kerr, Chicago found its paramour in Heinrich Hauser, a doctor turned *litterateur*, who visited the city in 1930. "This is the most beautiful city of the world," he wrote, "a technical dream in aluminum, glass, steel, cement and artificial suns, strange as another planet. Fantastic as one of H. G. Wells' novels come to life. The future of civilization has been anticipated." And he found the people just as interesting: "Something in the atmosphere of this city enfolds me like a warm bath. The people here are generous and primitive in an unconscious way. The instincts are strong." Chicago's women, he found, were beautiful, but somewhat to be pitied:

> A new type of women. They are beautiful. Their movements are flighty, like wild things, so worried are they by the autos in crossing the street. Their skin is wasted and heavy-pored from the gas-filled air of the metropolis. The roughness of the streets makes them tenderer, weaker, and thereby more lovable. The type of the future will be a suffering one.

It might be added that Hauser saw much of the seamy side of Chicago also, not only from his residence in one of the city's cheap hotels—a "gangster hotel" he called it—but also from his interviews and visits about the city with Dr. Ben Reitman, a socialist philanthropist of the day.[63]

Another defender of the city was Louis Schulthess who found that in Chicago success was not the consequence of what you know as in Boston, where you come from as in Washington, or what you have as in New York, but rather what you can do.[64]

6. *The "Wild West" and Beyond*: There was for Germans a special lure in the real West, the "Wild West" of American history. The works of Karl May portraying the adventures of his Apache nobleman, "Winnetou," and of "old Shatterhand," his frontier hero, had already passed from the first to the second generation of

[62]*5 Minuten Amerika*, 155.

[63]*Feldwege nach Chicago*, 152-216. Quotations with permission of S. Fischer Verlag.

[64]*Durch den amerikanischen Kontinent*, 119.

German readers.[65] And the somewhat more realistic account of hunting and adventure in the Wild West by Friedrich Armand Strubberg[66] had reached its ninth edition.

The interest in the days of the frontier continued throughout the Weimar period. Karl May's work still found an uncritical audience little concerned with the authenticity of his stories and Strubberg's book passed through eight more editions during this period. In 1927 Friedrich von Gagern added to the German reading list on the American West his "frontiersman book" in which he sought to bring over into German the little known writings of James Fenimore Cooper and other tales relating to "pathfinders, chieftains, and leather-stocking men."[67] Popular publications still found interest in the stories of the West also, for example, the colorful series, strikingly illustrated, by Joseph Delmont in *Die Woche*—"Going West, the Way of the Pioneers" and "Cowboys in Winter."[68]

The passing of the days of adventure but not of the lure of un-tamed nature, of outdoor life, and of strong men was reflected in the vignettes of life set forth by Paul C. von Gontard in his book, *West vom Mississippi. Bilder aus den unpolierten Breiten des heutigen Nordamerika* (*West of the Mississippi: Pictures of the Un-polished Reaches of Contemporary North America*).[69] Gontard pictured the new days of the Texas cowboy, with the picturesque "longhorns" and the romantic gunfighter having disappeared from the scene. In their place were the sturdier, more tractable, more profitable Hereford bulls, and the modern cowboy still in love with his horse and the round-up, but better paid and more settled in his ways than earlier.[70] Similarly, he found that the ravaging Indians of the past had given way to the idyllic life of Chief "Tawakptiwa" ("Evening Sunshine") of the Taos tribe of New Mexico, content now with his lands and his fat cattle, but still

[65]See Joseph Wechsberg, "Winnetou of der Wild West," *The American West*, I, No. 3 (Summer, 1964), 32-39.

[66]*Amerikanische Jagd- und Reiseabenteuer aus meinem Leben in den westlichen Indianergebiete*, originally published in 1858.

[67]*Das Grenzerbuch. Von Pfadfindern, Häuptlingen, und Lederstrümpfen* (Berlin, 1927). The indebtedness to Cooper is indicated in the preface, vii-ix.

[68]XXX, No. 42, 1353-1355 (October 20, 1928); XXXI, No. 4, 111 (June 26, 1929).

[69](Berlin, 1928).

[70]Ch. II.

holding to the old ways of his people and sanctioning the beating by his tribesmen of his son, "Joe," whose medical training had led him to desert Indian clothes and customs.[71]

Gontard's book still breathed the lure of unsettled wilderness and wasteland, of struggles against great natural obstacles, and of unexpected wealth. On one occasion this was the dramatic realization by a trio of gold-seekers that before them in the hills of Arizona lay four-footed gold—the plentiful supply of rabbits which they began to ship into southern California to compete with the much more expensive poultry of the area.[72] On another, it was the dramatic strike of a rich oil gusher.[73] And the "Greenhorn" still found the West a place of misadventure, via a fleecing by professional gamblers on the train.[74]

Other Germans, too, followed the lure of the great Western reaches. Prof. Adolf Reichwein loaded up his Model T Ford with camping provisions, sought out the Anaconda copper mines of Butte and the silver mines of Philippsburg, the wheat fields of "Bitter Root Valley" of Montana, the dairy farmers of North Dakota, and the beauties of the Yellowstone. In the West he found

> the real America, where nothing is smooth and finished, where everything is still in the first stages of civilization, in its beginnings, in hopes, in plans, in construction, where the people still speak with iron-like conviction of unlimited possibilities.[75]

Another who traveled by car was Josef Ponten, who with his wife and another traveling companion went by truck from Florida across the Gulf states into Texas and on into Arizona and New Mexico, the principal interest of their journey being the Pueblo Indians. Ponten, however, published only a small portion of his fascinating descriptions of the lonesome wastelands and the lives of its decimated red-skinned inhabitants during the Weimar period.[76]

Accounts of adventurous "bumming" visits across the West

---

[71]Ch. X.   [72]Ch. VI.
[73]Ch. VII.   [74]Ch. V.
[75]*Blitzlicht über Amerika* (Jena, 1930), 42-75.
[76]"Indianische Pueblos," *Kölnische Zeitung*, September 22, 1929; "Vom unbekannten Amerika," *ibid.*, January 12, 1930. The full account of the journey appeared 1937 as *Besinnliche Fahrten im Wilden Westen*.

found interested German readers both before and after the First World War. Karl Ey (Meyer) told of wanderings through the West "with 100 marks" and of Omaha, the cocaine center of the region, a city where an innocent German-American was railroaded for the murder committed by one of the political leaders of the city.[77] Kurt Faber related "the erring journeys and adventures of a greenhorn."[78] Oskar Kollbrunner described his "driftwood" wanderings through the West[79] and "Jack Omaha" his adventures with "crooks, charlatans, and redskins."[80]

Most German travelers, however, went by sleeping car, admiring the natural marvels of the Yellowstone, of the Yosemite valley, and the Grand Canyon, the raw but colorful beauties of the Arizona desert, and the lush wealth of California. Somehow the nagging, nasty criticisms of America faded away in the presence of these great reaches of land still to be developed, in the realization of the immense labor which was still being expended in converting a wilderness into settled land. The West confirmed the belief of the German visitors that the United States was still very much "a colonial land," but it stilled their cavilling against urban materialism.

Thus Anton Erkelenz, visiting Salt Lake City with its broad streets, its many flowers and parks, its tasteful one-family homes, and listening to the magnificent organ performance in the Mormon tabernacle, reflected that fifty to seventy years had been all that had been devoted to transforming a wilderness into civilization.[81] Perhaps Alfred Kerr expressed more frankly than most Germans were willing to the thought that accompanied the views of new cities and green farms growing up in formerly arid and unproductive regions:

> Yankee power! They created out of the wilderness a paradise. They reached toward the stars and the stars gave their all.[82]

[77]*Mit 100 Mark nach USA. Ein deutsches Schicksal in Amerika* (Berlin [1930]), 52-74.

[78]*Rund um die Erde. Irrfahrten und Abenteuer eines Grünhorns.*

[79]*Treibholz. Irrgänge eines Amerikafahrers.*

[80]*Wilde Fahrten im wilden Westen. Mit Gaunern, Gauklern und Rothäuten unterwegs* (Hamburg, 1927).

[81]"Quer durch das amerikanische Festland," *Die Hilfe*, 1925, No. 17, 365-366.

[82]*Yankee-land*, 111.

There is in the German accounts of visits to the Yellowstone, the Grand Canyon, the Yosemite valley, little to set them off from a typical American view, except, perhaps, the almost poetic quality of their descriptions.[83] They praised the efficiency of conducted tours, the provision of hotel and camping facilities, the concept of park service for the enjoyment of all. Always the size impressed—Yellowstone Park as large as all Bavaria. The democratization of recreational facilities and the linking of the auto and the enjoyment of nature were repeatedly praised.

And for most Germans, California was a place apart. Their impression of lush growth, of wealth was enhanced by the fact that most emerged from the scrub-grown areas of the Southwest into the greenery of southern California. Alfred Kerr found there a true feeling of good fortune: "You feel in California not only the warmth of the blue heaven (which, as is known, laughs), but also the warmth of the most recently won human progress and the most recently gained opportunities for labor."[84] And Felix Salten spoke of "the wealth displayed in blinding, overwhelming nakedness."[85]

The cities of the West coast also received a more favorable appraisal than those of the East. Los Angeles suffered under the burden of its Hollywood connections, but its rapid growth, its combination of bustling business and tropical living found it favor. For Rudolf Hensel it was "the city of the three 'F's' "—"Fruit, films, and foreigners (tourists)." Skyscrapers and advertising lights were not, he felt, "so wild" as in New York, and the whole city made "an impression of dignity and cultivation." The women, he added, had even discovered that they could get along without lipstick. And the hundreds of thousands of "villas" lining the broad avenue were separated neither from one another nor the public by fences. "Free under the sky and equals among equals," they made an impression of being joined together like a "family in a common, but unusually splendid park of enchanting beauty."[86]

Lajos Steiner was in agreement. "This struggle for existence," he wrote, "has not taken on such crass forms as elsewhere in

[83]E.g., Salten, *5 Minuten Amerika*, 84 ff.; Anton Erkelenz, *Amerika von Heute*, 14-27.

[84]*Yankee-land*, 6.

[85]*5Minuten Amerika*, 103-104

[86]*Die neue Welt*, 137.

FIGURE 1.—The continued popularity of Indians and the West in emphasized in this sketch from the widely circulated German weekly *Die Woche*, 1928, 1353.

America. I have noticed none of the nervous, tense haste which impressed me in the great cities of the East. One has time to enjoy the sunny side of existence and to rejoice that he is alive."[87]

Even more than Los Angeles, San Francisco won its praise. It was for the German visitor unquestionably America's most popular city. "The pearl of the West Coast," Lajos Steiner called it, "a fortress of the white race against the yellow people who live beyond the Pacific."[88] "One thinks of Brussels, perhaps even of Rome," wrote Doctor of Engineering Gottfried Huldschiner, as he strolled up and down the hilly streets and admired the pleasant perspectives which the city offered, "but then one looks around, finds himself at the other end of the world in San Francisco, and he wonders, wonders."[89] In contrast, Dr. Bernhard Goldschmidt, one of the highly critical visitors of the period, found San Francisco a mixture of Paris and Vienna and wrote that he was more at home there than in any other city in the country.[90]

Rudolf Hensel, however, found no trace of European air there and was enchanted by "the strange, wild, east-west mixture of men of all peoples, colors, and races" and by a plant world which amazed him with its luxuriousness and beauty.[91] Franz Friedrich Oberhauser found it "freer, sunnier, and not so sober, earnest and hard" as New York. He spent a night in Chinatown—his guide a German from Munich who had come over ten years earlier and stayed, perhaps because of the excellent quality of Chinatown beer![92]

The cities of the Northwest also attracted their share of visitors much impressed by the omnipresent lumbering operations and by the search for culture even in this remote region. Dr. Rudolf Hensel admired the roses of Portland and the "villas" which nestled among them, but added, "In every step one senses how young all of this still is; everywhere the egg shells of colonial times are still there. But everywhere there are also the moves toward the new,

[87]*Unter Palmen*, 125.

[88]*Ibid.*, 100-103.

[89]"San Francisco," *Vossische Zeitung*, August 7, 1923.

[90]*Von New York bis Frisco*, 34-36. Similar, Kurt Faber, *Rund um die Erde*, 218.

[91]*Die neue Welt*, 151.

[92]"Amerika von der anderen Seite," *Kölnische Volkszeitung*, June 30, 1929; "Nacht in Chinatown," *Kölnische Zeitung*, August 25, 1929.

and one asks himself how it will all look after twenty years."[93]
Bernhard Goldschmidt was particularly impressed with the keen
sense of enterprise and the optimism of Seattle.[94] Another visitor
described with astonishment the creation from scratch of an entire
lumbering city complete with individual homes for workers, parks,
artificial lakes, hospital, and schools.[95]

7. *Once over Lightly*: One city demands attention separate from
considerations of sections and regions—Washington, D. C. Most
German travelers sought to visit it. Almost all praised it as the
worthy showplace of a democratic state, "the salon of America,"[96]
"the Rome of the New World."[97] Rudolf Hensel reported that his
friends had called Washington a "European city" as though that
were an advantage (which he doubted). But the "agreeable quiet-
ness" of the city did not, he found, make it European. Washington
was "absolutely American," American in its youth and in its rapid
growth:

> American are the broad streets, the many parks, and very
> particularly American the extremely broad vistas which lie
> between the capital and Potomac Park; no European city
> would set aside such a gigantic area simply for purposes of
> display. American are above all things the Greek gables, Ionic
> and Doric columns which appear in masses (nowhere is there
> so much antique as in America) and just as American the
> splendid Washington monument, which in Europe would not
> be one-third as high.[98]

"The center of political life," wrote Franz Westermann, "has nowhere else in the world found such an imposing symbol as in
Washington."[99]   Herbert Eulenberg noted the propriety of the

---

[93]*Die neue Welt*, 173-174.   [94]*Von New York bis Frisco*, 16.

[95]Longview, Washington. Feiler, *Amerika-Europa*, 26-31; *cf.* Ernst Prosinagg, *Das Antlitz Amerikas. Drei Jahren diplomatische Mission in den U. S. A.*
(Wien, 1931), 154-155.

[96]Sandor Friedrich Rosenfeld [Roda Roda], *Ein Frühling in Amerika*
(München, 1924), 129.

[97]Kühnemann, *Amerikafahrt*, 30.

[98]*Die neue Welt*, 242-243. Paul Fechter, an architect, came to a much less
favorable evaluation. Too much space, he said, had been left between the
great buildings in Washington—they were not in harmony with their "Raum."
"Der amerikanische Raum," *Deutsche Rundschau*, CCIX (April-June, 1929),
47-59.

[99]*Amerika, wie ich es sah*, 153.

massive use of marble and wrote that the Capitol lighted at night was "like an alabaster crown raised up to the stars, as though created to bring erring mankind under one noble and holy power."[100] And Alfred Kerr added that the spotlights which created this vision "make the love of country not a stern must—no, an attraction."[101]

Individual travelers noted many American cities which have not been mentioned. Cincinnati, Milwaukee, and other "German" cities attracted much less attention than might have been anticipated. Perhaps Felix Salten provided the answer—although Cincinnati and its surroundings gave the impression of a city on the Rhine, its German character was past—"Vorbei."[102] Personal experiences often affected the observations—for Heinrich Hauser Columbus, Ohio, was simply a love affair with "Ellen!"[103] Smaller cities often repelled the visitors with their monotony, their disarray, their sense of incompleteness and neglect.[104] As Salten left one of the smaller cities of California, for example, he noted the nondescript and disorderly appearance of the town and its outskirts, bade his good-bye with the thought that he would never see it again, and added, "I hope so."[105]

German travelers, therefore, tended to present vignettes of widely varying character and validity. They ranged broadly across the country, but their observations were eclectic and superficial. Impressions of sections were built more largely upon reading and previous knowledge than upon direct observation. German readers would have had to plow through a veritable mountain of "America books" to put together an overall view of the American landscape with any real depth.

[100]"Die Stadt Washington," *Vossische Zeitung*, May 25, 1923.

[101]*Yankee-land*, 27.

[102]*5 Minuten Amerika*, 189-199.

[103]*Feldwege nach Chicago*, 220-222.

[104]E.g., "Persius" [C. L. Lothar], *Der Meteor. Charakterbilder und Streiflichter aus der nordamerikanischen Welt* (Magdeburg, 1928), 11-12.

[105]*5 Minuten Amerika*, 114-115.

Chapter IV

AMERICA'S POLYGLOT SOCIETY

he Raising of the Bars: The years 1921 and 1924 had marked a turning point in the history of the United States, felt German observers. The immigration laws of those years, suggested Arthur Feiler, signified the breaking away from its origins on the part of a "colonial country":

> One no longer wishes to be a new world, no longer a refuge for the burdened and oppressed, no longer an object of the longings and hopes of the adventurous in old Europe. The men who, having themselves all derived from such an entry, have taken possession of the land are now closing its door. They say that it belongs to them—that they are now numerous enough, that they do not wish a new flood. America shall no longer belong to mankind, but rather only to the Americans.[1]

And Moritz Bonn felt that the change in laws had altered the whole symbolism of the Statue of Liberty:

> The Goddess of Freedom whose mighty face turned towards Europe greets those who come into the harbor of New York is for many no longer the guide into the beloved land of freedom, but rather the angel with the flaming sword who guards the gate of paradise.[2]

More than ever before there was criticism of the American reception of the would-be immigrant and continued cries of disappointment from Ellis Island, "the Isle of Tears."[3]

---

[1]*Amerika-Europa*, 225-6. Quoted with permission of Verlagshaus Frankfurter Societäts-Drückerei.

[2]*Amerika und sein Problem*, 157.

[3]Horror stories of Ellis Island abounded in Germany during this period, typified, perhaps, by the romantic, novelistic account of "Jack Omaha," who

Some visitors believed the immigration laws reflected most largely the growing power of organized labor.[4] Others felt that they were designed to preserve an increasingly shaky Anglo-Saxon dominance.[5] Many Germans considered the laws the first step towards the creation of an American "race," the end of a profligate attitude which had made the United States a "mish-mash" of peoples. Some, however, regarded them as the prelude to the downfall of American civilization—its cultural and spiritual survival, suggested one writer, had been made possible only by the constant renewal of its strength from Europe.[6]

As soon as they landed in New York, German visitors became aware of the varied origins of Americans. They visited the quarters of the city which set forth melancholy reflections of the sights and smells of Naples, or sad reminders of the cafes of Madrid. They saw the exotic scenes of Harlem and Chinatown. They found New York clearly "a Jewish city, an Italian city, a Negro city."[7]

As they continued their journeys, however, they seldom pursued their study of minority groups in any orderly fashion. Their "America books" set forth random impressions and experiences rather than study and research. They remained overwhelmingly interested in the fate and fortunes of the German-Americans. Because American Jews were often of German origin and were sympathetic with Germany and its culture, the German visitors dealt extensively with their activities. They displayed great curiosity about and great sympathy for the American Negro. They were also interested in the Indians, the Asiatic peoples, and the Irish in the United States. Very little attention was given to the Americans of

---

escaped from its prison confines to go on to adventures in the Wild West: *Wilde Fahrten im Wilden Westen. Mit Gaunern, Gauklern und Rothäuten unterwegs.* Hartmuth Merleker provided a much more sympathetic account, noting also the reduced function of the island, in *Was weisst du von Amerika? Etwas von Überseereisen und vom Land und Leuten in Amerika* quoted in Chajim Bloch, *Das jüdische Amerika. Wahrnehmungen und Betrachtungen* (Wien-Brigittenau, 1926), 65-66.

[4]Bonn, *Amerika und Sein Problem*, 226 ff.

[5]*E.g.*, Venzmer, *New York ohne Schminke*, 43-44.

[6]Fritz Behn, "Amerikanismus in Deutschland," *Süddeutsche Monatshefte*, XXVII (1929), 672-674.

[7]Holitscher, *Wiedersehn*, 25. Or, as Gerhard Venzmer reported, New York was a city founded by the Dutch, inhabited by the Jews, ruled by the Irish, and now and then visited by the Americans. *New York ohne Schminke*, 71.

Italian, Scandinavian, or, with the exception of the Jewish group, of East European origins.

Although the German visitors often championed the cause of minority groups, their accounts frequently lacked real conviction. Few of them reflected genuine empathy with the groups described. The minorities were a part of "America's problems," the reverse side of the coin of well-being and prosperity, an excuse for criticism and cavilling. But even this was often forced. Those who proclaimed the prejudices of Americans were not always able to hide their own![8]

2. *Americans of German Origins—the Passing of the Hyphenated Americans*: "The German history is tragedy," wrote Eugen Kühnemann in his autobiography, and added, "One portion of this tragedy is German America":

> If we think of the more than five millions who came from Germany to America in the nineteenth century alone, this is the greatest German migration of all times. It was a tragedy that they had to leave the homeland. It was a more painful tragedy that they did not find there [in America] a [new] homeland in the fullest sense.[9]

Kühnemann, however, was one of a minority of German visitors who realized the pressure on their erstwhile countrymen to be both good Germans and good Americans, who remarked that the German emigrants had been abandoned by the homeland before they themselves deserted their spiritual moorings. Kühnemann, however, understood less fully than Moritz Bonn the dilemma of German-Americans during the First World War. Again and again Bonn sought to make his countrymen realize that they should not have expected active support from the Germans who had emigrated to the United States, that this could not have been reconciled with loyalty to the United States.[10]

Similar efforts were made by Kuno Francke, the famous art historian, whose presence at Harvard as the director of the museum for German art there had lent to the university a special interest for visiting Germans. Francke explained that he himself had been

---

[8]A case in point, Venzmer's description of racial problems in Europe—*New York ohne Schminke*, 129.

[9]*Mit unbefangener Stirn*, 205.

[10]E.g., *American Adventure*, 62.

placed in a quandary during the war when a German-American representative in Congress called a conference seeking to end the munitions trade which strengthened Germany's enemies. He had, he related, turned down the invitation to attend and had opposed the move advocated, because it ran contrary to American principles of non-interference with private property interests and because it might well have led to war with England. The latter consequence would have been of benefit to Germany but not to America:

> As one of German descent I could rejoice at such a conflict between the United States and Great Britain, since Germany would derive advantages from it. But as an American citizen I could not possibly support a policy which raised the peril of war for my own country.[11]

Most of the German visitors of the twenties, however, had little sympathy for the political weakness of the German-Americans during the war.[12] Many of them rehashed the stories of German sufferings in the war period and reminded their countrymen that most of the German-Americans, now designated "Americans of German origin," had defended the position of the homeland during the conflict and aided it in the evil days which followed. But in spite of verbal homage to the "martyrdom of the soul" which German-Americans had suffered, there remained the notes of sadness and of criticism.[13]

The visitors from abroad were most distressed by the catastrophic decline of German culture in the United States during the war. The disuse of the German language, the lack of interest in German literature, occasioned a chorus of chagrin. Many of the visitors searched vainly for bookstores which dispensed German books or shops where newspapers from the homeland could be obtained and bemoaned the loss of what once had been a profitable overseas market for German authors.[14] Even without the loss of

[11]*Deutsche Arbeit in Amerika. Erinnerungen von Kuno Francke* (Leipzig, 1930), 64-65. Quotations here and later with permission of Felix Meiner Verlagsbuchhandlung, Hamburg.

[12]See Rudolf Hensel's comment on the irritation on the part of German-Americans occasioned by this attitude. *Die neue Welt,* 79.

[13]*E.g.,* Erich von Salzmann, "Das Deutschtum in Amerika," *Vossische Zeitung,* February 15, 1921. For an answer to criticisms by home-land Germans, see Wilhelm Müller, *Die Deutschamerikaner und der Krieg* (Wiesbaden, 1921).

[14]Hartmuth Merleker. "Wenn man in New York deutsch lesen will," *Vossische Zeitung,* August 13, 1924 .

Alsace-Lorraine and other territories, suggested Roda Roda, one of the popular literary figures of the day, the loss of the cultural ties which had existed with German America "would have been in itself an enormous and particularly painful defeat for the German people."[15]

The explanations of this "defeat" were similarly detailed in most of the America books. Most Germans who had come to America, pointed out the postwar visitors, had been "little people" with relatively little education. They very seldom spoke High German and often had had little more connection with the culture of the homeland than the Bible and the psalter.[16] "Mostly farmers, artisans, laborers, they lacked the framework of education which always provides the strongest national backbone," one observer phrased it. And he added that they had scattered broadly across a vast country in which they lived quietly to themselves, concerned with their own life and ways, not those of the country in which they had settled. When the Romans had created an empire, he suggested, it was the officers who came; the British had colonized with both officers and men; but Germany had sent abroad an army without officers.[17] Other visitors echoed the criticisms of disunity, division into blocs and groupings, excessive individualism, and the willingness to accept rule rather than to assume responsibility themselves.[18] German-Americans had been "good naturedly stupid" in respect to the workings of American democracy.[19] They had shown none of the astuteness and aggressiveness of the Irish, who had, as a consequence, maintained their influence in America. "Yes, if we had been Irish, if we had understood as did the Irish how to exploit our significance as a power factor in the political balance, America would never have entered the war," was a complaint which Arthur Feiler found prominent among the German-Americans he met.[20]

15[Rosenfeld] *Ein Frühling in Amerika*, 42-44.

16*E.g.*, Dr. Paul Rohrbach, "Die Deutschamerikaner und Deutschland," *Kölnische Zeitung*, March 20, 1923.

17Wolfgang Kraus, "Die Brücke über den Ozean," *Die Hilfe*, 1919, 475-477. A very similar explanation was given by Ludwig Müller in one of the most widely used handbooks on America—W. Fischer *et al.*, *Handbuch der Amerikakunde*, 105-106.

18*E.g.*, Kurt Hassert, *Die Vereinigten Staaten von Amerika*, 128.

19Schönemann, *Die Vereinigten Staaten*, I, 309-312.

20*Amerika-Europa*, 225.

Some of the visitors raised the question whether the fate of Germans in America was to be paralleled by that of the homeland itself. Thus Friedrich von der Leyen, a strongly nationalist Professor of Philosophy at the University of Cologne, wrote:

Disunity, lack of leadership, short-sightedness and the sense of being uprooted from the homeland, these brought the misfortune [of the German-Americans]. The fate of these overseas Germans should provide for our homeland an unforgettable lesson appropriate to our days. If German minorities in European countries are still oppressed and misused, as minorities have never before been so misused and if the dignity of the homeland is threatened for centuries to come, will we also go under as the Germans of America have gone under?[21]

The new Germany, the Weimar Republic, some of the travelers discovered, found little understanding among Germans in the United States. They had come to America from imperial Germany—this was the image they had preserved of the homeland—and the "black-white-red" of imperial Germany found more enthusiasm than the "black-red-gold" of Weimar. "In bourgeois German-Americans," wrote Wilhelm Sollmann, one of the able defenders of the new state, "lives a Germany which no longer exists." Weimar, he warned, should seek to provide these Americans of German origin with better understanding of changes in the homeland.[22]

Other travelers disagreed with this judgment. Dorothee von Velsen found curiosity rather than hostility predominant.[23] And other travelers found that it was exactly the remnants of the old Germany, "the caste spirit," the continued use of titles, and "the holy awe" in which bureaucrats were held which repelled German-Americans and lessened the sense of loyalty to the country from which they had emigrated. One German-American observed during a three weeks return to the homeland more unpleasantness on the part of officials than he had experienced in fifteen years in America![24]

[21]"Amerikanische Eindrücke: Deutscher Unterricht und Deutschtum in den Vereinigten Staaten," *Kölnische Zeitung*, December 7, 1929.

[22]"Schwarz-Weiss-Rot in Amerika. Zur Psychologie der Deutschamerikaner," *Vorwärts*, November 21, 1925.

[23]"Eindrücke aus Amerika," *Die Frau*, XXXVII, 390-391 (April, 1930).

[24]Reported in Donatus Pfannmüller, *So sah ich Amerika. Reise von Fulda nach Chicago* (Essen, 1931), 173-175.

The sense of decline, of a failing culture, was, however, more disturbing than political weakness on the part of German-Americans. One of the later expressed his own deep concern at the rapidity with which his fellow-countrymen put aside German culture in their new surroundings:

> It is not a pleasant feature of the German national character, this effort to assimilate so unearthly quickly foreign speech, foreign customs, foreign usages, with a complete relinquishment of one's own national characteristics, . . . by this rapid erasing of his nationality the German makes the very poorest impression on the foreigner whose features he seeks to copy—What, indeed, should the latter think of a man who has so little respect for himself, who thinks so little of his nationality that he turns handsprings to rid himself of it?[25]

This feeling that Germans coming to the United States allowed themselves to be Americanized too rapidly was quite prevalent. One of the most popular guidebooks for emigrants published during the period warned those who left that they should hold fast to their cultural possessions.[26] And many visiting Germans considered that their erstwhile countrymen had, indeed, accepted an inferior cultural status. Prof. Alfred Forcke, for example, wrote caustically:

> Almost every educated German who emigrates to the United States gradually comes to resemble the Americans and unconsciously takes on something of their being and their point of view. This involves no progress. By permanent separation from the mother country he descends to a lower cultural level.[27]

As suggested below, however, German judgments of cultural achievement were heavily ethnocentric. And Friedrich Schöne-

[25]Ernst Voss, *Vier Jahrzehnte in Amerika. Gesammelte Reden und Aufsätze* (Stuttgart, 1929), 58.

[26]Johannes Saalfeld, *Wie komme ich in den Vereinigten Staaten vorwärts? Winke und Ratschläge für Auswanderer nach die Vereinigten Staaten von Amerika unter besondere Berücksichtigung der Kopfarbeiter und nicht Handwerker* (Dresden, 1926), 6, 17. The accounts of would-be immigrants to the United States during this period were often discouraging. Sagas of the problems of new entrants were presented by John Lassen, *Das andere Amerika. Bilder, Skizzen, und Reiseschilderungen* (Leipzig, 1924) and Oskar Kollbrunner, *Treibholz; Irrgänge eines Amerikafahrers.*

[27]"Aus dem Land der grossen Kinder," Berlin *Tägliche Rundschau*, February 6, 1920.

mann pointed out that in spite of the loss of German speech and the neglect of the great heritage of German literature, German-Americans had made an immeasurable contribution to American life. They had, he suggested, provided the first real countering of the Puritan spirit; they had brought from home a love of life and a joyful spirit to moderate the coldness and sobriety of Calvinism. German music, he added, had already made its impact in America. German concepts of drama were beginning to find their way into American usage.[28] Rudolf Hensel found in the placards of coming concerts, the statues in public parks, the names of spiritual heroes decorating American libraries a reflection of respect for German cultural accomplishment.[29] Others pointed out that the Steuben society, the only large-scale organization of Americans of German descent remaining, in spite of its political insignificance, was winning a rapidly increasing respect for Germany after the dark days of the war.[30]

But through all of the more perceptive accounts ran the warning, "German-America is an artificial conception; Americans of German descent are Americans first and only vaguely conscious of a former homeland; Germany is not represented in the United States by a politically active bloc dedicated to its interests." Those Germans who wished to do so could find this viewpoint eloquently expressed by the German-American best known in the homeland, Kuno Francke. In a parting message for his fellow German-Americans, Francke seemed to confirm the fears of the highly nationalist visitors:

> More than ever today, after the sad collapse of the larger part of the German cultural heritage which was won here in the hundred years before the war, I am convinced that this cause can be given no worse service than through political groupings which are held together by nothing except common ancestry or common economic interests. To be sure the German-American has the sacred obligation to remember what worthy treasures he possesses in German customs, speech, literature, and art. Directly in the service of his new home-

---

[28]*Die Vereinigten Staaten*, I, 310-311.

[29]*Die neue Welt*, 83.

[30]Dr. Paul Rohrbach, "Die Deutschamerikaner und Deutschland," *Kölnische Zeitung*, March 20, 1923, and "Die Präsidentenwahl und die Deutschamerikaner," *ibid.*, October 25, 1924.

land he should more truly and expressly cultivate these treasures of the old homeland than is often the case. But above all he should be aware of his obligation to take part in all the great strivings of the political, social, and spiritual life of America in an outstanding, unselfish, and unlimited fashion. By relying on his descent, by standing aside from the mighty stream of American public opinion, by priding himself on the German accomplishments of the past or future, he will awaken no American sympathies for Germany. Individual accomplishments of great merit, accomplishments in the field of industry, of finance, of government, of education, of science, of the reform movements in city, state, and federal government, of welfare activities, of philanthropy for idealistic goals, in short, of all the best things which have won for the America of today its imposing position in the world—these are the things through which the German-American can best and most effectively serve not only himself, not only the life of America, but also his old fatherland. This is my parting greeting to the German-America of the future.[31]

Francke's words were well-conceived and prophetic. The day of the hyphenated American had passed. German efforts to distinguish German-Americans from other Americans proved increasingly futile in the years which followed.

3. Irish and Jewish Americans—Friends of the Germans: German visitors to the United States after the First World War were predisposed toward sympathy with all groups who seemed like the German-Americans to have suffered from the dominance of the "Anglo-Saxons." They were particularly friendly to the Irish and the Jews who had become defenders of the German cause during the war.

As noted above, the Germans regarded the Irish as more effective in American politics than the German-Americans. German visitors in the postwar period paid some respect to their defense of German-Americans during the war and sympathized with them

[31]*Deutsche Arbeit in Amerika*, 91. Mrs. Schönemann added that the "Nichtmehrwissen" (forgetfulness) of immigrants had been replaced by a "Nichtwissenwollen"—they no longer *wanted* to know of the homeland. German America, she complained, had lost every connection with the homeland. Could she have done so, she would have packed the Schiller and Goethe statues in the park in San Francisco in her suitcase and taken them home where they belonged! "Eine Vortragsreise durch Nordamerika nach dem Kriege," Berlin *Tägliche Rundschau*, November 24, 1930.

in their difficulties with prohibition and with the Ku Klux Klan.[32] On the whole, however, they received less than minimal attention as compared with that given the Negroes and the Jews.

The only thoughtful commentary on the role of the Irish in American life was that of Friedrich Schönemann, who wrote that in America "a new Celtic type" had developed, with much of the "vitality and heritage of fantasy" of the old Celts. The Irish, suggested Schönemann, had brought to the American soul not only the warmth of feeling but also "a certain melancholy and sentimentality." The Irish had strengthened American interest in music, with a preference for the Latin, particularly French, music, although the cause of Beethoven had been advanced by their efforts. They gave to America an outstanding modern composer, Edward MacDowell, whose work gave assurance that the development of native American music in the future was not only possible but probable. And Irish literary talents were reflected, said Schönemann, not only in the humor of Finley Peter Dunne's "Mr. Dooley," but also in the writings of Henry James and William Dean Howells, whose ancestry showed strong Irish components.[33]

The Jewish influence in the United States received, however, much more attention from German visitors than did the Irish. To a considerable degree Weimar Germans found a strong sense of identification with the cause of Jewish Americans. Ludwig Lewisohn's book *Against the Stream* had been translated in 1924 and was very widely read. The impatience of his cultured and creative soul with a hostile environment awakened universal German sympathy.[34] Very probably Lewisohn's writings had a larger and more permanent impact in his old homeland than in his new.

"New York," wrote another German *litterateur*, Roda Roda, "is the most Jewish city in the world, a Jewish Florence."[35] German visitors found the eastern metropolis the major haven of American Jews and believed they dominated much of its political and social life. The travelers rejoiced at the Jewish preservation of the German language and were delighted by their interest in German culture. Four-fifths of the 10,000 New Yorkers studying German

---

[32]*E.g.*, Bonn, *American Adventure*, 64-69.

[33]*Die Vereinigten Staaten*, I, 265-267.

[34]*E.g.*, Review by Walter Kühne, "Vom 'Geist' Amerikas," *Geisteskultur*, XXXIV (1925), 142-146.

[35]*Frühling in Amerika*, 45.

at the time of his visit were Jewish, noted Friedrich von der Leyen, and he added,

> The Jews never lack the proper perception, and one must rejoice, therefore, that they place their trust firmly in the German [culture]. But the newest German poetry of Jewish character, which is not always very appealing, receives from these American German scholars and their supporters a strengthening not entirely desirable. However, in spite of everything, the interest for German is there again and increases constantly.[36]

The interest of American Jews in German culture was also underscored by Hans Goslar.[37] And one of the major guides for German immigrants suggested the likelihood of a friendly reception among Jewish families.[38]

The visitors from Weimar Germany, however, were much concerned by the extent of anti-Semitism which they found in America. Eduard Meyer declared that the sentiment was stronger in America than almost anywhere else and suggested, with a lack of realism that probably reflected anti-Semitism on his own part, that Germany's poor relations with America in the First World War had been in part due to their being represented by an ambassador of Jewish origin![39] Other Germans expressed their concern about American anti-Semitism; in some accounts one has the feeling he is reading about Nazi Germany rather than Weimar America![40]

The most careful and thorough study of the role of the Jewish element in America was made by the Viennese Jewish writer and religious leader, Chajim Bloch. His volume on Jewish America[41] is frankly derivative, which is justified, he explains, by the fact that although there are numerous volumes in English on the subject,

---

[36]"Amerikanische Eindrücke: Deutscher Unterricht und Deutschtum in den Vereinigten Staaten," *Kölnische Zeitung*, December 7, 1929.

[37]"Amerikas öffentliche Meinung," *Vossische Zeitung*, March 18, 1922.

[38]Msgr. Karl Spohr, *Der Auswanderer in Amerika. Vorteile und Nachteile* (Paderborn, 1930), 22.

[39]*Die Vereinigten Staaten von Amerika*, 172-173.

[40]See, for example, Bernhard Hans Zimmermann, "Volkstum und Glaube in den Vereinigten Staaten Nordamerikas," *Die evangelische Diaspora*, XIV, No. 3, 177-196 (January, 1932).

[41]*Das jüdische Amerika. Wahrnehmungen und Betrachtungen* (Wien-Brigittenau, 1926).

his is the first treatment in German. Unfortunately, the author's ill health restricted his visit to New York City, and his knowledge of Jewish activities elsewhere in America came to him second-hand.

The Jews of Europe, suggested Bloch, had been more tragically affected by the events of the First World War than any other people. The press for immigration into the United States rested strongly upon them. Of the four thousand would-be immigrants carried by the ship on which he crossed the Atlantic a large percentage were of Jewish background.[42] At the time of his visit, 1923, wrote Bloch, there were in New York City alone 1,700,000 Jews, a little less than a half of the estimated four million residing in the United States.[43] The earlier Jewish immigrants had been largely from western Europe and had been rapidly assimilated. The later immigrants, like Bloch himself, who was born in Galicia, stemmed most largely from eastern Europe.[44] These latter, he suggested, had in 1923 twelve Jewish theaters and seven daily newspapers. They held, he admitted, more closely to national characteristics, customs, and speech, than had the older immigrants.[45]

Although Bloch became aware of considerable anti-Semitism in the United States, he was favorably impressed by the extent of good relations between Jews and Christians. He noted with some amazement the conversion of churches into synagogues in areas where the Jewish population had increased. He related the story of a law case placing penalties against the misuse of the word "Kosher." He asserted that Jewish welfare societies and hospitals served non-Jews as well as Jews. And he praised the founding of the Committee for Friendship between Jews and Christians in Detroit.[46]

But Bloch was clearly on the side of the more orthodox approach to religious matters. He related with implied approval the stand of conservative rabbis against religious intermarriage, and his admiration for the reform leader, Rabbi Stephen S. Wise, was mingled with strong reservations in respect to his adoption of the ethical teachings of Christ as a part of a new Judaism.[47] On the

---

[42]*Ibid.*, 13-16.

[43]*Ibid.*, 50.

[44]So-called "Black Jews." See Zimmermann's account *(fn.* 40), 191.

[45]*Das jüdische Amerika*, 55-57.

[46]*Ibid., passim; cf.* Zimmermann *(fn.* 40), 193-194.

[47]*Das jüdische Amerika*, 85, 93-96.

other hand Bloch welcomed converts to Judaism and denied that it was exclusively connected with a "race" or "nation."[48] Among the curious phenomena he found in New York were the "Black Jews," the Negroes who claimed to be descended from the lost tribes of Israel. At the time he wrote, they had already established two organized religious communities and two synagogues.[49]

And Bloch also stressed the strong sympathy of American Jews for German culture and for the German fate in the world of the day. They had, he related, lent significant aid to welfare undertakings. They, like the Germans, knew what it meant to confront an unfriendly world.[50]

It should, of course, not be assumed that all Germans were sympathetic with the Jews. Bloch had encountered on shipboard some early "Swastika men."[51] Anti-Semitism was heavily evident in such books as "Jack Omaha's" adventure book[52] and Hermann Keyserling's *America Set Free*.[53] More subtle forms were found in comments such as that of Friedrich von der Leyen on Jewish poetry quoted above and remarks such as that of Arthur Holitscher, "Particularly difficult is it for the Jews in New York to preserve a sense of propriety [*Mass zu halten*]."[54]

In general, however, German visitors regretted only the restricted role of the Jews in American life. In 1920 Annalise Schmidt wrote that the greatest difference between the cultural achievements of Germany and America lay in the absence of the Jews from the "Schwabing circles," the culturally influential groups of America.[55] But by 1932 Friedrich Schönemann found a Jewish near-monopoly in literature, especially newspaper and book publication, in theater and artistic criticism, and in many of the academic professions. For no other immigrant group, he suggested, had America become quite so much "the land of unlimited possibilities."[56] And Hans Goslar added that since most of these leading personalities of

[48]*Ibid.*, 83, 116.
[49]*Ibid.*, 98-100.
[50]*Ibid.*, 43-46.   ,
[51]*Ibid.*, 20.
[52]*Wilde Fahrten im Wilden Westen.*
[53]*E.g.*, 86, 471, 516.
[54]*Wiedersehn*, 45. Holitscher criticized American anti-Semitism, however.
[55]*Der amerikanische Mensch*, 90.
[56]*Die Vereinigten Staaten*, I, 276. In spite of his move to Nazism a year later, Schönemann's main work reveals very little anti-Semitism.

Jewish blood came to America from southern Germany, the corresponding loss to Germany had indeed been great![57]

4. Lo! the Poor Indian!—and the "Asiatics": German sympathy was joined with curiosity and a kind of romanticism in respect to the colored minorities in America—the Indians, the "Asiatics," and the Negroes.

The conquest of the Indians, declared Professor Albrecht Penck, had strongly reflected the "Kampfnatur" (warlike nature) of the American. It had shown, he said, that a people with a highly developed sense of citizenship could act the part of a master race with complete brutality; that a people whose writers and learned men preached peace could with a cold smile condemn another people to destruction. "The will to power lives in every U. S. American; for him law is primarily that of the stronger."[58] And Rudolf Kindermann contrasted "the ruthless extermination" of the Indians in the United States with their treatment in Mexico—the erection of hundreds of schools and the toleration of old customs and usages.[59]

There was, of course, plenty of evidence provided by Americans to support this criticism. Helen Hunt Jackson's *Century of Dishonor* was well known among many of the visitors. The slogan that "the only good Indian is a dead Indian" found its echo in the travel accounts of the day. Only occasionally did a traveler suggest that the destruction of the Indians was in part occasioned by internecine wars among themselves and that very probably the total number of Indians at the time of the coming of the whites was not so much greater than it was in that post World War I era.[60]

The German visitors found racial prejudice much weaker in respect to the Indians than in respect to the Negroes. They attributed this to the fact that the Indians had opposed the Whites by force of arms, had never been enslaved, and were free from the inferiority complex which had troubled the Negro.[61] They had,

[57]*Amerika, 1922* (Berlin-Wilmersdorf, 1922), 122.

[58]*U.S.-Amerika*, 16-19.

[59]"Was können wir von Amerika lernen," *Volkswohl*, XXI (1930), No. 5, 175-183, 177.

[60]See, *e.g.*, Hensel, *Die neue Welt*, 98-99; Hassert, *Die Vereinigten Staaten*, 94.

[61]Alice Salomon, *Kultur im Werden. Amerikanische Reiseeindrücke* (Berlin, 1924), 174-175.

as a consequence, proved less assimilable than the Negroes, had retained customs and former ways of life on the reservations assigned them. Nevertheless they were lured by the superior privileges and culture of the whites, and miscegenation (although not so frequently mixed marriages) had reduced almost to half the number of pure-blooded Indians.[62] Mixture of Indians and Negroes also occurred frequently in the Southern states, the results not being exactly pleasing to the eye, suggested the usually tolerant Moritz Bonn.[63]

The Indians themselves, however, were regarded by the Germans as an attractive race—"All in all a handsome, proud race of men," wrote Rudolf Hensel, "splendid, the keen eagle nose which most of them have. Why they are actually called redskins cannot be understood; their skin color is not red but leather brown."[64] And the Germans felt that the Indians had left the United States a valuable legacy—the beautiful names applied to places often more sober in appearance; the love of outdoor life; and an enrichment of the literary and musical heritage.[65] At least one German visitor added chewing gum and rouge to the Indian contributions to American life![66]

The pueblo reservations in the American Southwest were those most visited. Although the visitors recognized the great advance made in the treatment of the Indians since the turn of the century, they remained skeptical of the possibilities of a real assimilation of them into the American population. The Indians, reported Alice Salomon, had tended to preserve their own culture over against that of the dominant race, whom they still hated, and the myth of a return to Indian dominance still had some currency.[67]

The romanticism of Indian life was largely gone by the 1920's. "O, alte Siouxherrlichkeit, wohin bist du geschwunden!" ("Oh, ancient glory of the Sioux, whence have you disappeared?" after the German song, "O alte Burschenherrlichkeit"), exclaimed Alfred Kerr, and added when the Indian dance of the Hopis was followed

---

[62]*Ibid.*   [63]*The American Adventure*, 39.

[64]*Die neue Welt*, 101.

[65]*Ibid.*; Schönemann, *Die Vereinigten Staaten*, I, 227-230.

[66]Waldemar Oehlke, *In Ostasien und Nordamerika*, 134-135.

[67]*Kultur im Werden*, 178; similar view, Hassert, *Die Vereinigten Staaten*, 96-97. An unusual picture of Indian life in the Cattaragu reservation was given by Dietrich, *U.S.A., das heutige Gesicht*, 32-36.

by the "collection" on the part of the chief, "Mean stinking world!"[68] And the German periodical, *Die Woche*, mournfully told its readers of Karl May's stories that the heritage of "Chingachgook" was a mournful one; nothing was left but the presentation of "shows," posing for photographs, perhaps a memorial in the waxworks museums. One lusty German traveler, *Die Woche* related, had joyfully discovered a "totem pole" in the midst of an Indian village, only to have its mayor—mayor, not chief—tell him that the Indians of the village were good Catholics. He had confused with totemism the symbol of the village barber. The only exception to *Die Woche's* sad story was Francis Nikawa, a member of the Blackfeet tribe soon to appear as a romantic singer in London.[69]

And Gustav Frenssen, the poet, summed up his impressions of the Indians he saw in America with the words:

> How ancient seemed the one with whom I spoke! As though he were three centuries old! There was something somnolent, strange to life in him. Certainly it was God's will that they [the Indians] died; they had become too old. But a guilt remains and the guilt will be paid. The earth in which they lie will bring the American people other things than flourishing crops, oil, and gold. That is the most remarkable thing about the people who live in this piece of earth, that they seem to believe they will for three hundred years and in all the future still be a happy and laughing people as they are now.[70]

"The Indians," suggested Alfred Kerr, "are more alert than the Negroes; therefore one loves them [in America]." "But," he added, "the Japs are more alert than both together; therefore one hates them."[71] Many of the German travelers visited Chinatown, either in New York or San Francisco.[72] Not many Germans, however, probed the world of Asiatic Americans very deeply. Alice Salomon, Friedrich Schönemann, and Rudolf Hensel gave somewhat more than passing references. Few other Germans were really concerned.

The problem of the Japanese, suggested those Germans who

[68]*Yankee-land*, 42, 64.

[69]*Die Woche*, 1923, No. 43, 41-43.

[70]*Briefe aus Amerika* (Berlin, 1923), 141.

[71]*Yankee-land*, 49.

[72]Franz Friedrich Oberhauser, "Nacht in Chinatown," *Kölnische Zeitung*, August 25, 1929.

dealt with the problem, combined racial and economic prejudice. Due to their industriousness and low standard of living, the Japanese had constituted a dangerous competition for the dominant whites. Nationalist organizations had raised banners against the danger of "inferior" races and created legends of spies among them.[73] The exclusion act which resulted had cast an unnecessary aspersion on the Japanese—the use of the National Origins law itself would have restricted total immigration to 250. The tension between Japan and the United States occasioned by this act was regarded by Alice Salomon as a threat to the whole western world posed by a possible joining of the colored races.[74]

The exclusion of the Japanese had, of course, been preceded some forty years by that of the Chinese. But both remained in modest numbers, especially in the West. There the German visitors often encountered the Japanese as hotel employees, "always alert, polite, friendly, smiling, industrious, and modest,"[75] and as agricultural workers and cooks.[76] The Chinese remained as cooks and fish handlers, impressing at least one German visitor with the beauty of their children: "The most beautiful, however, which mother nature has created in the human countenance, one finds in Chinese children. I believe that no people of the world, even the Italians, have prettier children than the Chinese."[77]

5. *Soulful Negroes in Soulless America*: The tone of criticism of American policy towards minority groups reached emotional heights in respect to the American treatment of its Negro population. "Here," in America, wrote Arthur Feiler in 1926, "one can study with horror how injustice, once perpetrated by a people, continues in later generations to consume it like a destructive poison."[78] And Hans Goslar, an official in the Prussian state government, called the Negro question in America "a bit of the Middle Ages in modern

[73]Schönemann, *Die Vereinigten Staaten*, I, 213-214; Bonn, *American Adventure*, 45-46; Salomon, *Kultur im Werden*, 182.

[74]Salomon, *Kultur im Werden*, 182. But Hitler in his "Secret Book" expressed understanding and approval of the American action. *Hitler's Secret Book*, 108.

[75]Hensel, *Die neue Welt*, 102.

[76]Salomon, *Kultur im Werden*, 181.

[77]Hensel, *Die neue Welt*, 102. "Persius" [C. L. Lothar] also dealt with anti-Chinese feeling. *Der Meteor*, 46-49.

[78]Feiler, *Amerika-Europa*, 245.

America," although he admitted it would be "a thoroughly tough nut to crack."[79]

Even more passionate were the words of Alice Salomon, the chief woman-suffragist of her day in Germany, who called the racial problem "the sore spot on the body of American social life," and went on to explain:

> Not only because many unsolved and perhaps insoluble tasks are involved, but above all, because here the sins of the past—and also much injustice and many violations of law of the present—cry out to Heaven. Because all words of freedom, of equality, of democracy, all the idealistic viewpoints of the American constitution, the great and beautiful words of noble leaders, cannot be maintained when measured against the lot of the colored peoples.[80]

These lines were typical of German criticism of the permanent subjection of one section of our population to "second class citizenry," of Ku Klux Klan activities, and of lynch justice.[81]

The genuineness of German sympathy, however, is subject to some qualification. The bitterness of wartime experiences was reflected in a general tendency to excessive criticism of American ideals and the American way of life. European fears of "Americanization" during the 1920's were reflected in efforts to "debunk" and disenchant. And Germans, themselves, were by no means free of racial prejudices. Europeans, suggested one visitor to America,

---

[79]*Amerika, 1922,* 63, 75.

[80]*Kultur im Werden,* 161. Quotation with permission of Verlag Ullstein G.m.b. H.

[81]The term "second class citizen" appears in a number of accounts, *e.g.,* Hassert, *Die Vereinigten Staaten,* 102; Dietrich, *U.S.A. das heutige Gesicht,* 26. Dr. Manfred Sell in "Die schwarze Völkerwanderung," *Kölnische Zeitung,* August 27, 1929, complained of the "inhuman degredation of thinking men to working animals," and Hensel, *Die neue Welt,* 103, particularly criticized the attitude of American white women towards the Negro. The spate of criticism of lynch activities during the First World War has been noted in Chapter I. See, *e.g.,* Anon., *Im Schatten amerikanischer Demokratie und Freiheit,* 57-65. Some Germans saw in the Ku Klux Klan revival of the 1920's the source of a possible American *Kulturkampf* (*e.g., Kölnische Zeitung,* August 8, 1924); others spoke of it as "American Fascism"—Anon., "Amerikanischer Faschismus: Das 'unsichtbare Kaiserreich' vom Ku Klux Klan," *Die Woche,* 1923, No. 18, 423-427. The most perceptive studies of the KKK are found in Arthur Rundt, *Amerika ist anders* (Berlin-Charlottenburg, 1926), 61-64, and Bonn, *The American Adventure,* 66.

could find little real anthropological distinction between blacks and whites. But, he continued, if a European asks himself, "whether he himself would accept equality with the Negro, or, indeed, would accept a position in which he himself was the subordinate and social inferior while the Negro was the supervisor and social superior—then his racial feelings assert themselves."[82] German prejudices had also been raised by alleged instances of lawless behavior on the part of French Negro occupation troops on the Rhine.[83] Some Germans saw in these problems of the French with their Negro troops and in the intensification of the racial problem in America a common retribution for an unjust war on Germany.[84]

Before the First World War, pointed out many German students, the problem of Negro-White relationships had been largely confined to the South. Some Germans were willing to suggest that the Civil War had been followed by a "too hasty freeing of the Slaves," to label the Reconstruction period "insane," and to applaud the establishment of stabler relationships in the South.[85] "Without doubt," wrote one of these,

> the Southern states east and west would be the best place for the Negro masses, if they were reasonably treated and educated by the Whites. This would in no way imperil the supremacy of the Whites during the next century. The Southerner is much better suited [than Northerners] for this task; on the average he knows the Negro better, is more accustomed to him, and also has more real liking for him than the Northerner, who imposes no legal limitations on the other race, but does not understand its soul and does not know how to deal with it.[86]

[82]Hensel, *Die neue Welt*, 103. One young German, however, who had occupied such a position, working under a Negro boss in cleaning bricks, etc., found his foreman kind, understanding, and always a source of good spirits. Hugo Cramer, *Als Junglehrer nach U. S. A., Erlebnisse eines Ehepaares* (Leipzig, 1932), 134-136.

[83]Hellmuth Pankow, "Die 'Vernegerung' der Vereinigten Staaten," Berlin *Tägliche Rundschau*, August 14, 1920. At the time an American philanthropist, Miss Ray Beveridge, spoke at Munich on "the black disgrace in the Rhineland." See *Der Welt-Spiegel*, March 6, 1920.

[84]*Ibid.*, *cf.* Scheffauer, *Das Land Gottes*, 224-225.

[85]Schönemann, *Die Vereinigten Staaten*, I, 237-238; Penck, *U.S.-Amerika*, 20; Paul Rohrbach, "Ein Blick in Amerikas Zukunft," *Kölnische Zeitung*, June 11, 1924.

[86]Schönemann, *Die Vereinigten Staaten*, I, 239. Quotation with permission of Deutsche Verlags-Anstalt, Stuttgart.

Similarly, another German wrote,

> In the South, at any rate, a tacitly acknowledged caste-system is in existence, and nothing wiser could have been invented. . . . Thus the Negroes need not feel humiliated; they can develop, as Americans, a racial pride of their own. And they will perhaps even build up a culture of their own, and this culture may even be acknowledged, by the non-American world, as America's most authentic culture.[87]

The South, however, fared badly in most of these travel accounts. "The Southern States," wrote one observer, "have paid for the attempt to maintain the feudal system, in the peculiarly harsh form of slavery, by economic backwardness in every department of life."[88] Southern lynch justice came in for vivid descriptions as the wartime "Hun" detailed graphically the brutalities of his erstwhile "humanitarian" opponent, who watched defenseless Negroes burned alive and then went home to supper with a sharpened appetite.[89] Germans recognized, as the 1920's moved to an end, some economic improvements in "the awakening South," and German newspapers labeled the year 1927 a "Bad Lynch Year" since "only" sixteen lynchings were recorded.[90] But the resistance to change in the South was cogently set forth by Moritz J. Bonn, who wrote:

> For fifty years the Southern whites have ignored the Fourteenth and Fifteenth Amendments to the Constitution, which gave the Negro the franchise, and evaded them by all sorts of "dodges," or have openly resorted to intimida-

[87]Graf Hermann Keyserling, *America Set Free* (New York, 1929), 38. Other German observers, although critical of "Jim Crow" laws, found the Negroes of the South happier and more suited to the climate than those of the North. Thus Holitscher, *Wiedersehn*, 137-140, reports on his first visit to the South that Southern Negroes were more attractive than Northern ones, their manners more appealing, and their educational progress encouraging. Professor Julius Hirsch (*Vorwärts*, July 2, 1929) expressed his impressions in verse—the translation is, of course, not quite literal:

"Tausend schwarze Negerlein   ("A thousand little Negro boys,
   die machen gross' Geschrei.   They make a big to-do.
Jedes fährt 'nen alten Ford   Each drives a beaten-up old Ford
   und ist vergnügt dabei."   Which makes him happy too.")

[88]Bonn, *The American Adventure*, 170. Also critical, Dietrich, *U.S.A., das heutige Gesicht*, 28; Persius [Lothar], *Der Meteor*, 42-45.

[89]Rundt, *Amerika ist anders*, 117.

[90]*Bremer Nachrichten*, April 16, May 19, 1929; L. Korr, "Der erwachende Süden," *Neue Zürcher Zeitung*, March 20, 1930.

tion. This revolt against the Constitution has become almost hallowed by use. No one thinks of appealing. The Federal authority never dreams of interfering against this breach of the Constitution by State Administrations, for public opinion has sanctioned it. There is an occasional decision in favor of Negro voters given by the Supreme Court; it is nearly always evaded by some clever constitutional dodge of the State legislature. And so long as public opinion condones this attitude there is no remedy against a defiance of the Constitution which as a matter of principle is far worse than the occasional outbreaks of lynch law of which the North is inclined to complain.[91]

For Negroes in the South, suggested another observer, the Statue of Liberty was a hollow irony.[92]

With World War I, however, the Negro question had ceased to be a purely Southern one. The American Negroes, suggested Arthur Rundt, were the only people in the world who could find in the events of the First World War a distinct source of betterment.[93] The opportunities of employment had been greatly increased by the expansion of the munitions industry. A tremendous exodus of Negroes from the South had begun. The course of exodus had led to the greater cities of the North, especially to New York, where Harlem had become an American Negro Zion. Housing difficulties and racial antagonisms had resulted in the creation of Negro ghettoes in every large city of the North. The movement had been attended with difficulties. The Negro death rate had increased with the effects of climate, poor housing, and disease. But the lure of the air of freedom had occasioned among the Negroes an ever-increasing "me, too."[94]

Germans, however, noted that white hostility to the Negro in the North had increased in the face of this migration and of competition for jobs. Racial prejudice was attended by violence in Northern cities.[95] German observers were critical of the exclusion

[91]Bonn, *The American Adventure*, 119. Quotation with permission of George Allen & Unwin, Ltd.

[92]Pankow, "Die 'Vernegerung' der Vereinigten Staaten," Berlin *Tägliche Rundschau*, August 14, 1920.

[93]*Amerika ist Anders*, 78.

[94]*Ibid.*, 73-74, 76 ("I, too" in original!); Bonn, *American Adventure*, 44; Dietrich, *U.S.A., das heutige Gesicht*, 28-29; probably the best summaries of Negro problems in the North are found in Schönemann, *Die Vereinigten Staaten*, I, 239-242, and Holitscher, *Wiedersehn*, 127-137.

[95]*Ibid.*; cf. Charlotte Lütkens, "Im Schlagschatten des amerikanischen Wirt-

of Negroes from American labor unions. They pointed out that this resulted in the use by factory owners of Negroes as strike breakers. They labeled the policies of American labor unions narrow and short-sighted.[96] Although the major source of discrimination in the North was to be attributed to workers' fears of economic competition, Germans also pointed out that acquisition of social equality in the North was proving as difficult as it had been in the South. "Over and over again," said Feiler, the Negro "bumps painfully against invisible walls from which a 'down, down, down with you' lashes out at him."[97] The place of the Negro remained in German eyes the most pressing, the most decisive question confronting the United States.[98]

In view of the later racialist mania of Nazi Germany, the liberalism of German views of the Negro in the 1920's is surprising. Most of these visitors denied the existence of real anthropological distinctions between black and white in America. The American Negroes were as much Americans as the whites, they believed. Their very appearance belied conceptions of physical inferiority. "There are among the Negroes," wrote Rudolf Hensel,

> the handsomest (*bildschöne*) of individuals, particularly among the women, who, moreover, understand how to clothe themselves with true refinement, possess a remarkable sense of color and choose with absolute security the color of clothing which best agrees with the nuance of their skin shading. . . . The many handsome individuals which one finds among the Negroes are evidence against the often-maintained ethnical inferiority of the Negro, since bodily beauty is seldom an accompaniment of inferiority or degeneration.[99]

Hensel, with the sharpened olfactory sensitivity of the non-smoker,

---

schaftwunders," *Urania*, 1928-1929, No. 8, 250-252; Erkelenz, *Amerika von Heute*, 123.

[96]*Ibid.* The criticism of Charlotte Lütkens, a well-known sociologist, was particularly caustic in this regard. One of the German labor periodicals, however, carried a strong defense of the White attitude, including an appreciation of the writings of Madison Grant and the statement that "the effort for absolute equality of rights and pay for all races is to be equated with cultural Harakiri on our part." Karl Valentin Müller-Königstein, "Amerikanisches— Arbeiterschaft und Rassenproblem," *Gewerkschaftsarchiv*, II, No. 3 (1925), 249-256.

[97]Feiler, *Amerika-Europa*, 249.

[98]*E.g.*, Hassert, *Die Vereinigten Staaten*, 104.

[99]*Die neue Welt*, 104.

found no evidence of "the certain sweetish racial odor" complained of by one of his countrymen![100] And facial expressions he found as moving and varied as those of his own countrymen and just as much a key to occupation and social status.[101]

Other Germans emphasized the obvious fact that the existence of large numbers of mulattoes and "white Negroes" indicated the absence of real physical repulsion between the races. The lure of racial mixture is an ever-recurring theme in these accounts—sometimes attributed to others, sometimes clearly present on the part of the writer! Dr. Hermann Lufft, an economics professor from Berlin, noted that in spite of all social prohibitions and stigma, mixed marriages continue to occur—marriages rather than illegal sexual intercourse—because of "the particular attraction or perhaps particular sexual and psychological *haut goût* imparted by remnants of black blood." Germans were among those involved in these marriages, he added.[102] And the delightful adventures of Manfred Hausmann included the pursuit of a light-brown maiden with the nose of an Aztec, "defiant" eye-brows, and a wisp of a blue veil.[103]

Germans often accepted it as axiomatic that racial mixture resulted in an intensification of the worst elements of both races, but more objective observers reported the vast accomplishments of those of mixed origins.[104] The more sophisticated travelers also emphasized the fact that it was the stigma of social inequality which increased the tendency to racial mixture and that in areas where

[100]*Ibid.*; *cf.* Hermann Lufft, "Weiss und Schwarz in der Bevölkerungsbewegung der Vereinigten Staaten," *Volk und Rasse*, III, No. 3 (July, 1928), 140; Penck, *U.S.-Amerika*, 21.

[101]*Die neue Welt*, 105; *cf.* Gustav Frenssen, *Briefe aus Amerika* (Berlin, 1923), 79.

[102]"Weiss und Schwarz in der Bevölkerungsbewegung der Vereinigten Staaten," *Volk und Rasse*, III, No. 3 (July, 1928), 140.

[103]*Kleine Liebe zu Amerika*, 97 ff. A similar theme, the account by *litterateur* Peter Scher of his experiences in a Negro night club in New York and the dancing of a white girl with a Negro musician, "New York wie ich es sah," *Frankfurter Zeitung*, November 18, 1924.

[104]Schönemann, *Die Vereinigten Staaten*, I, 237; Hassert, *Die Vereinigten Staaten*, 100-103. James Weldon Johnson's *Autobiography of an Ex-Colored Man* was translated into German as *Der weisse Neger: Ein Leben zwischen den Rassen* (Frankfurt, 1928) and occasioned interested comment in German newspapers, *e.g.* Franz Josef Fürtwangler, "'Weisse Neger!' Das Negerproblem in Amerika," *Vorwärts*, September 13, 1929.

equality was conceded, racial mixture had declined.[105] Germans were uniformly critical of the celebrated Rhinelander case in 1925, where a young wife involved in a divorce trial was forced to strip to the waist before judge and jury to prove that her husband must have been aware of her Negro blood prior to marriage. German sympathies were all with the wife as against a husband whose name had a strong German flavor![106]

C. J. Jung, the famous Swiss psychiatrist, found that Negro characteristics had permeated the American way of life even without the mixture of blood:

> The emotional expression of the American, in the first place his laughing . . . that inimitable Roosevelt laugh is found in its original form in the American Negro. The characteristic walk with relatively relaxed joints, or the swinging hips, which are seen so frequently on the part of American women, stem from the Negro; the dance is Negro dancing. The expression of religious feeling, the revival meetings, the holy rollers, and other such abnormalities, are strongly under the influence of the Negro—and the famous American naivete in its charming form, as well as in its less agreeable appearances, can easily be equated with the childishness of the Negro. The on-the-average uncommonly lively temperament, which displays itself not only at baseball games, but even more particularly in an unusual enjoyment of vocal expression, of which the ceaseless and boundless stream of nonsense in American newspapers is the best example, is scarcely to be traced back to German antecedents, but rather is much more similar to the "chattering" of the Negro village. The almost complete lack of intimacy and the massive sociability which breaks down all barriers is reminiscent of primitive life in open huts with the complete identification of all members of the tribe. It seemed to me as if in all American houses all the doors were always wide open, just as in the American country towns there are no garden fences to be found.
>
> It is naturally difficult to determine in detail what is to be laid to the symbiosis with the Negro and what may be laid to the circumstance that America is still a pioneering nation on virgin soil. But . . . the significant influence of the Negro on the national character cannot fail to be recognized.[107]

[105]Salomon, *Kultur im Werden*, 167-168.

[106]Paul Gutmann, "Nacktkultur," *Vorwärts*, December 5, 1925.

[107]"Die Erdbedingtheit der Psyche" in Graf Hermann Keyserling, Schule der Weisheit, *Mensch und Erde (Der Leuchter, Weltanschauung und Lebensgestaltung*, Achtes Buch. Darmstadt, 1927), 88-137, at 131-132.

The influence of the Negro on white civilization was not, of course, confined to America, Jung pointed out. But in Africa, for example, where the white man was in a minority, his yielding to primitive influence was catastrophic. "In America, however," he declared, "the Negro because of his minority relationship signifies not a degenerative but rather a specialized (*eigentümlichen*) influence, which on the whole is by no means to be described as unfavorable, unless one is possessed by a phobia against jazz."[108]

On the other hand, Jung found that the Negro influence was one largely exerted on outward manners and habits—not on the soul of the white American. Psychologically the whites rejected the Negro. The "hero figure" of American fantasy he found associated with the American Indian. In the dreams of many of his American patients, the Negro appeared as an expression of the less desirable side of their personalities. "So the American offers us," Jung concluded, "a strange picture: a European with Negro manners and an Indian soul."[109]

German observers noted with interest and approval the growing tendency of Negroes to develop a social awareness of their own significance and worth. They found much to criticize in the division between Negro intellectuals and the Negro masses and in the divisions among the intellectuals themselves. They were almost universally hostile to Garveyism, the movement to establish a Negro empire in Africa initiated by the Negro leader Marcus Garvey.[110] They applauded, however, the effort to create a sense of a racial mission:

> They are beginning to be proud of their African individuality, and to recognize their mission: their most important contribution to American life is not the absorption into their own nature of what belongs to America, but the preservation of their African nature and its impression on the American mind. They would like to establish their Ethiopian culture in the heart of America, borrowing nothing from America but her technical forms.[111]

---

[108]*Ibid.*, 133.   [109]*Ibid.*, 135.

[110]Schönemann, *Die Vereinigten Staaten*, I, 230 ff.; Salomon, *Kultur im Werden*, 170; Rundt, *Amerika ist Anders*, 78; Holitscher, *Wiedersehn mit Amerika*, 134-137. On Garvey's movement see Edmund David Cronon, *Black Moses: the Story of Marcus Garvey and the Universal Negro Improvement Association* (Madison, Wisconsin, 1955).

[111]Bonn, *The American Adventure*, 43. Holitscher in an earlier book,

Or, as another writer phrased it, "They find that mimicry is a surrender of their own value; that the Negro possesses much which is individual: the quiet grace of the race, paired with the spring-ready strength of relaxed limbs, spiritual agility, sagacity, and a high moral earnestness."[112]

These comments mirrored the fact that many Germans found more genuine creative culture among the American Negroes than among white Americans. Americans in general they found "soulless," superficial, materialistic—in short, "cultureless."[113] The Negro, in contrast, had a soul and was creating a culture. Although the German travelers, many of them dignified professors, weighty men of business, or public servants, almost universally condemned jazz *per se,* they recognized that it was an American creation differing markedly from African antecedents. "The Negro of American slavery," wrote Rundt, "sang along with his hard work a sad song." But even this, he continued, had its unusual variations of rhythms. "The end of slavery gave freedom to hands and feet. These hands and feet expressed the merriment and joy of life; freed from bonds, they beat the time of a new song." But only with the transfer of jazz to the great cities, only as it became "a mass action" on the floor of the Harlem night clubs, did jazz acquire its end character:

> It is entirely un-African.
> It is the animal freedom, to which the Negro, having landed in the teeming jungle of the World city, gives keen expression. No one threatens this freedom now.
> It is, in pure culture and without sophistication, the Negro-American Jazz: the rhythm of America mirrored in the blood of the colored man.[114]

But beyond jazz, beyond significant contributions in dance and in music other than jazz, Germans found Negro culture showing

---

Das amerikanische Gesicht (Berlin, 1916), 131, had reported an antagonism to the term "American": "Don't call us 'Americans'! We are not, as long as America treats us as it does now. We don't want to be called 'Americans,' we are Africans. We belong to a dark race. When there was talk of a war with Japan years ago, the sympathies of the young Negro, more or less disguised, were on the side of the Japanese—because the Japanese also belonged to a dark race!" Quoted with permission of S. Fischer Verlag.

[112]Rundt, *Amerika ist anders,* 77.

[113]See Chapters X, XI.

[114]Rundt, *Amerika ist anders,* 135-138.

signs of real significance. The native folklore, which had under-
gird earlier literary contributions of white authors, indicated an
innate gift of imagery.[115] Negro poetry and literature were in the
1920's beginning to have real significance. Germans were greatly
interested in these developments. Albert C. Barnes' able article
on "Negro Art in America" appeared in translation in the *Vossische
Zeitung* of Berlin, one of Germany's leading dailies.[116] Many of
the German travelers not only visited Negro night clubs, but also
Negro churches and Negro schools and many of them sought out
Negro cultural leaders.[117] Paul Schulz, a German translator and
free-lance writer, reported after his visit: "I myself met many
Negroes of the educated classes and loved their spirituality, their
temperament and their liveliness in discussions, their poetic souls,
and their receptiveness to art and music."[118]

Perhaps Hellmuth Pankow best summarized the prevailing
German view when he wrote,

> The colored man is awake, awake to a degree which exceeds
> the bounds of reason; he has become extraordinarily acute
> in hearing and sharp in vision, and his whole mind and
> being will from now on be directed to conquering with
> every means of civilization the culture, which alone lends
> to the being of men nobility and stature and is necessary
> to make our life really worth the living.[119]

In similar vein the poet Ernst Toller wrote, "The pain and injustice done to the Blacks will some day return to bring fearful consequences to America. . . . Today a troop of black pioneers is
fighting; tomorrow a self-confident army of millions will fight for
the rights of man."[120] Colin Ross, the world traveler, labeled the
racial question "one of the most serious issues confronting hu-

---

115Schönemann, *Die Vereinigten Staaten*, I, 242-244.

116January 6, 1925.

117The accounts of Rundt, Schönemann, Holitscher, and Bonn all pay
tribute to the progress of Negro education. Both Holitscher and Kerr sought
interviews with Du Bois, the latter astounded to hear the Negro leader drop
into fluent German in the telephone conversation preceding the interview.
Yankee-land, 200.

118"Eindrücke von meiner Reise nach die Vereinigten Staaten im Sommer
1926," *Zeitschrift für französischen und englischen Unterricht*, XXVII (1928),
209-217, at 215.

119Berlin *Tägliche Rundschau*, August 14, 1920.

120*Quer durch. Reisebilder und Reden* (Berlin, 1930), 78.

manity" and predicted significant change in the whole picture of the world in this regard.[121] Other Germans had no doubts of the success of the Negro in his surge for equality. "I consider it completely excluded from the bounds of possibility," wrote Rudolf Hensel, "that the blacks there will let themselves be held within the social status which has been assigned them. . . . Already in the next generation things will be very different."[122]

[121]*Die Welt auf der Waage*, 6.
[122]*Die neue Welt*, 103; 106.

Chapter V

GERMANY ADMIRES THE FIRST "WIRTSCHAFTSWUNDER"

America's *"Might"*: *"Wirtschaftswunder"*—"Economic miracle"—the term is familiar to Americans through its usage in the years since World War II to characterize the rapid recovery of West Germany. Few Americans realize that the term was first applied not to Germany but to the United States, that this was the designation which Germans gave to this country in those dark days after World War I when they first began to realize the tremendous power, the *Macht*, of America.

The author of the term, Dr. Julius Hirsch, had been for a time a Professor at the University of Cologne and then later a member of the German Ministry of Economics. In 1925 he wrote a series of articles for the *Vossische Zeitung* which were later gathered together into the book which bore this descriptive title.[1] His definition of his term stated briefly and pithily the great challenge of the United States to the rest of the world during the 1920's:

> The American economic miracle is basically this: *Reckoned in money the wages over there are four to occasionally even five times as high as in Germany* and in most other European countries. Also *the internal purchasing power of these wages is at least twice as much as with us.* But in spite of this *America is able to compete with us in all important areas* and

[1] Articles in *Vossische Zeitung*, February 14, March 11, 18, April 2, 16, July 25, 1925. *Das amerikanische Wirtschaftswunder* (Berlin, 1926)—see review by Theodor Marcus, "Das amerikanische Wirtschaftswunder," *Börsenblatt für den deutschen Buchhandel*, XCIII, No. 19, 98-100 (January 23, 1926). The present author's treatment of the German image of the American economy during the 1920's differs in many particulars but not in overall evaluation from that of Peter Berg, *Deutschland und Amerika, 1918-1929. Über das deutsche Amerikabild der zwanziger Jahre (Historische Studien* herausgegeben von Wilhelm Berges *et al.*, No. 385. Lübeck and Hamburg, 1963), 96-132.

THE FIRST "WIRTSCHAFTSWUNDER" 89

also with England. How is this possible? Does the explanation lie alone or even chiefly in the great natural riches of this fortunate land, or does it lie in the better economic organization, which has been so emphatically pictured for the German public under the names Fordism, Taylorism, and the like?[2]

Much of the sense of the miraculous derived from the rapidity of American progress. Never in world history, declared a German guide book of the period in dealing with the United States, had economic power developed so rapidly from an agrarian and plantation economy.[3] Or as Hirsch expressed it, "The economic balance of the world pushes ever more rapidly towards the West." Much of this, he added, had occurred during the war period itself and immediately afterward:

> So we saw suddenly documented before our own eyes this *unheard of displacement of all the power relationships of* the world. America a nation of still less than 115 million inhabitants as the arbiter and regulator of the mother continent, Europe, with its now helpless population of some 480 million; this same America that until the outbreak of the world war sought in Europe for money and capital and was still at the beginning of that great catastrophe in debt to European nations for four billion dollars has paid this entire debt; it has moreover become today the creditor of the Entente states for between 11 to 12 billion dollars and holds private credits for between 8 to 10 billion dollars of which over 4 billion dollars went to Europe.[4]

This accomplishment, he added, was mirrored in concrete signs of wealth. America's population, less than one-fifteenth of the total population of the world, possessed three times as many automobiles, three to four times as many radios as the rest of the world. It had one-third of all the railroads of the world and over one-half of its gold supplies. Three-fifths of the world's cotton, two-fifths of its coal, three-fourths of its oil production, half of its copper, and a fourth of its wheat were at its disposal. And all of this was reflected in massive consumption of food, clothing, and other needs. In America one-fifteenth of the world's people purchased in their retail stores more than the value of all the goods

[2]*Das amerikanische Wirtschaftswunder*, 21. Quotation with permission of S. Fischer Verlag.
[3]Fischer *et al.*, *Handbuch der Amerikakunde*, 83.
[4]*Das amerikanische Wirtschaftswunder*, 7-9.

crossing the frontiers of the world. Truly, America was "the richest land of the earth."[5]

In this recognition of tremendous economic accomplishment all travelers, specialists and non-specialists, pattern and non-pattern tourists joined. The United States was a new colossus. Its prosperity contrasted sharply with the cheerlessness and poverty of the homeland. The impact of everywhere-apparent wealth and strength struck each German tourist as he landed in New York. In most cases it had been anticipated but reality exceeded expectations. Even those who had earlier visited the United States were startled by the changes. Arthur Holitscher, for example, found that a whole "new generation of skyscrapers" had replaced those with which he was familiar.[6] And Hirsch laughingly told of the contractor for a skyscraper of twenty stories who was hurrying to meet his completion schedule since the building was scheduled three months later to be replaced by one of forty stories.[7]

The postwar visitors found "prosperity" enshrined as a kind of god. The belief in "the eternal light of prosperity," wrote one observer, had taken the place of "faith in the Grace of Heaven."[8] Another pictured the two as closely entwined: prosperity was the visible sign that God was pleased with His America![9] Most of the visitors were not greatly impressed by the economic crisis of 1921-22 in America. This was essentially a question of readjustment to postwar conditions.[10] By the end of 1922 the American economy was again in an upward swing. The comparison with Germany during the year that followed was enhanced by the use of the dollar as a yardstick for the decline in value of the German mark during the great inflation. In the midst of the growing crisis of the inflation, when the dollar already stood at a value of more than 21,000 marks, the *Vossische Zeitung* printed a reminiscent bit by Karl Helfferich describing Georg von Siemens' assistance in the financing

[5]*Ibid.*, 10-14; 150.

[6]*Wiedersehn*, 17; *cf.* Kühnemann, *Amerikafahrt*, 8—"On all sides giant buildings have shot up beside which the old skyscrapers seem petty."

[7]*Das am. Wirtschaftswunder*, 29.

[8]Dr. R. Burkhard, "Die Gefahr des Yankeetums," *Grüne Blätter*, XII, No. 32, 523 (August 10, 1930).

[9]Holitscher, *Wiedersehn*, 65-66.

[10]Erich von Salzmann, "Die amerikanische Krise," *Vossische Zeitung*, February 26, 1921; *cf.* Hans Goslar, "Amerika, 1922: die wirtschaftliche Lage," *ibid.*, February 18, 1922.

of the Northern Pacific Railroads. This little piece of fond recollection looked back to much different times and emphasized the great change in Germany's status.[11] When Alfred Tyrnauer wrote an article on "The Land of Milk and Honey" in the *Vossische Zeitung* of June 5, 1923, the newspaper in which it appeared cost its buyer 300 marks and the dollar was worth 71,000 marks!

Little wonder that few German observers gave more than a passing thought to the American "crisis" of 1924.[12] And little wonder that they were slow to recognize the onset of the depression after 1929. The quotation above about "the eternal light of prosperity" was written well after the days of the American stock market crash, and other Germans continued to write of American prosperity long after the time when Americans themselves were convinced that the horn of plenty had been emptied. Not until the very height of the depression did German travelers begin to speak of a land where things were now still and quiet, and problems of unemployment such as those observed at home were to be found.[13]

The reactions of Germans to this American prosperity, of course, varied all the way from envious hatred to poetic adulation. For many it awakened fears that Europe had become narrow and "Balkanized," that it would be a financial vassal of America.[14] Indeed, from the German vantage point, their homeland looked outward upon two great new giants, East and West, the United States and the Soviet Union. Although aware of vast differences between them, Germans found much that was similar—both were still relatively immature countries, semi-colonial in character; both worshipped material well-being, although they sought it in very different ways; both looked forward to a period in which they

[11]"Amerika und Deutschland," April 13, 1923.

[12]An exception, Hermann Lufft, "Der Krieg und die amerikanische Wirtschaftskrise," *Kölnische Zeitung*, July 27, 29, 1924.

[13]Oskar Sommer, *Amerika will die Zeit festbinden* (Berlin, 1927) predicted the coming of difficulties; most graphic depression pictures—"N.N.," "U.S.A. im Blitzlicht," *Europäische Revue*, VII, Part 1 (January-June, 1931), 93-96; Georg von Schnitzler, "Amerika—Frühjahr, 1932," *ibid.*, VIII, Part 1 (January-June, 1932), 375-358; Alfons Goldschmidt, *Die dritte Eroberung Amerikas. Bericht von einer Panamerikareise* (Berlin, 1929).

[14]Adolf Sonnenschein, *Eindrücke eines Verwaltungsbeamten von den Vereinigten Staaten. Vortrag* (Weltwirtschaftliche Gesellschaft zu Münster i. W., Heft 13. Leipzig, 1927), 1; *cf.* Hirsch, *Das am. Wirtschaftswunder*, 7.

would certainly play a greater role, while Germans saw their own country slipping into the back-stream of history.[15]

All through the 1920's the Germans engaged in a self-questioning search for the sources of prosperity in America. What was it that provided for the United States this high standard of living, this unquestioned well-being, when the homeland was struggling to survive? Did the answer lie only in the great material resources of America or were there also techniques of production and qualities of business management which contributed to this? What could Germany learn from this new giant which would help in its own advancement?

This search, of course, engendered in many cases efforts for imitation, for adoption of American business practices. With this imitation of business practices also came often an adoption of other aspects of American civilization, from jazz to American journalism and advertising. It was this trend towards imitation which gave rise to the controversy of the 1920's over the "Americanization" of Germany. Did this imitation carry with it dangers to German traditions and ways of life? Was the price of prosperity, if it could be achieved, the surrender of German culture? One group, wrote Moritz J. Bonn at the time, saw advancement in this Americanization; the other the "coming of a new storm of Huns led by a new Attila, who bears the features of Henry Ford or of Taylor."[16]

It was, of course, most comforting to find the answer to American well-being in the great extent and vast variety of resources of the United States. The size of the country they visited filled most of the German travelers with awed admiration and envy. In particular they were shocked by the great reaches of uncultivated land and the uncared-for forests from which older trees were not removed—as at home—so that the new might flourish and replace them. As one traveler summed it up, America was, of course, a land created by hard work, one where "labor alone determined the worth of men." "But," he continued,

> however powerful was American labor, how much was also given to them and fell freely into their laps! Into their laps fell that wonderful land. What a land it is. The land of the

[15]Prosinagg, *Das Antlitz Amerikas*, 278; Holitscher, *Wiedersehn*, 11-12; Colin Ross, "Russland und U.S.A.: die unfreisten Reiche der Erde," *Bremer Nachrichten*, June 4, 1929.

[16]*Die Kultur der Vereinigten Staaten von Amerika* (Berlin, 1930), 7.

broad spaces, the land of inexhaustible resources, the land of few men, the land in which the clock in the same moment strikes four different hours, 12 in New York, 11 in Chicago, 10 in Denver, 9 in San Francisco. The land in which all the climates of the earth work for its people, the land to whose population all the parts of the world have made their contribution. What are now 120 million men in a land which is seven and one-half times as great as Germany in its old boundaries, alone as great as all of Europe?[17]

This virtual worship of the bigness of America was not new. Before World War I a German had labeled the United States "the land of unlimited possibilities."[18] Now new names joined the old designations—"the land of milk and honey,"[19] "El Dorado,"[20] "the land of the record figures,"[21] "the meteor,"[22] "the wonderland of capital."[23]

Strangely enough few German travelers sought to see at first hand the exploitation of the mineral resources of the country or the real centers of production. Not one of them thought it worthwhile to devote a chapter in his America book to the coal fields of Pennsylvania and the industry of Pittsburgh! Few of them saw the iron barges of the Great Lakes, let alone visited the mines in the Mesabi range. One of the non-pattern travelers did stop at Duluth-Superior and discovered for himself the fantastic statistics of this city on the Lakes; although smaller than Duisburg-Ruhrort, it carried twice the traffic of the Rhineland city, was, indeed, the largest internal harbor of the world.[24] Another non-pattern tourist found himself among the great forests of the Northwest and observed how a lumbering company, which had exhausted its earlier supplies by the exploitation which Germans called *Raubbau*, "a robbing operation," created a new city to serve its needs.[25]

[17]Kühnemann, *Amerikafahrt*, 63.

[18]Max Ludwig Goldberger, *Das Land der unbegrenzten Möglichkeiten. Beobachtungen über das Wirtschaftsleben der Vereinigten Staaten von Amerika* (Leipzig, 1903).

[19]Title of article by Alfred Tyrnauer, *Vossische Zeitung*, June 5, 1923.

[20]Descovich, *Unsere Technik und Amerika*, 7.

[21]Jakob Dorfmann, *Im Lande der Rekordzahlen. Amerikanische Reiseskizzen* (Berlin, 1927).

[22]Persius [Lothar], *Der Meteor*.

[23]Title of article by Tony Sender, *Vorwärts*, December 14, 1926.

[24]Dietrich, *U.S.A., das heutige Gesicht*, 87-92.

[25]Longview, Washington, already mentioned in Ch. IV. Feiler, *Amerika-Europa*, 26-31; Prosinagg, *Das Antlitz Amerikas*, 154-155.

Most German travelers, however, contented themselves with peering from the windows of Pullman cars and calculating how the wastelands they saw would have supported—with careful cultivation and fertilization—half the population of the homeland.

2. *The "Great Henry"*: But much as they envied the material resources of America, many Germans found a more convincing explanation of American accomplishment in the nature of American men and methods. Thus Hirsch's book, one of the best of the contemporary analyses of the American economy, found five major sources of prosperity. Two related to geography—the richness of the land in natural resources and the absence of internal customs duties. The other three related to men and methods: "the peculiar economic energy of a people which has taken unto itself by natural selection the healthiest and most adventuresome of the peoples of thirty-five other nations"; "a particular working organization for production and transportation built upon a great labor shortage, enormously high real wages, and the exaggerated purchasing power created by this"; and an organization of trade and banking which had worked out better than its beginnings, coming in the long run to finance not only production and trade, but also use and consumption.[26] Many German observers were less measured and cautious in their judgments than Hirsch. For them the human elements of the American "economic miracle" were of predominant interest. Obviously Germany could not profit from envious study of America's gifts of nature. But she could profit by an examination of the men and methods by which the United States had accomplished a miraculous expansion of her industry.

For Germans both of these were symbolized by the towering figure of "the great Henry,"[27] Ford, the author of American "automobilism" and in European eyes the creator of a whole new concept of production and business views which they labeled "Fordism."

No German left America without having been overwhelmed by the consequences of Ford's activity. "The swarms of motorized ants"[28] which flooded the streets of the larger cities and moved in

[26]*Das am. Wirtschaftswunder*, 15.

[27]Designation by one of his most ardent admirers, Otto Moog, *Drüben steht Amerika. Gedanken nach einer Ingenieurreise durch die Vereinigten Staaten* (Braunschweig, 1928), 15.

[28]"Ameisengewimmel auf rollenden Pneus," Willy Sachs, "Amerikaner und Wir," *Kölnische Zeitung*, December 23, 1924.

perfect tempo to the changing traffic signals presented an almost traumatic vision to Europeans. The omnipresent auto became in their eyes an integral part of the American landscape even in the dusty reaches of the prairies.[29] The figures of comparison, almost eighteen million in the United States in 1924, one car for every six Americans, as compared to less than three-quarters of a million for the whole rest of the world, one car for every eighty-eight Frenchmen, one for every three hundred ten Germans, underscored American superiority.[30] And all of this they attributed to Henry Ford. To be sure the "tin lizzy," "*Blechbüchse*," was not attractive and the stream of traffic was dark and cheerless.[31] But the auto had been a source of "freedom"—particularly it had altered the whole life of the farmer.[32] Little wonder that German travelers regretted mournfully that there was no German "Volksauto,"[33] not even a "Ford Bicycle."[34]

But the name of Ford meant more to Germans than the provision of autos *per se*. It stood for a style of production—the apotheosis of the "laufende Band," the conveyor system of production, and for an attitude towards the conduct of business which contrasted sharply with those prevailing at home.

Few visitors missed the opportunity to see a Ford created before their eyes—to follow the highly developed "assembly march"[35] of the perfectly machined, interchangeable parts as they presented themselves at their appointed time to the workers on the assembly line, to see the product grow until the last workers filled the gas

[29]Hensel, *Die neue Welt*, 58.

[30]Feiler, *Amerika-Europa*, 78; Köttgen, *Das wirtschaftliche Amerika*, 32. Or, as a Berlin advocate pictured it, 32 factories in Germany produced 30,000 cars per year, while 60 factories in America produced 3,280,000 cars. Justizrat Dr. Waldschmidt, "Travel Impressions Gathered in the United States of America," *The Dawes Way*, I, No. 3/4 (1925), 31-35.

[31]Erich von Salzmann, "Die Grossstadt von Morgen," *Vossische Zeitung*, February 5, 1921.

[32]Hensel, *Die neue Welt*, 57; Alice Salomon, "Lebenstechnik: Amerikanische Eindrücke," *Vossische Zeitung*, April 17, 1924.

[33]Term used by Sonnenschein, *Eindrücke eines Verwaltungsbeamten*, 34, and by Kurt Heinig, "Das Auto als Gebrauchsgut," *Vorwärts*, November 27, 1925. An anticipation of Hitler's later concern with the Volkswagen is seen in his "second book," *Hitler's Secret Book* (New York [c. 1961]), 98.

[34]Moog, *Drüben steht Amerika*, 88.

[35]"Ein verwickelter Zusammenmarsch," Friedrich von Gottl-Ottlilienfeld, *Fordismus: Ueber Industrie und technische Vernunft* (Jena, 1926), 18.

tank, started the engine, and drove off the completed auto. Many of the observers realized that Ford had not originated the techniques he employed, that the assembly line itself was not a Ford creation.[36] What he had done, they realized, was to make use of existing techniques for his own purposes with a degree of creative imagination and skillful efficiency which gave him a special role in the history of the world's economic achievements.

One of the closest students of his accomplishments, Dr. Friedrich von Gottl-Ottlilienfeld, remarked that a whole "Ford-Philology" had come into existence, and that it was vitally necessary in evaluating Ford's activities to separate his technical accomplishments from his non-technical. To the former he applied the term, "Fordization," to the latter "Fordism." And both, he emphasized, must be separated from any confusion with "Taylorism," the enforcement of severe and strained work methods. By this he meant that Ford's assembly line had been planned for maximum efficiency and production, but not at the price of the conversion of his workers into senseless automatons operating under an elite of obnoxious work-supervisors, such as he believed Taylor's methods involved.[37]

This sort of definition of Taylorism was, of course, unfair to Taylor and his disciples, but reflected the fact that the Ford works themselves provided the most convincing rebuttal to charges that American production methods overstrained industrial workers.[38] Although Ford's methods of division and simplification of labor had made it possible for three-fourths of his employees to learn their jobs in a week's time, Ford had not sought to cheapen labor costs by an unjust tempo of work and had instituted a careful proc-

[36]E.g., Feiler, *Amerika-Europa*, 167; Hirsch, *Das am. Wirtschaftswunder*, 40-43.

[37]Gottl-Ottlilienfeld, *Fordismus*, 7-8.

[38]Edmund Kleinschmitt, a German who sampled American factory techniques from the worker's standpoint, wrote in his book, *Durch Werkstätte und Gassen dreier Erdteile. Das soziale Bild von Amerika, Ostasien, und Australien* (Hamburg, 1928), 12, "If one goes through the [Ford] factory with German industrialists and producers, [one finds] they are disappointed because the work tempo is a fully humane one. The clamor about the soul-shattering work methods, the so-called 'Americanism,' derives mostly from such American travelers who see here for the very first time modern industrial production methods." Kleinschmitt's own experiences as a Ford worker corroborated this view (33ff.).

ess of work rotation to counter job monotony. He had also taken the unusual step of creating positions where the physically handicapped might earn a normal working wage.[39] "Fordization," therefore, the creation of an improved technical system of production, was also closely related to "Fordism" as Gottl-Ottlilienfeld defined it, the employment of a creative spirit of personality. And Ford's business, he suggested, rested not upon "the spirit of organization," which he equated with Taylorism, but upon "the spirit of personality."[40]

It is somewhat difficult to realize in retrospect the tremendous impact of Ford's business concepts upon the world of the 1920's, when they first became fully understood in Europe. In essence, as Europeans saw them, they were simple—the principle that mass production at a low per-unit rate was far more desirable than lower production even at higher profits; that the constant concern of a mass industry must be price reduction; that high wages increase the market for mass-produced items and by creating an *esprit de corps* of the workers actually aid in increased production and hence are economically as well as sociologically justifiable. Along with this the concepts that no factory is large enough for more than one product, that nothing is ever so good that it can't be made better, and that an enterprise must be as free as possible from reliance upon outside capital loans and from the hindrances of middlemen in creating its product.

Ford, felt Gottl-Ottlilienfeld, had been possessed from the first with a desire for mass production, a passion for what his German interpreter called "technical intelligence"—"*Technischer Vernunft.*" Obstacles he had met like the knights of old—"First throw your heart before you, then spring after it." And, added Gottl-Ottlilienfeld, "Nothing is now or ever will be ripe and complete for Henry Ford! He is 'Dynamism' in all its power, actually as if 'activism' in the narrower sense of 'constant betterment' of a William James were spiritually incorporated in this most American of all industrial figures."[41] Fordism was essentially "a will to service," with a leadership called by "its self-assured will

[39]Hirsch, *Das am. Wirtschaftswunder*, 94-106; Irene M. Witte, *Taylor, Gilbreth, Ford. Gegenwartsfragen der amerikanischen und europäischen Arbeitswissenschaft* (München und Berlin, 1924), 60-61.

[40]Gottl-Ottlilienfeld, *Fordismus*, 13.

[41]*Ibid.*

to service, chosen by a process of natural selection."[42] Such a development, he added, was still far in the future in Germany.

Ford was the subject of an adulation almost pathetic in character during the 1920's. His German admirers vastly outnumbered his critics.[43] Germans followed his activities closely. They read with appreciation of his nostalgia for his past—his creation of a museum town at Greenfield Village in Dearborn, including an exact reproduction of Edison's laboratory. They hailed his autobiography with respect and perused its pages for a guide to their own problems. Only gradually did cynicism set in and some writers begin to express doubt that Ford himself had written the volume which bore his name and to note that it was virtually ignored in America. An increased measure of disillusionment in respect to the personality of Ford derived from his visit to Germany in the middle twenties. In an interview at that time he admitted unabashedly that he knew nothing at all of German politics, not even the name of Germany's president. All he knew of Germany, he said, was that the Jews were in control of affairs there as elsewhere in the world— "The Catholic Church is in the hands of the Jews; the unions and Stinnes and the Kaiser also under their control." These gibberings, suggested one newspaper commentator, would be unimportant except for Ford's wealth: "Henry Ford is one proof of with how little intelligence the world can not only be ruled but also exploited. The lord of the life and death of hundreds of workers is a spiritual nullity."[44]

Criticisms of Ford's lack of spirituality, however, weighed little in contrast to his achievements.[45] The creation of a vast industrial complex controlling raw materials as well as production, the equa-

---

[42]Ibid., 37.

[43]Among his most caustic critics was Dr. Arno Faldix, the chairman of the Economic Office in Düsseldorf, whose book, Henry Ford als Wirtschafts-politiker (München, 1925) denied that Ford had a system—his autobiography, said Faldix, set forth only contradictory, incoherent, and superficial judgments and prescriptions. (80-82)

[44]Hans Bauer, "Interview mit einem Krösus," Vorwärts, December 11, 1925.

[45]Moog in Drüben steht Amerika, 77, used Ford to prove his point that Americans just didn't want to be educated! Emil Müller-Sturmheim chose the figure of Gandhi for a contrast and suggested that, unlike Gandhi, Ford did not need to flee the present, for he had mastered it and proved that poverty and suffering were not necessary. Ohne Amerika geht es nicht, 70-80.

tion of Ford's name with the ideal of high wages, and the lure of
the optimism reflected in Ford's confidence that the United States
would not reach a saturation point in automobile production until
there were thirty million cars for a population of one hundred and
fifty million—all of these made Detroit an American mecca and
engendered a continuing "debate" in Germany over the question
of imitation.[46]

Some commentators simply dismissed the idea of possible imitation with the flat comment that if it were tried, German industrialists would make a mess of it as they had done with most
things since the war.[47] A more restrained observer pointed out that
there were, indeed, very serious obstacles besetting the employment of Ford's methods in Germany and that Ford's success in
America was to a considerable degree due to a favorable conjunc-
ture of time and circumstances in the postwar period which Ford
had shrewdly appraised and skillfully exploited to make himself
"one of the most gifted (*genialsten*) enterprisers of modern times."
But, he continued, a hard road lay before his would-be apostles in
Germany. Ford's great enterprises had been developed gradually—
any effort for rapid expansion would interpose the problem of high
interest rates on capital loans, which would in turn negate efforts
to keep prices down. Furthermore, he believed, the German worker
would not willingly accustom himself to being simply a link in a
chain, and the whole question of buying power was in such a state
of flux that the efforts of a single enterpriser to promote a drastic
rise by sharply increased wages would be doomed to failure; only
an effort of the whole complex of industrialists could succeed. All
that could be hoped for was a gradual improvement of production
and of buying power and even with the best efforts difficulties still
remained: the individuality of German purchasers and the narrowness of the German market—here, as in other complaints of the
day, was suggested the great advantage of a European-wide market
not to be realized until more than thirty years later.[48]

[46]Term used by Dietrich, *U.S.A., das heutige Gesicht*, 71. Witte in *Taylor,
Gilbreth, Ford*, 6, suggested that the common German approach favored
lengthening rather than shortening the workday. See her review of the
"debate," 62-74.

[47]Kurt Heinig, "Ford Problem und Arbeiterschaft: Was ein Gewerkschafter
bei Ford sah," *Vorwärts*, November 18, 1925.

[48]Dr. Erich Thieme, "Die Debatte über Ford," *Vossische Zeitung*, June
26, 1925, "Umschau in Technik und Wirtschaft." The term "common market"

As a consequence, imitation came slowly. It may be noted, however, that by 1928 the Ford exhibit in Berlin was an event celebrated by lights and fireworks at midnight, and by 1930 a Ford factory was underway in Cologne.[49]

3. *Taylorism and Its Opponents*: This debate over Fordism was a part of a larger controversy over the whole complex of American industrial techniques,"*Technik*," which Germans symbolized with the names of Ford, Frederick Winslow Taylor, and Frank Gilbreth. These names were identified with American *Arbeitswissenschaft*, the science of the proper employment of labor.[50]

The United States, of course, impressed all comers with the degree of mechanization of factory production. The American people, wrote Otto Moog, were "*das Volk der Technik*," "the nation of technology."[51] As Anton Erkelenz expressed it, in America, "thirty iron slaves" (horse-power) worked for every inhabitant.[52] Dismally, Alfons Goldschmidt imagined that he could see the conveyor belt stretching across the country from shore to shore.[53] But Emil Müller-Sturmheim wrote, "In the heart of Europe the machine is still a curse, in the heart of America already a blessing, tomorrow complete freedom."[54]

In its most extreme form Arthur Feiler found one completely mechanized and almost empty factory which proudly placarded its achievement: "A half million horse-power obey here one man, who sits at his desk."[55] In this factory the major problem of the workers was boring idleness. But by far the most common impression of American factories emphasized haste, "speed-up," the severity of effort on the part of the workers.

---

was used in those days to include Russia. *Cf.* Kurt Heinig, "Optimismus als Ausweg: die grossen Wirtschaftsfragen Amerikas," *Vorwärts*, December 12, 1925.

[49]Pastor Eilert, "Die amerikanische Gefahr," Berlin *Tägliche Rundschau*, June 24, 1928; *Kölnische Zeitung*, January 22, 1930.

[50]See Dr. Werner Mahrholz, "Amerikanische und europäische Arbeitswissenschaft," *Vossische Zeitung*, August 14, 1925 and Witte, *Taylor, Gilbreth, Ford*, 62-74. By 1924 there was even an "Arbeitswissenschaftliches Kongress" which met in Prague to discuss this American science of labor management, *ibid.*, 5.

[51]*Drüben steht Amerika*, 11.   [52]*Amerika von Heute*, 61-70.

[53]*Die dritte Eroberung Amerikas*, 74.

[54]*Ohne Amerika geht es nicht*, 68-69.

[55]*Amerika-Europa*, 164.

Gradually German observers came to realize that many of their assumptions about American factory methods were faulty, that the real difference between German and American factory labor lay not in the greater efforts of the Americans but in the more efficient employment of these efforts. There were in America, wrote Kurt Heinig, "no nervous employers." Things were done with a sense of balance, one not given by God but worked out by man as a parallelogram of social and economic forces. This, rather than the tempo of labor, really determined production.[56]

Perhaps the most comprehensive study of American technical methods published in Germany during the 1920's was that written by Emo Descovich an engineer. Descovich sketched critically the history of American techniques of labor management, emphasizing the contributions of Frederick Winslow Taylor, the American engineer who had risen from a position as a simple factory worker to that of foreman, master, and engineer. Taylor's study of waste motion in the labor of the workers at the Midvale Steel Company had accomplished a phenomenal increase of production.[57] But Descovich, in contrast to the harsh judgments of Gottl-Ottlilienfeld noted above, pointed out that Taylor himself had always warned that he was not creating a "system," that the effective employment of his methods required a harmonious relationship between employers and employees, and that the increase of wages paid as an incentive for the great increase of production desired must be really significant.[58]

The actual propagandization of Taylor's methods had come with the work of his disciple, Frank Gilbreth, after his death. But Gilbreth also added "the human factor," the problems of decline of productivity with the weariness occasioned by monotony and the necessity of replacement and rotation of workers.[59] And one German commentator declared in 1926 that in all of American industry only about 100,000 could be characterized as laboring under Taylor methods.[60]

The effort of German analysts, therefore, to draw lessons from

[56]"Das amerikanische Arbeitstempo," *Vorwärts*, December 8, 1925.

[57]Related, *Unsere Technik und Amerika*, 17-19.   [58]*Ibid.*

[59]Werner Mahrholz, "Amerikanische und europäische Arbeitswissenschaft," *Vossische Zeitung*, August 14, 1925.

[60]Fritz Naphthali, "Der Amerikabericht deutscher Gewerkschaftsführer," *Die Arbeit*, III (1926), 363-367, 367.

the work of these technical pioneers often came to the conclusion that not specifics but generalities were all important. What was involved was the careful management of the work of thousands of employees. The slogan which Feiler brought back from one American businessman was typical—"He who saves twelve thousand employees ten steps a day has accomplished a saving of fifty miles of energy."[61] Everything rested upon rather simple adjustments; "simplicity" and "concentration" were the real keys, declared one German engineer, and even more important was the "spirit" in which things were done—"only the spirit, the spirit alone, the nature of man's point of view, brings progress."[62] In technical reform, he suggested, the Americans followed the maxim of the old Prussian infantry: "Spring up! March!" In other words they waited until they were capable of making the large changes which were worthwhile; little, rapid springs in too great tempo would only bring losses.[63]

All in all, Germans saw the greatest differences between their industry and America's comprehended in the human factor, both on the part of management and of labor. Efforts to use American methods without understanding the spirit of them came a cropper.[64] The major differences between American and German production lay not in isolated techniques but in the whole framework of the handling of human labor. Basically, employers and employees must build a working association, joined in a common "fresh and merry struggle for dollars and progress."[65] For the prevalent Ger-

[61]*Amerika-Europa*, 166.

[62]Moog, *Drüben steht Amerika*, 46. One American visitor, James J. Davis, added emphasis to this stress on the "spirit" of the industrial enterpriser in his interview with a German newspaper. The European problem, he stated, was simply a question of "will power, of leadership, and of organizational knowledge." What Europeans needed to find was "the will to action." "Das Arbeitsproblem in Amerika," *Kölnische Zeitung*, August 15, 1925.

[63]*Drüben steht Amerika*, 24-25.

[64]*E.g.* in the Niles Works in Oberschöneweide, where a bonus plan for increased production had failed miserably—related by Dir. Dr. Ing. Litz, "Sozialpolitische Reiseeindrücke in den Vereinigten Staaten," Berlin *Tägliche Rundschau*, May 2, 1925. And Johannes Buschmann told of a Berlin banker who was able by labor-saving methods to fire 19 out of 20 employees, but looked completely blank when an American acquaintance asked him how much he had raised the wages of the twentieth! "Amerika—das Tor zu neuen Wegen der Kultur," *Zeitwende*, VII, No. 2 (February, 1931), 154-172 at 157.

[65]Moog, *Drüben steht Amerika*, 98-99.

man impression that American factory labor was one of forced strenuousness gave way frequently on closer view to the realization that American factory workers did not really work as hard as German workers, that their relations with their employers were much better, that even in assembly line labor the spirit was "more the passionate play of the sportsman than of the slave."[66]

There was, therefore, in the long run, more interest in the men who ran the factories in America and the workers who labored in them than in specific techniques of production. Here in the psychology of the enterpriser and of the men at the lathe Germans found the most convincing explanations of American prosperity and progress.

4. *The Lure of the Wealthy: Babbitt and His Breed*: "One of every 10,450 of us is a millionaire," declared the chief statistician of the United States Treasury Department in September, 1926. The statement was reported in a book by Carl Adolf Bratter on *American Industrial Magnates,* and Bratter drove the figures home by adding that seventy-four Americans had an *income* of over a million dollars a year and that the three richest Americans jointly controlled eight hundred millions of dollars.[67] Here, indeed, were titans worthy of study.

The attitude of German observers towards the great capitalists was surprisingly tolerant. Little of the spirit of the muck-rakers found reflection in their descriptions of American men of wealth. Even Socialist observers spoke of them with respect and often contrasted them with less civic-minded leaders at home. "Self-made," suggested one critic dolefully, was an expression of respect when used for American business leaders, but such "self-made" figures at home got little sympathy.[68] "Intellectual America makes fun, often unfairly, of its race of Babbitts," wrote Moritz J. Bonn. "Europe, which thinks itself so superior to them, admires and copies them."[69]

The German commentators did recognize that great ruthless-

[66]Paul Riebensahm, *Der Zug nach U.S.A. Gedanken nach einer Amerikareise, 1924* (Berlin, 1925), 20-21—on the Ford factory in Hamilton, Ohio.
[67]*Amerikanische Industriemagnaten,* 18-20.
[68]Karl Scheffler, "Self-made," *Vossische Zeitung,* March 7, 1925, Unterhaltungsblatt.
[69]*American Adventure,* 205.

ness had often been associated with the advancement of many of these leaders and that the middle class groupings had been injured by the process.[70] But not until the early 1930's did astute observers such as Friedrich Schönemann begin to note that the "Morganization of business" was leading to a sterilization of much of the national wealth and that "the blessedness of possession works increasingly against the pioneer-democratic concept of equality of opportunity."[71]

Through most of the twenties, therefore, a kind of hero worship attached itself to the great magnates. Yet much of this hero worship was based not on the conception that these magnates stood apart from or were different from Americans in general, but that they reflected in high degree the personality traits of their fellow countrymen. They displayed the "gaze towards greatness" which was a characteristic of every American.[72] They had derived from and helped to reinforce the immutable attitude of optimism which was a part of the American scene. This contributed, in turn, to the unusual daring which was associated with the American businessman: "Frightened hesitation is no part of his being."[73] As Adolf Sonnenschein, a German governmental official, expressed it, the American put all his emphasis upon the principle of accomplishment, the German on the principle of security. Each German approached the problems of life with the hope of maintaining the possessions he had received by inheritance and passing them on undiminished to his offspring. The sense of security, of holding to certainties, was an integral part of his being. In contrast, the American staked much on the future, held little to tradition, trusted his own abilities to accomplish success.[74] In Ford's maxim as quoted by one of his German admirers, there was a clear symbol of this: "Thou shalt not honor the past nor fear the future."[75] Or as Alfred Kerr reported it poetically, "The most earnest of all men in his daring is the Yankee. Without par as a planner. Without par as an executor of those plans. Hero without pathos. And withal soft—in comparison with us."[76] In many other ways, too, American

[70]Penck, U.S.-Amerika, 30-32.
[71]Die Vereinigten Staaten, II, 243 ff.
[72]Hassert, Die Vereinigten Staaten, 225.
[73]Bratter, Am. Industriemagnaten, 11.
[74]Eindrücke eines Verwaltungsbeamten, 35-37.
[75]Moog, Drüben steht Amerika, 47.   [76]Yankee-land, 41.

business leaders reflected the experiences of the past. Although Bratter gave a role of great prominence to Puritanism and Quakerism in the formation of the American business ethic, it was, he emphasized, not an *a priori* philosophy but one derived from many sources—the American pioneer spirit, the love of overcoming obstacles, the love of sport and records, the acceptance of change, the sense of self-respect, and the pride of accomplishment.[77]

The greatest of the leaders of industry, he suggested, had been set aside from the great masses of businessmen by three primary characteristics: 1. they understood their own times; 2. they were able to measure the past as well as the present and hence to understand progress; and 3. they were able to show the present generation how to create new and costly values.[78] Bratter's list of the greats included not only the ubiquitous Ford, but also Rockefeller—discussed without benefit of Tarbell; Carnegie, the "Krupp of American business," Gary, Schwab, William Andrews Clark, the Dodge brothers, Sinclair and Doheny—including the oil scandal, John Henry Patterson of National Cash Register, and Firestone.

The title of Bratter's book, *American Industrial Magnates*, had, of course, excluded the great financial leaders of the country, but some of the German commentators were aware of the great power and significance of the so-called "Investment Houses," such as that of J. P. Morgan, which exercised a kind of "dictatorship" over international long-term credit and a strong influence on the insurance business at home.[79] Hirsch pointed out that many banking concerns which Germans took to be independent were really a part of the Morgan complex. Morgan, he suggested, had a place in the American banking world similar to that held in Germany by Hugo Stinnes a few years earlier, and Wall Street itself was "the treasure house of the world."[80] Hirsch was also aware of the growing tendency towards concentration and integration in business and believed that Americans themselves were no longer following the anti-trust policy as originally conceived. Instead of seeking to

[77]*Am. Industriemagnaten*, 60 ff.

[78]*Ibid.*, 74.

[79]Charlotte Lütkens, *Staat und Gesellschaft in Amerika*, viii, complained that there was a "gap" in this regard, that no new material had been added to that set forth by the Pujo Committee in 1913. Even in these comments she was much more perceptive than most German commentators of the period.

[80]Hirsch, *Das am. Wirtschaftswunder*, 202-205, 210 ff.

destroy trusts, they were now satisfied with some measure of control which would ensure fair methods of competition on their part.[81]

In the long run, although German visitors discussed at length the importance of the personality of the businessman and the spirit in which he ran his business undertakings, they devoted little real effort to a direct appraisal of these things. On the one side they continued to hold to the preexistent image of Babbitt. On the other side they paid tribute to the "spirit of the business-

FIGURE 2.—Long before the time of Kennedy, the value of the rocking chair as an administrative aid was emphasized in this sketch from Hans Christoph Kaergel, "Kleinigkeiten aus dem grossen Amerika," *Die Bergstadt*, XIV (1926), 465-76.

man." Very few of the accounts record actual interviews with the businessmen themselves. Erwin Carlé provided the typical view of a businessman, whom he described dramatically: "He is a constantly reined-in motor. Everything in him pounds and hammers. He never stands still. He sees and hears all."[82] But Hans Christoph Kaergel provided a very different view from actual observation. In his article on "Little things out of big America" the sketch of a large and comfortable *Schaukelstuhl*, the rocking chair found in the office of the executive upon whom he called, indicated that the

[81]*Ibid.*, 60-64.
[82]*Amerikaner* (Leipzig-Gaschwitz, 1930), 32.

"rush" and "bustle" associated with business might sometimes be exaggerated.[83] Perhaps other clichés would have lost force with additional interviews.

5. Sears Roebuck and Chain Stores: Symbols of Standardization: The enormity of American production during the 1920's was matched by the size of its retail trade. Here, too, the lure of bigness and of the record figures at which they constantly cavilled drew the attention and study of the German visitor.

If the auto had "freed the farmer" from his bondage to the soil, the mail order house achieved even more—it integrated him into the business pattern of the country—"it drew the men of the solitudes, the inhabitants of the farms, of the country towns, of the widespread little and middle-sized cities into the great, unified, standardized market of America."[84] The catalog of Sears Roebuck had "the format and extent of the address-book of a city of millions." A million addressees received it. With all the special catalogs involved, the firm sent out fifty million catalogs a year.

The figures of this monstrous business were to Germans a symbol of the size of the American market. Eight million pairs of shoes a year, often 38,000 pairs a day; an average of 30 to 40 million orders a year for merchandise. And Sears Roebuck brought to the country areas the new goods of the great cities and imposed upon local retail firms the necessity of "keeping up with the times."[85]

Similarly, the chain stores worked to create a uniform market of foodstuffs and other wares. Already in the twenties, noted one observer, this was leading to the combination of production and sale on the part of many of these enterprises.[86] "Strangely enough," wrote Julius Hirsch,

> when I wrote my Habilitation thesis fourteen years ago on these enterprises, almost nothing was known in America about this whole movement. Today it is stronger there than elsewhere and [has brought about a] completely revolutionary alteration in trade and indeed in a degree which leaves every

---

[83]"Kleinigkeiten aus dem grossen Amerika," *Die Bergstadt*, XIV (1925/6), No. 5, 465-476 at 466.

[84]Feiler, *Amerika-Europa*, 149.

[85]*Ibid.*, 149-150.

[86]*Ibid.*, 151-152.

other country far behind it and in forms which can be very useful for German business if understood at the proper time.[87]

Not only had the chain stores themselves moved into predominant positions in groceries, cigar stores, and drug stores, added Hirsch, but their very existence forced independent merchants to work out cooperative arrangements for purchase and sale.[88] Typical of the chain stores and perhaps most impressive to the German visitor were the five and ten cent stores—Woolworth, Kresge, Penney's and the like—million dollar businesses upon a "two and four groschen" basis! The big question, suggested Hirsch, was whether this kind of business would come to Germany under native or American sponsorship.[89]

On the other side of the picture were the great department stores with their vast variety of goods. Here success was due to advertising, to "basement wear" selling—"In the long run cheapness is the most effective advertisement."[90] It was also due to some of the same spirit of "service" which had characterized the process of production: "The American department store, which assumes that the customer is always right, and accepts the justice of his complaints without inquiry and without hesitation, even when they are groundless, is not indulging in sentiment, but is displaying business common sense."[91]

All of these great retail enterprises were, of course, part of the great process of standardization of business in America. This was reflected even in the government—the most often mentioned agency, of course, the Bureau of Standards with its Division of Simplified Practice. This agency in working for the reduction of the numbers of types of beds, milk bottles, and bricks reflected the "will of the nation for uniformity of consumption."[92] And standardization was also, of course, encouraged and sponsored by the process of advertising and the provision of mass credit facilities. Julius Hirsch found in this process of standardization and in the uniformly accepted concept of business "service" a kind of "unconscious socialism" in a land strongly opposed to anything which smacked of Marxism.[93]

[87]*Das am. Wirtschaftswunder*, 168-169.
[88]*Ibid.*, 171-172.   [89]*Ibid.*, 172-174.
[90]*Ibid.*, 158.   [91]*Ibid.*, 232-233.
[92]*Ibid.*, 30-33; Köttgen, *Das wirtschaftliche Amerika*, 52-55.
[93]*Das am. Wirtschaftswunder*, 228-229.

6. American "Reklame"—Advertising and Installment Buying:
No feature of American business impressed the German observer more than the skillful if obtrusive use of advertising. They
were willing to admit that this was a peculiarly American contribution, that it had indeed in America become "a science of its
own." Its status was emphasized by its inclusion in university cur-
ricula and the establishment of research bureaus by business to
accumulate the statistics necessary to its constant improvement.[94]

The nature of American advertising, as Germans saw it, reflected the superficial and childlike character of Americans. It indicated that the American public did not really know what it
wanted; it had to be told. Advertising, wrote one observer, was
"the art of suggesting wants to the consumer," "the art of arousing
desires and putting the likely consumer in the right mood for
buying the right goods."[95] To do this the advertiser skilfully employed "business psychology." He appealed to the ideal of beauty,
to love of children, and to patriotism.[96] This was done in the
most elementary fashion possible—of this the slogans were a clear
sign. Often the visitors were more impressed by the mottoes which
came from private sources than those employed by the big cigarette
and soft drink firms, for example, "It's cheaper to send your
washing to the laundry than your wife to the hospital!" Arthur
Feiler was particularly intrigued by one which he found in a lonely
stretch of highway: "Hot dogs, Ice Cream, Lemonade—100% service." This he found especially American—100% service, even for
the lowly hot-dog-eater![97] The childish nature of these slogans, the
delight in "Licht-reklame," lighted advertising signs, and the basic
appeals to egotism confirmed the German view of the United States
as the land of the "big children." They were consistently critical
of the excessive use of advertising and of its extension into such
areas as church attendance and funerals.[98]

[94]Feiler, *Amerika-Europa*, 152-153; Kaergel, "Kleinigkeiten aus dem grossen
Amerika," *Die Bergstadt*, XIV (1925/6), No. 5, 465-476 at 466.

[95]Bonn, *American Adventure*, 211.

[96]Hans Goslar, "Amerikanische Reklame," *Vossische Zeitung*, March 25,
1922.

[97]*Amerika-Europa*, 153.

[98]"Amerikanismus," *Weser Zeitung*, June 12, 1929. Erwin Stranik, "Das
Land der Gegensätze," *Der getreue Eckart*, IX, No. 6 (March, 1932), 428-432,
repeated in detail the advertisement of an American funeral parlor and added,
"Here it must be a pleasure to die."

On the other hand, they were rather ruefully aware of its effectiveness. The greatest accomplishment of American business, wrote one observer, had been to hammer into the public "the Monroe Doctrine of industry: imported clothes are luxury, home-made suits, as much as possible exactly alike, are staples."[99] This was, of course, a vital achievement, because ninety per cent of all sales were registered on the home market.

Along with the cavil, there was, of course, some appreciation and admiration. Advertising was one sign that the American businessman was closer to his consumers than was the German. It did indeed expand the overall demand for goods and help to produce the prosperity of the twenties. The more objectionable forms of advertising were tending to disappear; "truth in advertising" was one aspect of business ethics which was beginning to take hold.[100] In German considerations of possible adaptations, however, there was a major obstacle—the lack of nation-wide periodicals with a broad reading public. There was no German *Saturday Evening Post*.[101]

Closely related to the advertising process were two other particularly American methods of expanding business—the premium system and installment buying. In the premium system with its premium catalogs and special offers (the predecessor of the trading stamp craze) was found a novel way to create a permanent clientele. One German observer retold with obvious approval the story of the employment of this scheme by such companies as the Quaker Oats Company, the Texas Music House in Houston, Parker Oil Company in Cleveland, and others. His appreciation for the ingenuity of these firms and their appeal to the psychology of their consumers emphasized the author's point that business psychology was more highly developed in America than in Germany. A case in point was the Thalhimer Bros. Clothing Company in Richmond, Virginia, which ran a contest for boys

[99]Descovich, *Unsere Technik und Amerika*, 63-64. Oskar Sommer wrote that when he raised with an American business man the question of importing German cement, the latter told him that they were already selling cement in Boston under the production price to keep out Belgian competition. *Amerika will die Zeit festbinden,* 26.

[100]Paul Wallfisch-Roulin, "Deutsche und amerikanische Geschäftspraxis und Geschäftspsychologie," *Betrieb und Organisation,* 1924, 101-103.

[101]Karl Berg, "Amerikanischer Wirtschaftsgeist," *Volkswirtschaftliche Blätter,* XXVII (1928), No. 12, 412.

by printing 5,000 buttons with only 16 duplicates and supplied a new outfit for the boys who could bring in the duplicates.[102]

And installment buying occasioned constant comment, much of it critical. "The Yankee lives on installments," was the prevailing charge.[103] The whole practice of credit-rating came in for study and examples: "Frau Mayer, Chicago, Midway 11, is quite wealthy and good for all orders, but inclines to cheating"; or "Mr. Stauffer, New York, Broadway 115, is well provided, but pays rather slowly since he is inclined to live beyond his means."[104] Able economists, however, pointed out that the system was essentially sound, that it really made better sense to advance credit for the consumption of goods than for their production, and that it had greatly expanded business in spite of losses in bad times.[105] As Moritz J. Bonn stated it, "In the nature of things, however, it is very much better for a business to have claims upon its ultimate customers than to owe money to its contractors and bankers."[106]

7. *Other Views of the Business Kaleidoscope*: Sketched out above have been the features of American business which drew the greatest amount of attention. Perhaps the slaughter houses of Chicago should have had their place among them. The lure of blood, of the technical aspects of this operation accompanied by some charges of sadistic handling of the animals, drew the attention of a great number of the visitors.

Strangely lacking, however, in the studies of American business were careful evaluations of American finance. Julius Hirsch gave some attention to the subject but wrote largely from the vantage point of secondary study rather than of interviews and observations. The stock market lured few observers, and the offices of the bank presidents attracted those who came for specific purposes rather than to write America books! An exception, however, was the insurance business, which attracted attention because the lack of

[102]Paul Wallfisch-Roulin, "Deutsche und amerikanische Geschäftspraxis und Geschäftspychologie," *Betrieb und Organisation*, 1924, 101-103; "Amerikanische Reklame und Verkaufsmethode," *ibid.*, 145-147.

[103]Felix Schmidt, "Der Yankee lebt auf Abzahlung," *Weser Zeitung*, September 3, 1925.

[104]Wallfisch-Roulin, see *fn.*100.

[105]Feiler, *Amerika-Europa*, 160-161.

[106]*American Adventure*, 214; *Geld und Geist. Vom Wesen und Werden der amerikanischen Welt* (Berlin [1927]), 83-91.

social security arrangements in this country boomed this business. "Fifty million insurance companies," suggested one German traveler, as he ran over the figures mentally, was "a business of skyscraper format." Seventeen billion dollars worth of new insurance written in 1927—to bring the total to a monumental ninety billion dollars—this, felt the German, was a reflection of the sense of independence of the American, who cared for these vital concerns himself.[107] An insurance man himself, he was amazed at the degree of state supervision. Although he recognized that this increased administrative costs and, as a result, premiums, he pointed out that it also eliminated real competition in setting rates and regarded this as justifiable.[108]

Other specialized interests were often reflected in travel accounts. Cement makers visited America to find the roads there constructed with a care and quality they had not anticipated. Much as they admired American road building, however, they did not feel there was much need to emulate American methods at home. German roads were not likely to develop at the rate of those in America or street parking ever to assume the importance at home that it had in the United States![109]

Electrical techniques were also a lure. The Berlin electrical net was closely modeled upon American examples in New York and San Francisco, and prominent leaders in this field journeyed to America for inspiration.[110]

8. *Labor and Labor Unions*: The Germans were also interested in those who might be considered the "victims" of this great business establishment—the workers and the farmers. The problems of the workers in America received much greater attention than did

[107]Hensel, *Die neue Welt*, 109.

[108]*Ibid*.

[109]Stadtdirektor Feuchtinger und Dr. Ing. Neumann, *Bericht über eine Studienreise in den Vereinigten Staaten von Amerika* (Charlottenburg, 1925); Direktor Alfred Müller, *Meine Reise nach Amerika. Vortrag gehalten auf der Sommerversammlung des Vereins deutscher Portland-Cement Fabriken vom 8. bis 10. September 1926 in Hannover* (Charlottenburg [1931?]).

[110]E. Rühle, "Meine Amerikareise und ihre Anwendung auf den Ausbau der Netze der Berliner Städtischen Elektrizitätswerke A.G.," *Elektrotechnik und Maschinebau*, XIV, 405-415 (May 30, 1926); Dr. Felix Deutsch (German General Electric), "Meine Eindrücke in Amerika," *Spannung. Die A.E.G. Umschau*, I (1927-8), 129-133, 168-172.

those of the farmers. Few agricultural experts or farmers visited the United States, whereas a considerable group of labor union leaders and ordinary workers came to this country. An agency of the "Wirtschaftshife der deutschen Studentenschaft" established an American Work Student service, which sent student workers to a two year apprenticeship in the Ford Motor Company, the Hudson Coal Company, the Pennsylvania R. R., Swift and Company, United Aluminum Company, Textile Machine Works, Westinghouse, International Harvester, and others.[111] As a consequence the problems of labor and of labor unions were much better understood than those of the farmer.

Both of these groupings, however, in German eyes were very different from their counterparts at home. Neither could really be regarded as classes. Indeed, one of the greatest secrets of American business, in German eyes, was this lack of distinction between employer and employee—both were "comrades in labor."[112] In America, wrote Alma Hedin, everyone is a democrat, even the millionaire; in Europe everyone seeks to be an aristocrat, even the worker.[113] And Otto Moog added his praise of the American view:

> In no other land is manual labor so respected and so highly valued as here. One feels instinctively that men cannot satisfy their basic needs with speeches, reading, and writing, that one cannot export printed paper in exchange for foodstuffs and that the first and most important task is to exploit the riches of nature. And so it comes about that we in Germany with [our pride in] educational and spiritual accomplishments carry on an irresponsible luxury while we are in material want, while the American half-consciously neglects the spiritual life and lives in material excess.[114]

Furthermore, the worker did not think of himself as occupying a fixed position of subordination to his employer. He expected to move onward and upward. "Every living, healthy American," wrote Julius Hirsch, "believes that he carries in his knapsack the future key to the wealth of J. P. Morgan."[115] Or in an-

---

[111]Anon., "Als Arbeiter in den Grossbetrieben der Vereinigten Staaten," *Kölnische Zeitung*, September 16, 1928.

[112]Pfannmüller, *So sah ich Amerika*, 170.

[113]*Arbeitsfreude. Was wir von Amerika lernen können* (Leipzig, 1921), 55.

[114]*Drüben steht Amerika*, 12.

[115]*Das am. Wirtschaftswunder*, 69.

other phrasing, no American considered himself a worker for life—
"Forward with head and elbows—that, too, is Americanism."[116]
Indeed, workers often owned considerable shares of the business
which employed them. This had, of course, been particularly true
of Ford employees but extended beyond them. Arthur Holitscher
noted that 60 per cent of the stock of the streetcar lines in Philadelphia was held by their employees.[117]

Beyond this lack of real distinction between workers and their
bosses there was also a general lack of really serious workers'
problems. The high wages of the day were universally admired.
Not only did they expand the natural market, but they aided in
technical change. Moog, for example, demonstrated that the labor
savings involved in a new turntable would pay for the change in
a year's time in America, whereas it would take three years in
Germany.[118] And, as has already been noted, observers discovered
that the much bruited pressure on labor was largely imaginary
and that there was none of the deception on the part of the
workers which existed in Germany.[119] Workers and employers
were joined in "a partnership in profit"—the "participation of
the many in the profits of the few."[120]

Nor did the assembly-line process of production pose real
mental hardships for the workers. The conveyor belt need not
connote spiritual slavery, noted Riebensahm. The American
worker accepted it as a device by which he was freed from the
harder part of his labor.[121]

German laborers and labor leaders visiting the United States
during the 1920's were almost invariably impressed by the lack
of importance of socialist movements or thought in this country.[122]

116Paul Rohrbach, "Was heisst Amerikanismus?" *Deutsche Monatshefte*, V,
subvol. II, 469 (November, 1927).

117*Wiedersehn*, 102-103.

118Moog, *Drüben steht Amerika*, 33-36.

119*Ibid.*, 98-99; *cf.* Hirsch, *Das am. Wirtschaftswunder*, 38.

120Bratter, *Am. Industriemagnaten*, 12.

121*Der Zug nach Amerika*, 11. Riebensahm's comments agreed with those
of the French worker Hyacinthe Dubreuil, whose account of fifteen months'
work in the United States was translated and widely read in Germany
(*Arbeiter in USA*. Leipzig [1930?]). See Paul Lang, "Amerika von Europa
aus gesehen," *Schweizerische Monatshefte für Politik und Kultur*, X (1930/1),
514-515.

122*E.g.*, Paul Löbe, "Eindrücke aus Amerika," *Vorwärts*, Nov. 17, 1925.

This they attributed to the high wages, the prosperity, and the nativism of American workers which rejected foreign intrusions. Alfred Tyrnauer suggested that even the poorest-paid American workers were capitalists by European standards.[123] Prosperity was also the motif stressed by Rudolf Kessel, one of the German work students in America, who asserted that "the economic peacefulness" of the worker was simply a matter of the "good times."[124]

Charlotte Lütkens, the sociologist, however, pointed out that actually the United States still stood "at the entry way to organized capitalism." America was facing problems which Europe had already experienced, although it had not solved them. "The completely immeasurable fullness of social relationships and divisions, which have become for Europe a very threatening reality which we cannot ignore, is in the U.S.A. still somewhat in flux and therefore occupies a much smaller place in social discussions."[125]

America, she concluded, was in a stage of "pseudo late capitalism."[126] Another observer expressed a similar evaluation. In his eyes, there was a dichotomy. America was in the highest stage of capitalism, but its social organization was still decisively determined by its youth, its colonial character. He, too, anticipated that time would bring the class system of America closer to that of Europe.[127] For many German socialists, probably writing largely from the standpoint of wishful thinking, time would bring greater opportunities in America for socialist points of view.[128]

German observers found the labor movement itself not really a labor movement in any European sense of the term but one which followed business principles and ideals.[129] This, they sug-

[123]"Amerikanische Arbeiter," *Vossische Zeitung*, August 16, 1923.

[124]"Ist der amerikanische Arbeiter wirtschaftsfriedlich?" *Kölnische Zeitung*, July 29, 1928. One socialist worker explained American working class passivity as due to the use of film propaganda—August Siemsen, "Soziale Betrachtungen eines Arbeiters in USA," *Gewerkschaft*, XXXII (1928), No. 43, 1189-1190.

[125]"Europäer und Amerikaner über Amerika," *Archiv für Sozialwissenschaft und Sozialpolitik*, LXII (1929), 615-630 at 615. Similar, Feiler, *Amerika-Europa*, 194-195.

[126]*Staat und Gesellschaft in Amerika*, 1.

[127]Fritz Naphthali, "Der Amerikabericht deutscher Gewerkschaftsführer," *Die Arbeit*, III (1926), 363-367.

[128]*E.g.*, Tony Sender, "Arbeitskämpfe in Amerika. Die Kehrseite der Medaille," *Vorwärts*, December 15, 1926.

[129]Heinrich Pollak, *Die Gewerkschaftsbewegung in den Vereinigten Staaten* (Jena, 1927), 303-322. Also dealing in detail with the conditions of

gested, was "an unavoidable consequence of the economic system based on an inanely emphasized concept of private capitalism." Only a "dollar union" was possible in such a country![130] The basic consequence was a kind of "labor-union capitalism" (*Gewerkschaftskapitalismus*).[131] Labor unions became training organizations, political pressure groupings, integrating agencies for labor. They guaranteed high production in return for employer concessions and accepted these by contract. This was found in particular in the unions dominating the clothing workers and the railroad employees.[132]

Different in approach, but no less business-like in procedure was the American Federation of Labor, which obtained high praise from the majority of German observers. Some of them were willing to suggest that its principles might be studied with profit by German labor unions, which had allowed themselves to become too heavily enmeshed in politics.[133] Dr. Hermann Lufft in his biography of Samuel Gompers related that this labor leader's work had left a legacy of "Gomperism" which joined together the austerity of the Puritan with a sense of the proprieties of life, of an appreciation of each man's worth, and of the need for patient constructive work rather than "social brutality." This was, he felt, a combination which needed emulation in continental Europe.[134]

Other observers were critical of the political powerlessness of labor. "The judicial scandal of the murder of Sacco and Vanzetti could only transpire in this country," wrote a young German worker. "The whole world protests, only America does not. Of politics the American worker knows nothing. To him it makes no difference what happens to his working class brothers."[135]

American workers, the activities of labor unions, profit-sharing schemes, etc. is Fritz Tänzler, *Aus dem Arbeitsleben Amerikas. Arbeits-verhältnisse, Arbeitsmethoden und Sozialpolitik in den Vereinigten Staaten von Amerika* (Berlin, 1927).

[130]Martin Wagner, "Amerikanische Gewerkschaftsprobleme," *Die Arbeit*, I (1924), 359-363.

[131]Feiler, *Amerika-Europa*, 214 ff.

[132]*Ibid.*, 214.

[133]Pollak, *Die Gewerkschaftsbewegung in den V.S.*, 334.

[134]*Samuel Gompers. Arbeiterschaft und Volksgemeinschaft in den Vereinigten Staaten von Amerika*, 189-190.

[135]August Siemsen, "Soziologische Beobachtungen eines jungen deutschen Arbeiters in USA," *Gewerkschaft*, XXXII (1928), No. 43, 1189-1190.

The German critics realized, of course, that American labor had many specialized problems. One was the dispersion of industry into many small cities often widely separated from one another, which made centralized control difficult. Often, however, they pointed out that the difficulty of bringing together different types of workers was greater than that of bridging distances—hence the particular nature of the American Federation of Labor. Another was the problem of integrating immigrants into national groups, and Germans stressed the connection between labor unions and the raising of immigration bars. But this latter action was not, asserted Charlotte Lütkens, entirely due to the labor unions. Middle-sized capitalists moving into later stages of capitalism, she suggested, also favored immigration restriction because of the advantages of standardization and of increasing consumer demand. The simplicity of the needs of the immigrant made him a hindrance in this process.[136] At any rate, there was much German sympathy for this action, an assertion of its economic justification. Dr. Heinrich Pollak, one of the closest students of the American labor union movement, suggested that the decline of immigration had already aided the work of the labor union movement.[137] With the exclusion of Negro labor from the existing labor unions, however, there was much less agreement. This would, declared the critics, only serve to drive the Negroes into the service of employers as strike breakers.[138]

Many German observers were horrified by the lack of social security arrangements—of unemployment or old age insurance in the United States. Although some admired the spirit of rugged individualism which this involved—on the part of the workers as well as of their employers—many pointed out that this posed serious problems for the future. On the other hand they were greatly impressed by the employer-sponsored welfare arrangements of many industries, including not only these basic matters of security but also the refinements of entertainment at lunch and work-time recreation. A popular book by Alma Hedin, the sister of the famous Swedish explorer, devoted itself to this matter with much appre-

---

[136]"Europäer und Amerikaner über Amerika," *Archiv für Sozialwissenschaft und Sozialpolitik*, LXII (1929), 615-630 at 617.

[137]*Gewerkschaftsbewegung*, 286 .

[138]Charlotte Lütkens, "Im Schlagschatten des amerikanischen Wirtschaftswunders," *Urania*, 1928-29, No. 8, 250-252.

ciation for American accomplishments. She found much attention to cleanliness, to sobriety, and to the care of workers and a recognition that welfare work paid for itself and benefited the nation as a whole, lessons which might well be studied back home:

> The Americans bring matters to completion to which we can't force ourselves to give full attention and hence we save our honor by criticizing. That is stupid of us and we would be acting more wisely if we sought to learn from them as they have learned from us in the past and are still learning.[139]

She believed the National Cash Register Company in Dayton, Ohio, to be the best example of American welfare capitalism.[140] Her most earnest proposal was for female factory inspectors to act as sort of factory mothers to cushion the monotony of work and provide a personal element in what was otherwise such an impersonal undertaking.[141] Like most European observers, she concluded that in America "every kind of labor is an honorable office and the name of worker is a title of honor."[142] There was not the effort to conceal one's labor in a factory which was found in Europe. There was no real proletariat in America unless it was that of the Negro and the foreign immigrant.[143] The transition between working class and middle class was almost imperceptible in an America where eighty per cent of the locomotive engineers' children went to college![144]

9. *The Farmers*: Just as there was no real proletariat in America, so also, concluded German observers, there was no real farming class equivalent in its ideals or practices to the European peasantry. The farmer, like the worker, was a member of the business class, with the same search for profit, the same spirit of business enterprise. The farmer, wrote one critic, "knows neither status (*Stand*)

---

[139]*Arbeitsfreude*, 47-53. Whether more Germans read the book for her observations or the fanatically nationalist "greetings to the German people" of her brother, which served as a foreword, might be debated.

[140]*Ibid.*, 133-162. Tänzler dealt in considerable detail with such items as profit-sharing, share-holding by workers, and factory welfare institutions in *Aus dem Arbeitsleben Amerikas*, 75-134.

[141]*Arbeitsfreude*, 37-43.

[142]*Ibid.*, 175. Or as Donatus Pfannmüller stated it, "All work which is paid for is worthy of honor; everything else is play." *So sah ich Amerika*, 170.

[143]Fritz Naphthali, see *fn.* 127.

[144]Feiler, *Amerika-Europa*, 213.

nor calling (*Beruf*), but rather only gain (*Erwerb*)."[145] Schöne-mann agreed with this observation, pointing to the contrast be-tween a satisfied and stabilized farming class in Germany and the restless and impatient rural population in America, the latter striving for the advantages of city civilization and failing to win a real connection with or feeling for the land.[146]

To the farmer, also, as to the businessman, technology was "a friend."[147] American agricultural missions to Germany reflected a high level of accomplishment. One such mission in 1929 empha-sized the great need for German agriculturists to improve means of distributing milk, to develop standardized sorting procedures for eggs, fruits, and vegetables, and to bring animal diseases under control.[148] Germans were also impressed by the training provided in American schools of agriculture, by the dissemination of scien-tific knowledge to the farmer through the extension services of these schools, and by the widespread use of machinery in farming.[149]

But advancing techniques did not in the 1920's mean pros-perity for the American farmer. Germans became aware of the exist-ence of a "flight from the land," of a chronic agricultural depres-sion.[150] Most Germans did not regard American agricultural prob-lems as fundamentally critical. There had been an expansion of agriculture, they noted, during the war. It was rather natural that there should now be a contraction and a return to normal balance. The American farm worker calculated one observer, produced three times as much as his German counterpart and earned 159 per cent more than farm workers in the four leading European countries.[151]

Nevertheless, it did seem an enigma to most German visitors

[145]A. E. Günther, "Amerika und Europa," *Deutsche Handelswacht,* XXXVIII (1931), 100.

[146]*Die Vereinigten Staaten von Amerika* in *Handbuch der Kulturgeschichte* hrsggbn. v. Heinz Kindermann, Abteilung 2, Heft 3, 147.

[147]Georg Kühne, *Von Mensch und Motor,* 70 ff.

[148]Viktor Baur, "Amerikaner über die deutsche Landwirtschaft," *Kölnische Zeitung,* May 6, 1929.

[149]Feiler, *Amerika-Europa,* 120 ff.

[150]The best analyses are Wilhelm Vershofen, "Eine Studienreise in den Vereinigten Staaten," II, III, *Die Hilfe,* 1924, 363-364, 423-424; Dr. Julius Hirsch, "Vom Landhunger zur Landflucht," *Vossische Zeitung,* July 2, 1925, and "Frei-land," *ibid.,* July 15, 1925.

[151]Hirsch, *Das am. Wirtschaftswunder,* 23.

that in a country where only one-fifth of the soil was being used for agriculture, there should still be a surplus and that in a country where industrial workers received such high wages, eggs, butter, milk, and sugar sold more cheaply than in Germany.[152] Germans noted the problem with particular interest because it involved a clear line of self-interest—the recovery of Germany was of moment to Americans because thereby the sale of American foodstuffs could be increased, and the prosperity of the farmer would in turn assist in the disposal of German finished wares.[153]

Germans also noted with interest the operations of great producer cooperatives in the United States. Their efforts to limit production in order to preserve higher prices were watched in the light of German predictions that those at home might sometime attain a monopolistic status. But, as Arthur Feiler noted, there was a fundamental fallacy in the work of American cooperatives. On the one side, they urged limitation of production to encourage an increase of prices. On the other side, they worked strongly for the betterment of production methods. And temporary success in maintaining prices, as with the wine-grape producers in California, had led only to a catastrophic expansion of production, which in this case had shaken the foundations of the whole financial system of the state. Still, efforts to obtain state assistance for farmers had been unavailing, and Feiler saw as their only hope the eventual expansion and unification of the cooperative movements.[154]

10. Fading of the Vision: Economic America, then, was seen by the Germans of the 1920's through the rose-colored glasses of observers largely interested in employing their observations to occassion changes at home. Few of them really sought a comprehensive view of the American economy or studied it in organized fashion. Those who presented the fullest and clearest views were those who based their conclusions largely on American accounts and analyses. Yet the lure of the accounts of "those who had really seen for themselves" was great. Many of these travel accounts were produced in multiple editions of thousands, even hundreds of thousands, of copies each. In the long run the trend for imitation

[152]Vershofen, "Eine Studienreise," *Die Hilfe*, 1924, 364.
[153]*Ibid.*
[154]Feiler, *Amerika-Europa*, 141-145.

was one which did not seek specific techniques or practices as a model for changes at home, but rather sought to describe and propagandize an American "spirit" of business enterprise.

With the coming of the depression in America, the drama began to fade. The vision of bread lines and unemployment, of stillness and disarray, intensified the criticisms of the United States which had already existed.[155] The depression, stated Moritz Bonn, was largely the consequence of the lack of a sense of international responsibility on the part of the United States. To conquer the depression, Americans would have to realize that their economic life was closely intertwined with that of the rest of the world. But Bonn regarded the situation with pessimism. Although there were signs that political and economic leaders in the United States were becoming aware of the close ties between America and the rest of the world, the American people gave little evidence of a greater sense of responsibility for the world's affairs.[156]

Bonn was correct in this estimate. A year after he had written those observations, the United States at the World Economic Conference made a decisive turn back towards renewed economic nationalism. Germans, however, were similarly self-centered. The vision of American prosperity was more real than that of idle factories and unemployment. Probably for many Germans the National Socialist movement possessed some of the spirit and dynamism which they had admired in the United States.

[155]For depression accounts see sources noted in *fn.* 13.
[156]*"Prosperity":Wunderglaube und Wirklichkeit im amerikanischen Wirtschaftsleben* (Berlin, 1931), 177.

Chapter VI

AMERICAN DEMOCRACY IN THE
BUSINESS AGE

Hostile *Preconceptions*: "The United States of America was the first modern democracy of significance, the first popular effort to transform democratic feelings and thoughts into a comprehensive state-system, a mighty administrative apparatus, and into social life; indeed, for a long time America counted as a synonym for democracy." Thus wrote Friedrich Schönemann in 1932 and followed the statement with a friendly and objective analysis of the strengths and weaknesses of the American symbol.[1] In this sympathetic approach to his subject Schönemann differed from many of his countrymen. Most German observers of the American political scene were inclined to highlight the shortcomings and hypocrisies of its democratic government.

The two books most virulently critical of the American political system were written by authors who knew the country well but were not by temperament disposed to make balanced judgments. One of these authors, Herman George Scheffauer, was an American, but spent most of his later life in Germany and wrote during the twenties as a spiritual expatriate. The other was Adolf Halfeld, a German journalist whose long residence in the United States had not modified his antipathy toward it. Both denied the existence of true democracy and freedom in the United States.

"While America, as its chief of state proclaimed," wrote Scheffauer, "fought for democracy, it became itself a victim of a ruthless and unfeeling autocracy of the worst sort."[2] Now, he declared, "We stand confronted by the sad fact that the land of freedom has become the land of oppression. It is the land of industrial feudalism and of the aristocratic (which means in

---

[1] *Die Vereinigten Staaten*, II, 3.   [2] *Das Land Gottes*, 47.

America, the capitalist) reaction. Government for and by the people, America's highest pride, has more than ever become the government of the moneyed oligarchy."[3] And Halfeld, who also pictured the American government as a "business state," added, "The people see in this leadership of wealth not only no endangering of its constitutional prerogatives, but rather a necessity, criticism of which would be blasphemy."[4] Like most foreign observers of the period, both writers made much of corruption, of "boss" rule, of what they felt to be the cynical disregard of public interest.

Perhaps it was unavoidable that the hostility of the war and the influence of wartime propaganda should carry over into the postwar period. Perhaps it was also unavoidable that the feelings engendered by American wealth and prosperity would occasion a resentful view of American politics. At any rate German sober factuality was notably missing from most observations of this phase of American life. Not until 1924 was James Bryce's famous work on the United States and its government translated into German.[5] And not until Schönemann's work of 1932, referred to above, was there a really thorough German accounting of the workings of American democracy. As one author suggested, the Germans of the twenties followed patterns—in dealing with the Far East, they were interested in philosophy; in dealing with the United States, they studied economics.[6] Politics, as well as many other aspects of American life, were of secondary interest. Then, too, many observers were not really competent to judge the workings of American politics. As one critic suggested, one must know the workings of government at home thoroughly in order to understand political procedures and practices in another country.[7]

2. *The Concept of Democracy*: Most German observers did recognize the overall acceptance of the democratic concept. As Arthur Feiler expressed it,

> The foundations of the state and its constitution are, it must be recognized in advance, the common property of the whole people and stand beyond every struggle, indeed

[3]*Ibid.*, 11.   [4]*Amerika und der Amerikanismus*, 71.

[5]See Josef Aquilin Lettenbaur, "Die amerikanische Verfassung und ihr Historiker James Bryce," *Hochland*, XXII, 1-17 (April, 1925).

[6]Brinkmann, *Demokratie und Erziehung in Amerika*, 7.

[7]Lettenbaur, see *fn.* 5.

beyond discussion. Not only is the republic, but also democracy—the government of the people, by the people, for the people—deeply rooted in the history as well as the faith of the people: it is utterly excluded that a person, a group, or a party openly attacks it. This democracy is also not pure fiction. No matter how large, for example, the powers of the President are, he can no more than Congress or anyone else carry out a policy against the will of the people; he who wants to effectuate a political measure must either possess the agreement of public opinion or win it.[8]

American democracy had, of course, developed out of American history. As Schönemann expressed it, it began "not with an idea, but with a circumstance; not out of doctrine, but out of life."[9] Beginning in revolution, it was accompanied by an acceptance of change. "*The popular conception of Revolution in America*," wrote Moritz J. Bonn, "*is a conception of something creative and not of something destructive.*"[10] Absolute democracy had never been a part of America, but the original form of the New England "town meeting," felt Schönemann, had cast a long shadow. He regarded the government of the United States in the post World War I era as "a large-scale nationally-organized local town meeting," and suggested that many existing problems reflected the discrepancy between the institutions of an earlier day and contemporary circumstances. All in all, as he saw it, American democracy had derived from three major influences: "the beginnings in a Wilderness, without the advantages or disadvantages of century-old institutions and traditions; the 'frontier' (in the sense of a settlement and free land frontier); and the decisive role of the middle classes with their good solid industriousness and efficiency, but also with their lack of social courage and their basic fear of public opinion."[11]

3. The Role of Public Opinion: Most German observers regarded public opinion as a destructive force rather than a positive one. Schönemann in his earlier writings had strongly castigated the country's propaganda mill during the First World War, labeling

---

[8]*Amerika-Europa*, 272. Quoted with permission of Verlagshaus Frankfurter Societäts-Drückerei.

[9]*Die Vereinigten Staaten*, II, 5.

[10]*American Adventure*, 87. Italics in original.

[11]*Die Vereinigten Staaten*, II, 6-7.

many of the writings of that period "producers of madness"—they were designed to inculcate maniacal hatred.[12] In his study of "the art of influencing the masses," written in 1925, he included the scathing statement, "In the entire world there are hardly any [other] popular masses who can be so easily led about by the nose or stirred up emotionally as the Americans."[13] Herman George Scheffauer pictured the superficialities and hypocrisies which public opinion imposed upon the would-be official:

> The man who begins a public career in the United States must be a master of the jargon of patriotic and moralistic "cant" which the great masses love. He must give the impression of possessing an open, cheerful, democratic freedom of spirit; he must in fearless and knightly fashion play the role of the cheekiest hypocrite in order to win public, financial, or social success. He must have the ability to win the good will of the common man; he must turn to the women and arrive at an understanding with the parties, the newspapers, the capitalists, the political machine, and even with the political bosses of the electoral district. He must howl with the wolves and turn with the winds. This constant necessity to make compromises and to give in explains why men like [Theodore] Roosevelt were to fall apart morally during the war.[14]

Ferdinand Tönnies, one of Germany's better known sociologists and economists, agreed that American public opinion prized "smartness," cleverness, ruthlessness. Success redeemed everything. But, like Feiler, he also stressed the acceptance of the democratic concept and believed that public opinion often transcended individual or class interests.[15]

4. The Position of the President: German observers felt that the American President was the most likely beneficiary as well as vic-

---

[12]" 'Wahnsinnsmacher,' Amerikanische Kriegsliteratur," *Vossische Zeitung*, February 26, 1921.

[13]*Die Kunst der Massenbeeinflussung in den Vereinigten Staaten von Amerika*, 25.

[14]*Das Land Gottes*, 63.

[15]*Kritik der öffentlichen Meinung*, 182, 269, 355-358, cited in Ernst Fraenkel, ed., *Amerika im Spiegel des deutschen politischen Denkens. Aeusserungen deutscher Staatsmänner und Staatsdenker über Staat und Gesellschaft in den Vereinigten Staaten von Amerika* (Köln und Opladen [c. 1959]), 281-284.

tim of these caprices of public opinion. His office was regarded as
one of the most irrational aspects of the American scene. Too
frequently Germans measured it by the standards of its wartime
status, and hence they considered the President's powers too great
to comport with true democracy. "Therefore, all the critics are
agreed," wrote one German student of the American political
system, "that the President of the United States in actuality exer-
cises a greater power than, for example, any one man in England,
and that even among the crowned heads only the Russian tsar had
an advantage over him."[16] Eduard Meyer, the historian, agreed,
but suggested a different simile:

> It depends, therefore, solely on the personality of the
> President how much use he wishes and can make of the
> power which is at his disposal. Constitutionally, this power
> is quite extensive, much larger than that which the King
> of Prussia and the German Kaiser exercised under their
> constitution; it can only be compared with that of the
> Pope.[17]

Fritz Linn, the author of a carefully written study of the position of the American Presidency, regarded the powers of that
office as subject to great variation. The American President, he
wrote,

> stands in the central point of political interest for the great
> mass of citizens. . . . All eyes are directed upon him; his figure
> is visible to all, and occupies the fantasy of the people, in
> contrast to Congress, whose activity takes place most largely
> behind closed doors in the sessions of countless committees.[18]

"The office of President," he continued, "offers to a strong personality gifted with powers of suggestion an outstanding possibility
of overrunning all constitutional limitations to make himself the
undoubted leader of a great nation."[19] But, he suggested, the
American President was not likely to be "a seductive (*mitreis-
sender*) leader of the masses, but rather a respectable citizen, who

---

[16]Julian Borchardt, *Demokratie und Freiheit. Eine Untersuchung über
das parlamentarische System und seine Wirkungen in den westlichen Kultur-
staaten*, I, *Amerikanische Freiheit* (Berlin, 1918), 13.

[17]*Die Vereinigten Staaten von Amerika*, 211.

[18]*Die staatsrechtliche Stellung der Präsidenten der Vereinigten Staaten von
Amerika*, vii.

[19]*Ibid.*, 141.

distinguishes himself by dependability and personal integrity." The consequence is that there are possibilities of extraordinary variation in the powers of the President. He "may begin the first half of his term of office as the dictator of the nation and finish the last half virtually powerless."[20]

Moritz J. Bonn joined Linn in his more cautious approach to the interpretation of the Presidency. He pointed out that the American government differed radically from European parliamentary governments—the office of the President was the only part of the government which was truly "responsible," and this was a responsibility to the people, not to Congress. There was no way to overturn the government under normal circumstances, added Bonn. "The Government is absolutely safe; it can never be turned out, but it may be quite unable to accomplish anything." Indeed, said Bonn, "there is in normal times no Government weaker than that of the United States."[21] Although the President, suggested Bonn, was "always idealized no matter what his real qualities may be," real leadership after the election was not expected or obtained.[22]

On the other hand, Linn believed that from the turn of the century on, in spite of variations, there had been a growth in the meaning of the Presidency. This was in part due to the greater significance of the nation and the President's role in the formation of foreign policy, in part to his position as party leader.[23] In this judgment of the dynamic role of the Presidency, Linn was joined by Wilhelm Cohnstaedt, who regarded the office as the most democratic element in the political life of the United States.[24]

5. *Political Parties*: Although the President was in some ways the embodiment of party government as well as of the authority of the

[20]*Ibid.*, 141-143.

[21]*American Adventure*, 83-84.

[22]*The Crisis of Capitalism in America*, 169-171.

[23]*Die staatsrechtliche Stellung der Präsidenten*, 143-144.

[24]*Amerikanische Demokratie und ihre Lehren* (Frankfurt, 1919). German political theorists frequently joined the words "plebiscitary" and "presidency" in describing the office of the American chief executive. See Hugo Preuss, *Staat, Recht, und Freiheit*, 385-386, cited in Fraenkel, ed., *Amerika im Spiegel des deutschen politischen Denkens*, 285, and the author's *The Death of the Prussian Republic: a Study in Reich-Prussian Relations, 1932-1934* (Florida State University *Studies*, XXXI. Tallahassee, 1959), 17-18, 51 ff.

state, Germans tended to see him as freer of the demands of the party system than other agencies of the government. Germans found the American party system irrational, illogical, and detrimental to the public interest. This is not surprising. The domestic scene in Germany prior to World War I had provided a concept of political parties very different from that which they saw in America. Until 1918 German political parties had been far more the focus of *Weltanschauungen*, philosophies of life, than the center of practical political action. The almost completely pragmatic approach of American political parties mystified observers searching for clearcut political programs and points of view.

Germans generally concluded that parties in America had lost all of their original meaning. Eduard Meyer, for example, suggested that the two major parties had indeed grown up out of very different conceptions of the state and had set up for themselves sets of "sanctified principles." "But," he added, "in actuality these have long ago become obsolete."[25] Schönemann agreed: "They (the parties) exist because they have existed."[26] Of all the principles dividing the Democrats and Republicans, he felt, only the position on the tariff issue remained clear cut.

6. Corruption: Corruption was a direct consequence, in German eyes, of this pragmatism of the parties. Most party men, said Meyer, ignored principles: "So unconcealed personal ambition of the lowest type has become the driving factor in political life."[27] The unscrupulousness of party bosses and political rings, the ignoring of the public will received top billing in most accounts. "Without ideals and completely materialistic (*mammonisiert*), a piece of machinery with thousands of wheels, whose completely mechanical weight is set in motion at election times by the pressure on a button exerted by a single campaign manager, controlled in all its utterances by local functionaries, who remain unseen behind the outward scaffolding, that is the American party," wrote Adolf Halfeld.[28] Similarly, Fritz Linn found the American political party "in theory, thoroughly democratic and above reproach," in

25*Die Vereinigten Staaten*, 228.
26*Die Vereinigten Staaten*, II, 115.
27*Die Vereinigten Staaten*, 229.
28*Amerika und der Amerikanismus*, 69.

practice serving not the interest of the people, but manipulated by party committees in behalf of interested groups.[29]

A few German observers recognized that these observations were too severe, that the sensationalism of the press magnified the actual extent of corruption.[30] Schönemann, perhaps best described the American scene as he wrote,

> Corrupt and vulgar politicians are easily found everywhere in the United States, but far more often good will is joined to unfitness for office and mediocre ability. By sober observation, therefore, one sees along with the occasional outstanding accomplishments, which are, of course, found seldom enough anywhere, and much evil corruption, a good broad measure of practical ability and business-like industriousness, of practical and humanitarian sobriety, and, finally, of that success with which the American, like other men, is endowed in spite of all his human shortcomings.[31]

Political parties, he added, although they were in truth a part of the "unseen government" of America, were responsible not only for the damages and corruption involved, but also for the accomplishments and success of the government.[32]

7. *Congress: the Seen and Unseen Governments*: But Schönemann as well as other Germans found much to criticize in the workings of the American Congress. Although Congress followed English parliamentary precedents in its bicameral organization, it was purely American in operation. The lower house, Schönemann reported, was popular and "shows clearly all the ups and downs of the democratic movements. Its members are often maids of all work, employment mediators, political agents, common advisers, while the senators are regarded as persons to be respected—sages and prophets."[33]

But the committees of the House of Representatives, named by the Speaker, Schönemann found, were irresponsible and un-

---

[29]*Die staatsrechtliche Stellung der Präsidenten*, 16. For similar comments linking parties and corruption in the United States see Max Weber, *Politik als Beruf*, as cited in Fraenkel, ed., *Amerika im Spiegel des deutschen politischen Denkens*, 262.

[30]*E.g.*, Sonnenschein, *Eindrücke eines Verwaltungsbeamten*, 15-24.

[31]*Die Vereinigten Staaten*, II, 138-139.

[32]*Ibid.*, 131.

[33]*Ibid.*, 47, 50.

observed agents.[34] Fritz Linn agreed. "No one," he wrote, "is responsible for the whole complex of laws determined upon by Congress. Above all, however, planned action and unity is lacking. Often laws determined upon in the almost wholly isolated committees conflict with one another. This is revealed in a disagreeable fashion, particularly in the budget and in financial legislation."[35] As a consequence of this chaotic system, declared German school principal Adolf Reichwein, practically every law had its "joker."[36] Schönemann warned, "The greatest danger for America's political democracy lies in this form of 'unseen government.' "[37]

The Senate, of course, figured in German accounts as the seat of privilege and wealth. This body with its long speeches, its filibusters, and its influence over foreign policy was regarded as evidence of the conservatism which German observers attributed to the American political system. Gradually, however, Germans came to realize that some of the prominent figures of the Senate were men of real ability, and sympathetic and realistic sketches of them were published in the newspapers.[38]

8. The Role of the Supreme Court: More unfamiliar to Germans and hence of greater interest was the functioning of the American Supreme Court. Its role in the process of judicial review, its lack of responsibility, its function of fitting the Constitution to the modern tasks of government—all of these came in for both approval and criticism. The survival of the Constitution was most largely due to the court's work, as Germans saw it. "If the Americans were a people more concerned with principles, more pedantic and theoretical," wrote Schönemann, "they would have been left stranded by this constitution."[39] Both he and Fritz Linn suggested that with the difficulty of amendment involved, the expansion of the Constitution by way of judicial interpretation had been of overriding importance. "The most important changes of constitutional

[34]*Ibid.*
[35]*Die staatsrechtliche Stellung der Präsidenten*, 13.
[36]*Blitzlicht über Amerika*, 13.
[37]*Die Vereinigten Staaten*, II, 51.
[38]*E.g.*, series in *Kölnische Zeitung* called "Scherenschnitte aus dem amerikanischen Kongress," during 1927—William E. Borah, March 6, 1927; Jim Reed, August 29, 1927; George Norris, September 4, 1927; Nicholas Longworth, September 18, 1927; etc.
[39]*Die Vereinigten Staaten*, II, 21.

law have been introduced by an altered interpretation of the old provisions."[40]

9. *Civil Service vs. Bureaucracy*: The entire administrative process of both federal and state governments carried with it one element extremely disturbing to German observers. Although the huge number of public officials amazed them (every thirtieth American a public official), there was no class of people who made the public service a profession for which they particularly trained and who developed a particular set of ideals associated with the work they undertook. There was no real equivalent in America of the government bureaucracy in Germany. America was a "Beamtenstaat" without a "Beamtentum."[41]

The German sociological grouping conveyed by the word "Beamtentum" or bureaucracy was, suggested the German sociologist Charlotte Lütkens, only "a special instance of that great in-between class for which the label 'intellectual middle class' (*'geistiger Mittelstand'*) has become customary."[42] In an America where material success dwarfed all other considerations, she suggested, there was no room for a class which was set apart by its possession of education. Most intellectuals, she asserted, soon after completing their educational work deserted their cultural pursuits and lost consciousness of a separate identity. As a consequence, she concluded, American intellectuals did not constitute a particular social group nor did they seek their proper role in governmental activities. In America, in the place of the German professional officialdom, was a broad dispersion of interest in government, which meant that "the peculiar objectivity and class honor of the [German] officialdom" was lacking.[43]

In place of the bureaucracy in America was a hidden class, one with its own approach to life and own set of moral standards—the politicians who manipulated the party machines. The politicians were indeed specialists, she suggested, in "organizational and election tactics." Like John J. Mahon, one of the political "bosses" of

[40]Linn, *Die staatsrechtliche Stellung der Präsidenten*, 9.

[41]Sonnenschein, a "Verwaltungsbeamte," for example, could find in America no equivalent for the kind of position he held in Germany. *Eindrücke*, 15-24.

[42]*Staat und Gesellschaft in Amerika*, 133; *cf.* her article, "Über Bureaukratie und Parteimaschine in den Vereinigten Staaten," *Archiv für Sozialwissenschaft und Sozialpolitik*, LX (1928), 280-301 at 281.

[43]*Staat und Gesellschaft in Amerika*, 109.

that era, they "delivered the goods."[44] To their influence Miss Lütkens attributed the corruption which she saw. "Perhaps only the Balkan countries can be compared to the United States in respect to the role of the professional politician, if one considers the unscrupulousness of the corruption and the extent of the tendency to seek public office only for the sake of extraordinary monetary advantages."[45] Although Lütkens felt that the Civil Service system marked a beginning in the process of bureaucratization, she noted that American civil servants still remained differentiated from the European *Beamtentum* in their lack of "a specific 'class honor,' of a social and moral tradition and probably also of a group exclusiveness."[46]

Schönemann, on his part, although less concerned than Lütkens with the sociological defects of a bureaucracy-less society, stressed the cost and inefficiency of government. Ordinarily, he said, government moved along in orderly fashion, "because the average American, when he receives an office, brings to it a certain practical sense and some business experience. He comes, in contrast, to the average German, very much as a practical man to public affairs." "But," he added, "as soon as particular factual knowledge becomes necessary for his administrative tasks, he fails, and the most beautiful trust of the largest imaginable election majority doesn't help him." The modern state system demands in administrative positions, he emphasized, even down to the lower echelons, a particular "suitability, preparation, and a schooled and tested experience." The American Civil Service system, he, like Lütkens, felt, was not really solving this problem.[47]

10. An Elected Judiciary: Perhaps no area of American government suffered more, in the estimation of German observers, from this amateur influence than the judiciary. The concept of elected judges was one to which they found no means of reconciling themselves. "That the filling of judicial seats by popular election has

---

44Lütkens, "Über Bureaukratie und Parteimaschine," [see *fn.* 42], 284-86.

45*Staat und Gesellschaft in Amerika*, 111. Her volume was, of course, written hard on the disclosures of the Teapot Dome scandals which got much play in the German press—*e.g.*, "Oel und Politik in Amerika: Der Teapot Dome Scandal," *Kölnische Zeitung*, April 24, 1928.

46*Ibid.*, 118.

47*Die Vereinigten Staaten*, II, 42-44.

led to the most extreme conditions of evil," said Eduard Meyer, "is self-evidently clear. Thereby the most doubtful personalities, if they know how to make themselves popular, gain judicial seats, and even if they are not actually corrupt, these popularly elected judges are often completely uneducated and without any knowledge of the law."[48] Schönemann, on his part, admitted that the process of popular election of judges had made them more democratic, but agreed with Meyer's criticism: "Popularity, honorable mediocrity, and even a blind zeal for the public welfare offer, however, no guarantee of a really modern judiciary, which is unthinkable without a creative but technically experienced corps of jurists."[49]

11. The Confusion of State and Local Government: Germans found the relationships of federal, state, and local government in America complex and confusing. In state and local government, as in the federal, there was no real differentiation between "administration" *per se* and government. The consequence was an overextended governmental mechanism at all levels. The "federal analogy" led to a duplication on the state level of the wasteful patterns of the federal government. As for local government, said Schönemann, "In no country of the world are there such countless overlapping districts of local administration."[50] Furthermore, the degree of public interest declined as the governmental unit involved became smaller. "The result of this is a clear consequence of the nature of the system; exactly that part of the government which touches the daily life of the people most closely functions worst of all and blemishes their democracy."[51] German writers detailed the story of Boss Tweed and his gang and that of other bosses in other cities. They found the cynical attitude of these exploiters of the public purse well exemplified in the published comments of Boss John J. Mahon, who made "politics his business."[52]

Many Germans were unaware of the progress of reform efforts. Schönemann described the movements for city commission and city manager plans, but noted the relative slowness of progress in

[48]*Die Vereinigten Staaten*, 224.
[49]*Die Vereinigten Staaten*, II, 103.
[50]*Ibid.*, 74.   [51]*Ibid.*, 81.
[52]Lütkens, *Staat und Gesellschaft in Amerika*, 114.

this area.[53] Eduard Meyer noted the fact that without some progress in this regard, the existing prosperity would not have been achieved.[54]

For many of the defects of government in all areas, Germans blamed not the system but the people themselves. Schönemann found the greatest obstacle to political leadership in America in the lack of "the schooled willingness" of the popular masses to be led. "Between 'Hallelujah!' and 'Crucify him!'" he said, "the American electorate vacillates in short swings back and forth."[55]

Count Keyserling, on his part, complained of the tendency of Americans to "privatism," to exalt private interests over everything that could not be classed as such, and the tendency to think of and treat everything in terms of private interest.[56] This led, in his view, to the American tendency to put up with the political system regardless of its weaknesses.[57] Adolf Halfeld's views were quite similar. He believed Americans lacked a sense of feeling for the whole; they had no conception of the state as a closely knit community.[58] Arthur Feiler found the explanation for political indifference in America in the existence of prosperity: "Things are going too well for the country. Therefore political matters here do not take a central place in people's thoughts and emotions." Even corruption, he was told by Americans, could be ignored—the country could afford it.[59]

12. Diagnosis and Prognosis: All in all the German view of the American political scene was not one marked by great sympathy. Germany was, in these years, struggling to make democracy succeed at home. Many Germans had from its beginning found the Weimar experiment distasteful. It was a "party state," strongly influenced by socialism during portions of its existence, and lacking

---

[53]*Die Vereinigten Staaten*, II, 78-80. C. A. Bratter also sketched the reform movements, the drive towards the use of referendum, initiative, and recall, and the move towards city commission governments in "Amerika, unser demokratisches Vorbild; seine Einrichtungen und seine Schönheitsfehler," *Welt-Echo* (Berlin), April 16, 1919.

[54]*Die Vereinigten Staaten*, 227.

[55]*Die Vereinigten Staaten*, II, 28.

[56]*America Set Free*, 276.

[57]*Ibid.*, 287.

[58]*Amerika und der Amerikanismus*, 58.

[59]*Amerika-Europa*, 284.

the authority and traditions which Germans respected. Undoubtedly some German criticisms of American democracy were designed to raise questions in respect to the sister republic at home.

On the other hand, an amazing aspect of German comment on American democracy is the slight degree of real interest displayed. There were no discussions, for example, as to whether the German supreme court (*Staatsgerichtshof*) should adopt the principle of judicial review as exemplified by the American Supreme Court. There was no debate as to whether the German cabinet system was better or worse than the American. Perhaps ordinary travelers regarded these matters as the prerogative of the *Beamtentum*.

There was, however, considerable debate over general principles, over the validity of the American example of democracy *per se*. The opposing viewpoints were well exemplified in the writings of the conservative historian Eduard Meyer and the more liberal economist Moritz J. Bonn.

Meyer found the whole concept of majority rule unwise. The Americans, he suggested, had as their ideal the acceptance of the view of the majority in all phases of life, economic and social as well as political. The German, although he accepted the rule of a minority, demanded that this minority rule in the interests of all, and he insisted that individual freedom be protected from the oppression of the majority. Thus Germans preserved a much greater freedom than did Americans in respect to the development of the personality of the individual.[60]

Moritz J. Bonn was not entirely in disagreement with Meyer. He, too, believed that the actions of a democracy without an "established authority" were often subject to ill-considered decisions. "In a democracy," he wrote, "as a rule, action is nearer to words than in countries with a firmly-established authoritarian government." As a consequence, there was, he felt, "a tendency of democracy to sudden, spasmodic, and violent action." This was, he added, particularly true in the United States for, "The American mind is double-barrelled, so to speak; it is highly rationalistic, but at the same time thoroughly emotional."[61] On the other hand, Bonn had, in the version of his book designed particularly for his own countrymen, spoken somewhat more optimistically:

[60]*Die Vereinigten Staaten*, 243-245.
[61]*The American Adventure*, 111-113.

Democracy is not always wise, it is not always strong. But it has, in spite of all false steps, broken the bonds by which the rulers held the ruled in dependency. Conditions in American prisons may cry out to heaven; the persecution of Bolshevists may flush the cheeks of liberal Americans with shame. These are remainders of the time when fear was a political motivation . . . . There may also be corruption in political life today; but there are no more slaves.[62]

America stood, therefore, suggested Bonn, as a civilization which gave hope for a society of free men and free women in which political fear would be ended by democracy, economic dependence by high production, and fear for one's soul by a faith in God. America, he believed, might well become "the cornerstone of civilization."[63]

[62]*Die Kultur der Vereinigten Staaten*, 294.
[63]*Ibid.*, 296.

Chapter VII

AMERICA'S "VENUS COSMETICA"

he Coldly Beautiful Ladies: An American author whether writing in the twenties or today would only with caution and trepidation approach such a topic as "American women." Such reticence did not mark the German writers of the twenties. They discoursed on the subject with abandon, with self-assurance, with conviction of their own authority. They wrote with a curious mixture of admiration and disdain, of praise and criticism. German assessments of the feminine world in the United States were even more subject to the stereotype and the cliché than those dealing with other subjects. The American woman is perpetually "a girl." Grandma and granddaughter are scarcely discernible one from the other.[1] She is artificially beautiful—a "Venus Cosmetica."[2] She displays outwardly a smile but is inwardly cold, self-centered, "soulless." And each one looks exactly like her nearest neighbor.[3]

Most Germans were truly superficial in their view of American women; they stopped with the *Schminke*—the rouge and lipstick which horrified the foreign observer in this "rouge and powder land."[4] Forgetting that such adornment had been employed in European courts, they accused the American girl of

[1]Sonnenschein, *Eindrücke eines Verwaltungsbeamten*, 7.

[2]Hans Trausil, "Venus in Amerika," Berlin *Deutsche Allgemeine Zeitung*, November 24, 1926: "It would be wrong to believe that Venus America is born from cold cream, emerging as a finished beauty product from the waves of cosmetic essences. Just like the material wealth of the men of this land, so also is the ethereal beauty of its women in by far the majority of the cases the product of hard work and dearly purchased, insofar as it is not the consequence of racial mixture and breeding for a series of generations."

[3]*E.g.*, Rundt, *Amerika ist anders*, 65.

[4]Dr. Paul Rohrbach, "Vom amerikanischen Leben," *Kölnische Zeitung*, September 9, 1923.

aping the Indian.[5] They were (perhaps properly so) repelled by make-up's constant employment and its replenishment in public places.[6] Universally, they regarded it as a sign of standardization, a form of leveling, a clear indication of inward emptiness.[7] Since they visited the great metropolitan areas more frequently than towns and rural regions, they saw most frequently the business women of the day, whose reserve, developed to cool the ardor of American "wolves," froze the marrow of the visitors from abroad. They lack "the German romanticism of love," wrote one observer. "In spite of all fire," complained another ruefully, American women remained cool and self-centered.[8] And Alfred Rundt, in many areas sensitive and understanding, took exception to Anatole France's argument that "a hateful world" of Puritanism and materialism could not bring forth such magnificent pictures of femininity. These pictures, said Rundt, reflected only outward beauty; they were portraits without grace:

> A constantly maintained smile, which displays the whitest teeth between red, moist lips; a free, bold, curious glance, free words, free gestures, a play of the body in which apparent shyness and boundless surrender cross one another—all of this whips up desire, seems to reflect an unbounded warmth of passions.
> But behind the warmth stands—nothing.
> Or so little, that it is nothing in comparison with that which without being sought is engendered [in the viewer], is promised.[9]

The street scene lent vivid confirmation to the judgment that the American male slaved to clothe his wife in excessively expensive garments. Clearly many an American woman was a *Luxusfrau,* "a luxury wife."[10] In "Fairyland U.S.A." even the shop girls were "dollar princesses," who put themselves into perpetual debt to provide the fur coats and silk stockings which they displayed

---

[5]Hans Tischert, *Es interessiert Europa (Amerikanische Reiseeindrücke)* 2. aufl. (Berlin, 1928), 109.

[6]Reinhard Weer, "Amerikanerin. Paraphrase über ein helles Thema," *Neue Schweizerische Rundschau,* XIX, 154-169 (January, 1926), 154-156, 162.

[7]Goldschmidt, *Von New York bis Frisco,* 13.

[8]Gustav Frenssen, "Die Amerikanerin," *Vossische Zeitung,* June 16, 1923.

[9]*Amerika ist anders,* 65.

[10]Feiler, *Amerika-Europa,* 296.

with such obvious self-satisfaction.[11] For in America *Schönsein,*
"being beautiful," was obligatory.[12]

And in spite of all their criticisms, few of the visitors denied
the success achieved in this universal undertaking. High nutrition
and high standards of cleanliness—America's "bathroom culture"
—made this possible. But beauty was a standardized thing, a universal ideal to be sought in a process of conformity, rather than
an individualized conception as in Germany.[13] The German women
reading the America books of the twenties found much to temper
possible jealousy of their sisters overseas.

Moreover, caution was in order on the part of the foreign
visitor! The American beauties were to be seen and admired
discreetly. It was, reported the German visitors, a part of American tradition that high honors were to be given to women, an
excessively staid and moral tone employed in daily intercourse with
these lovelies, who might haul one before a judge if the stranger
addressed a careless word. The lonesome refrain of the unattached
male in Germany—"May I accompany you a little ways?"—was,
suggested one observer, an unknown melody in America.[14] "The
revolt against sin" on the other side of the Atlantic, concluded the
Germans, had established a highly moralistic standard of conduct.[15]
There was, as a consequence, a kind of sickening "sentimentality"
attached to the feminine side of life in America.[16] The American
woman was as "sweet as a teenager" in Europe, but without substance.[17] The tone of social relationships was reflected in the
radio of the day with the "whispering, muted, tremulously com-

[11]Goslar, "Der amerikanische Mensch," *Vossische Zeitung,* June 22, 1922.

[12]Tischert, *Es interessiert Europa,* 105-109.

[13]*Ibid.*

[14]M. Heiden, "Eva von New York," *Vossische Zeitung,* July 18, 1925.
Another comment on the place of women in the proceedings of American
courts appeared in "Amerikanische Justiz," *ibid.,* November 22, 1922, where
the release of a woman guilty of the hammer-slaying of a rival for her husband's affections was reported—"She admitted everything, but smiled so be-
guilingly that the male jurors did not have the heart to place the noose on
such a fascinatingly smiling creature. So Mrs. Phillips was released and only
her hammer was confiscated. But in case of need she can buy a new one."

[15]Bonn, *American Adventure,* 285.

[16]Erich von Salzmann, "Sentimentality," *Vossische Zeitung,* February 18,
1921.

[17]Tischert, *Es interessiert Europa,* 105-109.

plaining and enticing singing, intermingled with sighs and ranging from baritone to tenor tones."[18]

2. *The "Girls" Come to Europe*: If there was doubt in the mind of the German reader of the truth of these observations in the America books, they were dispelled by the arrival of "the girls," the touring dance groups which conquered the European stage. One German writer described this advent in vivid but critical tones. The newcomers were, he suggested, different from the "Gibson Girls" of an earlier period, who had exemplified the peaches and cream of sweet sixteen. Bypassing Rubens and improving on Venus, they engaged in a kind of "mass drill gymnastics," a process of "group dissolution and reunification with the precision of a machine." Vividly they displayed the lack of individuality existing in America and the ideal of the perpetual girl: "The matured and cultivated woman, the intelligent woman of thirty or forty of Europe: for these no one has an interest." And, he added, "These girls are dollar machines set into motion." Although America since the war had won the victory of the bobbed hair, of the fox trot, and of "the girls" over old Europe, the latter remained "spiritually richer, more individual, than America."[19]

3. *Family Life: the Domesticated Male*: Family life in America, wrote many German observers, rested under the controlling hand of a matriarchate.[20] A hold-over of colonial and pioneer days when women were scarce and hence particularly desirable, this was reflected in modern society in a kind of fetish worship. Indeed, complained one observer, the existence of a masculine God was a subject of some doubt in America![21] In the home the woman was the dominant figure constituting what Count Keyserling described as "a higher caste."[22] Married as well as unmarried women enjoyed a degree of independence unknown in Germany. That an American wife might not only earn her own living but also have her own clubs and host parties at which the man of the house never

[18]Holitscher, *Wiedersehn*, 161.

[19]Dr. Fritz Giese, "Das tanzende Amerika," *Velhagen & Klasings Monatshefte*, XLI, subvol. II, 544-548 (July, 1927).

[20]Holitscher, *Wiedersehn*, 158-159.

[21]Bonn, *American Adventure*, 271.

[22]*America Set Free*, 271.

showed his face seemed a strange state of affairs to Germans.[23] They felt that this often led to a neglect of the domicile which made it a house rather than a home.[24]

The cliché view of the American male pictured him returning home scarred by battles in the market place only to take over a vast array of household duties which the wife had failed to perform. One German set forth these obligations in verses of pretended scorn for the unreconstructed immigrant who had failed to observe the niceties of American life:

> You demand from your wife, If I can trust my eyes,
> That she rise each morning to prepare your breakfast.
> My, what are you thinking of? Do you mean you're from over there on the Rhine
> Where one is allowed to mistreat his wife this way?
> It is *your* duty to do that and many other things besides.
> If you also have children, it is unavoidably your task,
> To see to it, with much pleasure, that they are always happily asleep (at night),
> Since it just isn't fair, that she should also have to do that.
> Afterwards, it's your job, as ordered, to bring her the various things she needs.
> If you come home in the evening and she is still out,
> Make no great to-do about it; first, you must make the beds,
> Then naturally you must cook, no need to rest your bones,
> Since it just isn't fair, that she should also have to do that.
> Then when she comes home in the evening, press her tightly to your breast,
> As you did it before you were her husband.
> All this you must learn, dear fellow, if you want to make good
> All the shortcomings of your marriage, and as I see the matter
> You will then in the future be the ideal married man.[25]

[23]*E.g.*, Eduard Meyer, *Die Vereinigten Staaten*, 162-163.

[24]Alice Salomon, "Amerikanischer Winter," *Vossische Zeitung*, March 30, 1924.

[25]Cramer, *Als Junglehrer nach U.S.A.*, 39-40. German of verses translated in text follows:

Du verlangst von deiner Frau,	Seine Frau kann schikanieren?
Wenn ich meinen Augen trau,	*Deine* Pflicht ist's, das zu machen,
Dass sie aufsteht jeden Morgen,	Und noch viele andere Sachen.
Dir das Frühstuck zu besorgen.	Wenn du auch noch Kinder hast,
Ja, was fällt denn dir da ein?	Ist es unverzeilich fast,
Meinst, du bist dort von dem Rhein,	Sorgst du nacht mit viel Vergnügen,
Wo man ohne viel Genieren,	Dass sie immer glücklich liegen,

Obviously Germans took over-seriously much of the humorous comments on family life that circulated in newspapers and conversation. More sober observers pointed out that domestic help was much harder to come by in America than in Germany and that the average housewife really confronted a more formidable load of domestic duties than did many of their German counterparts.[26]

Nevertheless, the superior role of the woman in the household was tremendously disturbing to Germans. They considered that American women were made over-masculine as a consequence and that American men were weakened in character and determination. One of the various problems which Count Keyserling described in American society was the "infantilization" of the men and a solution, he felt, needed the assistance of the women themselves.[27]

Women were also held to be dominant in the cultural sphere. They were, noted Eduard Meyer among many others, "spiritually much superior to the men"—"they are clever and lively and employ with great skill the womanly art of setting themselves out to advantage."[28] And Charlotte Lütkens, the sociologist, referred to them as the "custodians of the nice things" of life.[29] It was likely, wrote Arthur Feiler, that a family forced to choose between a college education for a son or for a daughter would give the nod to the latter.[30] As a consequence, reported Alice Salomon, the

---

Denn das geht nun doch nicht gut,	Dass sie dieses auch noch tut.
Dass sie dieses auch noch tut.	Kommt sie abends dann zurück,
Nachher hast du, wie befohlen,	Selig sie ans Herze drücke,
Ihr verschiedenes zu holen. —	Wie du damals es getan,
Kommst du abends dann nach Haus,	Als du noch nicht warst ihr Mann.
Und sie ist noch immer aus,	Alles dies musst du lernen,
Mache denn nicht viel Gesichten.	Lieber Mann, willst du entfernen,
Erst muss du die Betten richten.	All die Mängel deiner Ehe;
Dann natürlich muss du kochen,	Und wie ich die Sache sehe,
Brauchst nicht schonen deine Knochen.	Wirst du in die Zukunft dann,
Denn das geht nun doch nicht gut,	Der ideale Ehemann.

[26]Toni Harten-Hoencke (Mrs. Schönemann), "Amerikanisches Frauenleben," *Süddeutsche Monatshefte*, XXVII (1929), 660-63.

[27]*America Set Free*, 351-52. Adolf Halfeld treated this problem under the title "Kulturfeminismus" and suggested that the "manliness of the American spirit had been placed for the eternal future in question." The result was an alteration of "the natural relationships" of the sexes—not only a dangerous but "almost pathological" problem. *Amerika und der Amerikanismus*, 209 ff.

[28]*Die Vereinigten Staaten*, 163.   [29]*Staat und Gesellschaft in Amerika*, 155.

[30]*Amerika-Europa*, 296.

educational level of the wife was on the average above that of the husband.[31] Richard Weer found tradition undergirding the cultural superiority of women in America. There had, he suggested, developed a division of tasks between the marriage partners in which the women had gained the custody of those things which went beyond necessities:

> As a consequence, all things of spiritual life, all of the higher and more decorative matters, all refinements became her field. She had time to see and cultivate beauty; she could give to art her smile and feel herself blessed by it in return; yes, she could even win from hard and dogmatic learning a lighter, friendlier side.[32]

Rudolf Hildebrand agreed with these observations but suggested sourly that American women used culture as the reins by which they directed society. America's materialist toughness was all a facade—the men who created the business world of the United States were the slaves of the women, who had made it an aphorism that the status of civilization was to be determined by the degree to which the men had been "tamed" by the women.[33]

Germans were also impressed by the great influence exercised by women in areas such as philanthropy, pacifism, and temperance.[34] American women, suggested Alice Salomon, were possessed of a "passion for service" derived more from generosity of the heart than from understanding. This passion for service, she wrote, "shows itself in all areas of social life" and "is a grandiose effort to create a culture of the personal life, a humane-ethical culture. It comes closer to a synthesis of thought and action, of spirit and life, than the culture of countries whose form is until now exclusively determined by the men." Miss Salomon wrote at length of the "heroic" work of Jane Addams, Lillian Ward, and Carie Chapman Cott and praised the "womanly activism" which this displayed and the role of women in America in the field of politics as well as philanthropy.[35]

---

[31]*Kultur im Werden*, 26.

[32]"Amerikanerin. . ." [see *fn.* 6], 158.

[33]"Feminismus in Amerika," *Neue Schweizerische Rundschau*, XXI [Jrg., also numbered Vol. XXXIV], 55-62 (January-June, 1928).

[34]Sophie M. Dulles, "Die amerikanische Frau und der Weltfriede," *Süddeutsche Monatshefte*, XXI, subvol. II, 182-185 (June, 1924).

[35]*Kultur im Werden*, 105, 110-145.

Friedrich Schönemann also admitted the significance of American women as the advocates of "causes." The American woman crusader, he noted, displayed a curious mixture of "intellectual revolt and personal conventionality" very different from that of her counterpart in Europe. But the effectiveness of her work was clear: "In the United States not a single great national movement is possible any longer without the influence and cooperation of the women."[36]

4. *Sex Life*: Lacking, however, on the part of American women, charged many of the visitors, was the actual feminine, the sense of domesticity, of order and cleanliness in the home, and above all "the inward surrender" (the sense of subordination and accommodation to the wishes of the husband), the "spirit."[37] Count Keyserling concluded that American women were, as a consequence, completely incapable of love in the European sense.[38] He and other German observers decided (it is never very clear how they reached such a horrendous conclusion!) that American women were "undersexed." In comparison with European women, wrote Bruno Dietrich, American women were possessed of a "much more weakly developed sexuality."[39] Alice Salomon agreed, but graciously added that this defect was compensated for by the broad variety of activities into which American women entered![40] Keyserling felt that both men and women in America were sexually weak and looked to the American flora for an explanation. In America, he suggested, grew great sequoias and other plants. But "the vitality of the air" which produced these generated "only activity (*Betriebsamkeit*) not real strength." As a consequence the American was "sexually and erotically weak." He suggested, however, that modern teaching about hormones might carry an explanation of these matters—perhaps in the future.[41] Others agreed with Keyserling's appraisal, but believed sex shortcomings due most largely to the heavy hand of Puritanism, which had made the woman synonymous with "the flesh" and had soured the natural joys of marriage.[42]

[36]*Die Vereinigten Staaten*, II, 371-372.

[37]Meyer, *Die Vereinigten Staaten*, 163; cf. Schönemann, *Die Vereinigten Staaten*, II, 373.

[38]*America Set Free*, 409 ff. [39]*U.S.A., das heutige Gesicht*, 7.

[40]*Kultur im Werden*, 27-28. [41]*Mensch und Erde*, 23.

[42]Schönemann, *Die Vereinigten Staaten*, II, 372-373.

In view of these assessments of American sex activities, the translation by the Schönemanns of Judge Ben Lindsey's book, *The Revolution of Modern Youth*, was something of a bombshell in Germany. There was some relief in knowing that the natural instincts found expression in America more often than had been assumed. Heinz Pol, in reviewing the German edition, wrote that after reading this book "even the most educated, cultured European will no longer be able to say that America is an unspiritual, soulless, money-making, and sport-record land. They are superior to us because they have more courage; more courage in flying, more courage in money-making, but also more courage in tearing down gods even though they be national saints."[43]

Gustav Frenssen, the poet, had already suggested that the "purity" of the American maiden might exist more in appearance than actuality, that Puritanism and Anglo-Saxon traditions had led to much "cover-up." The American girl, he wrote, "is strongly sexual; yes, some say to me entirely sexual; but this is hidden under all kinds of clever games. She keeps herself under control and gives herself . . . if not out of . . . (what she's going to get from it?), still with careful consideration."[44] And Moritz J. Bonn also wrote that with the decline of Puritan ideals that of withdrawal and shyness had also declined—"She can do with her body what she pleases. She does it."[45] Anna Tizia Leitich suggested that the dominance of the American woman, the acquisition of the status of "a great lady," was primarily to be explained by sex: "How did they do it?—not with logarithms, or hunger strikes, or doctoral dissertations—with the bedroom-slipper. Exactly, my ladies."[46]

American "technique" even entered into sex. The American girl, suggested Arthur Rundt, had passed a milestone in her moral history with the advent of the "kiss-proof lipstick," and Count Keyserling assured his readers that many American girls carried with them a *Pröservative* "for any case of need."[47]

Sex also entered increasingly into American entertainment. Most German male visitors sampled the delights of the American

[43]*Das blaue Heft*, IX, No. 14, 421-425 (July 15, 1927).
[44]*Briefe aus Amerika*, 96-98.
[45]*Geld und Geist*, 171. Bonn was also influenced by the Kinsey report.
[46]*Amerika, du hast es besser* (Wien, 1926), 74.
[47]*Amerika ist anders*, 67; Keyserling, "Die Verjüngung Amerikas," *Kölnische Zeitung*, July 19, 1930.

burlesque show, and those at home read with amusement Manfred Hausmann's description of the strip-tease routines [in one show] of "Miss Raiben, Miss Rogers, Miss Duval, Miss Merit, Miss Keny, Miss Robinson, Miss Bee, Miss Sloane, Miss Fawell, Miss Grey."[48] To these diversions for the married man tired of his wife, as Holitscher regarded it, was now added "the strange new concept of sex appeal" which came from "that grotesque city," Hollywood. But, noted Holitscher, in spite of contests for supremacy as "vamp" or "sheik," no machines had yet been invented to register sexual excitement graphically![49]

Sober observers, however, discounted the validity of the conclusions derived from Judge Lindsey's book. Judge Lindsey, remarked one of the contemporary analysts of the American scene, was better known in Germany than in the United States.[50] Many still admitted that the social relationships of men and women in America were "sounder and more natural than in Europe," perhaps due to the life-long association of boys and girls in coeducational schools, which mitigated the sense of separation often burdening the German teenager, especially the male.[51] As Eugen Kühnemann expressed it, "At the time of my first return home from America the greatest fortune of American life seemed to me the wonderful naturalness and true friendship in the relationships of young American men and women. Had I only been able to imagine something of this sort possible in my own youth!"[52]

Nevertheless, many Germans considered marriage in America to be too often divorced from the erotic drive. Alice Salomon reported that the bachelor girl could have everything she wanted without marriage and, unlike the German girl who accepted a proposal when she hoped she might be happy with the man who presented it, the American girl accepted it only when she was sure she would be unhappy without him![53] Frequently marriage was simply a joining of efforts for material well-being on the part of

[48]*Kleine Liebe zu Amerika*, 313-314.

[49]*Wiedersehn*, 95-96, 163-164.

[50]Ludwig Müller in W. Fischer *et al.*, *Handbuch der Amerikakunde*, 118.

[51]Hans Goslar, "Der amerikanische Mensch," *Vossische Zeitung*, April 22, 1922; similar, Hugo Graf Lerchenfeld-Köfering, "Meine Reise durch die Vereinigten Staaten," II, *Hochland*, XXI, 166 (November, 1923); Friedrich Dessauer, "Amerikanische Reisebriefe," *ibid.*, XIX, 345 (December, 1921).

[52]*Amerikafahrt, 1932*, 38.

[53]*Kultur im Werden*, 26.

the marriage partners rather than for the grounding and rearing
of a family. Young couples, asserted several German writers, were
likely to postpone children in favor of the purchase of a Ford,
and children were often treated as unfortunate and disturbing accompaniments of marriage. "If he would," wrote Dr. Paul Rohrbach, "Henry Ford could congratulate himself on the fact that
every year he has kept millions of children from being born in
America."[54] Abortion, reported another writer, was in America
considered a reasonable means of avoiding undesired issue.[55] The
result was that too many American women, well educated and
culturally advanced, became "overcultivated garden flowers without
a blossom."[56]

The consequence was that too frequently the house was not a
home. Well-equipped as were American houses, they failed to develop the sense of attachment, the feeling that they provided a
private retreat from the pressures of the outside world which the
German sought.[57]

5. *Children*: As for children, when they did come, they quickly
assumed a mastery of the domicile. Parents became the "slaves"
of a spoiled brood, who dominated the life of the family. Under
the aegis of "everything for the kiddies," wrote one visitor, in
family priorities the child came first, the wife second, then nothing
for a while until finally was reached "the lord of creation," the
man of the house, who served all the rest.[58]

This conception was intensified by the very widely read little
book written by Vivi Laurent. Under the title of *Vivis Reise*
(*Vivi's Travels*) she told of her experience as a Swedish maid in
many American homes.[59] The omnipresent spoiled brats in her
account and the between-the-lines apparent cultural superiority
of maid over employers could not fail to leave their mark on the
many German readers. At the same time the generosity and kind-

[54]"Was heisst Amerikanismus?" *Deutsche Monatshefte*, V, subvol. II, 469-
470 (November, 1929).

[55]Meyer, *Die Vereinigten Staaten*, 164.

[56]Hensel, *Die neue Welt*, 88; *cf.*, Bonn, *American Adventure*, 284.

[57]Salomon, "Amerikanischer Winter," *Vossische Zeitung*, March 30, 1924.

[58]Erkelenz, *Amerika von Heute*, 39.

[59]*Vivis Reise. Ein Jahr als Dienstmädchen in Amerika; das Abenteuer
einer schwedischen Studentin.* Übersetzt von Nora Feichtinger (2 vols., Gotha,
1925-1926).

ness of the American women she served were underscored by her.

As is indicated in a later chapter, however, closer German observers approved strongly of American educational methods and admitted that the American treatment of children brought an earlier maturation on their part.[60] One German after ten years in America returned to Germany to complain of the "atmosphere of hate and lovelessness and doubt" which he saw. "I believe," he charged, "that one sees in Berlin in a month more roughness with children (I don't mean criminal actions but rather little signs of lovelessness and meanness) than in New York in five years."[61]

6. *Beyond the Superficial*: The foregoing has dealt most largely with the typical German assessments of the feminine side of American life. The dominance of the cliché and the stereotype is clear. But there were some Germans who found the nuances, the exceptions, the more logical explanations behind the appearances. Carl Brinkmann, a visiting educator, explained that the cosmetics kept both husband and wife content with the maintenance of the fiction of youth.[62] Marta Wassermann, a German poet and novelist, undercut the assumption that all American women were alike as she drew perceptive word pictures of seven American women of vastly different types and character.[63] Not the least interesting of her sketches was that of Ethel Waters, the Negro singer-dancer, whose art she found presenting "everything decked out with the purest innocence; not a fold in her tightly drawn skin knows anything of lust or abasement and on her tender, brown cheeks rests the reflection of a mature, motherly love."[64]

Dorothee von Velsen, a German feminist leader, was impressed by the great eagerness and ability of American women to absorb new knowledge and understand new points of view.[65] And Richard Weer concluded that American women had the advantage of "a

[60]Schönemann, *Die Vereinigten Staaten*, II, 194.

[61]Hermann Lufft, "Aus meinen amerikanischen Erfahrungen," *Deutsche Arbeit*, XI (1926), 24-38.

[62]*Demokratie und Erziehung*, 32.

[63]*Eine Frau reist durch Amerika* (Berlin, 1928). Published under her pseudonym Marta Karlweis.

[64]*Ibid.*, 120. The remarkable accomplishment reflected in this description is emphasized by a reading of Ethel Waters' autobiography, *His Eye is On the Sparrow* (Garden City, New York, 1951).

[65]"Eindrücke aus Amerika," *Die Frau*, XXXVII, No. 7, 390 (April, 1930).

freedom, which shows itself openly in a manner of life lighter, less forced, and more suited to the nature of women than is accorded to them in Europe." He wrote that they accommodated themselves with ease to various levels of well-being, managing with dexterity and grace the entertainment of a visitor even in one of the little kitchenette apartments of the professional woman in the cities. They remained in control of themselves at all times, especially in erotic situations, even though the use of alcohol might be involved.[66]

Dr. Julie Langen presented German readers with another view of the bachelor girl in America—life in the Y.W.C.A. She praised the institution with its conveniences, its sense of democracy, its opportunities for physical well-being and cultural advancement, but suggested that efforts to introduce such an institution in Germany would fail, not only due to cost, but also due to "the different way of thought and social attitude of the German woman."[67]

Many of the observers presented a rather strange mixture of sour-grapes criticism and unwilling admiration. Thus, Gustav Frenssen, the poet, whose surmise that the sex morality of American women was largely a sham has already been mentioned, wrote:

> The life of the American woman is more independent than that of the North European. She holds down good positions, is more appreciatively handled by the men folk; everything is allowed her. Her life is therefore more colorful, fresher, freer; she is therefore more choosy and self-possessed [in her actions]. Sober and completely without shyness she gives her photograph to the newspapers where the northern European would hold back. . . . In her secure self-consciousness she gives herself only when she desires it with her whole heart or understanding. The American woman is lighter, more light-footed, more elegant than that of Northern Europe. She is more problem, excitement, play. She is a great flirt and enjoys the game according to her temperament. Thereby she is a good comrade of both her male and female friends. She is soberer than the North European. She cannot pour out enthusiasm [Schwärmen]. . . . She is strongly sexual, yes, some say to me entirely sexual, but this is hidden under all kinds of clever games. Her beautiful appearence, fullest care of her body, short, beautiful, and loose clothing work into

[66]"Amerikanerin, Paraphrase über ein helles Thema," *Neue Schweizerische Rundschau*, XIX, 154-169 (January, 1926).

[67]"Heimleben der berufstätigen Frau in Amerika," *Daheim*, LXII, sub-vol. I, No. 6 (November, 1925).

the blood. But she has herself fully under control, remains cool in spite of all fire and gives herself . . . with careful consideration.[68]

American moral standards also found defense as well as criticism. Among the defenders of the American system was Dr. Rudolf Kindermann, a local government official in Germany, who proclaimed the need of Germans to relearn chivalry:

> What appears to us on the one side a ridiculous over-valuation [of women], is on the other side a thoroughly ethically founded higher respect, which has been by us unfortunately too often lost. Such details as the prohibition against an approach [to women] on the streets, etc. are indications of a chivalrous feeling. Our culture-Bolshevists may describe it as prudery, but there is a sound kernel within it, a piece of the good old customs. Should we not also in this respect be able to learn from America?[69]

Prof. Friedrich Schönemann referred to the moral standards of Americans as involving "a rather strong *Spiessbürger* philosophy in its better sense."[70] And Mrs. Schönemann (Toni Harten-Hoencke) declared that the prevalence of divorce in the United States was simply a sign that the American woman refused to put up with the kind of shoddy treatment that German husbands accorded their wives: "She demands from her partner unquestionable loyalty and chivalry and does not hesitate long in giving up a marriage which is in her view no longer a proper one." But Mrs. Schönemann also suggested that the American wife often lacked the ability to give herself passionately and fully to her husband and hence remained dissatisfied with married life and sought through new partners to fill a void which lay not within the husband but within herself.[71]

Perhaps the most perceptive and understanding appraisal of the psychology and style of life of the American woman was contained in a book published not too long after World War I. Written by Annalise Schmidt, it sought to analyze the character

[68]*Briefe aus Amerika*, 97-98.

[69]"Was können wir von Amerika lernen?" *Volkswohl*, XXI, No. 5 (1930), 175-183 at 180.

[70]*Die Vereinigten Staaten von Amerika* in *Handbuch der Kulturgeschichte*, 174.

[71]"Amerikanisches Frauenleben," *Süddeutsche Monatshefte*, XXVII (1929), 660-664 at 661.

of the American and did so more successfully than many of the later studies.[72] Miss Schmidt commented on the "charm, naturalness, and freedom of behavior" of the American woman. These traits were, she said, most largely explained by her "sense of self-respect" (*Selbstgefühl*) which gave her the basis for a far-going freedom of expression:

> These warm-blooded beings have a vital sense of self-respect, which gives them a true and quiet, not false, recognition of their own being, a judgment concerning themselves which is a compromise between their innate feeling of self and that which is matured and made conscious by their experience.[73]

Although American women were not intellectual, they had, she felt, much "psychic fantasy" which allowed them to judge clearly themselves and their acquaintances. Each woman developed her own style, a natural one unlike the inculcated ones in Europe:

> They recognize clearly the power which a woman has. They know how a woman displays everything—fineness, strength, intelligence, race—so that in every situation she acts as is required: her surrender is not quick and self-forgetting, but since she is conscious of her worth, it is all the more sweet and passionate.[74]

As for her relationships with her husband, the higher tone of respect for women in America did not reveal the weakness of the man. Quite the contrary:

> The American men do not feel the necessity of imposing their authority and of releasing on the female members of the family their repressed desires for power. Not because they are less intellectual or softer than European men. But rather because the struggle for life, the unbounded conquest of the world of a self-chosen work gives their natural quest for power a great and always newly-challenging objective, and each is confronted with a task in life and does not have to hem himself in in a dependent position.[75]

The woman, on her part, said Miss Schmidt, displayed a large share of the will power which was a special characteristic of Americans. They were *not* sentimental in the European sense, not holding passions long beyond their usefulness as in unhappy love af-

---

[72]*Der amerikanische Mensch. Vom Wesen Amerikas und des Amerikaners* (Berlin, 1920). Miss Schmidt also wrote on Bolshevism and infant care.
　　[73]*Ibid.*, 73.　　　　　[74]*Ibid.*, 74.　　　　　[75]*Ibid.*

fairs. They were lively and awake. As a consequence, they brought to marriage "a larger psychological reserve" than did Europeans. Moreover, "the art of the erotic, in spite of flirtation . . . plays no such a dominating, pervasive role as in Europe." The American husband, she added, continued the gallantry of pioneer days in a way "reminiscent of the days of the troubadours" and displayed tenderness to his wife without the loss of manliness.[76]

It was the woman, continued Miss Schmidt, who began to create in America the graces of social intercourse, striving not only for the material things of life but also for the niceties, "the spiritual imponderables." In this search she employed the term "success" in the same sense her husband used it in the business field: a dress or a party was "a success." But she did not forget that it was her husband who created the values "which she takes in her womanly hands and forms with her womanly heart and spirit."[77]

"America," concluded Miss Schmidt, "is not exactly wealthy as respects creative cultural values. But the art of womanliness which American wives possess is such a value." It was particularly in the great area between the Alleghenies and the Pacific that she found what she regarded as the true type of American womanhood: "With her supple and powerful fullness of body, her activeness and charm, her independence, and her self-created glorification of the nature of womanhood."[78]

In similar tone Emil Müller-Sturmheim declared American women were the descendants of pioneer heroines who had braved the hardships of the frontier and the perils of Indians at the same time that they had acted to prevent the brutalization of society, founding schools, teaching the children, creating the centers of spiritual and social intercourse and thus becoming "the guardians of the holy flame of the spirit, of the soul of man." Upon them, indeed, rested a large measure of that which had become the greatness of America.[79]

Alice Salomon expressed her views less poetically but more personally as she wrote, "Always, even after my first visit to the states, it was clear to me that—should I come once again to the world as a woman—I would only wish to be born in the United States."[80]

[76]Ibid., 75.   [77]Ibid., 76-78.   [78]Ibid., 78.
[79]Ohne Amerika geht es nicht, 55.   [80]Kultur im Werden, 24.

Chapter VIII

"CULTURELESS" AMERICA: BABBITT AND THE ARTS

olonialism and Puritanism: The lack of culture in America was a favorite theme of German visitors in the twenties. The unity of the voices proclaiming the nullity of American cultural accomplishments is astounding. But few of them found it necessary to define the term or set forth their frame of reference. Culture—Germany had it; America did not!

Between the lines the definition of the term often varied. For many it did not involve so much actual accomplishments in art, music, literature, philosophy, and education as an attitude of appreciation for the things of life which were essentially non-practical. For many it was to be measured not so much by anything concrete as by the existence of leisure for reflective thought and creative accomplishment. The bustle and activism of American life was a clear evidence that this did not exist. For many Germans the term connoted creative accomplishment clearly related to the nation itself and peculiar to it— separate and apart from outside influence. That America might have "a bad mixture of derivatives" (*schlechter Abklatsch davon*) from European culture did not change their hostile appraisals.[1] In many accounts there was clear evidence that the negative impression of the Germans reflected disappointment at the lowly place accorded German thought, German literature, and German music.

Two notable defects on the part of the German observers themselves tended to accentuate their depreciation of American culture. First of all, as a whole they were abysmally ignorant of American accomplishments in this sphere when they arrived. American studies had never been a real part of German university

[1]Prof. Alfred Forcke, "Aus dem Land der grossen Kinder," I, Berlin *Tägliche Rundschau*, February 6, 1920.

153

programs. Where attention was given this subject, it formed a subordinate and neglected phase of the English studies program.[2] The ignorance of American literary history on the part of the visitors, for example, was nothing less than astounding. And for American culture in general there was no appreciative summary before that of Friedrich Schönemann, produced as part of his general work on the United States in 1932 and expanded somewhat in the early years of the Nazi regime as part of the cultural handbooks of the world edited by Heinz Kindermann.

Secondly, the preoccupation of the visitors with the great cities and the narrow view of these which the Germans obtained walled them off from more appreciative assessments of American culture. Many of them had been ivory-tower scholars at home whose knowledge of and experience with many aspects of life in Germany itself was minimal. Hence, as Anton Erkelenz, a member of the German Reichstag, complained, many Europeans on the second day of their arrival in America proclaimed it had no culture.[3] They looked about with a homesick longing for green hills and the cathedral spheres nestling quietly in the valleys between them and saw instead a hateful, modern scene which repelled them.

Whenever a German traveler came with a well-defined mission, a lecture trip or a survey of American museums for example, he began to make exceptions. Such was the case with Eugen Kühnemann, the Goethe expert from the University of Breslau, as has been seen in an earlier chapter. Kühnemann's lengthy lecture trips left him much less harsh in his appraisal of America than many of his less traveled colleagues.[4] The tone of evident surprise in Dr. Bernhard Goldschmidt's discovery that Princeton University offered an atmosphere of culture much like that at home is another case in point. Goldschmidt immediately suggested the need of caution in evaluating America.[5]

It must be stated emphatically that the great majority of German travelers of the 1920's failed to reflect in their accounts of their visits to the United States the high standards of scholarly objectivity associated with their own country's cultural achievements. One can only underscore the statement of Friedrich

[2]Sigmund Skard, *American Studies in Europe*, I, 256 ff.
[3]*Amerika von Heute*, 80.
[4]*Amerikafahrt, 1932*, 11 *et seq*. See sketch in Ch. II.
[5]*Von New York bis Frisco*, 84-88.

Schönemann in the Foreword to his study of the United States published in 1932: "Most of our America literature is neither a compliment for our thoroughness and our sense of history, nor even for our open-mindedness or real cosmopolitanism."[6]

German preconceptions of America involved a two-fold assumption: one, that the United States remained essentially a "colonial" country; and, two, that the cultural heritage of America was predominantly "Anglo-Saxon" and "Puritan." These views were so often repeated that examples could be chosen from dozens of accounts. Professor Josef Hengesbosch of the University of Frankfurt-on-the-Main expressed the colonial aspect when he asserted that the United States was indeed a nation, but could say with the South Sea Islanders, "We are young, exceedingly young." Youth, he added, might be an asset, but culture required "planting" and "cultivation" and these had not yet taken place in America.[7] Similarly, Hans Goslar, a ministerial councillor in the Prussian state government, wrote that in America things were too much "in a process of formation and fermentation" for the country to have found its cultural mission.[8]

Professor Alfred Forcke, an Orientalist at the University of Hamburg, took the term used by the Indian poet Rabindranath Tagore, and wrote his travel letters "from the land of the big children." This meant, he explained, that Americans engaged in superficial thinking rather than going to the heart of things and were guilty of mental laziness, credulity, exaggeration, excitability, and vacillation! Culturally, he rated the United States not only behind the advanced nations of Europe, but also behind the Indians, Chinese, Japanese, Swedes, Dutch, and Swiss, suggesting hesitantly that they might be in advance of the Serbs, Bulgars, Czechs, and Latin-Americans. Goethe's famous verse he altered to read, "There are no castles, no ruins, no old cities, no historical buildings and monuments; everything is new, sober, and boring."[9]

Another observer, Richard Müller-Freienfels of Berlin, cau-

[6]*Die Vereinigten Staaten,* I, xiii.
[7]"Amerikanismus und Kultur," *Gelbe Hefte,* IV, subvol. II (1928), 895-902.
[8]"Amerikas Geistesleben, 1922," *Vossische Zeitung,* March 11, 1922.
[9]Designation of level of cultures Forcke's—"Aus dem Land der grossen Kinder," I, Berlin *Tägliche Rundschau,* February 6, 1920; III, *ibid.,* April 30, 1920. The depth and thoroughness of Forcke's own pronouncements were contradicted by his very faulty allusions to American history!

tioned that observers were labeling "American" things which existed at home:

> Actually, all these things [mass measures, capitalism, business, etc.] strike the European who comes to the United States so grossly and harshly that he often completely overlooks the fact that he has all these things at home, even if also actually mingled with and moderated by forms of life which are founded in his older culture.[10]

But, he continued, these other forms were exactly what was lacking in America:

> those difficultly grasped things which one is accustomed to gather together with the word "tradition": ancient social differences, a native art, a science and philosophy pursued without concern for practical applications, all those things which are not measurable and cannot be expressed in monetary terms.[11]

The lack of these deprived America of the claim to culture; it was only a "civilization."

Impressions of newness also repelled Walter Behrendt, the director of the German Ceramics Society in Berlin, who found in a brief country excursion "the impression of the provisional and unformed, of the incomplete and becoming."[12] And Alice Salomon, the German feminist, entitled her travel report, "Culture in Formation" (*Kultur im Werden*) suggesting, "The American people is still too young to have a cultural tradition," and adding, "the soul of the American has not yet grown into the new" which he has conquered.[13]

Professor Arthur Salz, an economist, regarded the United States as a "land without a Middle Ages," a country which had manifested an "overextended puberty" and had as a consequence carried over into the maturity of industrialism many features of its youth. But Salz believed that there was room for optimism. The First World War had been followed by a debate over values in the United States, and there was a possibility that this country across the Atlan-

---

[10]"'Amerikanismus' und europäische Kultur," *Der deutsche Gedanke*, IV, 30-35 (July, 1927).

[11]*Ibid.*

[12]"Aus dem Tagebuch einer Amerikareise," *Kunst und Künstler*, XXIV, No. 3 (1925), 18-23, 61-67, 97-99.

[13]*Kultur im Werden*, 63, 65.

tic would now create a culture suitable to its democratic character. His own answer to American cultural problems was cultural pluralism—a larger role to the maintenance of the cultural backgrounds of its varied national groups.[14]

In similar words but somewhat more sympathetic tone, Anton Erkelenz, a member of the German Reichstag, proclaimed that it would, indeed, take a thousand years for the United States to have its own culture, but this would then be "probably something new and better" than that of Europe:

> It is not the mission of this land to copy Europe. Probably there are already here too many European imitations, because they wish to create artificially that which Europe has of beauty. One day they [the Americans] will joyfully destroy most of these imitations because they will find that they do not reflect their own spirit.
> For this is the mission which this land has, like all others, to discover its own being, to fulfill its task of presenting itself [before the world]. And if one puts his ear to the ground, then one hears millions of forces at work to forge and shape this individual being. There is, indeed, the danger that it will be brought to finished form before it has been inwardly matured.[15]

And Erkelenz was optimistic for the future—the spirit of colonial life, he believed, was passing; solid achievements were being made by a class of educated and artistically oriented men whose numbers grew larger each year.[16]

The Catholic lay brother Donatus Pfannmüller echoed the same thought in different words when he suggested that in America a culture was developing which was more appealing than "the tired culture or 'unculture' of old Europe."[17] And Alfred Kerr, the poet, in the midst of repeated emphasis that the criticism of the American soul and of American culture was simply a sign of jealousy of a more fortunate nation, "a hocus-pocus of swindlers," proclaimed also that America would not just create *a* culture, "but a still greater culture" than that of Europe.[18]

[14]"Das Land ohne Mittelalter," *Weltwirtschaftliches Archiv*, XXXIII (1926), 90-117.
[15]*Amerika von Heute*, 80-81.
[16]*Ibid.*, 89.
[17]*So sah ich Amerika*, 277-278.
[18]*New York und London*, 88-89, 104.

Another German visitor took violent exception to the clichés which were circulating. Emil Müller-Sturmheim denied that it was proper to label the United States a country having no history. It had a history of glorious achievement in contrast to that of Europe, which set forth "an unbroken chain of wars, beginning in the Roman period and reaching into modern times, wars which never had the excuse of ethical or moral purposes and are only to be ascribed to the aggressiveness and acquisitiveness of individual rulers."[19] And, he continued, although it was true that America had not yet produced a Goethe, a Molière, a Voltaire, a Kant, a Beethoven, or a Tolstoy:

> The gleaming sun of these geniuses and their countless talents are even yet today veiled by a heavy fog from the mass of the people and also from the little throng of men who determine the history of the European states. They are lonely islands in the ocean of flatness and spirituallessness which covers Europe even today.[20]

The "genial intuition" of America had solved many problems still troubling Europe: the future of mankind lay in binding together European culture and European methodical thinking with the sense of justice and the genial intuition of America.[21]

Unfortunately the pronouncements of Kerr, of Erkelenz, of Pfannmüller, and of Müller-Sturnheim were also "lonely islands" in the ocean of German superficiality. Most German observers still prided themselves on the old and inherited and condemned the newness and lack of tradition of America.

One aspect of the German emphasis on newness and youth attached itself to the conception that America was still essentially an Anglo-Saxon cultural colony. This carried with it an emphasis on the "Puritan" aspects of American life. The term "Puritanism" was used in a much broader sense than that involved in the American connotation. It comprehended a whole range of moralistic and religious viewpoints attached to such things as "religiosity," "fundamentalism," "sex-prudery," "asceticism," "narrowness," etc. The German antagonism to the ideal is often surprising. German Lutherans had little patience with the moral severities of their fellow Protestants. Prohibition was a case in point. The attach-

[19]*Ohne Amerika geht es nicht*, 31.
[20]*Ibid.*, 36.
[21]*Ibid.*, 40-41.

ment of connotations of virtue to drinking ice water rather than beer was in itself convincing proof of the lack of spiritual depth of Americans!

Perhaps one of the severest indictments of American Calvinism was that set forth by Annalise Schmidt in her study of "the American man." Calvin's teachings had been, she declared, "harsh and inhumanitarian" and "directed towards a rationalization of one's entire life." The "searching of the heart" which laid emphasis on constant "work on one's soul, tireless self-repression, a deeply-burdened sense of sinfulness" occasioned "perversities, superficialities, self-deceptions, idiosyncrasies." In the harshness of nature in the New World people were pressured "to give up our dreams and longings in order to show of what stuff we are actually made." God was conceived of as so sovereign that "to search for him was frivolous." Puritan churches were "so whitely painted, so abstract and Godless, that certainly a God with a free, warm, and open heart could not have stopped there for a short Sunday visit." "The dangerous aspect of the Puritan teachings lay and lies," she warned, "in its repression of everything spontaneous, sensate, in its moralistic evaluation of things."[22]

If many of these observations might have been applied to the Puritan colonies of New England, what is surprising is the insistence of German observers upon the continuing impact of this ideology. Moritz Bonn in his *American Adventure* wrote of the "Puritan Twilight" but stressed more the continuance of these ideals than their decline.[23] Undoubtedly the decline of religious observance and sincere faith among the German intellectuals contributed to their unexpressed aphorism that religious faith and culture were not reconcilable. However, some of the reflection which they recommended to Americans might have led them to the recognition that German cultural traditions had reached their greatest heights prior to the decline of German "religiosity."

Puritanism, of course, also carried with it in German minds an emphasis on the Anglo-Saxon nature of American culture. The postwar period naturally tended to emphasize this. The wartime propaganda of the Anglophiles still found its echoes, and German culture in America showed little sign of recovering its former role.

[22]*Der amerikanische Mensch*, 9-11.
[23]Ch. 6, 244 ff. Bonn had also noted the "falling of the [Puritan] pillars" in his book *Geld und Geist*, 104-190.

The beginning of concern about the new immigration carried with it also an emphasis on "Americanization," which did indeed tend to underscore Anglo-Saxon ideals. Hence, Germans, whose appraisal of Anglo-Saxon culture in England was not exactly a friendly one, were even less inclined to find its reflection in the United States very appealing. As the expatriate Herman George Scheffauer phrased it, "The Anglo-Saxon element,—and that is the factor in the United States in which Puritanism is most deeply rooted,—is artistically unproductive."[24]

2. *The Babbitt Concept*: Beyond the charges of Puritan and Anglo-Saxon dominance, but indeed directly related to them and reinforcing and confirming them, was the widespread adoption of Sinclair Lewis' Babbitt symbol as a satisfying explanation of American life. The dominance of materialism over cultural fields was thus made crystal clear. Arthur Feiler, for example, though he still labeled the United States a colonial land, denied that its youth was a convincing explanation of its lack of cultural achievements. After all, he pointed out, the population was to a high degree derived from the most musically gifted peoples of Europe. But only the Negro music had developed on this side of the Atlantic. The answer lay in the atmosphere of materialism, the quest for economic success, and the accompanying depreciation of cultural attainments. But Feiler saw hopeful signs of transition towards better things.[25] Many of his countrymen did not.

Richard Müller-Freienfels emphasized the "simplicity" of American civilization, the lowness of the spiritual level, and said that this gave newcomers from abroad the opportunity to relax and let their cultural antecedents slip from them; it was easy to adjust to circumstances and "become American." In the search for material progress and well-being the mixed races of America found a common ground. The lack of culture was a kind of "overcompensation" for the differences between peoples of different origins.[26]

One of the strongest expositions of the assessment that American life was Babbitt-oriented appeared in the book *America and*

[24]*Das Land Gottes*, 205.
[25]*Amerika-Europa*, 310-315.
[26]" 'Amerikanismus' und europäische Kultur," *Der deutsche Gedanke*, IV, 30-35 (July, 1927).

Americanism (*Amerika und der Amerikanismus*) of Adolf Halfeld. On its cover it bore the inscription,

> The culture of Europe, in particular of Germany, developed by tradition, is threatened by America with its concentration on materialism and the mechanization of life. Rationalization on the American example is trump, regardless of whether it kills the human in mankind.

And throughout, Halfeld emphasized the standardization, the leveling of culture, the tendency to replace spiritual matters with the ideal of success and progress. Main Street, the center of each new town desirous of becoming a city and reproducing the sterile patterns of all American cities, was indeed the symbol of American culture.[27]

Joined to the Babbitt concept was that of American pragmatism —the measuring of things by their usefulness. Art was, in America, suggested Curt Glaser, neglected because it served no real purpose, had no rationale in the pattern of American life. But to a German one criterion of culture was that it should not seek utilitarian values. It would, felt Glaser, require time until Americans realized this. But, he added, it had taken Europeans centuries to realize that art must exist for its own sake, must be sole ruler in a kingdom where things were not measured by practical objectives.[28]

3. Jazz, "Kitsch," and Skyscrapers: There were in German eyes many symbols of America's spiritual and cultural poverty. Perhaps the outstanding was the universal and omnipresent jazz. The twenties saw it in its hey-day in America and in Europe. As has been seen above, although most Germans viewed jazz critically, it also had its defenders willing to recognize that it was a form of art, but one created not by the American as commonly understood but by the

---

[27]*E.g.,* 109. The concept was also given emphasis by the book of an American, Edgar Ansel Mowrer, published in the United States as *The American World* (New York [c. 1928]) but translated as *Amerika, Vorbild und Warnung* (Berlin, 1928). Although Mowrer provided warnings that Europe was labeling as "Americanism" much which had been derived from its own civilization and emphasized the declining *élan vital* of European culture, reviewers were wont to summarize the book with the words "spiritual democracy and machine organization triumph and Babbitt purchases the world." *Kölnische Zeitung,* July 16, 1928.

[28]*Amerika baut auf* (Berlin, 1932), 113.

Negro.[29] American jazz was, indeed, by the reports of some observers, closer to Africa than European jazz was.[30]

Some observers, however, tied it to American cities rather than to the jungle. After describing the polyphony of sounds produced by "water-gurgling sprinkling cans, swinging saws, howling pot covers, primitive forest tones of buzzing sticks, bells, saxophones, etc.," Dr. Fritz Giese declared that these were joined

> to a suggestive, close-cut disciplined rhythm. A rhythm just as harassed, just as concentrated, just as determined as the brutal turning tempo of the industrial machine, the speed of the racing car, the momentarily changing lighting [and darkening] and constant rotation of the lighted advertisements on the business houses.

And Giese described one band in New York with appropriate symbols:

> First it rattles like the air-pressure pump in the subway; suddenly a dog is run over by an auto bus; just as unexpectedly the gas stove explodes; then one hears the whining sound of the elevator motor. This instrument sounds off like a motor horn in haste; the other hums like the carpet sweeper; in the midst of it purrs in eternal calm the ventilator. Swinging cranes, locomotive steam, telephone snarls, back-fires of motorcycles—this and everything else is actually caught and melted into a musical film full of emphatic express-train tempos.

Jazz carried with it the pulse of the city, of industry, of Fordism, of Taylorism.[31]

American music other than jazz seldom received notice from German observers. Most of them seem to have been unaware of serious interests or any native creativity in this field. Dr. Ernst Kunwald, longtime director of the Berlin Philharmonic Orchestra, spent the last years of the war in internment in the United States.

[29]*E.g.*, Rundt, *Amerika ist anders*, 135-138.

[30]Eduard Büchler, *Rund um die Erde. Erlebtes aus Amerika, Japan, Korea, China, Indien und Arabien* (Bern [c. 1921]), 15—"Es war dies die berühmte amerikanische 'Jazzband'-Musik in ihrer Originalauflage. Ich will mich über sie nicht etwa lustig machen, sie hat ja ihren Siegeszug über den ganzen Erdball angetreten und erfreut mit ihren rhythmischen Tönen das Tanzpublikum in London wie in Paris. Allerdings hat sie auf dem Wege nach Europa etwas von ihrer negerhaften Originalität eingebüsst."

[31]"Das tanzende Amerika," *Velhagen und Klasings Monatshefte*, XLI, subvol. II, 544-548 (July, 1927).

He returned to Germany in 1920 to report that German music had held before and even during the war a dominant and respected role in America. He also praised American orchestras and noted the beginnings of native work in this area.[32] Siegfried Wagner, the son of the great composer, visited the United States in 1924 in behalf of funds for the continuance of the Bayreuther Festspiele, and although not entirely satisfied with the financial results, he considered his trip "an undoubtedly great artistic success."[33] And Hans Goslar found the New York and Chicago opera and the performances of musical concerts in these cities an exception to his general impressions of cultural mediocrity.[34]

Not until 1931, however, did Germans learn directly of the larger scope of American music, when Ambassador Frederick M. Sackett sponsored a festival of American music in Bad Homburg, July 6-8. The *Frankfurter Zeitung* carried on this occasion an account by the American music critic Irving Schwerké, which described in some detail the history of American music and the various schools and composers represented in it. Schwerké told his German readers that the United States had created independent forms and significant musical values:

> Modern American music does not exhaust itself in jazz as is, unfortunately, much too much believed. Rather, it strives for many-sidedness, to comprise both the primitive and the artistic. American national music seeks to derive creativity from the most differing kinds of sources and to be representative of the greatly varying elements of which the American nation consists.[35]

Schwerké's account, however, attracted little attention and Ambassador Sackett's festival does not appear to have altered German views. For most Germans jazz remained the typical if not the only American contribution to music.

After jazz, the second most persistent irritant to the cultural sensitivities of German visitors was the American theater as displayed on stage and screen. For the tone of this form of art the favorite German work was *Kitsch*, meaning gaudy and showy trash. America's sound films were, wrote Arthur Holitscher, "A Niagara of

---

[32]"Amerika und die deutsche Musik," *Vossische Zeitung*, July 22, 1930.
[33]"Meine Amerikafahrt," *Deutsches Musikjahrbuch*, 1925, 276-278.
[34]"Amerikas öffentliche Meinung," *Vossische Zeitung*, March 18, 1922.
[35]"Amerikanische Musik," *Frankfurter Zeitung*, July 4, 1931.

'unculture.' "[36] Nevertheless, Hollywood was a mecca for a number of the travelers in America. They went there most largely to find ammunition to arm pre-existent complaints. These centered on the superficiality and naïveté of the movies, particularly the universal "happy ending." The latter was, to Germans, a clear sign that the American didn't want to be challenged by the theater; he wanted his sensibilities tickled, his fancies flattered, his sense of optimism confirmed. One German critic thought Charlie Chaplin the epitome of what was wrong with the movies—his great success was due most of all to the fact that he reflected typical American naïveté, childishness, practicality. And he had led the way to the spreading abroad of these traits.[37]

Alice Salomon declared that the Hollywood production of the "Ten Commandments" began as a mighty spectacle produced with the common American search for a record number of people, animals, wood, nails, cables, and other assorted items of production, but had quickly degenerated from a highly conceived version of history into "a modern thrill story, with moralizing tendencies emotional and sentimental." It would, she said, be totally improper to speak of it as art.[38]

The same criticisms applied to Broadway productions. As Eric Reger pictured it, "sentimental buffoonery, catchy operettas, costly reviews" were most likely to have success: "Recipe: at least one great role which can be carried off, dreadful acting with an idyllic admixture, and above all a good and happy ending." Then the play might go on for weeks, or months, or even years. For Reger, this state of affairs was not really funny; it was a tragedy:

> The tragedy of a mechanized people that has been conquered by the machine. The raging speed of technical development has destroyed the soul, the sensibilities, the human character. Feeling for art has no longer a basis.

And, felt Reger, there was little hope for the future. These were not the defects of youth but permanent qualities:

> The taste tendency of Americans is, however, not naive but sophisticated, seeks not for excitement but for titillation, not

[36]*Wiedersehn*, 170.

[37]Gerhart Pohl, "Charlie Chaplin, Ein Symbol für die amerikanische Kulturdämmerung," *Die Glocke*, XI, subvol. I, No. 13, 406-408 (June 27, 1925).

[38]Salomon, *Kultur im Werden*, 96.

for drama but for sensation. Where is in this the child? Where is the possibility of maturity?

For him "theater culture" was non-existent in America. The tempo of life, the lack of separation from material things, the intensive search for enjoyment all prevented the development of real art.[39]

One German writer, however, strongly presented the opposing side. American drama represented, he said, the psychic needs of the public; it was a concern of the people as a whole. On the other hand, the much vaunted German tragedy was no longer popular in Germany itself; it was "an affair of the cultured few" rather than a genuine expression of Germany's soul and traditions. The German theater, he said, would gain a much broader support if it abandoned such delusions and fitted itself more closely into the tempo of the times as the American theatre had done.[40] And another observer, critical of much that he saw, had to admit that there were indeed some very able American actresses, some of them the equals of any on the stage in Europe.[41]

There were, however, no defenders of the American "music-girlie shows." As one critic described them. "They are textually and musically irresponsible, at their best pompously decorative but clumsily butchered; they exist because of the silken shine of the stockings, because of the low-necked dresses; and their sour humor exhausts itself on prohibition."[42] Another critic bemoaned the transfer to the European stage each year of some new dance form displaying an eccentric or exotic motif—"Fish dances," "jitter dances," Charleston. American dance groups displayed the standardized, the routine, the typical, which was a part of American life; they reflected its leveling tendencies, its superficial optimism and good cheer.[43]

Most Germans were also vehemently negative in respect to another field of American cultural endeavor—architecture. Here

[39]"Drama und Kritik in Amerika," *Kölnische Zeitung*, February 28, March 3, 1925.

[40]Carl Werckshagen, "Amerika erobert die Bühne," *Vossische Zeitung*, July 12, 1924.

[41]Gustav Kauder, "Die Kunst am Broadway," *ibid.*, November 20, 1920.

[42]*Ibid.*

[43]Dr. Fritz Giese, "Das tanzende Amerika," *Velhagen und Klasings Monatshefte*, XLII, subvol. II, 544-548 (July, 1927).

the anti-skyscraper, anti-utilitarian emotions of the visitors erupted vehemently. Most visitors saw New York with awe and loathing. Typical was the reaction of the artist, Walter Curt Behrendt, who found New York beautiful from a distance:

> The charming magic of the light, of the smoke and mist over the water, which mercifully veils all details, gives this universal and by form and measure peculiar city mass a surprisingly artistic effect like the realization of the dream of an exaggerated architectural fantasy.

But after a closer view, he described the city as "a hateful stone desert" built at the expense of the souls of its inhabitants:

> The city format of Manhattan is hopelessly and finally ruined; a place incomparably blessed by nature has been tastelessly spoiled and only the force of an elementary catastrophe could bring a solution in that it would create the opportunity of starting over again. This is no place where men live, where an honored work can be served. This is the inferno and the devil was its contractor.[44]

For some of those who came a second time, the effect was more fearful on the second visit than on the first. Thus Arthur Holitscher, returning in 1929, found that all picturesqueness had disappeared. "A new generation of skyscrapers" had grown up, "a heavy, weighty construction of power, awesome and individual," making New York a city "strange and cold."[45]

Eugen Kühnemann, the Goethe expert, who had known New York before the war, returned in 1932 and was, like Holitscher, impressed with the new and awesome growth. But, unlike Holitscher, he saw accompanying signs of a new artistic creativity:

> Giant buildings near which the old skyscrapers appear puny have shot up on all sides. Striding along the streets one looks high up along the framework of the buildings, high above to the stars in the heaven, which in this neighborhood seem unreal. The summits of the buildings make the city between the monstrous heights a kettle in which life pulsates with frightful alarm. In it the thickly-pressed throngs of people, all the women and girls painted like a mask and all apparently the same in expression, seem a pulsating fantasy of the senses.

[44]"Aus dem Tagebuch einer Amerikareise," *Kunst und Künstler*, XXIV (1925), No. 2, 61-66.

[45]*Wiedersehn*, 11, 17-25.

The men seem small. All of their human quality disappears before the monstrous element of the fearful city, which, in itself a superhuman, demoniac being, mocks all little human things. Man's creation has grown over his head. And yet man has created it and he struggles to satisfy the needs of his creativity which has not lost its power. The artistic thought has begun to become master of the mass. It forces it under the rule of form. The coming American beauty announces itself in astonishing accomplishments.[46]

Other lay observers also found the skyscraper not so artistically shocking as they had anticipated. Alice Salomon, for example, wrote, "The skyscraper of today is no longer just a particularly tall building, a building with many stories, but rather a structure with a new, utilitarian, and esthetic style."[47]

Some of the more professional observers were openly laudatory and regretted only the maintenance of European styles in circumstances where they were not appropriate. They bemoaned the misoneism of their countrymen. Edmund Schüler, for example, wrote that the skyscrapers were not a purely American creation— the cathedrals had had similar connotations. City regulations rather than the character of the people had prevented their construction in Europe. But the skyscraper, he declared, had come into existence "out of a new spirit of the times" rather than because of any actual lack of space. Its origins he attributed to Louis Sullivan, and its first artistic format had been displayed by the Wainwright building in St. Louis. Sullivan's maxim, "Form should follow function"—"a new time, a new form," had gained acceptance and acclaim after his death. Now the tendency to build banks like Greek temples, Gothic churches, or Renaissance business buildings was giving way to an unadorned style more in keeping with their purpose. And skyscrapers, predicted Schüler, would become a form of real art:

> Who would not recognize the depth of power which is reflected in these works and these words [defending the purely functional in architecture]? . . . Nothing strong has ever appeared in the world which did not in the end find its ultimate expression in an individually artistic deed, almost without wishing it. The skyscraper is, naturally, not the only example [of modern artistry] and it has, indeed, not yet

[46]*Amerikafahrt, 1932,* 9.
[47]*Kultur im Werden,* 98.

attained its own fulfillment, but it is certainly one of the most important and most obvious bearers of the new and mighty form of life involved in modern urban civilization, one of the first sons [sic] of a new style.[48]

Two other German architects also found in American skyscrapers the signs of "an independent sense of form," "a creative energy of the first order," which had "finally returned to the recognition that the problem of all architecture is a cubic-rhythmic one." They, too, praised "the faultless sense of proportion" of American skyscrapers and their tendency to free themselves from "the unflattering mask" of European forms. For them the hero of skyscraper architecture was John Wellborn Root, whom they considered the most significant innovator in this move towards an independent style.[49]

However, it was a third American architect, Frank Lloyd Wright, who gained much broader recognition in Europe than did Sullivan or Root. His accomplishments were called "a summary of American achievements having universal implications."

> He goes in everything back to the very beginnings of construction and wins from this starting point clear and constantly progressive new forms for all architectural purposes. His incomparable richness of talent brings to his sense of the Romantic feeling for form an enchanting unity with the tenderness of the Japanese and the severity of the Egyptian. Against Root's elementary monumentality he places the unerring security of his proportions sublimated in a genial and dynamic construction.[50]

Wright was, of course, concerned not only with the building of skyscrapers but also with the construction of individual homes. And here, too, Germans found that he achieved new art:

> The most of his country houses, fitted into the ocean-like endlessness of the prairie, are very low, joined with, indeed

[48]"Der Wolkenkratzer," *Kunst und Künstler*, XXIII (1924), No. 6, 228-239. Schüler incorrectly identifies Sullivan with the given name "Arthur." For other favorable comments on the new trends in building skyscrapers see Fritz Schatthöfer, "Die Himmelslinie. Aus meiner amerikanischern Reise," *Frankfurter Zeitung*, January 20, 1927; Georg Swarzenski, "Europäisches-Amerika," *ibid.*, January 30, 1927.

[49]Ludwig Hilbersheimer and Udo Rukser, "Amerikanische Architektur," *Kunst und Künstler*, XVIII, No. 8 (1920), 537-545.

[50]*Ibid.*

pressed down toward the earth, and as a consequence the interior rooms spread out horizontally from one another. Therefore these houses do not seem like some grotesque thing which has grown out of the earth, they appear native to the soil and fitted to it, like the farmhouse.[51]

Two German architects of genius followed directly in Wright's footsteps. One was the Austrian-born Richard Neutra, who came to the United States in 1923 and attached himself to the circle about Wright. Four years later he published in Stuttgart his description of *How America Builds* (*Wie baut America*), directed largely to those who "are in accord with the contemporary" (*Bejahung der Gegenwart*). Neutra pointed out that mass methods could produce "a new refinement, which scarcely finds its equal in the most unusual luxury objects of other times," and sought to describe the tremendous improvement in techniques which was being displayed in the architecture of skyscrapers and dwelling houses.[52]

A year later Erich Mendelsohn published his picture book of his American travels accompanied by a foreword which indicated he was not yet "in accord with the present." America on the whole he regarded as exemplifying "the whole monstrosity of a negative civilization" "whose culturelessness can be hidden neither by the painter's brush nor by expanded verticals." But Mendelsohn did find "hopes for a new world," did note the improvement of skyscrapers by accommodating them to their technical purposes—"out of naked utilitarianism comes abstract beauty."[53] And in spite of his negative commentary on American architecture, Mendelsohn conceived a great admiration for the work of Wright and before the end of the twenties was bringing to German city buildings much of Wright's spirit.[54]

Wright, of course, found caustic criticism as well as praise in Germany. Paul Ferdinand Schmidt wrote in 1931 that Wright's genius had come to an end prior to World War I and that the

[51]*Ibid.*

[52]*Gegenwärtige Bauarbeit amerikanischer Kreise. Wie baut Amerika?* (Stuttgart, 1927), 2 and *passim.*

[53]*Amerika. Bilderbuch eines Architekten* (Berlin, 1928). Folio. Unnumbered.

[54]Arnold Whittick, *Erich Mendelsohn* (New York, 1956), 69-71 and following.

postwar period had shown a notable decline in his abilities.[55] Wright, in answer to German criticism, suggested that too many of the critics were seeking to reduce his ideas to a "style" rather than recognizing them as an imaginative approach, an effort to join composition to surroundings. His work, he said, must be judged in *Gestaltist* fashion, as a whole, rather than as a source of technical solutions to technical problems.[56]

There were, of course, Germans who admitted the genius of exceptional individuals like Frank Lloyd Wright, but denounced the constant repetition of style of housing found both in city and country in the United States. For them America had "a culture of the common form." [57] Some answer to this charge was provided by an article on American housing by Gustav Ludwig, published in 1924. Ludwig provided an unusually sympathetic description not only of American homes but also of their furnishings.[58]

Ludwig dealt most largely with middle-class, moderate-income homes. These he found more interesting than those of the wealthy, which were likely to model themselves after foreign styles. The average American, believed Ludwig, was possessed of a deep love of nature ("not expressive and not demonstrative, but deeply rooted and alive in his subconscious"), and a strong desire to have his own land and his own home.[59] As a consequence, he often willingly assumed the task of an arduous journey to his place of employment and accepted a home which might well require the use of his ingenuity to complete it for comfortable living. Furniture as well as the house was standardized, but its quality was good. The overall effect Ludwig found much less shocking to artistic sensibilities than did many European visitors:

> In spite of all these constantly repetitive factory-produced mass products the comfortable little houses and dwelling

[55] "Der Untergang des amerikanischen Genies," *Sozialistische Monatshefte,* LXXIII, 770-774 (August, 1931). Adolf Behne also considered that Wright had less influence than formerly, but regarded this as unfortunate. "Amerikanische Architektur," *Vossische Zeitung,* April 14, 1923.

[56] "Meine Kritiker zwischen Rhein und Donau," *Frankfurter Zeitung,* August 25, 1931; in the same issue a defense by Walter C. Behrendt, "Wright oder Corbusier?"

[57] Julius Hirsch, "Kultur der Gleichform," *Vossische Zeitung,* July 25, 1925.

[58] "Wohnen und Bauen in den Vereinigten Staaten Amerikas," *Zeitschrift für Geopolitik,* 1924, No. 10, 636-644.

[59] *Ibid.,* 639.

rooms breathe a certain atmosphere of well-being. The rooms are small; the houses, mostly one, seldom two-storied, have relatively flat roofs and are therefore comfortably spread out, with their lower windows immediately joining the garden, with which they fit together in one pattern and which the housewife tends with great love and much understanding. The dwelling rooms are low, mostly paneled in wood; with the comfortable fireplace, with the horizontally-divided sliding windows and broad sliding doors everything goes into breadth instead of height and gives the rooms, aided by the bright sunny light which floods in and the richly used floral decorations, a certain individual charm. The constantly repeating form of furniture and equipment lose their individual impression in the overall effect. Also the cheapness of the typical furniture is erased by the good form and good technical quality [in which it is produced]. The ambition to furnish the house in modernistic fashion finds little support. The dwelling rooms also lack, of course, the beautiful, old, inherited house decorations which one still finds with us, which are of course not always utilitarian and practical but always beautiful in form and material, and examples of artistic craftsmanship.[60]

Ludwig also took account of the growing use of apartment buildings, which he described in tones of praise, and of tenement areas, which he considered one of America's greatest dangers for the future. But his overall appraisal was strongly favorable:

On this subject it is possible after this detailed discussion to determine, in summary, that by far and away the greater percentage of the population lives well; indeed, in comparison with all other peoples of the world, the English not excepted [they are] better [housed], and have, accordingly, reached the highest stage of dwelling culture, the better civilization. This judgment is not altered by [the condition of] the urban proletariat, which only outlines the sharp contrast of light and shadow.[61]

4. The Vain Search for Beauty: In the areas of painting and sculpture as well as in music most Germans believed that Babbitt had killed the artistic spirit. One visitor reported cynically that for the American the art of painting was sufficiently displayed

[60]*Ibid.*, 641.
[61]*Ibid.*, 644.

in the colors of his Cadillac![62] Another related that when he asked Americans the names of their most respected artists, none could mention more than a couple of them and those named varied from person to person.[63]

Others added to their disdain for American creative work their trenchant criticisms of American art collectors. These philanthropists who drained off Europe's cultural treasures were, they believed, motivated not by the spirit of art but by that of exhibitionism. Art collections were one way of displaying great wealth and for many of the collectors provided an excellent form of investment.[64] William Medinger proclaimed that all such art collections were useless; art deprived of its surroundings was sterile:

> The poorest Tyrolean village, the narrowest Italian alleyway will remain for us a more artistic experience than the most refined museum of a skyscraper city. The *genius loci* is neither to be bought nor constructed. Culture torn loose from its home ground sinks down to ordinary civilization.[65]

Some Germans, however, saw positive gains from the work of the collectors. Alice Salomon suggested that not all of them were so lacking in artistic appreciation as German critics suggested; an American museum was the only one to collect Manet's work during his lifetime![66] This interest in the collection of art created a growing group of American art critics concerned with "educational work." Although the attitude of superiority and the dogmatism of these "teachers" might repel Europeans, they were sowing the seeds of future progress. Curt Glaser wrote that to expect too rapid a progress would be like believing in utopias, but he did praise the spirit of sharing displayed by the collectors and did admit that the collecting group had been educated in artistic appreciation in an astonishingly short time.[67] And August L. Mayer saw the spread of city museums across the country as pro-

---

[62]Dr. R. Burkhard, "Die Gefahr des Yankeetums," *Grüne Blätter*, XII, No. 32, 522-526 (August 10, 1930).

[63]Glaser, *Amerika baut auf,* 114.

[64]*Ibid.,* 126.

[65]*Amerikanische Eindrücke* in *Vier Reden auf dem Kongress der interparlamentarischen Union, 1925* (*Veröffentlichungen der deutschen Völkerbundliga in der Tschechoslowakischen Republik*, No. 7. Prag, 1927), 23.

[66]*Kultur im Werden*, 98.

[67]*Amerika baut auf*, 130-136.

viding centers for the "propaganda of good art" and regarded the "enlightening efforts" of the director of the city museum at Minneapolis, as skillful.[68]

Few of the German observers were aware of or particularly interested in native developments in the field of painting. George Grosz, the German painter, in his journeys about America found no kindred souls, regarded the students in art schools in New York as not particularly gifted, and took more time to tell of his experiences in the burlesque theater than he devoted to art museums or art schools.[69] An exception, however, was Hildebrand Gurlitt, Professor of Architecture at the Technical University of Dresden and later director of the art museum in Hamburg, who named as examples of a new tendency to creative painting such figures as Charles Sheeler, Charles Demuth, John Marin, and Preston Dickinson. Gurlitt proclaimed that "the specific American [in recent painting] seems to me to lie above all in a very unusual refinement of taste and a highly developed love of the purely esthetic" which he believed made an appealing contrast to what he called the "all-too-gross of the Germans." Gurlitt predicted that these American painters would create worthwhile accomplishments based upon their own experience in their own country.[70]

5. *The Literary World: Libraries, Newspapers, Literature*: In the world of the written word Germans were also more likely to praise Americans as collectors than as producers. The public library movement gained broad approval from German visitors. "America," wrote Arthur Feiler,

> possesses in its major cities and in its chief universities splendid libraries, with a completeness of collections which spans the entire world production, with a monumentalism of the

[68]"Von modernen amerikanischen Kunstsammlungen," *Kunst und Künstler*, XXI (1923), 298-300.

[69]"Briefe aus Amerika," *Kunst und Künstler*, XXXI (1932), 273-278, 317-322, 433-443.

[70]"Jungamerikanische Maler," *Vossische Zeitung*, July 15, 1925. Gurlitt, however, failed to include Joseph Stella or Marsden Hartley, who were strongly picturing American life and foreshadowing the creation of beauty from the very things repugnant to German observers. Art historian Georg Swarzenski was also quite defensive in his evaluation of American art and its potentialities. See "Europäisches-Amerika," *Frankfurter Zeitung*, January 30, February 6, 19, 26, 1927.

housing of them, with a provision of comfort for the user, and with the assignment of monetary funds for continuing collection and expansion which can only make the German think with sharpened sorrow how far behind we got here in the twelve years of the war and postwar era.[71]

Feiler pointed out that the New York Public Library compared favorably in size and holdings with the British Museum, but that the latter served only scholarly study, while the New York Public Library served a public of eight millions.[72] Friedrich Schöne-mann in similar fashion detailed the great accomplishments of the public library movement and praised the efficient and practical methods of providing for public use which accompanied it.[73]

The most significant account by a professional librarian was that provided by Hermann Escher, Head Librarian of the Zentral-bibliothek ("Central"—municipal library) in Zürich. Escher paid glowing tribute to the service of American libraries in the cause of popular education, in the creation of general knowledge of library practices, and in the development of the habit of making use of their resources. He warned, however, that this carried with it the danger that the books might be "read to pieces" and future generations deprived of access to them.[74]

Some Germans, however, admitted the beauty and commodious-ness of the large public libraries in the United States, but asserted that the building itself often exceeded the contents in quality.[75] In German eyes American creativity was as lacking in the literary field as in the fine arts.

The negativism of the German observers found its starting point in the newspapers. These shared with jazz and the movies the profound disgust of the visitors. Albert Lorenz joined "the *Kitsch* flood of the movies" with the "boarding-house diet of the

[71]*Amerika-Europa*, 314-315.

[72]*Ibid.*

[73]*Die Vereinigten Staaten* in *Handbuch der Kulturgeschichte*, 194-195.

[74]*Aus dem amerikanischen Bibliothekwesen. Beobachtungen und Studien* (Tübingen, 1923), *passim*, especially 71-77. Escher's book is the most thorough study of the subject written in German. He visited New York, New Haven, Providence, Boston, Cambridge, Pittsburgh, Washington, Baltimore, Philadelphia, and Princeton, and wrote on state, county, and city public libraries, specialized libraries, and business libraries.

[75]*E.g.*, Father Jakob Overmans, "Amerikanisierung des Geistes," *Stimmen der Zeit*, CXVIII (1930), 161-173 at 167-168.

newspapers,"[76] and Hans Christoph Kaergel spoke of "the newspaper sickness" in America and cartooned the state of speechless stupefaction which that medium imposed upon its readers in the New York subway.[77] The newspapers in America, charged other observers, avoided the significant for the trivial. Their purpose was not to inform but to arouse and excite. Their reports of crime and violence, their lack of interest in serious things, their reduction of everything to the comprehension of the child made them a serious obstacle to cultural progress.[78] Nor did the "reform" periodicals which professed to correct the weaknesses of the newspapers really succeed in this task. Even Mencken's *American Mercury* lacked real substance.[79] Furthermore, the poor quality of the newspaper reacted unfavorably upon reading in general and reduced the spiritual quality of books published in the country.

Unlike jazz, the newspapers found no really committed defenders. Emil Dovifat, a professor of journalism at the University of Berlin, did recognize the great technical achievements of American journalism and asserted that its level of responsibility was rising, but he denied that it approached the very important overall cultural preparation which existed in Germany or that it had gained the real sense of mission of the newspaper which was of vital importance in both countries.[80]

American literature in general was also regarded as insignificant. This negative appraisal was explained in part by pure ignorance. Friedrich Schönemann was to remark at the close of the period that far too many Germans were discussing American literature without ever having actually read much of it.[81] A collection of "readings" in American literature published in Germany during the period contained a strange mixture of writings from little-known authors and even included one sketch of English origin![82] Almost none of those who discussed American literature save Schönemann himself and Walther Fischer, another specialist in the

[76]"Amerikanismus," *Volkserzieher*, 1928, Beilag, "Der Bücherfreund," 1.

[77]"Kleinigkeiten aus dem grossen Amerika," *Die Bergstadt*, XIV (1925/1926), No. 5, 465-476 at 474.

[78]Penck, *U.S.-Amerika*, 132; cf. Overmans [see *fn.* 75].

[79]Overmans [see *fn.* 75], 164.

[80]*Der amerikanische Journalismus. Mit einer Darstellung der journalistischen Berufsbildung* (Stuttgart, 1927), 9, 237-243.

[81]*Die Vereinigten Staaten*, II, 409.

[82]Magda Winkler, *Sketches of American Life* (Stettin, 1929).

field, indicated any awareness of American literary figures prior to 1900 other than Walt Whitman and Ralph Waldo Emerson. By and large the assumption that there was a virtual vacuum in American literary production derived from the preconceived judgment that America was too young, too busy, and too materialistic to have a literature. By constant repetition the assumption became an aphorism.[83]

Some of the negative appraisals derived from an over-emphasis on the importance and validity of the current American cultural pessimism. H. L. Mencken's caustic comments on the American scene won many accolades: he was "although of course much smaller and later, an American edition of Voltaire."[84] After all, Mencken said what Germans expected to hear and were glad to listen to. Similarly Sinclair Lewis' Babbitt explained and capsulized the American for Germans. American criticisms of his having been chosen as the first American author to receive the Nobel prize in literature gained little sympathy from Germans.[85] Ludwig Lewisohn also attracted more attention in Germany than in America. His Jewish background did not prevent the Germans of the twenties from an emotional identification with his frustrations in seeking a place in this strange and unfriendly New World.[86] But even the critics failed to gain real respect from the Ger-

[83]Here and there, more sober appraisals appeared. Karl Arns wrote an appreciative account of "Moderne amerikanische Dichter," *Zeitschrift für französischer und englischer Unterricht*, XXIV (1925), 140-145. Schönemann provided several studies: "Köpfe des literarischen Amerikas von Heute," *Leipziger Illustrierte Zeitung*, Nr. 4385, 438-439 (January 3, 1929) and "Die amerikanische Literatur von Heute," *Deutsche Rundschau*, CCXX (1929), 67-72. Fritz Schatthöfer found in Dreiser's *American Tragedy* elements comparable to Stendhal's novels: "Das amerikanische Rouge et Noir," *Frankfurter Zeitung*, January 23, 1927. However, several articles by the expatriate Hermann Scheffauer reinforced the negative note: "Amerikanische Literatur der Gegenwart," *Deutsche Rundschau*, CLXXXVI (1921), 215-222; and "Whitman in Whitmans Land," *ibid.*, CCI (1924), 255-262. As a consequence, even some of the more scholarly articles parroted the prevailingly negative appraisals; *e.g.*, Walter Damus, "Der Amerikaner und seine Literatur," *Zeitschrift für französischer und englischer Unterricht*, XXIX (1930), 111-120, 202-209, and Hans A. Joachim, "Romane aus Amerika," *Die neue Rundschau*, XLI (1930), 396-409.

[84]Hans Zbinden, *Zur geistigen Lage Amerika* (München, 1932), 38.

[85]Ernst Untermann, "Der junge Geist in Amerika," *Sozialistische Monatshefte*, LXXIII (37. Jg., 1931), 351-354.

[86]See, *e.g.*, Walter Kühne, "Vom Geist Amerikas," *Geisteskultur*, XXXIV (1925), 142-146.

mans. There was, suggested Adolf Halfeld, a great gulf between criticism and real creativity. No really creative group existed in America. The younger generation was "striking matches," but there was nothing to burn.[87] Gustav C. Müller found the new generation of "American intelligentsia" comical and futile—although possessed of the attitude of "Nietzschean supermen," they never really rose above the surroundings they so despised and, indeed, made fundamental reform more difficult by the ill-repute which their superficiality gave to the word "intelligentsia."[88] Müller found much more promising beginnings in the "New Humanism" in America led by W. C. Brownell, Irving Babbitt, and Paul Elmer More. Here, in a "new Platonist" turning back from the industrial world of the day to the very earliest roots of America, to a Puritanism freed from dry mythology and from the narrowness of provincialism, Müller saw some hope of progress.[89]

Another German critic, Franz Zimmer-Telsing, was more strongly impressed by the "new idealism" in America, personified in the work of Ralph Waldo Trine and Orison Swett Marden. This was, he said,

> a new powerful effort to lead men of a mechanistic time period back to the spiritual sources of their strength and, in the midst of an economic crisis, whose extent we are not yet able to judge, to prepare for a rebuilding of life, and to give this life an idealistic basis upon which we must place the man of the new day as soon as he, after the inner and outward disintegration of our days, has become again ripe enough for the higher values of life.[90]

Related closely to Emerson's idealism, this new school stressed the creative power of thought for the deepening of life's enjoyment as well as for knowledge. Thought, wrote the German observer, gained in the writings of the "new idealist school" something of the nature of material force, of physical actuality. As such, it cut counter to German conceptions and was not of itself fully acceptable, although its ethical concern was to be praised.[91]

[87]*Amerika und der Amerikanismus*, 176.

[88]"Die amerikanische Intelligentsia," *Zeitwende*, VI, No. 8 (August, 1930), 169-172.

[89]"Der 'neue Humanismus' in U. S. A.," *ibid.*, VII, No. 3 (March, 1931), 250-257.

[90]Franz Zimmer-Telsing, "Der amerikanische Neuidealismus," *Hochland*, XXI, 503-514 (August, 1924).   [91]*Ibid.*

Another critic turned European criticisms back on Europe itself. This was Hans Zbinden, Professor of Cultural Sociology at
Berne, who presented his views on the German radio in 1928 and
later published them in the midst of the depression. America's
economic difficulties, he suggested, were no more serious a problem
than the shadows lying across the spiritual life of the country. But
he heralded a time of change, part of a turning point in world history. Current judgments on America, he declared, had been grossly
faulty: "No country in the world has been so unjustly libeled, none
more critically judged, than has in the last decade the continent
of unlimited possibilities."[92] Europeans had ignored the signs of
change—"While Europe is blindly copying some of the worst features of 'Americanization' within the U.S.A., the leaders of a new
generation [in America] are engaged in a conscious and energetic
struggle against 'Americanization.'" This was signalled by a cultural pessimism, "an inexplicable longing and a dissatisfaction"
with things as they were.[93] In the forefront of change Zbinden
found Edgar Lee Masters, Van Wyck Brooks, H. L. Mencken, and
J. E. Spingarn. The center of change lay outside the universities,
which provided anything but real leadership. The remnants of
Puritanism, of Pragmatism—the absence of an American "problematic"—hindered progress, but America was, he said, "richer than
Europe in unbroken, youthful fighting spirit, in the open-minded
drive for new forms."[94]

In similar fashion Hans Tietze pointed out that cultural criticism had been a part of the American scene ever since the time
of Whitman. The depression, he believed, had matured and
ripened America; it would now be able to deal more fundamentally
with the cultural problems which beset it.[95]

The critics dealt with above have demonstrated the growth
of German interest in contemporary American literature. But few
of these literary critics had a scholarly knowledge of earlier periods.
Overall evaluation rested largely in the hands of two pathfinders
in the field of American studies in Germany, Walther Fischer
and Friedrich Schönemann. Fischer produced the only major

[92]*Zur geistigen Lage Amerikas*, 7.
[93]*Ibid.*, 9.
[94]*Ibid.*, 43.
[95]"Das amerikanische Kulturproblem," *Zeitwende*, VIII, No. 9 (September,
1932), 181-189.

literary history of the United States published during this period. Unfortunately it was limited in its coverage to the period after the Civil War. Schönemann wrote with perception of Mark Twain, served as a review critic of contemporary American literature, and worked throughout the period on a literary history destined never to be published. However, in his general work on the United States published late in the period, and in his volume on the culture of the United States published early in the Nazi era, he gave extensive consideration to American literature.

Fischer's literary history was more a sketch than a detailed analysis of the period it covered.[96] More than three-fourths of the volume was taken up with a selection of reasonably well chosen texts going beyond literature *per se* to exemplifications of political and philosophic thought. Similarly the portion of the volume devoted to summarizing American developments was also considerably broader in scope than literature as the term is commonly employed.

Fischer's basic evaluations were not particularly revolutionary. He found the themes of democracy and Puritanism dominating the whole of American thought and culture. Puritanism, although it had lost some of its original dogmatism and asceticism, provided a continuing thread not really lost in either Emerson or Whitman, not fully contradicted by William James or entirely rejected by many of the contemporary cultural critics. Puritanism had carried with it ethical values:

> The feeling of one's own sinfulness, bound up with the conviction that one could secure his own selection by making good in the hard fight for existence and in restless labor, created that striving for self-fulfillment, that intensification of the inward life of the individual, and that steeling of the will, which we must above all place on the ethically positive side of Puritanism.[97]

But Puritanism, said Fischer, had carried with it also "a depreciation, even a complete misevaluation of all artistic values" and in the long run had led the believer away from his chief objective, a

[96]*Amerikanische Prosa. Vom Bürgerkrieg bis auf die Gegenwart (1863-1922)* (Leipzig, 1926). Fischer had anticipated portions of this in his article "Über einige Beziehungen der Literaturgeschichte der Vereinigten Staaten zur amerikanischen Kulturgeschichte," *Die neueren Sprachen*, XXXI (1923), 39-55. This article also dealt with earlier portions of American literary history which Fischer bypassed in his book.

[97]*Amerikanische Prosa*, 18.

way of life pleasing to God.[98] The joy of living had been destroyed as artistic relationships were interpreted in narrow and sterile fashion. Transcendentalism, also, in spite of its Platonic and neo-Platonic overtones, had retained the Puritan conception that a moral purpose is to be found in all things and the ethic of activism which saw the goodness of thought only in its execution.[99] And Walt Whitman, who was, felt Fischer, closely tied to the Transcendental movement, had made the spiritual struggle of the individual a part of the larger effort of all men to find "identity" with one another, with all their fellow men. Even William James' pragmatism had in the long run led to the somewhat contradictory premise of "Meliorism"—the hope of a better future. This was a form of continued Puritanism:

> Such a Weltanschauung, however, "a universe with only a fighting chance of safety" . . . is a matter of strength, of objectivity, of largeness of heart. It is also the matter of the old Puritans, who in faith (or in spite of their faith) worked for salvation in spite of Predestination: "Those Puritans who answered 'yes' to the question: Are you willing to be damned for God's glory? were in this objective and magnanimous condition of mind."

But amazingly, continued Fischer, although Josiah Royce might criticize William James's pragmatism and stand on the ground of pure idealism, both thinkers arrived at similar theological speculations: "The long-inherited Puritan spirit lives in both, although in differing degrees."

Puritanism, admitted Fischer, was one of the chief banes of the existing cultural critics in America. Sinclair Lewis with his view of the Middle West as "double-Puritan," "prairie Puritan on top of New England Puritan," H. L. Mencken with his sharp criticisms which added to Middle Western Puritanism also a Southern Puritanism, were typical. The closest approach to real progress along new lines Fischer found in the work of J. E. Spingarn who asserted that the moral approach of both Puritans and anti-Puritans was faulty—a true philosophy of life must be derived from the immersion of one's self in an appreciation of the work of the artist, for the artist's creation by its very artistic nature represents the creation of a personal philosophy of life.[100]

In the field of literature proper, Fischer displayed a sympa-

[98]*Ibid.*, 19.   [99]*Ibid.*, 20.   [100]*Ibid.*, 31.

thetic and understanding criticism. Emerson and Whitman received only passing attention since their halcyon days had preceded Fischer's point of departure, the American Civil War. William Dean Howells he saw as "a much softer, quieter temperament with greater literary culture [than Mark Twain]," who bound the pre- and post-Civil War periods together. "Of all Americans," wrote Fischer, "he is undoubtedly the artist whose works convey to the European reader the most European tone." Henry James also received special attention from Fischer because of his careful search for details of character and his philosophical preoccupations. But James, the naturalist, remained in Fischer's eyes still the Puritan, "basically an earnest moralist."[101] With him the American novel, believed Fischer, reached "an artistic summit." After James, Fischer's attention turned to novelists of lesser stature who worked, however, in areas underscoring native regions and traits, producing that which Germans denominated *Heimatkunst*. Such were Mrs. Margaret Deland's story of New England Puritanism, George Washington Cable's accounts of the Louisiana Creoles, and S. Weir Mitchell's pictures of the Pennsylvania Quakers.

Late in the nineteenth century, noted Fischer, had begun the development away from the romantic to the realistic—the search for "undisguised factuality in the name of democratic art. . . ."[102] Frank Norris, the most gifted of American naturalists, never achieved full realism—there lived within him "a romantic trait, a longing for the boundless of which the symbol [wheat] became for him the most characteristic expression." "So," summed up Fischer, "this 'objective' Naturalist finished his work actually not logically but rather driven by his 'Will to believe,' in an idealistic conception of the course of world events."[103] Upton Sinclair, on the contrary, moved strongly into purely Marxian views.[104] In the later period, writers such as Joseph Hergesheimer, Theodore Dreiser, and John Dos Passos broke thoroughly with Puritan traditions, although Dos Passos remained purely American with his conception of "the unity of feeling" which bound Americans together coast to coast. But the expositors of "programmatic naturalism" had never received the acceptance given to more recent cul-

[101]*Ibid.*, 52.
[102]*Ibid.*, 57.
[103]*Ibid.*, 58.
[104]*Ibid.*, 59.

tural critics, such as Sinclair Lewis, whose criticisms were aimed not only at American bourgeois society but at bourgeois society everywhere.[105]

Fischer devoted extensive attention to the short story, considering it the most typical American literary development. It had permitted literary figures of truly popular character to appear:

> Therefore, however, they have, unlike the Brahmins of the East, grown up with the people and give them, without esthetic doubts, what they most desire: on the one side the glorification of the raw world about them by rosy-colored romanticism, primitive sentimentality, and hand-made melodrama; on the other side raw, grotesque humor in whose trait of monstrous and improbable exaggeration may be recognized something like a hidden longing of the people for the metaphysic.[106]

Thus with Bret Harte the "tale" of Edgar Allan Poe had evolved into a somewhat less refined but more easily managed genre descending so far that literary style sought the "cheap effects" and "effusion of sentimentality" which was attached to the work of O. Henry. But Fischer's appraisal was largely favorable. Criticizing Bret Harte for his "sentimentalism" and "theatricality" and Mark Twain for the "constitutional pessimism" of a part of his work, he came to a more sympathetic view of Mark Twain's stories of Huckleberry Finn and Tom Sawyer, a praise of the artistry of George Washington Cable and of Joel Chandler Harris, and particularly favorable note of the stories of Ambrose Bierce. Even in O. Henry's work, in spite of the criticisms previously mentioned, there was, said Fischer, "an undoubtedly artistic element" which should not be overlooked.[107]

As for the essay, Fischer did not ignore Mencken but gave special notice rather to Paul Elmer More, Brander Matthews, and J. E. Spingarn.[108] As a whole, he believed American literature had freed itself in part from its English traditions; it had become "more national and more cosmopolitan at the same time." Many western influences other than English had affected it, and it in turn had had an even stronger effect upon Europe. Although it still belonged in part within the Anglo-Saxon tradition, consider-

---

[105]*Ibid.*, 60-64.   [106]*Ibid.*, 38.
[107]*Ibid.*, 38-46.
[108]*Ibid.*, 64-65.

able segments of approach and philosophy could no longer be fitted into an English pattern.[109]

Like Fischer, Friedrich Schönemann was by predisposition and training a literary historian and critic. His doctoral degree having been won in the field of German literature, Schönemann employed a nine-year stay in America as the springboard by which to become Germany's most prominent postwar specialist in "American studies." Writings in the area of literary criticism continued to employ his pen, in particular studies of "American humor" and of Mark Twain, as well as a criticism of American literary critics.[110] But unlike Fischer, Schönemann never harnessed his talents fully to this single field; rather he sought a broad understanding of American life and thought in all its ramifications. Many of his perceptive and objective although sometimes critical assessments have been noted above. His *magnum opus, Die Vereinigten Staaten von Amerika* (*The United States of America*) was published in two volumes in 1932. Strangely enough, there is no chapter in the work devoted purely to a summation of accomplishments in the literary field. Rather, in every segment of his discussions Schönemann adduces references to the field of literature which are intimate, exact, and usually sympathetic. It is unfortunate that Schönemann never completed and published his projected literary history of the United States. It would undoubtedly have been a significant addition to Germany's Americana.

As it was, Schönemann left behind as his most significant piece of literary criticism, the book *Mark Twain als literarische Persönlichkeit* (*Mark Twain, as a Literary Personality*). Mark Twain had had, suggested Schönemann, a particular predilection for German thought and ways and had found in Germany an answering interest and respect.[111] The German problematic was reflected in Twain's inner agonizing over the nature of man in which he hovered between love and scorn and came in the long run to a pessimism which reflected in part his disappointment that his own best and deepest thoughts had not been recognized and appreciated.[112] But Twain differed from the German in his conscious and thorough-going revolution against the traditional,

[109]*Ibid.*, 66-67.
[110]See biographical sketch in Chapter II.
[111]*Mark Twain als literarische Persönlichkeit*, 5.
[112]*Ibid.*, 20-26.

and inherited.[113] He reflected the trust in one's self of Emerson and Transcendentalism.[114] Yet he ended in a pessimism which did not accord with this spirit of self-reliance. Mark Twain was, said Schönemann in summary, "Much broader and more meaningful" than many of his critics were willing to admit:

> He was full of contradictions: that makes him typical of humanity and in particular a true child of his time and of his country. He was uncommonly many-sided and often suffered as a consequence. He was also full of struggle. This gives his life and work often the character of something unresolved. All in all he was a highly individual, outspoken, and great personality, who gave even his weakest writings an individual note and pressed upon his strongest and most mature works the stamp of extraordinary human values and true artistry.[115]

Within his *magnum opus* on the United States Schönemann displayed a broad and perceptive knowledge of American literature.[116] Schönemann used these literary references, however, as a framework upon which to evaluate the cultural traditions and ways of thought of the United States. Although he was by no means uncritical, he was on the whole more friendly and sympathetic than those who wrote upon the basis of a narrower and shallower knowledge of the subject.

Schönemann, in spite of a strong preoccupation with the adverse effect of Puritanism, regarded it as "by no means lacking a sense of beauty."[117] Moreover, he did not employ the term as the sole key to American literature and culture. Although not present until the time of the Civil War, a distinct "sans-culottism," a spirit of revolt against European culture, had made itself felt in the period following.[118] Moreover, in all fields of culture, America had

---

113*Ibid.*, 78-83.

114*Ibid.*, 107-108.

115*Ibid.*, 11.

116As noted above, these are interwoven with Schönemann's overall evaluations of American civilization. See, *e.g., Die Vereinigten Staaten*, I, 141, 229, 243; II, 173, 250 ff., 271, 316 ff., 323, 329, 344, 373, 378 ff. It must be admitted, however, that Schönemann, like other German critics, gave an emphasis to the writings of some Americans who have not loomed large in later judgments—notably Ludwig Lewisohn, who was a favorite subject of German observers, and William Eleazor Barton, a Chicago clergyman who wrote a series entitled "The Parables of Safed the Wise." *Ibid.*, II, 416-417; 462, fn. 39.

117*Ibid.*, II, 373.   118*Ibid.*, 378.

followed "a more or less conscious eclecticism"—"Behind France or Germany stood for him [the American] mankind itself, not just Europe." And, Schönemann added, "This is in itself not to be wondered at, it is indeed entirely human and wise, but the individual, culturally-advanced nations of Europe keep forgetting it and are always disturbed anew [as they discover] that they themselves do not mean *everything* to the American."[119] Because of this and because of the lack of the problematic in American philosophy, the superficiality in its essay literature, and "the happy ending" psychosis in lyrics and novels, uninformed Europeans had been led "to an underestimation of American earnestness in life and American thinking as a whole." "The American," he wrote, "appears, however, more thoughtless than he really is, just as in the contrasting case the German appears less practical than he actually is."[120]

But Schönemann felt that America's cultural development required a greater appreciation for past history. By this he did not mean a worshipping at European shrines. There were dangers in this as Goethe himself had pointed out:

> For Goethe the values and disadvantages, even danger, of history were clear as he freed from obstacles (*einräumte*) America's right to its young, present-oriented, and relatively traditionless culture. The developing American world was to him more vital and interesting than the European cult of the eternal yesterday. This ought to give the intelligent Europeans of today something to think about when they feel able to dismiss American culture with a word.[121]

However, Schönemann felt that American pragmatism, particularly as reflected in Dewey's stress on the utilitarian in history—history as a guide to present action—tended to rob history of its function of facilitating spiritual depth and cultural enrichment.[122]

In spite of pragmatism, however, and in spite of the concern with the present, Schönemann believed that in America there slumbered in the unconscious "an extraordinarily important and attractive historical heritage" upon which Americans would draw

---

[119]*Ibid.*, 379.
[120]*Ibid.*, 388.
[121]*Ibid.*
[122]*Ibid.*, 388-391.

more fully in the future.[123] Hellas and Rome had left strong marks upon American consciousness.[124] But the influence of the European Renaissance and European Humanism on American thought was more tenuous and narrower.[125] And the Romantic movement in Europe had been broader in scope than that in America. America had chosen to follow some of the manifestations of the movement—"that idealizing, rosy-coloring, poetizing impulse which leads beyond the drabness of daily life, that interruption of a static cultural status, that adventure in a new world. . . ."[126] But America had never obtained the true sense of the German Romantic, the analysis of feeling in the appreciation of art and in the conception of religion. And the American had never found real identity with the idealization of the Middle Ages which had been a part of the European Romantic—for this his Protestantism had posed too strong a barrier. Not until after the First World War had America overcome some of its antipathy to the Middle Ages with the founding of the "Medieval Academy of America." Perhaps, felt Schönemann, this might lead to the recognition that much light for modern civilization was to be found in the "dark Middle Ages" and to the final conquest of Puritanism itself.[127]

In final summary Schönemann noted that American philosophy and culture had attained a level far above that recognized by many European observers. They were determined by four basic factors: "the close relationship to nature of the Americans, their historically-formed habits of thought, their eclecticism, and the new tone of their life."[128] There were really two Americas—the East with its closer ties with Europe; the more purely American Middle and Far West. "In both Americas," he suggested, "the 'Anglo-Saxon' soul contends with the spirit of the new, non-English immigration." And in neither had the dollar-quest destroyed appreciation for spiritual values. Rather, Schönemann wrote, "Life in America also mixes unending manifolds and the American will and the American intellect cannot be typified by the skyscraper in the one

123*Ibid.*, 392.
124*Ibid.*, 397.
125*Ibid.*, 403.
126*Ibid.*
127*Ibid.*, 403-407.
128*Ibid.*, 407.

case, the colonial style in the other."[129] And again, " 'Americanization of the soul' means to us simply a mass corruption of the
spiritual life, but the truths of American life are by no means so
simple." In America, declared Schönemann, leisure was producing
a new kind of public, with more libraries and books than any
where else in the world. And too many judgments were being
passed uncritically on American literature:

> People talk too much *about* American literature and by no
> means read it enough to justify true judgments. Or they
> think that from the often entirely accidentally translated
> books of mediocre value of the last century it is possible to
> understand the whole literature, [a standard of scholarship]
> which in all cases much contradicts our much prized "histori-
> cal tradition."[130]

The American, said Schönemann, did indeed seek success in
life. But in so doing, he did not lose his idealism: "He stands
firmly on the ground of this life of so-called actuality and yet is
not lost in the present, since he has his fantasy."[131] He makes
plans for the morrow and rejoices in their success. On the ground
of this success he tends to idealize his experience and to underscore
the practical.[132] He sees the spirit of God in all things and all men.
Transcendentalism was "the real and natural beginning of an
American philosophy of life."[133] But the deification of experience,
reflected in William James' Pragmatism, had tended not only to
confuse psychology and philosophy but also to replace the previous
securities of morals and faith with a skeptical and energetic rela-

---

[129]*Ibid.*, 407-408.

[130]*Ibid.*, 409. The comment on accidental translations is given substance
by the listing of school texts on America available in 1930—see Walter Damus,
"Amerikanische Schullektüre," *Zeitschrift für französischer und englischer Unterricht*, XXIX (1930), 665-667. Eugen Kühnemann also pled for the provision
of better chosen views of the United States: "Let us have the books which give
a full impression of American or German life translated into the corresponding
language. Let us begin with the fascinating children's books, so that the
American childhood joys are transferred to the German youth, the German
maiden, and in reverse, the German to American children." Kühnemann
stressed the need for a translation of *The Rise of American Civilization* by the
Beards, which was not translated into German until after World War II.
Amerikafahrt, 1932, 15.

[131]*Die Vereinigten Staaten*, II, 412.

[132]*Ibid.*, 413.

[133]*Ibid.*, 419 ff.

tivism.[134] This had been broadly reflected in the writing of history and in literature:

> This relativism [displaying itself] partially as passion without judgment spread into all phases of American cultural life. It destroyed the old self-reliance and self contentment of the pioneer, took from the old, inherited optimism its religious and moral supports, and also destroyed especially the blind faith in the wisdom of the American average voter.[135]

It had undergirded the protest and reform literature which circulated, and there was in American criticism, lyric, novel, and drama "no longer any unified and harmonious feel for life." This movement had not been entirely desirable. Much of life and art had been "dismembered, demeaned, and robbed of its innermost life, and therefore every sense of the poetic as well as the respect which is the condition of religious thought as well as of the grace of living and the soul of fine literature."[136] America was, therefore, in the midst of a cultural crisis, a search for a new Humanism. But in this search she was not alone: many of the same problems existed in Europe. And Europe was not only engaging in misjudgment but confirming her own lack of energy when her critics persisted in labeling cultural problems "Americanism" as though these problems really did not concern Europe, were really not a part of common problems confronting the two continents.[137]

6. *Science and Medicine*: In one area of cultural achievement Germans recognized a high degree of accomplishment in America. This was in the area of the natural sciences and related fields of medicine. Many Germans, however, tended to equate this area with "technology" rather than with "culture." German doctors and veterinarians returned with praise of new hospitals and approval of the respect which their professions held in the United States.[138]

[134]*Ibid.*, 425-427.   [135]*Ibid.*, 427.
[136]*Ibid.*, 427-428.
[137]*Ibid.*, 429-435.

[138]*E.g.*, Dr. Fritz Grünbaum, "Reiseeindrücke in Nordamerika," *Deutsche Medizinische Wochenschrift*, LVI (1930), No. 49, 2100-2101; 50, 2145-2146; 51, 2185-2187; Nils Lagerlöf, "Eine Studienreise nach Nordamerika," *Münchener Tierärztliche Wochenschrift*, LXXXII (1931), No. 46, 555-559; No. 48, 579-582; Prof. Oscar Gans, "Amerikanische Reiseeindrücke," *Klinische Wochenschrift*, VI (1927), No. 41, 1957-1960.

Friedrich Dessauer, the German physicist, visited the United States and brought back admiration of its scientific achievements and a hope for mutual exchange of scientific information. But Dessauer himself defined culture as separate from science, finding America's way to true culture leading through "a long, stony road" and requiring "suffering" before it should come to fulfillment. But fulfillment would come, he believed.[139]

7. *In Retrospect*: The Weimar period in Germany was, indeed, not one which found the United States reaching heights of cultural accomplishment. For many of the German criticisms there was a certain amount of genuine justification. What irritates is, of course, the exaggeration and the superficiality, the willingness to generalize from surface manifestations. And then there is also the unspoken frame of reference, the so much prized German *Kultur*. The conception that a differently formed civilization and culture must be judged by more universal standards, that one nation appraising the accomplishments of another must be prepared at the same time to submit its own to careful scrutiny, found little reflection in the myriad German writings on America. At the same time it must also be emphasized that in this era when Germany suffered from economic stress, when she was experimenting with a new form of government considered by many of her people alien in character, her cultural traditions remained her most secure, her most prized possession. German visitors forced to admit at the outset that America had become politically and economically powerful could, perhaps, not be blamed for emphasizing American cultural deficiencies. In so doing, however, they undoubtedly enhanced the cultural misoneism which was a factor in the success of Nazism.

[139]"Nordamerikanische Reisebriefe," *Hochland*, XIX, 331 ff., 460 (November, December, 1921). Dessauer's letters were reprinted in 1922 under the title *Auslandsrätsel: Nordamerikanische und Spanische Reisebriefe* (München, 1922) and then again in 1962 as part of *Kontrapunkte eines Forscherlebens. Erinnerungen; Amerikanische Reisebriefe* (Frankfurt am Main, 1962).

Chapter IX

TEACHERS AND PROFESSORS

𝔖 *chool and Life*: "The close relationship of the school to life [in America] brings it about that students are bound to their schools with ties of great love and that not only [academic] knowledge (*Wissen*) but practical ability (*Können*) and the teaching of practical activities are strongly cultivated." Thus wrote Otto Dorner, a German school teacher in Essen, after a visit to the United States in 1928.[1] Dorner was one of the many school teachers and professors who formed a significant portion of the visitors to the United States during the Weimar period. Some of these were exchange professors or representatives at international conferences. But many came at considerable personal sacrifice to see at first hand the nation now accepted as the most powerful in the world and to study its educational methods.

A disturbing thought must have troubled some of these visitors. If the victory of Prussia over France in the war of 1870-1871 was the victory of the Prussian school master, then, obviously, the victory of the United States in the First World War must show the superiority of the American educational system, or at least of some aspects of that system. But Germans were much too proud of their cultural heritage, of their own educational traditions, to accept this thesis. In their eyes America was still a backward "colonial" country whose cultural accomplishments were virtually nil. Wartime propaganda had denied the existence of real democracy in the United States. America's prosperity in the postwar period generated envy and supported charges of American materialism. It was a tribute to the open-mindedness of some German teachers that they were able to peer beyond the superficial and evade prejudice to emerge with the discovery that American educa-

[1]"Vom Bildungswesen in den Vereinigten Staaten," *Die neueren Sprachen*, XXXVII, 617-642 (December, 1929), 638-639.

tion had its strong points as well as its weak ones. A few became missionaries for changes at home designed to reflect some of the spirit of education in the United States.

There was, of course, a great gap between American and German educational philosophies of this period. In German eyes education was essentially the learning of subject matter, the acquisition of knowledge. In American eyes it was the development of the abilities of the individual and of his personality.[2] In Germany, suggested one visiting teacher, the basic purpose of education was the transfer of the cultural heritage; in America, the development of the human being with his inherited and acquired characteristics.[3] Or as Arthur Feiler, the author of one of the most popular "America books" of the day, expressed it, in America, "less value is assigned to the amount of knowledge and almost none at all to its depth; the chief goal is the ability of the student to attack the subject practically and to deal with it systematically."[4]

This drive toward practicality in American education found both favorable and unfavorable responses. Friedrich Schönemann, one of the most prolific and thoughtful of the German Americanists of that day,[5] argued that the lack of philosophical clarity in the American system (which he also found in Europe) led to awkward stumblings:

Their schools like their culture lack moral fiber: the broad philosophy of life, the uplifting sense of a national concept of propriety (*Volkssittlichkeit*). The successful businessman, today the decisive factor of all educational work in the

[2]*Ibid.*, 638. It should be noted that the differences between American and German educational practices and philosophy had been trenchantly set forth by a German-American author in 1910. But few of the postwar commentators appear to have been aware of this book by a former school superintendent, who published a variety of volumes in Germany. Wilhelm Müller, *Amerikanisches Volksbildungswesen* (Jena, 1910).

[3]Sebald Schwarz, Lübeck, "Was ist für uns in Amerika zu lernen?" *Deutsches Philologenblatt*, XXXVI, 630-633 (October 17, 1928), 631. Schwarz had also described the four months visit of the twenty-five members of the *Zentralinstitut für Erziehung und Unterricht* (Central Institute for Education and Instruction) in which he took part, commenting on the financial sacrifice it imposed and deploring the absence of school administrators. "Die Schulfahrt des Zentralinstituts nach Nordamerika," *ibid.*, 556-557 (Sept. 12, 1928).

[4]*Amerika-Europa. Erfahrungen einer Reise*, 94.

[5]Schönemann's experiences with the American educational system have been described in Chapter II.

United States, is himself most of all lacking in purpose and measure and hence unsuited to set the necessary spiritual goals for the schools.

This task, declared Schönemann, was the prerogative of the creative philosopher who knows how to think and to live.[6]

Other Germans, however, pointed out that at home the schools stood to one side of society, somewhat apart from it, whereas in America they were rooted deeply in the stream of national life.[7] They were impressed by the concern of American schools for their social surroundings and the accompanying social problems.[8] And they were astonished by the sense of national unity which they created. Although some complained that American schools promoted "black and white thinking" and "hurrah patriotism,"[9] most regarded the American development of a sense of citizenship and civil responsibility as a worthy accomplishment.[10] The overall evaluation by a visiting evening school teacher was almost panegyric:

> It [America] is the exemplary nation of unity and harmony, of tolerance, of an ideal democracy, of the separation of church and state, of the absence of class spirit, class rule, and traditions obstructing progress, of the one-class school [*Einheitsschule*], of the unobstructed opportunity for advancement for everyone, of a general effort for education, of a strong sense of the responsibility of the individual to society and [the advancement of] social progress, of a common willingness to make sacrifice for sanitary, medical, religious, artistic, and scientific purposes, and, finally, even of a burgeoning young art, philosophy, and science.[11]

[6]*Die Vereinigten Staaten*, II, 171.

[7]Dorner [see *fn.* 1], 640; *cf.* Schwarz [see *fn.* 3], 630.

[8]Kurt Richter, *Reisebilder aus Amerika. Jugendwohlfahrt in den Vereinigten Staaten (Veröffentlichungen des Preussischen Ministeriums für Volkswohlfahrt aus dem Gebiete der Jugendpflege, der Jugendbewegung und der Leibesübungen*, VI (Berlin, 1929), 68.

[9]Fritz Morstein Marx, "Jugend und Radikalismus in den Vereinigten Staaten," *Zeitschrift für die gesamte Staatswissenschaft*, XCIII (1932), 98-106 at 99.

[10]*E.g.*, Emmy Beckmann, "Schule und Erziehung der Vereinigten Staaten anknüpfend an den Kongress des Frauenweltbundes in Washington," *Deutsche Lehrerinnenzeitung*, XLII, No. 19, 169-172 (September 1, 1925).

[11]Fritz Kellermann, "Amerikakunde im Abendgymnasium," *Das Abend-Gymnasium. Zeitschrift für das deutsche Abendschulwesen und den Erwachsenen Unterricht*, Year 1929, No. 4, 23-28 (November, 1929), 25.

The author of the lines quoted above, Fritz Kellermann, was not the only German schoolman to feel that the much-prized traditions at home stood in the way of progress. Kurt Richter, a ministerial adviser in the Prussian Ministry of Public Welfare, wrote similarly: "Certainly we should not sink into materialism and we should uphold our thousand year old culture. However, it could do no harm if we made our educational work conform somewhat more closely to the demands of practical life. The excessive emphasis on history and tradition can act as a barrier to progress."[12] Otto Dorner wrote approvingly of the "joy in experimentation" in American schools, and Sebald Schwartz, a teacher in Lübeck, agreed, portraying these experiments as an effort to make the student a more vital part of the educational system than he was in Germany.[13]

German teachers were impressed by the value attributed to education by the public in America, although they pointed out that the low standards of teacher pay seemed inconsistent with the high evaluation it received.[14] In America, they noted, "education" was a slogan, a magic word which obtained universal enthusiasm.[15] "The people as a whole," wrote Professor Erich Hylla, "regard the public school as *their* school; there is no important part of the school system to which this or that group of the people is denied entry."[16] German school teachers were impressed by the close relationship of schools and parents, by the easy and unembarrassed visitation by parents which provided a direct control over the work of the schools.[17]

They were also astounded by the rapid expansion of the American educational system. One German teacher pointed out

[12]*Reisebilder*, 45.

[13]Dorner [see *fn.* 1], 625; Schwarz [see *fn.* 3], 631.

[14]The criticism of pay and social standards for American teachers was quite general. Perhaps the most careful study of the question was by Reinhold Lehmann. "Hemmungen und Hoffnungen im Erziehungswesen der Vereinigten Staaten," *Neue Bahnen. Illustrierte Monatshefte für Erziehung und Unterricht*, XXXII, No. 5, 164-166 (May, 1921).

[15]Penck, *U.S.-Amerika*, 51; Dorner [see *fn.* 1], 620; Kühne, *Von Mensch und Motor, Farm und Wolkenkratzer*, 100.

[16]"Der Geist des amerikanischen Bildungswesen," *Hochschule und Ausland*, IX, 7-13 (January, 1931), 9.

[17]Reinhold Lehmann, "Schule und Öffentlichkeit in den Vereinigten Staaten," *Neue Bahnen*, XXXII, No. 6, 189-193 (June, 1921), 193.

that the United States was seeking to accomplish in the half century of time which had passed since 1870 that which had required centuries in Germany. German educators noted with interest the efforts to get public and private support for this expansion, and admitted that the willingness of the wealthy to support the educational cause was much greater in America than at home.[18]

2. Elementary Schools: Feminism and Politics: The varied aspects of the American educational system received markedly different appraisals by German educators. Perhaps least criticized were the elementary schools, although they were categorized as being dominated by women teachers and, as a consequence, one of the symbols of what Germans labeled "cultural feminism" in America. In the eyes of most Germans, American women exercised an excessive influence on cultural matters—they were the only leisure class, the custodians of the "nice things" of life, the creators of a society which was too soft and feminine.[19] On the other hand, the American elementary school was the ideal of many German educators, the model for the *Einheitsschule* (unified school) at home, which would bring together divergent classes for a common education. They were particularly impressed by the efforts to extend educational advantages to remote rural areas by means of school busses and consolidated schools.[20]

Germans also admitted that the American child was brought more quickly to assume responsibility in school and developed maturity and self-reliance earlier than the German child. As Schönemann explained it:

> Under her [the woman's] influence the child obtains his rights early, indeed is often handled as a miniature adult from the time he is three or four. In the extreme this winds up in a sentimental cult of the child, whereas we Germans place all the emphasis on the adult. Both methods are faulty, but the American method is for the development of

[18]Lehmann [see *fn.* 14].

[19]Lütkens, *Staat und Gesellschaft in Amerika*, 195. Schönemann denied the propriety of the term "cultural feminism," although he did agree that there was "a certain pedagogical feminism." *Die Vereinigten Staaten*, II, 194-195. A caustic description of the role of women in education is found in Dr. Paul Rohrbach, "Vom amerikanischen Leben," *Kölnische Zeitung*, September 9, 1923.

[20]*E.g.*, Dorner [see *fn.* 1], 624.

character less dangerous, since it develops all the instincts of independence astonishingly quickly.[21]

American education found its most fundamental appraisal at the hands of Professor Erich Hylla, then serving in the Prussian Ministry of Education. A visit to the United States in 1926 resulted in the publication two years later of his volume *Die Schule der Demokratie; Ein Aufriss des Bildungswesens der Vereinigten Staaten (The School of Democracy; a Sketch of the Educational System of the United States.*[22] Hylla's appraisal of the elementary school provided a thorough-going assessment of its internal organization, methods of instruction, and experimental approaches. Generally, the appraisal was favorable. He praised reading and writing methods, which produced the rapid advancement of the beginning student in these skills, although he was concerned with the superficiality which he found accompanying them.[23] He found much of value in the study of science in the elementary years when the teacher was competent.[24] He approved of the extension of learning into the fine arts and music to a degree unknown in Germany.[25] His major complaint rested with the area of the social sciences, particularly history and geography.[26] On the other hand, he found in America, as also in Germany, a movement towards *Gesamtunterricht*, essentially the core curriculum. He was much interested in this and much impressed with the project method.[27] As he pointed out in a later portion of his book, such methods emphasized the central position given in America not to "materials" but to "people," not to subjects, but to children.[28]

Hylla was clearly very much sold on what was then known as "Progressive Education." As he summarized its consequences, the American student gained "greater freedom from restraint, greater liveliness, more self-confidence and initiative." But, he added, "The breadth, the fundamental character, and many-sidedness of knowledge and also the formal learning, above all in the abstract or

---

[21]*Die Vereinigten Staaten*, II, 194.

[22] (Langensalza, Berlin und Leipzig, 1928). For a sketch of Hylla's life see Franz Hilker, "Erich Hylla—65 Jahre," *Erziehung*, V (1952), 374-375.

[23]*Die Schule der Demokratie*, 24-27.

[24]*Ibid.*, 33.

[25]*Ibid.*, 36-37.

[26]*Ibid.*, 31-32.

[27]*Ibid.*, 39-43.   [28]*Ibid.*, 135.

more properly expressed 'theoretical' thinking, leave, compared with our standards, much to be desired."[29]

Both Hylla and Schönemann, as well as other German educators, were disturbed by the ties between party politics and education. German paternalism, wrote Schönemann, was absent, but party politics took its place, expressing itself not only in the choice of teachers, but also in the choice of textbooks, which often exercised a kind of "tyranny" over teachers. The teacher's conduct and attitude outside classes was far from free; he must be "secure" and patriotic. But, in spite of everything, noted Schönemann, "high intelligence and a good manly heart must not be subject to complete defeat, or how else would one still find in America so astonishingly much teaching enthusiasm and such selfless work and responsibility in the area of public education."[30]

Although German educators noted the varying division of the public school system into an 8-4 or 6-3-3 sequence, they paid little attention to the junior high school as such. One exception was Friedrich Schönemann, who found that this section of the American system operated "entirely in the rhythm of American democracy." Schönemann's attitude towards the junior high, much in contrast with his view of high schools *per se*, was highly favorable. Although he found it then "too young" in usage to evaluate fully, he reported favorably upon its offering of "try-out courses" and considered it to be the "most interesting part of a greater reform movement."[31]

3. The High School: Achilles Heel of American Education: American high schools were more criticized than any other part of the educational system. Undoubtedly this was because they differed so greatly from schools of the same level at home. Universally German observers attributed the lack of preparation of college and university students to the poor standards at the high school level (probably they found many American colleagues prone to

[29]*Ibid.*, 145; see also Hylla's chapter on Private Schools and Progressive Education, 203-214.

[30]*Die Vereinigten Staaten*, II, 198-200 *cf.* Hylla, *Schule der Demokratie*, 122-128.

[31]*Die Vereinigten Staaten*, II, 213-214; Hylla pointed out that the American junior high school carried into effect the project then being discussed in Germany of lengthening the *Volksschule* period as a trial time for movement into higher schools. *Schule der Demokratie*, 62.

the same judgment). It became an aphorism that American college students had not arrived at the beginning status of their German counterparts until they reached the junior or third-year level.[32]

Opinions varied on the basic rationale of the high school. For some it was another aspect of the "free road for the advancement of the able," an upward extension of the one-class school (*Einheitsschule*).[33] It was, said Erich Hylla, a cosmopolitan institution which gathered everyone into its fold.[34] Others, such as Schönemann, found that the deluge of numbers flooded out concepts of real education. The high school, he declared, was the Achilles heel of American education. It was a "mass school," serving to some degree the public welfare and the "melting pot," but dealing inadequately with academic matters. The excessive emphasis on "social affairs" had led to the neglect of intellectual work.[35] Schönemann was joined by Otto Dorner in his criticism of the great spread of subject matter from auto mechanics to Latin, mathematics to home economics. Both regarded the high school student as having excessive freedom of choice among these varied fields.[36] Hylla suggested that this was rendered even more a "patch-work" process by the lack of a terminal examination which would bring it all together.[37]

The most criticized aspect of the American high school was the inadequate and faulty instruction in foreign languages. The German visitors found French largely monopolizing the field and even this inadequately taught. They attributed the dominance of French not only to the First World War, but also to the traditions of friendship dating back to the American Revolution and to the appeal of French culture and dress to the women, who exercised so much influence on American education.[38]

The more perceptive observers, however, pointed out that the

[32]*Die Vereinigten Staaten*, II, 217; Penck, *U.S.-Amerika*, 50.

[33]Richter, *Reisebilder*, 38; Walther Lietzmann (Göttingen), "Das amerikanische Schulwesen," *Frankfurter Zeitung*, August 17, 1931.

[34]*Schule der Demokratie*, 68 ff.

[35]*Die Vereinigten Staaten*, II, 202-204.

[36]*Die Vereinigten Staaten*, II, 202-204; Dorner [see *fn.* 1], 628, 638. See also Paul Oestreich, "Volksbildung in den Vereinigten Staaten," *Deutsches Philologenblatt*, XXVII, 648-650 (December 24, 1919) and Hylla, *Schule der Demokratie*, 77-78.   [37]*Ibid.*, 79.

[38]Dorner [see *fn.* 1], 629-630; Lietzmann [see *fn.* 33]; Brinkmann, *Demokratie und Erziehung in Amerika*, 78-79.

American high school could not really be judged by European standards. It was a peculiarly native product, seeking, in Schöne-mann's view, its way between the Prussian *Volksschule* and the English college. In spite of all his criticisms he admitted that some of the best high schools produced outstanding products.[39] And Otto Dorner was impressed by the sense of cameraderie which existed in the high schools between teachers and students, and the community interest and concern found even in the giant in-stitutions of the day.[40] For Professor Hylla, the status of the American high school emphasized the fact that Germany and the United States confronted two opposing problems: the United States needed to make better provision for the proper education of its spiritual leaders, which required special schools for the more capable scholars; Germany, in contrast, needed to extend the opportunities of education to the capable members of all classes so that a larger portion of its population might acquire the neces-sary educational maturity.[41]

4. Colleges and Universities: Low Standards and Political Tyr-anny: American universities and colleges fared little better in German hands than did the high schools. With the exception of the best-known universities, especially those of the East, they were considered blighted by the deficiencies of the high schools and the adverse effects of athletics.[42] Harvard, they counted a great "world university"—it was well known to Germans because of the long residence and activity there of the German art historian Kuno Francke.[43] Johns Hopkins they considered the most similar to German universities.[44] Yale received a friendly sketch.[45] But many

[39]*Die Vereinigten Staaten*, II, 224.

[40][See *fn.* 1], 628.

[41]Hylla, *Schule der Demokratie*, 80.

[42]E.g., Paul Rohrbach, "Studenten und Universitäten in Amerika," *Köl-nische Zeitung*, September 16, 1923; for an example of the German views of American "sport" see the lampoons by Joachim Friedrich, *Vossische Zeitung*, December 19, 1922; June 15, 1923.

[43]See, for example, Friedrich von der Leyen, "Amerikanische Eindrücke; Deutscher Unterricht und Deutschtum in den Vereinigten Staaten," II, *Köl-nische Zeitung*, December 10, 1929.

[44]Penck, *U.S.-Amerika*, 48; Meyer, *Die Vereinigten Staaten*, 175.

[45]Dr. Ludwig Stein, "Die Yale-Universität. Gänge durch Amerikas Hoch-schulen," *Vossische Zeitung*, April 9, 1924.

of the lesser known universities were regarded as being backward and unenlightened. Commentators spoke slightingly of the "prairie universities" of the Midwest and the Bible-centered schools of the South.[46]

The lack of distinction in American usage between the word "college" and the word "university" often troubled Germans.[47] Germans tended to direct their severest criticism at the "colleges," often equating them not only with exclusive concern with undergraduates, but also with inferior instruction and accomplishment. An exception was Dorothee von Velsen, a free-lance writer who visited Bryn Mawr, Wellesley, Radcliffe, Vassar, and Smith. As she described American colleges,

> their most characteristic feature is rural calm. . . . It is to be kept in mind that a college by no means corresponds to our university or wants to do so. It comprises approximately our *Prima* [last year in the college preparatory school] and four beginning study semesters [at a university]. The lectures are easily comprehended, the seminar exercises resemble closely our secondary school methods. Only after graduating from college, by which the B.A. . . . is given, does the actual scientific work (post graduate work) begin at the university.

She added that the differences between the American higher educational system and the German often made it difficult for the German exchange student. He resented the discipline of forced attendance and prescribed curriculum. He often missed the "religious pathos" which accompanied the presentation of philosophical matters in Germany. But, she promised, if an exchange

[46]Term "prairie universities," Bonn, *The American Adventure*, 191, and more critically, *Geld und Geist*, 162 ff. But Bonn did suggest that in all of these a nucleus of superior students and professors tended to separate themselves from the generality and that these bore comparison with their German counterparts. Schönemann wrote that "the new universities of the Midwest have made history in American education. From them has come the democratizing of all education." *Die Vereinigten Staaten*, II, 227. Another German professor, Georg Kühne, also found the lesser-known universities much more impressive than he had anticipated. *Von Mensch und Motor*, 103 ff. It might be noted that Upton Sinclair's *The Goose Step* provided for the low evaluation of American universities the same kind of moral support which Mencken's writings provided for criticism of American cultural accomplishments in general. See, *e.g.*, Dr. Paul Rohrbach, "Studenten und Universitäten in Amerika," *Kölnische Zeitung*, September 16, 1923.

[47]See Hylla, *Schule der Demokratie*, 83.

student freed himself from traditional viewpoints, "then he will feel how very differently, especially in the colleges, the whole man is conceived of than in our universities and day schools." Signs of this were to be found in the close relationship of students and professors, in the extension of the curriculum into the fields of art, music, and the theater, and, "an invaluable factor," the self-government of the student body. "The tone is free, hearty, considerate, and polite; the relationship to the teachers surprisingly close."[48]

Miss von Velsen was not the only German observer to speak approvingly of the close relationship between student and professor in America. Friedrich Schönemann accepted with good humor his designation at Hunter College as "Doctor Dutchie" and found at Harvard students who maintained friendly relations with him in spite of the war years.[49] Schönemann also praised the willingness of American students to work for their university education, often at tasks which would be considered menial in Germany.[50]

Carl Schneider, who returned from teaching at Wittenberg College in Ohio to hold positions at the Herder Institute in Riga and later teach at Leipzig, added a denial that lack of serious purpose was a valid criticism of American students:

> Certainly, the completely impossible educational system directed towards the average student, the girl teachers, the mechanized university, the [dominance of the] financial viewpoint [on life], the unworthy "credit system," the conscious elimination of all personal responsibility, and the oppression of the capable on democratic grounds show the great dangers and fears of Americanism, but it is clear to me that a generation is growing up, which in spite of these things, or actually in tough, active struggle against them—in the Hegelian sense— seeks the way to the spirit. The Rah-Rah boy and the hysterical coed are not typical of American students.[51]

Nevertheless, serious criticism of the American system of higher education predominated. Although exchange professor Albrecht

[48]"Eindrücke aus Amerika," *Die Frau*, XXVII, No. 7, 393-394 (April 21, 1930).

[49]"Neun Jahre Amerika: Erlebnisse und Erfahrungen," Berlin *Tägliche Rundschau*, November 4, 1920; "Meine amerikanische Studenten: Erlebnisse und Betrachtungen," *ibid.*, January 7, 1921.

[50]*Ibid.*; *cf.* similar comments by Arthur Feiler, *Amerika-Europa*, 101-103.

[51]"Von Amerika und dem 'Amerikanismus,'" *Die evangelische Diaspora*, X, No. 3 (August, 1928), 116-131 at 124.

Penck was pleased to see how easily those in the lower academic ranks moved up to the higher, he raised the question how university professors who taught in the "school master" fashion of the first two years, with attendance marks, notes to the deans, and sloppy, uninterested students, could adapt themselves to the upper two years.[52] Another observer called the instruction in the lower classes "a spiritual motion picture performance"—the lectures must be simple; they should be accompanied with jokes, not be difficult to follow; at best provided with illustrative slides.[53] Somewhat more soberly, Professor Hylla emphasized the lack of training in independent study and the tendency to create hasty and unjustified generalizations which he found in American universities.[54] A Swiss writer found the whole instructional group mediocre, charging that American universities were filled with "attentive but completely mediocre teachers, routinists without spiritual significance, without the will or ability for outstanding accomplishment." As a consequence, he concluded, many of them became mere warehouses of learning turning out their annual products, the graduates.[55] Professor Hylla also labeled undergraduate education in America a *Betrieb*, a factory process, marveling that American professors could find time to do any research at all in the face of their teaching and counseling functions. And he advised that Germans should *not* imitate these conditions.[56] On the whole, German visitors were certain that German professors were better off in pay, social position, and intellectual accomplishments than their American counterparts.[57]

The broad extension of the university curriculum into the practical fields horrified most of the visitors, although a few defended it and considered it "fortunate" that the German division between the university and the "technical high school" did not

---

[52]Penck, *U.S.-Amerika*, 57-58; Brinkmann, *Demokratie und Erziehung*, 63-64, discusses the beginnings of the Junior College movement seeking to separate the unprepared first two years from the years of the more mature upper division.

[53]Anon., "Eindrücke vom geistigen Leben in den Vereinigten Staaten," *Börsenblatt für den deutschen Buchhandel*, Year 1928, 85-89 (January 24, 1928), 86.

[54]*Schule der Demokratie*, 92-93.

[55]Zbinden, *Zur geistigen Lage Amerikas*, 21.   [56]*Schule der Demokratie*, 95.

[57]Penck, *U.S.-Amerika*, 77-78; *cf.* Rohrbach, "Studenten und Universitäten in Amerika," *Kölnische Zeitung*, September 16, 1923.

exist in America.[58] In two subject fields Germans acknowledged outstanding achievement on the part of American universities. These were psychology, with the contribution of American pragmatism, and sociology, where institutions in the United States stood as pioneers in many respects.[59] In some universities these were combined as social psychology.[60]

Academic freedom in American universities was in the eyes of the visitors conspicuous by its absence. They considered American university professors much more hemmed in by public pressures than German ones.[61] American university presidents came in for diatribes for their weakness before the public and the various agencies of control, for their lack of scholarly attributes, and for the petty internal tyranny they exercised.[62]

Professor Hylla also suggested that conditions in American universities were likely to get worse before they got better. He saw the American higher educational system confronting a crisis in respect to admission problems with serious dangers of being overcrowded:

> The college must more and more prepare itself to become a school for the masses, must largely reject the thought of selection not only in respect to its students' social origins but also in respect to their degree of ability, suitability [for college life], and even their degree of preparatory education. The problem of over-crowding is one of the burning contemporary problems even of this school [level].[63]

Although Hylla did not approve of this lack of selectivity and could not understand the American failure to recognize the un-

[58]Brinkmann, *Demokratie und Erziehung in Amerika*, 50-51; Penck, *U.S.-Amerika*, 56.

[59]On psychology, *ibid.*, 54-55; Schönemann, *Die Vereinigten Staaten*, II, 422 ff.; on sociology, the able study of Andreas Walther, *Soziologie und Sozialwissenschaft in Amerika und ihre Bedeutung für die Pädagogik* (Leipzig, 1927).

[60]*Ibid.*, 27-48.

[61]See, for example, Penck, *U.S.-Amerika*, 65; Joachim Friedrich, "Amerikas akademische Freiheit," *Vossische Zeitung*, August 31, 1923.

[62]"The president of a great [American] university," wrote Eduard Meyer, "is one of the mightiest men on earth; he unites in one position the place of a German Minister of Culture or his adviser for university matters, of the Rector and of the Dean and along with this of a Minister of Finance." *Die Vereinigten Staaten*, 183; *cf.* Schönemann, *Die Vereinigten Staaten*, II, 220; Penck, *U.S.-Amerika*, 59-70.

[63]*Schule der Demokratie*, 100.

wisdom of spending money in offering educational advantages to students who could not make use of them, he did approve of the Junior College movement which seemed to promise some separation of the high-school-like first two years of college from that which was of real university level.[64]

Another American innovation also gained some plaudits. This was the experimentation in the cooperation of universities and businesses in combining technical and academic education.[65] Carl Brinkmann, Professor of Political Science at Heidelberg, thought that this made the acquisition of higher education of direct value to the career of the student, whereas in Germany the first advice given the newly graduated doctoral student was that he forget all he had learned.[66] Although Brinkmann recognized that this system carried with it some dangers to the intellectual and spiritual side of education, he believed these dangers were successfully overcome within the universities concerned.

It should also be noted that the more sober German observers regarded American graduate work as entirely respectable. Hylla wrote, "But where the doctoral title or a professional degree equivalent to it is sought, the recognized, great universities demand serious, scientific work which can well stand comparison with that directed to this end in English, French, and German universities."[67] Carl Schneider related his experiences with American graduate students whose "understanding, deep religious earnestness, and unwearied persistence" compared favorably with those in Germany.[68] And both Brinkmann and Schönemann warned their German colleagues that they were evaluating American universities with a standard which ignored shortcomings at home. Germany, too, they said, had its "crip courses" (*Paukkurse*) and its "dissertation factories."[69]

And Eugen Kühnemann, in spite of his love for Goethe and his rhapsodic promotion of German culture, defended the national spirit and the overall objectives of American colleges:

[64]*Ibid.*, 101-103.

[65]Brinkmann, *Demokratie und Erziehung*, 53-59.

[66]*Ibid.*, 56.

[67]*Schule der Demokratie*, 95.

[68]"Von Amerika und dem 'Amerikanismus,'" *Die evangelische Diaspora*, X, No. 3, 116-131 (August, 1928), 124.

[69]Brinkmann, *Demokratie und Erziehung*, 41, 67-68; Schönemann, *Die Vereinigten Staaten*, II, 234-235.

The ideal [of American colleges] is not primarily that of educating men and women so that their knowledge will bring secure ability in technical fields. The scientific [intellectual] man as such is not equated with the fully-developed academic man. The emphasis is primarily on life rather than on knowledge. They [the graduates] are to be completely developed Americans, leadership figures to whom the nation shall look upward. Everything is in this highest sense service to the nation. Everything is subject to unending improvement. What may be lacking of spiritual achievement will come.[70]

5. *Adult Education*: Adult education in America was given high praise. Germans regarded it as a most significant part of the process of assimilating immigrants.[71] It also aided the cause of citizenship and democracy. Kurt Richter of the Prussian Welfare Ministry saw in Rochester gray-bearded men and old women sitting beside young men listening to a woman teacher who could not yet have been twenty years of age, a situation impossible in Germany.[72]

And the Chautauqua institutes for summer education combined with vacation were also much admired. Anton Erkelenz found that his countrymen had been able to copy American methods of making money but had not yet found their way to emulating this significant cultural institution.[73]

6. *The Contrast with the German Scene*: As has been seen above, German teachers and professors examining the American scene were disposed by their pride in the cultural traditions of their country to find much to criticize in America. They also confronted a somewhat hysterical fear on the part of public opinion at home of being "Americanized"—of being brought to give up the spiritual values which they treasured, to become "mammonized" and bowed down with the practical things of life, to surrender the prestige of intellectual accomplishments. In spite of these obstacles a significant number of German educators spoke strongly in defense of the American educational system, praised the effort to meet the problems of life and criticized the educational system at home which encouraged day dreams and avoidance of the problems

[70]*Amerikafahrt, 1932*, 25.

[71]Dorner [see *fn*. 1], 634; *cf*. Hylla, *Schule der Demokratie*, 233-242.

[72]Richter, *Reisebilder*, 41-42.

[73]*Amerika von Heute*, 35-36.

of life. Professor Erich Hylla summed up the contrast of the two systems in trenchant words:

> The American educational ideal—so may we briefly summarize it—is different from the German, because the American ideal of living is a different one. The American ideal demands above all education of the *masses*, only secondly education of the specially gifted. We regard as the goal of education the development of intellect (*Vergeistigung*) and wish to bring the student to *think, understand,* be able to present a thing; the American demands from education that it create *activity*; it expects that the educated man will know how to maintain himself in life. German education results all too often in a situation by which the vision is lost in the past, in historical connections; *American* education teaches the student to look into the future. German education often makes the student all too ready to flee the rough world of reality into a rosy but unreal realm of ideas, at least for some leisure hours; American education does not withdraw its eyes from life, from the world of reality with all its difficulties, but imparts the robustness needed to meet it with optimistic courage and to work for the creation of a better reality.[74]

In similar language, Professor Brinkmann answered the criticisms of American childishness by proclaiming its value in meeting life:

> Therefore, there is for me something appealing, yes I might say something fully manly, not something warped and saccharine in the childlike side of American life. One senses behind it the free spirit of the healthy young organism, which faces the world adventurously, freshly, fully-awake, and with the self-reliant instinct of the boxer meets with step and counterstep the new and difficult but somewhat amusing situations which present themselves.[75]

And Otto Dorner found seven specific areas in which the American educational system was superior to that at home:

1. The respect of the entire nation for education *per se*;

2. The unity of educational concepts in spite of local differences of administration;

3. The fact that the higher education (high school) was free;

[74]"Der Geist des amerikanischen Bildungswesen," *Hochschule und Ausland*, IX, 13 (January, 1931).

[75]*Demokratie und Erziehung*, 21. Quotation with permission of S. Fischer Verlag.

4. The decentralized system of controls which allowed experimentation;

5. The various efforts being made to allow the gifted to advance more rapidly;

6. The close relationship between school and life which resulted in the great love of students for their school; and

7. The development of this love of schooling by the nature of the relationships existing among the teachers, between children and teachers, and between the parents and their children's school.[76]

The effect of these writings upon German educational philosophy and practice is difficult to assess. Their appears to have been little direct emulation of the American example. But it served to reinforce and solidify reform movements already underway in Germany.[77] It also provided one area in which the German rejection of "Americanization" became somewhat less vehement and positive. As a consequence, it left for the period after World War II a certain residue of good will upon which the educational reforms of that period could be built.[78]

[76][See fn. 1], 638-639.

[77]Oestreich [see fn. 36] noted the influence of American practice in Germany. But see appraisal of Oestreich's relatively minimal influence on reform in R. H. Samuel and R. Hinton Thomas, *Education and Society in Modern Germany* (London, 1949), 68-69. Jürgen Henningsen, *Die Neue Richtung in der Weimarer Zeit* (Stuttgart [c. 1960]) deals with developments in the field of adult education which might be classified as influenced by the United States but does not so label them. The *Einheitsschule* movement probably proceeded on its own initiative rather than the support of the American example—see description by Theodore Huebner, *The Schools of West Germany: a Study of German Elementary and Secondary Schools* (New York, 1962), 17-18.

[78]Huebner's book cited in the previous footnote is the best study of this subject.

Chapter X

"GOD'S OWN CHILDREN"

Religiosity and Fundamentalism: German observers viewed the church-going American with a mixture of amusement and cynicism, counteracted by much unwilling respect and some very real reverence. All of them acknowledged the high place accorded religion in American life. The critical observers were inclined to find evidences of childish superstition and pronounced Phariseeism, to raise doubts of the sincerity or depth of religious convictions, and to emphasize disparities between faith and practice. Sunday was "Lord's day-Ford's day," suggested an Evangelical pastor who found churches vying with the delights of an automobile excursion.[1] But those who studied the American churches most closely, whose views were based upon the soundest research, came away praising the basic piety and will to Christian service, in spite of all the apparent shortcomings. "Everything is less troubled and less burdened over there than it is with us," wrote an officer of the German Evangelical church. "Above all the churches play a significant role in public life, find extensive attention paid by the newspapers to their activities and personalities, and carry on in respect to public and social affairs a great deal of activity attended by some success. Things are very much different over there [in this respect]."[2]

The Americans were imbued, as the Germans saw it, with a highly developed "religiosity." The term conveyed an impression

[1]Devaranne, *Amerika, du hast's nicht besser,* 62-71.

[2]Direktor D. Steinweg, "Nordamerikanische Reiseeindrücke," *Das evangelische Deutschland,* VI (1929), 38. It might be noted that Wilhelm Müller, who had provided an excellent pre-World War I book on American education, had also written an able study of American religion—*Das religiöse Leben in Amerika* (Jena, 1911). Apparently few of the visitors of the 1920's had read this volume, however.

of an emotionalized response to religion, a propagandized status accorded to the religious establishment. It must be remembered that the generation of Germans who came to the United States after World War I was profoundly affected by the scholarly criticism of Christianity which had played a significant role in nineteenth century German scholarship. There was, as one of the visitors, Hermann Sasse, a German Protestant pastor, admitted, a profound cleft between the church and the cultural world back home. Religious skepticism had heavily undermined religious faith in Germany; it had made few inroads into the American consciousness.[3] It was, therefore, virtually a correlative of pretensions to scholarship on the part of the German visitors that they should emphasize the childishness and naïveté of religious life as they observed it in America.

On the other hand, the majority of German religious leaders who came into close contact with American life were favorably impressed. Many remained critical of the status of American theological studies, but the majority found the tone of friendliness and comradeship among American Christians appealing and the depth and breadth of religious observance and faith a welcome contrast to a homeland where the pastor no longer held the place of prestige which had once been his. In America, wrote Dr. Hermann Werdermann, one of the most perceptive and self-critical of all the Germans to visit the United States during the 1920's, "for many millions, many more people than in Germany, the practice of piety and church activity is something fundamental, a major characteristic of their life." It was, he added, the "dollar land" where one found the strongest exemplification of the Bible verse, "Man lives not by bread alone." It was there that one found the strongest struggle against materialism emphasized in America's "Sunday living, its idealistic and Christian striving."[4]

Most German observers found in the word "Puritanism" the major explanation of the strength of American faith. It was in Puritanism that the Swiss evangelical pastor Adolf Keller found the "dynamism" which he considered characteristic of American

[3]Hermann Sasse, *Amerikanisches Kirchentum* (Berlin, 1927), 9; *cf.* Adolf Keller, "Aktivismus und Fundamentalismus in Amerika," *Süddeutsche Monatshefte*, XXV, 673-675 (June, 1928).

[4]*Das religiöse Angesicht Amerikas. Einzeleindrücke und Charakterzüge* (Gütersloh, 1926), 6.

Protestantism.[5] Puritanism, said Keller, had placed its firm stamp on the entire history of American church life. During the long conflict with the wilderness it had been reflected in "the will to struggle, the harsh demands of conscience, the inward sense of personal independence"—those qualities which had made the American people strong and great.[6] And even in the business world of the twenties, Puritan qualities had survived within the influential representatives of American Protestantism—"the earnestness, the stern simplicity, the pursuit of high ethical ideals, the fixity of character created by the power of a determined will to serve God and to conquer the world for Him."[7] Too often, Keller admitted, Puritanism had taken a negative approach to Christian problems: the fight against evil by asceticism and prohibitionism (not only in drink, but in other areas).[8] This could, indeed, lead to hypocrisy, but Keller agreed with Lord Bryce's statement that hypocrisy was less present in America than anywhere else in the world. There was in America, he said, "an unconditional surrender [to God], a stormy impulse in which the whole energy of faith is directed towards the conquest of the world for the practical realization of [religious] ideals."[9]

German visitors were amazed by the continuing "fundamentalism" of American religion. The term received varying definitions: "a stern Bible belief and fanatical Separatism within almost all the great evangelical churches";[10] "the acceptance of the verbal inspiration of the Bible and adherence to chosen basic dogmas, such as the Virgin birth, the atonement by the blood [of Christ], resurrection, and the return of Christ";[11] "the belief in the literal, personal, physical, visible, imminent return of Christ as king on this earth."[12] Fundamentalism, as Schönemann saw it, involved "a mass orthodoxy,"[13] and made it suspect in the popular view to

[5]*Dynamis: Formen und Kräfte des amerikanischen Protestantismus* (Tübingen, 1922).

[6]*Ibid.*, 10.

[7]*Ibid.*

[8]*Ibid.*, 11.

[9]*Ibid.*, 11-12.

[10]Schönemann, *Die Vereinigten Staaten*, II, 248.

[11]Keller, "Aktivismus und Fundamentalismus," see *fn.* 3.

[12]Karl Bornhausen, "Fundamentalismus," *Die Christliche Welt*, XXXVII (1923), 49-50, 746-747.

[13]*Die Vereinigten Staaten*, II, 249.

be an atheist. "The theme of God is not to be discussed in good society," declared Adolf Halfeld, for belief in the Declaration of Independence and in God are common marks of the good citizen.[14] Americans reacted emotionally against "the infamous poison of German theology which is prepared by the devil himself," "the arrogantly, strong and insidious growth of the stinking new theology made in Germany."[15]

The year 1925 had, of course, seen the classic conflict of Darwinism and fundamentalism in the Scopes trial. But the conflict over the doctrine of evolution both preceded and followed this highly publicized event. The early twenties marked the beginning of prohibitions against the teaching of evolution in the schools. This was often harnessed to anti-German feelings and to charges of moral decay in Germany: "Monkey men make monkey morals," or "Germany took on Darwinism, used it literally for the development of the philosophy that might makes right, and threw itself on the helpless world." Fundamentalism bore in German eyes many similarities to what they saw as Ku Klux Klan fascism.[16]

But not all of the German observers joined in the common laughter concerning the monkey trial or in the depreciation of the mass orthodoxy which prevailed. Arthur Holitscher declared:

> that tough, fanatical clinging to the Holy Scriptures is a moral factor in America which one must regard earnestly. In the conflict between conscience, the religious tendency of the American of today, and his economic power position in the world which rises to heights beyond sight, the Bible offers the firm post, the anchor, which prevents the deepest spiritual disintegration in the storming conflicts and contradictions of worldly life.[17]

And Heinrich Frick, Professor of Theology at the University of Marburg, wrote that the spiritual commitment of the American went not half-way like that of the European but to the end and carried with it the courage of convictions (*Konsequenzmut*) of a seventeen-year-old.[18]

[14]*Amerika und der Amerikanismus*, 79.

[15]Bornhausen, "Fundamentalismus," see *fn.* 12.

[16]Bornhausen, "Faszismus und Fundamentalismus in den Vereinigten Staaten," *Die Christliche Welt*, XXXVII (1923), 235-243.

[17]*Wiedersehn*, 72.

[18]"Amerikanische Reiseeindrücke," *Die Christliche Welt*, XL (1926), 897-901.

Adolf Keller saw America in the beginning stages of a religious crisis which was an older and more familiar one in Europe. Indeed, the United States was as yet, he suggested, not completely aware that it faced such a crisis, and the commonly employed solutions for it were not fundamental ones. As a consequence, there was, said Keller, little effort to reconcile theology with the criticisms of science and scholarship. Americans sought to escape the controversy completely, either by a retreat into fundamentalism or a jump forward into religious forms basically ethical rather than theological.[19] Friedrich Schönemann considered this absence of understanding of dogma and of interest in its improvement a danger to spiritual progress.[20] But Schönemann noted that there had always been in America individual free-thinkers who escaped the bonds of conformity to deal with existing problems, and Bornhausen regarded the Unitarian religion as the "religion of the educated" which might be expected to provide forward motion.[21]

2. *The Multiplicity of Faiths*: If the first overwhelming impression of the German in respect to American religious observance was "religiosity," the second was "denominationalism." Germany itself was divided about half and half into Protestant and Catholic. The Protestant portion had tended to amalgamate Lutheran and Calvinist traditions under the aegis of the word "Evangelical." In contrast, the role of Catholicism in the United States was quite restricted, while Protestantism was reflected in a bewildering variety of expressions. Hermann Sasse called this combination of sects "a chaos," pointing out that its origin reflected not only the varied backgrounds of the immigrants who came, but even the time at which they came, so that the Lutherans in America might be divided into three groups, those from the pre-nineteenth century immigration unaffected by higher criticism at home, those who were influenced by the Erlangen theology, and those who were part of the Prussian union movement.[22] But Lutherans were only one of numerous competing sects. The consequence of this variety was that startled Germans found a village of ten thousand souls often having seven competing churches.

[19]"Aktivismus und Fundamentalismus," see *fn.* 3.
[20]*Die Vereinigten Staaten*, II, 249.
[21]*Ibid.*, 251 ff.; Bornhausen, "Fundamentalismus," see *fn.* 12.
[22]*Amerikanisches Kirchentum*, 28.

Adolf Keller, the Swiss evangelical observer, felt that the characteristics of the Protestant groups in the United States were somewhat different from those at home. The Presbyterian denomination, to which he gave first mention, derived from the reform movements of Calvin, Knox, and Zwingli, and was marked by a strong emphasis on teaching, dogmatic orthodoxy, and democratic government. Methodism he characterized as a warm "Christianity of experience and deed." The Baptist element, he said, emphasized strongly a personal Christianity along with the belief in adult baptism. The Anglicans were most like the English church from which they derived. The Congregationalists displayed great variety of theology, while the Lutherans tended to be more rigidly dogmatic than at home and less willing to cooperate with other Protestant groups.[23] Hermann Werdermann added that the social groups concerned also tended to vary—the wealthier elements being found with the Episcopalians and the Congregationalists, the broad masses with the Methodists and the Baptists. Werdermann, like most German observers, regarded the splintering of religion into a sum total of two hundred denominations as unfortunate. It produced, he suggested, a state of affairs which conflicted with any conception of a single Christian church.[24]

However, Werdermann and other Germans believed that a number of circumstances combined to render religious division less catastrophic than it might otherwise have been. One of the most significant, said Werdermann, was the fact that in America the real "anchor point" of religion lay in the individual congregation rather than in the denomination even in those groups where centralized control was strongly emphasized. The congregation was of such a size that the pastor could always maintain close relationships with its members. The members of the congregation knew one another and developed a closeness of spirit. They were bound together by social as well as religious ties—a kind of early Christian "Agape" existed among them. Even athletics had its place in the church—baseball within the sanctuary!—and sometimes movies and dancing. As for the pastor, his role extended beyond matters which were purely spiritual. All in all, suggested Werdermann, the congregational concept was so strongly emphasized in America

[23]"Die religiöse Krisis in Amerika," *Centralblatt des Zofingvereins*, LXXII, 594-602 (1932).

[24]*Das religiöse Angesicht Amerikas*, 209.

that there was no real conception of "church" *per se*, neither in the strongly defined sense of the Catholics nor in the vaguer but still significant notions of German Protestants. This was, he felt, unfortunate. The congregation needed to be part of a larger unity to preserve its true meaning and significance.[25]

The voluntary nature of church membership also tended to mitigate the effects of denominationalism. German visitors were amazed at the willingness of Americans to give monetary support for church activities. The very necessity of the congregation to raise funds for its support, to draw up its budget, and to plan for future needs and for missionary work increased the religious spirit of the congregation and avoided some of the problems that existed in Germany where the state played a role in this process.[26] Moreover, the act of joining a particular church was much more significant in America than in Germany: "One does not . . . belong to the church by birth, but rather through a decision, a personal resolution, a confession."[27] These elements were also bound up with the strongly pronounced "activism" in American church life, which is discussed below.

Furthermore, German observers of the late twenties were already finding breaches being made in the walls between American denominations. Thus Hermann Sasse related that at the Hartford Theological Seminary he joined in a seminar with theologians from twenty-five different churches, and their placement with specific denominations was often by chance, with even unbaptized Quakers becoming the pastors of Congregational churches! And both Sasse and Werdermann related the famous case whereby Dr. Harry Emerson Fosdick became pastor of the Park Avenue Baptist Church in New York, although not himself a Baptist.[28] The Germans were also strong in their praise of the efforts of the Federal Council of Churches to create bridges between denominations and to work together in common religious purposes—as, for example, in a religious census of a community not for the benefit of *a* church but for *the* church.[29] They hoped that the Federal Council through

---

[25]*Ibid.*, 212-220.

[26]*Ibid.*, 214-215.

[27]Keller, *Dynamis*, 6-7.

[28]Sasse, *Am. Kirchentum*, 29; Werdermann, *Das religiöse Angesicht Ams.*, 211-212.

[29]*Ibid.*; *cf.* Keller, *Dynamis*, 22-27.

its activities would help to create for all of the Protestant groups the sense of a larger unity above and beyond the one particular congregation to which they belonged.

3. The Land Without a Counter-Reformation: Most of the German observers were either Protestant or agnostic, and few had much to say about the Catholic Church in America. Their predominant impression was that of overwhelming Protestantism, and a number of them pointed out that the lack of Catholic influence had strongly affected the American cultural pattern. Friedrich Schönemann, for example, characterized the United States as the "land without a counter-reformation" and as having long lacked "a sense for the Middle Ages."[30] The Catholic Church, he suggested, was regarded as not strictly American, first because it depended so largely on the newer immigrants, and secondly because it was universal in scope. During the First World War it had been more moderate in its patriotism than the Protestant denominations. It offered Americans in the post-war era a freer form of living than did the non-German Protestantism and opposed "all narrow, moral reform movements, such as Prohibition, etc." Hence, Schönemann believed that Catholicism had a role in America very much in contrast with that in Europe—supplementing "the cold orthodoxy of middle class Protestantism" with "a somewhat more realistic, warmer, and more popular" religion.[31]

Catholic visitors to America were probably less numerous than the Protestant ones, and fewer of them appear to have had literary inclinations. At any rate there are not many "America books" by Catholic authors. Father Franz Weiser saw large sections of America, but his travel account was light and superficial. So far as Catholicism itself was concerned, he took pride in its unity, the able work of its teaching Sisters, and the success of its schools in the field of sports.[32] The Catholic lay brother Donatus Pfannmüller found much kindness and generosity in his reception everywhere and America more appealing than anticipated.[33] Apparently German Catholic clergy did not often find opportunities for lengthy work in the United States as did some of the Protestants, or if so, they did not write books on the subject.

[30]*Die Vereinigten Staaten*, II, 390-406.   [31]*Ibid.*, 259-263.
[32]*Im Lande des Sternenbanners* (Regensburg, 1933), 65-70.
[33]*So sah ich Amerika, passim.*

As a consequence, there does not appear to have been any German study of the status of American Catholicism comparable to those dealing with the Protestant groups. The closest approach, appearing in a Catholic periodical, gives evidence of being an evaluation by logic rather than an appreciation based upon fundamental study and travel. The author, one Karl Schaezler, bemoaned the fact that the "average American knows very little about Catholicism that does not derive from the polemics of Puritan clergy." But Schaezler could not really regard Catholicism as at all suited to the American scene:

> A religion which is so strongly rooted in mystery and strives for that which is beyond the senses, for which reason does not count as everything and outward success on earth counts for nothing, such a religion must be in its essence completely foreign to the character of the average American of today.

And in a cultureless America, declared Schaezler, the American Catholics were drawing back to a self-centered interest in the church rather than exercising an influence on the world about them. The cultural contributions of American Catholics were negligible. There was, as a consequence, no bright future for Catholicism in America:

> In America, if no change occurs in this situation, not only is no Catholic Renaissance to be expected in the appreciable future and, indeed, all signs of this are lacking, but American Catholics will in the long run not even be able to maintain their hard won position.

Only through a strong and concerted effort to make its influence felt in cultural matters, Schaezler warned, would American Catholicism be able to survive and expand.[34]

Another Catholic spokesman expressed a similar view. "The conquest of Americanism," he wrote, and he meant in Germany as well as in the United States, was "a Catholic educational objective." Americanism, he declared, was "nothing other than a particular form of a new heathenism."[35]

Protestant authors, however, noted that the prospects of Ameri-

[34]"Amerika und die Katholiken," *Hochland*, XXVI, No. 6, 657-660 (March, 1929).

[35]Dr. Adolf Bruck, "Die Überwindung des Amerikanismus—eine katholische Bildungsaufgabe," *Volkswohl*, XXI (1930), No. 3, 90-99.

can Catholicism were not entirely bleak. Karl Bornhausen and Friedrich Schönemann pointed out that Ku Klux Klan activities reflected a fear of the growing strength of the Catholic Church, which had survived the First World War less damaged by controversy than the Protestants. And Schönemann added that the democratization and Americanization of that church in the United States and the fact that it offered its members a freer form of life than did the non-German Protestant groups were winning it new attention.[36]

4. Activism: Christ among the Skyscrapers; the Social Gospel: In contrast to pessimistic evaluations of the future of the Catholic church in America, most of the accounts of Protestant fortunes were highly optimistic. Adolf Keller, whose book has already been noted, indicated his view of American Protestantism in the title he gave the volume, "Dynamis," "the moving force." The concept of activity which the term implied, of a close relationship between church and life, permeated the accounts of most of the visitors.

For some, of course, American religious idealism carried with it a sour taste. One such critic contrasted the concept of "Jesus Christ amidst the skyscrapers" with the realities of the harsh reception of immigrants on Ellis Island and the lack of concern for one another she found on the part of Americans. Christ didn't rule America, she proclaimed, and the idea of replacing the Statue of Liberty with a statue of Christ she found most inappropriate. If such a statue were erected, she stated, it would have to be one of Christ suspended on the "golden cross" of America.[37]

Although this was an extreme expression of the criticism of American materialism, and one contradicted by most serious observers, there was a very strong current of concern in respect to the entry of the market place into the church itself. This derived very

[36]Schönemann, *Die Vereinigten Staaten*, II, 261-64; Bornhausen, *Der christliche Aktivismus Nordamerikas in der Gegenwart* (Giessen, 1925), 11. A. Pfeffer, editor of the Munich *Allgemeine Rundschau*, also sketched the history of the German Catholics in America, their critical position under the pressure of the Ku Klux Klan, but their survival and strength in spite of obstacles, as witnessed by flourishing religious orders and an extensive press. "Ku-Klux-Klan, Deutschtum, und Katholizismus in Nordamerika," *Allgemeine Rundschau*, XX, No. 5, 50 (February 3, 1923).

[37]Clara Mendel, "Jesus Christus zwischen den Wolkenkratzern," *Weser Zeitung*, August 25, 1925.

largely from the methods of increasing monetary contributions by unseemly appeals on the part of some ministers. Arthur Holitscher, for example, recounted an incident in which the pastor started the circulation of the collection plates with the comment that the church in America had created the existing prosperity and the collection ought to be a "proper even if small requital for this."[38] Another source cited the slogan, "Invest your money in God."[39] And Werdermann described the money-drawing tactics of the traveling evangelist who even sold his fountain pen in his fund raising efforts, but with the accompanying comment that this was not, of course, typical.[40]

Perhaps even more disturbing to Germans, indeed verging close to sacrilege, was the tendency to identify Christ and the successful American businessman. Undoubtedly the origins of the idea lay in Bruce Barton's widely read volume, *The Man Nobody Knows*. There, indeed, Christ was pictured as a man of organizing ability, a man who used catch phrases similar to modern advertising techniques, a man who rose from humble beginnings to great success. And there was even the comparison of Christ's ideal of service to humanity to that of the American businessman, whose first ideal (supposedly) was selling a product useful to the masses rather than making a fortune. Arthur Holitscher reported that the idea of Christ as "the first American" was being carried widespread across the nation by a league of prominent business men who sought to emphasize the idea of "service." For Americans, he suggested, "Menschendienst"—"service to men"—meant also "Gottesdienst"—"service to God"—and was virtually a religious concept. "Christ is the unseen honorary president of all such unions and conventions [devoted to human service]."[41] Another critic declared that Americans were going even a step further and claiming the dear Lord himself as the first American because of His technical ability: he employed anesthesia to perform the operation on Adam by which he produced Eve![42]

[38]*Wiedersehn*, 56.
[39]"Amerikanismus," *Weser Zeitung*, June 12, 1929.
[40]*Das religiöse Angesicht Ams.*, 58-59.
[41]*Wiedersehn*, 65-70.
[42]Dr. R. Burkhard, "Die Gefahr des Yankeetums," *Grüne Blätter*, XII, No. 32, 522 (August 10, 1930)—citing sermon of a Baptist preacher in Los Angeles.

As usual in this area, the concept aroused less concern among the professionals than among the laity. The Rev. Hermann Sasse, after describing Barton's book, wrote that it sought to show that if Christ were still living, he would approve American civilization in principle:

> The basic ideal of this piety is that Christianity is something which belongs to this given world and to this American civilization. Between Christianity and civilization there exists a pre-established harmony. They do not cover one another, as every American would admit at once, since we are not yet perfect Christians and our civilization is still incomplete, but they both work toward the same goal: the perfection of the church coincides with the perfection of civilization.[43]

Sasse, like other serious students of American church life, then proceeded to explore the many facets of what Germans designated "American Activism," the concept that religion is embodied more strongly in deeds than in beliefs. Sasse's tone of profound respect was shared by Hermann Werdermann, by Adolf Keller, to a considerable degree by Heinrich Frick, and reluctantly by Karl Bornhausen. All of those who made careful study of the religious establishment of the United States during the 1920's rejected charges of hypocrisy and praised the sense of sacrifice and service which it embodied.

All American church membership, suggested Keller, was the reflection of a conscious choice, "a confession." In this confession dogma and formulae were of significance—"But the best confession is the [Christian] deed."[44] This sense of a need to express Christianity in action, said Keller, was the most important factor in the vitality of American religion:

> A vital and well-developed lay activism, such as most of the American churches possess, keeps alive that personal element, that full-hearted participation and inward warmth involved in this Christian world, gives the individual believer the opportunity for sacrifice and so fills his life and his convictions with active drives and personal sacrifices.[45]

From this activism, the American, continued Keller, expected "that a goal would be reached, a practical consequence would

---

[43]*Am. Kirchentum*, 14.
[44]*Dynamis*, 7.
[45]*Ibid.*, 8. Quotations with permission of J. C. B. Mohr Verlag.

result."[46] Religion was, therefore, combined with the pragmatism of William James: "This religious pragmatism lies in the blood of the American." American Protestantism, therefore, was "a dynamic Christianity, that sets in motion not so much the understanding or the feeling as the will, takes in hand mighty initiatives and presses with all its force toward accomplishments, action, practical changes, occasionally indeed at the cost of inwardness and depth [of feeling]."[47]

This tone of pragmatism comprehended in the so-called "social gospel" permeated the whole work of the church. It was a concept of a "seven day religion," not one restricted to Sunday alone.[48] In the Sunday service, noted Werdermann, the sermon dominated the whole proceedings, and the gospel of Christ's love and of the Christian's responsibility in consequence of it formed the motif. Werdermann made, perhaps, the most thorough and sympathetic study of the subject of any German. He summarized the substance of more than thirty American sermons which he had heard. He copied down innumerable sermon topics and read extensively on the subject. Frequently, he suggested, the Bible text provided only the launching pad for a discourse far removed from theology—"Are wedding bells a delusion?"; "What it costs not to be a Christian"; "Why do women use powder?" and "Is kissing a sin?" The real measure of the sermon was, he found, "closeness to life."[49]

Similarly, Sasse also stressed the effort of the churches to create "the vision of a reconstruction of human society" proceeding from "a deeper conception of the Gospel," accompanied by "shame that the church had been so long . . . 'a silent watchdog.' "[50] He added a listing of the goals of the Federal Council of Churches set up in 1908, such as the ending of child labor, the protection of women workers, and improvement of the unfavorable position of the American worker.[51] He pointed out that the goals of the Federal Council had found a sympathetic reception on the part of some enterprisers and declared in summary:

[46]Ibid., 12-13.
[47]Ibid., 13-14.
[48]Bornhausen, Der christliche Aktivismus Nordams., 16.
[49]Das religiöse Angesicht Ams., 238-239.
[50]Am. Kirchentum, 118.
[51]Ibid., 119-121.

The churches of America are therewith making for the whole world an experiment, whose outcome is not yet to be seen. Europe, in general, accords to church life, its power and effectiveness, particularly in social and political matters, an influence upon public opinion, but scarcely anything more effective. Our religious conceptions lead us no longer to expect to gain everything from effort, from the organization and good will of human forces, and has taken on a good portion of patience in waiting and enduring hope in [place of] the former optimistic activism. America, especially the Middle West, thinks otherwise in this matter. Great practical tasks, world-wide visions are to her motives for the greatest efforts even in the area of church and religious activities, and a young, optimistic faith expects much from this human dynamism devoted to the purposes of the Supreme Being. But in this struggle it still remains to be seen whether behind the programs and proclamations, behind the resolutions of commissions and conferences, behind the demands of individual leaders and groups, yes, even behind the whole range of these efforts, stands the awakened feeling of the religious masses, the conscience and the determined will of all the church-going people; whether the faith of a great community of a Christian nation is effective in this matter.[52]

In a similar manner, Adolf Keller spoke of "the will to service" which he found need of in the Old World as in the New.[53] But both he and Werdermann expressed the fear that this social welfare work might be "a flight from a deepening [of theological knowledge] in a horizontal direction." Nevertheless, he admitted that in the face of social need, of the problems of immigration, of the Negro question, and of the problems of providing church facilities for such a broad geographical area, this dynamism was much needed.[54] The American, declared Werdermann, looked for the kingdom of God on this earth—it was not to be an accomplishment of some later day but of the present. American preaching might be theologically faulty, but it gave a powerful drive for the expression of practical piety. And in America the church and the working class remained on good terms, not holding themselves separate and apart as they did in Germany. Concern for child labor, the work of women, the safety of workers, etc. had made the church an institution acceptable to American laborers.[55]

[52]*Ibid.*, 125-126.   [53]*Dynamis*, 15.   [54]*Ibid.*, 16.

[55]*Das religiöse Angesicht Ams.*, 251 ff.; cf. Keller, *Dynamis*, 111-118. Paul Knapp, a member of a German YMCA club, reported also, as he attended a

Many of the clerical commentators also found the linking of the church and the prohibition movement proper and desirable. German impressions of the effects of prohibition were often more favorable than the views of Americans as they look back upon that era. Some German visitors, in spite of speak-easies, found far less evidence of drunkenness than existed at home and considered that the movement had aided the working man and his family to remove one obstacle to their material and spiritual well-being.[56]

They also spoke of the work of the churches in developing racial understanding. These churches had been from the first, said Keller, the educators and leaders of the Negroes and their spokesmen. And he added, "The Negroes belong with their deep and inward religiosity among the truest members of the churches, and understand in spite of all identification as [Christian] brothers that this is not the same as a withdrawal or lifting of all social bars between races." Consequently, he predicted, they would continue to establish their own churches, largely Methodist or Baptist in denomination, within the larger Southern churches. Also, Keller added, the responsibility for finding a solution of the racial problem had been laid upon the heart and conscience of the Christian people of America.[57]

But American religious dynamism expressed itself not only at home but also, and perhaps more strikingly, abroad. With the objective stated by I. R. Mott, the leader of the Student Voluntary Mission Movement, "The Evangelization of the world in this generation," Americans had taken a leading role in the missionary movement. Their activism had been communicated to the Edinburgh World Missions Conference in 1910 and had won the hearts

---

World Congress of Christian Young Men held in the United States, that the American YMCA clubs were much more concerned with social ideals and philosophy than the German ones, where a confessional emphasis obtained. *Fahrten und Erlebnisse in Amerika* (Königsberg [1931]), 17-18.

[56]The most careful study of prohibition and its effects was Marta Küppersbosch, *Das Alkoholverbot in Amerika. Die Nationale Prohibition in den Vereinigten Staaten und ihre volkswirtschaftliche Bedeutung* (München, 1923). Defense of the prohibition law is found in Sonnenschein, *Eindrücke eines Verwaltungsbeamten*, 8; Devaranne, *Amerika, du hast's nicht besser*, 27; Hans Goslar, "Amerika, wie es isst und trinkt," *Vossische Zeitung*, April 15, 1922; Keller, *Dynamis*, 108-111.

[57]*Dynamis*, 104-107.

FIGURE 3.—"The Liquor War." Sketch from Hans Christoph Kaergel, "Klein-igkeiten aus dem grossen Amerika," *Die Bergstadt*, XIV (1926), 465-76.

of all its delegates.[58] Moreover, Americans had made dramatic and direct contributions to missionary work. At the time Keller made his appraisal there were in America 167 missionary boards and an army of 12,000 missionaries abroad.[59] The American missionary movement differed from those abroad in the significance of the work of women in this area.

Keller found the American contribution to missionary work the product of "a great, worldwide vision, of an active, religious fantasy." But he also noted some drawbacks—the fact that this missionary work was too often the key to commercial activity, and that there was too much impatience joined to it, too much faith in numbers and rapid accomplishment. This often led to superficiality and outward effects rather than real accomplishment measured by deep, inward change on the part of those who had been the objects of the missionary activity. But in spite of all faults, he stated, the missionary movement did portray the outcomes of "an energy of love."[60]

Bornhausen, on his part, dealt at length with the activity of American missionaries in Africa, China, and Japan, noting that too often in the past they had ignored native religions and cultural life, a defect they were beginning to repair.[61] But he feared the consequences of the unconscious nature of the American, "the born propagandist," who sought to make over into the American mold those to whom he preached. This was, felt Bornhausen, a danger in the mission field even as it was in Germany itself.[62]

5. Christian Science, Spiritualists, and Evangelists: It was, of course, to be expected that foreign visitors would devote considerable attention to those aspects of religious life in America which were novel for them. The Christian Science movement held in this respect undisputed first place. Few German visitors failed to mention it.

The German attitude toward the burgeoning movement founded by Mary Baker Eddy was often quite favorable. At least it was a native American development. It combined American op-

[58]Bornhausen, *Der christliche Aktivismus Nordams.*, 19-20.
[59]*Dynamis*, 93.
[60]*Ibid.*, 96-98.
[61]*Der christliche Aktivismus Nordams.*, 35.
[62]*Ibid.*, 47.

timism with religious orthodoxy and American pragmatism.[63] Moritz J. Bonn called Christian Science "the most successful ecclesiastical foundation of modern times" and praised it for freeing believers from the fear of Hell and replacing "the stern God of the old Puritans" with one who made men glad and happy. It had, he added, also "infused fresh life into the forms of American architecture" and made the church "no longer a reformatory where the natural instincts are disciplined by prison rules, but a psychological clinic in which inhibitions are removed and Freudian complexes resolved."[64]

The most thorough German study of Christian Science during this period was contained in the series of articles by Stefan Zweig on "The Life and Teachings of Mary Baker Eddy."[65] Zweig drew a word picture of Mrs. Eddy's life which devastatingly laid bare her human weaknesses, but he softened his caustic criticism with an acknowledgment of her will power and ability to inspire and inflame her auditors. He also paid tribute to the resolute effort she gave to the production of her first book, *Science and Health*, which he labeled one of "those most remarkable books of a private theologian, those meteoric works which, though completely uncohesive, strike down from the heavens into the midst of their times."[66] It was, he said, a weird concoction:

> The swindlerish and the creative alternate in a pattern of wild chess moves; the most contrary influences whirl about in confusion; Swedenbourg's astral mysticism is joined with popular knowledge from ten-penny books; near a Bible quotation there are excerpts from New York newspapers; dazzling pictures are drawn next to the most ridiculous and childlike statements; but, undeniably, this mass of whirling words is always hot; it glows and quivers and steams from spiritual passion; it produces the most wonderful bubbles; and if one stares long enough into this constantly glowing, boiling cauldron, one's eyes begin to burn. One loses sober understanding and feels himself transported into Faust's

[63]Schönemann, *Die Vereinigten Staaten*, II, 285-286.

[64]*American Adventure*, 270.

[65]"Das Leben und die Lehre der Mary Baker Eddy," *Die neue Rundschau*, XLI (1930), Part I, 610-641; 770-799; Part II, 14-60. The greater part of this appeared in translation by Eden and Cedar Paul in *Mental Healers: Franz Anton Mesmer, Mary Baker Eddy, Sigmund Freud* (Garden City, New York [c. 1932]). However, the first of Zweig's essays which traced her early life is omitted.   [66]*Ibid.*, Part I, 786.

witch's kitchen and believes that, like him, he hears "a hundred thousand fools" speaking. But the circling chaos presses constantly upon one single point; again and again Mary Baker-Eddy hammers this one and only idea into one's skull until one is more stunned than convinced. Looking at it solely as a spiritual accomplishment, as the achievement of a fully untaught, uneducated woman, one must recognize as magnificent how she with the feverish drive of her obsession spins this idea in increasing fury until sun, moon, and stars, the entire universe, rotate about it.[67]

Throughout Zweig pictures a fanatical and tyrannical personality alienating friends and converts but always pushing forward the promulgation of her beliefs. In the end result, he suggested, she had acquired "a permanent place among the pioneers of psychology, of the science of the soul, illustrating once more that in the history of the human spirit the uninstructed and unteachable impetuosity of a seeming simpleton may do as much for the advancement of thought as all the exponents of accredited doctrine."[68]

Spiritualists also received notice and condemnation from Germans, who rejoiced at their exposure.[69] But far more attention and much more critical comment was reserved for mercenary evangelists and sensationalist preachers. Holitscher described at length the services conducted in Manhattan by one Dr. Christian F. Reisner with an accompaniment of a boy's choir, a lady's brass quartet, sandwiches and apples, movies, and fiery denunciations of his opponent Mencken. Reisner, said Holitscher, combined all of the qualities of "the naive, primitive, and at the same time practical and pragmatic American enterpriser."[70] And Werdermann detailed at length the course of a St. Louis revival meeting with the sweating evangelist, the personal testimonies, and the "conversions": "For many it is only a straw-fire, this conversion, and many need their repeated, even yearly, awakenings."[71]

6. Christianity and the Star-Spangled Banner: The cynical German journalist Adolf Halfeld discussed religion in America under the heading "the American God," and employed such sub-headings as

[67]*Ibid.*

[68]Following Eden and Cedar Paul translation, *Mental Healers*, 247.

[69]Graf Carl von Klinckowstroem, "Neues von amerikanischen Schwindelmedien," *Kölnische Zeitung*, November 6, 1929.

[70]*Wiedersehn*, 84-89.   [71]*Das religiöse Angesicht Ams.*, 50-53; 58-59.

"the Nation created by the Grace of God" and "God's Own Children."[72] Other Germans, though less critical, commented on the presence of the American flag in all the churches, the patriotic tones of various sermons, the use of patriotic songs as part of the church services, and the strongly nationalist position taken by many American pastors.[73] "In America," suggested Schönemann, "religion is still a national affair. . . ."[74]

As a consequence, suggested many observers, the vaunted separation of church and state was often misleading. This doctrine, declared the visiting professor of religion Heinrich Frick, ignored "the extraordinarily strong influence of the churches on the public and the expressed recognition of them by public opinion."[75] He and other Germans cited many exceptions to this alleged separation—the use of chaplains by Congress, the proclamation of Thanksgiving Day as a national as well as a religious holiday, and religious observances in the schools. The church, they pointed out, reinforced the efforts of the state internally by the assistance it gave in the "Americanization" of immigrants; it advanced the interests of the state externally through the work of foreign missions, which often brought trade along with the Gospel.[76] All in all, stated Schönemann, "Although there is no 'official religion,' still unofficially the Christianity of the churches is recognized as a self-evident basis for the life of the state."[77]

Frick, on his part, believed that the absolute separation of church and state had outlived its usefulness and augured difficulties for the future position of the church. He found the institution of religious instruction in the schools of New York and other parts of the East a successful experiment, wisely defended by the churches as a necessity in constructing a Christian community. This involved no creation of a state church, but the recognition that religion was neither entirely "an affair of the state" nor "an affair of the individual" but "a public affair." What should be created, he suggested, was a situation in which

---

[72]*Amerika und der Amerikanismus*, 78-83.

[73]*E.g.*, Werdermann, *Das religiöse Angesicht Ams.*, 242-243, 248-249.

[74]*Die Vereinigten Staaten*, II, 244.

[75]"Amerikanische Reiseeindrücke," 6, *Die Christliche Welt*, XL (1926), 434-437.

[76]*Ibid.*; *cf.* Schönemann, *Die Vereinigten Staaten*, II, 244-247.

[77]*Ibid.*, 247.

the religious communities would be recognized as public forces, protected and indeed supported, but on the basis of free relationships with the state, which will provide freedom of movement for every popular trend. Over against the concept of a stabilized state church an instable relationship; and over against a purely private matter shoved away from public view, an expressly cultivated public concern.[78]

And, Frick added, this was the solution which was likely to be adopted with respect to the organized Christian churches in America in the near future.

Frick's optimism was shared by most German observers. They regarded the role of the churches as secure and firm. The churches were the counterpart of American prosperity and democratic government. "The truth of the lessons of a democratic social organization is, accordingly, clearly apparent to the American," wrote Hermann Sasse. "The truth of the Gospel is to him equally evident. The task of theology, therefore, is to combine the two and bring them into agreement." In America, he believed, there was such widespread recognition of the connection between progress and God's grace that the church was universally accepted as confirming and supporting the whole complex of the national civilization.[79]

7. *The Future of the Faith*: The tone of optimism in the appraisals of America's churches by many German visitors has been reflected in much of the discussion above. But this did not prevent some very trenchant criticism.

The most serious deficiency in the American religious establishment, felt many of its German students, lay in the absence of depth both in theological training and in the nature of the sermons preached by American pastors. Werdermann, it has already been seen, praised the closeness to life, the practicality, the activism of American churches. These things were, he admitted, seriously lacking in German churches. But he added a warning to Americans:

If in Germany the kingdom of God is conceived of and preached about perhaps too much as a matter of afterlife and the extra-temporal and thereby features of the preaching of Jesus are neglected which look towards the realization [of

[78]"Amerikanische Reiseeindrücke," 7, *Die Christliche Welt*, XL (1926), 529-533.

[79]*Am. Kirchentum*, 16.

His kingdom] here on earth, in America, on the other hand, the other-worldliness of the kingdom of God and the majesty of God are pushed too much into the background; yes, they almost disappear into that which takes place on earth and which the Christian and the man does as an individual.[80]

The consequence, he suggested, was that the stream of religion in America was broader, but not so deep as in Germany. In both countries efforts were being made to correct these deficiencies—in Germany to increase the influence of religion on everyday life; in America to find greater inwardness and religious depth.[81]

Part of the difficulties in America, suggested Werdermann, lay with the lack of preparation of theological students. Often without full high school training, seldom with preparation in Latin let alone Hebrew or Greek, most were not really capable of fundamental Biblical scholarship. On the other hand, he admitted, they brought with them earnestness and zeal, and some of their deficiencies in books of knowledge were made good by study in "the book of life."[82]

Studies in American seminaries, related Werdermann, included courses unknown in German institutions: "Religious education," "Sociology," "Rural life," etc. His concern about this dispersion of work was voiced even more strongly by a Pastor Joseph Bauer, writing in Germany's Reformed Church periodical, who described a Chicago "divinity school" which he said did not deserve the name. Nothing of real "Godliness' was taught; its professors offered exemplifications of "historicism," "sociological pragmatism," and "behaviorism." True theology was completely ignored.[83] Werdermann, similarly, had found exegetical classes at Eden Seminary weaker than in Germany due to the shortcomings of both sudents and professors. Again, therefore, the American pastor received far more practical training than his German counterpart, but also a much more superficial one.[84] Too many pastors, especially those in the smaller towns with competing churches, tended to preach "more loud than deep."[85] But, he added, they lived closer to their

[80]*Das religiöse Angesicht Ams.*, 252.
[81]*Ibid.*, 253.
[82]*Ibid.*, 262-263.
[83]"Universitätstheologie in U.S.A.," *Reformierte Kirchenzeitung,* **LXXX** (1930), 44-45.
[84]*Das religiöse Angesicht Ams.*, 266-267.
[85]*Ibid.*, 290.

congregations than in Germany and in spite of their deficiencies they were held in respect by those they served.[86]

And, lastly, denominationalism in America tended to deny the concept of a single God for all. The efforts to breach the divisions have been noted above, but many of those from abroad were somewhat skeptical of American ecumenical efforts. Sasse noted that real unity was only possible upon the basis of substantial doctrinal agreement.[87] But Keller wrote that an actual "immanent Christian unity" existed. It was only necessary to realize this; and America, he added, brought to this problem more energy and optimism than any other nation.[88] And, in a similar vein, missions-inspector Steinweg wrote, "One has, in spite of the strong church divisions, the picture of a certain unity of church life not only in forms but also in views."[89]

Perhaps Keller also suggested best the future role of American churches when he set forth his conclusions at the close of his book:

> The American soul has, however, not yet reached the limits of its strength. It is still young, dynamically constituted, boundlessly optimistic, hungry for action. . . . To her the task has been given for today, to carry this fire [of faith] out into the wide world, to give vent to her new dynamic impulse, and to do deeds which we cannot do.[90]

From America, he stated, was to be expected more than material aid. She could give to religion "a vital drive, an out-pouring of spirit and love, a challenge of man's conscience."[91] But for Europeans, he added, remained the task of deepening the soul, of finding the rich inwardness, the quiet faith which joins together this world and the next by a continuing search for new truths.[92]

---

[86]*Ibid.*, 301-302. Keller's appraisal was similar. American seminaries he suggested, trained "preachers" rather than theologians. *Dynamis*, 91-92.

[87]*Am. Kirchentum*, 48.

[88]*Dynamis*, 155, 159.

[89]"Nordamerikanische Reiseeindrücke," *Das evangelische Deutschland*, VI (1929), 38-40.

[90]*Dynamis*, 162.

[91]*Ibid.*, 83.

[92]*Ibid.*

Chapter XI

"AMERICANISM" AND THE "AMERICANIZATION" OF GERMANY

The Search for Generalization: In 1929 as Arthur Holitscher looked about him at the rapidly changing countenance of New York City, his thoughts sped halfway across the world to the Ukrainian city of Kharkov. Different in size, both revealed change and growth. He recalled that a People's Commissar in the Kremlin had once commented on the twin roles of the United States and the Soviet Union:

> We and they—are the two poles of contemporary time. But one day we shall no longer be poles; rather the two ends of development will run together, strive with one another, drive violently into each other [*ineinanderschlagen*]. Thus it will come about, and the result will determine the fate of mankind.

And Holitscher added: "Two worlds and the same time, two aspects of power grown from a common root, [dedicated] to the service of mankind from the same instinct, the same unfolding of will power, of the secret, unrecognized, but ever active energy of human thought and feeling."[1]

America, then, was one of the two great symbols of the new world which confronted Germans and other Europeans after World War I. Instinctively, there was somewhat more sympathy for the United States than for the Soviet Union.[2] But the German could study neither with real detachment. They were a part of his own "problems"; each posed a particular kind of menace to that which he held of value. Of the two, America perhaps impinged more sharply on his consciousness than the Soviet Union. Scholars and businessmen, teachers and preachers, doctors and lawyers, wide segments of the German population were met daily by the chal-

[1]*Wiedersehn*, 12. Quotations with permission of S. Fischer Verlag.
[2]See, for example, Prosinagg's comments, *Das Antlitz Amerikas*, 278-279.

lenges of what they called "Americanism." But even as they used the term, many were aware of its meaninglessness. It was a symbol of nameless fears of the future; it was a sign of dynamic change and great accomplishment. It aroused more emotion than reflection, more feeling than logical thinking.[3]

One of the less felicitous books of the well-known dramatist Herbert Eulenberg was a crude satire relating with would-be humor the adventures of "Amerikanus." Returning from the land of the giants to that of the pygmies, he and two friends, "Paukenschlag" ["drum beat"] and "Lafette," formed an "American club." With a flag of fourteen stripes (to keep off bad luck) and much poor poetry, they kept alive the memory of the great days of their travel abroad.[4] The unconcealed malice of this satire found its reflection in most of the "America books" and articles of the twenties. Their authors wrote with a purpose—the hope of arresting the tide of "Americanization" in Germany. But between the lines lay hopelessness and futility—they were seeking to sweep back the tide with a broom. Frustration increased their anger. And it vitiated their objectivity.

It seems obvious that the majority of visitors to the United States during the Weimar era came to see what they wanted to see—to enjoy the satisfaction of bolstering pre-existent fears, of reinforcing pre-existent judgments. This is clear from the tone of the books which they wrote, which set forth generalizations on America beginning with the first day they stepped from their trans-Atlantic steamer. And the passion with which these generalizations were made indicates that their basis was more often an emotional than a rational one.

For a second and smaller group of German travelers the cliché generalizations were familiar and were repeated, but enough objectivity remained to allow aberrations from standardized viewpoints, sudden gasps of surprise at that which was different from what had been anticipated, and occasionally even the realization of the need for an overall re-evaluation.

There was, of course, a small minority of "Amerika-Schwärmer," enthusiastic apologists. Many of the "America books"

[3]This chapter was written before the author had read Peter Berg's, *Deutschland und Amerika, 1918-1929*. Berg's treatment of this theme is strikingly similar to the author's in many places—see 132-153.

[4]Herbert Eulenberg, *Amerikanus. Amerikanische Lichtbilder* (Wien, 1924).

critical of the United States refer with disdain to the "flood" of books praising the overseas "wonder." But the circle of literary admirers seems amazingly small—Alfred Kerr, Emil Müller-Sturmheim, Otto Moog, Rudolf Hensel, Carl Brinkmann, Arthur Feiler, Adolf Keller, Erwin Carlé (Rosen), Hermann Lufft, Alfred Rundt, Hermann Werdermann, Anton Erkelenz, Friedrich von Gottl-Ottlilienfeld—these and others wrote of the United States with some friendship and appreciation. But *"Schwärmer,"* "enthusiast," the word seems fitting only with respect to Kerr. Obviously many of the critics were concerned with non-literary opponents. Obviously they were troubled by a mood, an atmosphere, which surrounded them in Weimar Germany. And they sought to counter it more on the basis of metaphysics than on the basis of factual observations and fully documented conclusions.

The "America books," then, were strongly stamped with the personal equation. For many of their authors they were part of a search for themselves, part of an effort to define their own *Weltanschauungen* or to assure themselves of the rightness of the existing *Weltanschauungen*. They could not, therefore, restrict their coverage to sections, or topics, or limited chronological periods. They needed to interpret America as a whole, to reach generalizations explaining and clarifying the New World and relating it to the Old. These generalizations, however shaky their foundations, comprised a declaration of faith—in most cases a renewed allegiance to European traditions; in a few cases, a call for the spirit of progress and of adjustment to new conditions and patterns of life.

2. *American "Characteristics"*: In 1922 one of the cartoons in *Der Welt-Spiegel*, the weekly illustrated edition of the *Berliner Tageblatt*, portrayed "the gent Teddy" suffering a "tragic moment"—he had just discovered that his efforts to look like an American were a failure. Pictured was a foppishly dressed German boy hunched forward in an ill-fitting jacket across whose path strode a real American, portrayed as a well-built and impeccably dressed man, whose figure expressed energy, and whose countenance revealed assurance and determination.[5]

But if "Teddy" was disappointed that he didn't look like an American, there were many Germans of his day thanking God

[5]May 28, 1922.

that no resemblance could be discovered between themselves and these unpleasant figures from abroad. The caricature of the American which emerged from the travel accounts of the period was anything but flattering.

In many respects the 1920's produced a much darker view of the American than that which had existed prior to the First

FIGURE 4.—The popularity of the ice-cream soda (instead of beer) was satirized in this sketch from Hans Christoph Kaergel, "Kleinigkeiten aus dem grossen Amerika," *Die Bergstadt*, XIV (1926), 465-76.

World War. Until then the most famous portrait of the American produced by a German was that drawn by Hugo Münsterberg. Münsterberg had found the American marked by five leading characteristics: "the spirit of self-direction,"[6] "the spirit of self-realization,"[7] "the spirit of self-perfection,"[8] "the spirit of self-assertion,"[9] and "the spirit of self-satisfaction."[10] Although these characteristics

[6]*The Americans*, tr. E. B. Holt (New York, 1907), 3-34.
[7]*Ibid.*, 230-254.
[8]*Ibid.*, 348-364.
[9]*Ibid.*, 531-557.
[10]*Ibid.*, x—"whose story I have forgotten to include in this volume."

were mentioned in the postwar period, they were stated in such exaggerated terms that the positive connotations were virtually lost.

Predominant—it has already appeared in many forms in the preceding portions of this volume—was the charge that Americans were purely materialist in their view of life. No one stated it more emphatically than did Adolf Halfeld in his *Amerika und der Amerikanismus* and perhaps no one more picturesquely than one of the reviewers of his book who noted that it dealt with the brutal rule of the God "money," and with "mechanized mass-man, over-burdened with his work, dully feminine, insecure, [living] in the soulless stone deserts of the city."[11]

A part of this materialism was the worship of success, the love of figures, of "records," of "prosperity."[12] Also implied was a willing acceptance of the processes of mechanization and standardization of life. As Joseph Draim saw it, this was the major component of Americanism, which he defined as "a spiritual attitude and viewpoint on life which sees the true goals of existence in the raising of living standards, in material success, in technical progress, and in the accumulation of power and wealth."[13]

This overemphasis of the material resulted, believed many Germans, in what they labeled the "soullessness" and "culturelessness" of Americans. As Draim phrased it,

> Under the influence of Americanism the dominance of economics over man's personal life and his cultural accomplishments sets in. In modern economic life the human personality declines in its meaning and in its display of spiritual qualities; individuality is caught up in the whirlpool of production and can scarcely maintain itself in the presence of machinery directed toward pure gain. Tied to a scientifically conceived division of labor, man is changed to a machine and by the uttermost spur to his working power, he becomes an object of exploitation. Everything personal and living freezes under the stern law of economic return. Eco-

[11]"Amerikanismus: Betrachtungen zu dem Werk Halfelds: Amerika und der Amerikanismus," *Der Volkserzieher*, 1928, Beilage, "Der Bücherfreund," Blatt 1.

[12]This and other characteristics dealt with below form a part of the "Abriss des amerikanischen Volkstums," in Adolar Angermann, *The Ways of the Americans. Lesebuch zur amerikanischen Wesenskunde für Oberklassen* (Bielefeld, 1932), 88.

[13]"Der Amerikanismus," *Pharus*, XXIII (1932), No. 10, 237-241 at 238.

nomic values and viewpoints are alone significant, all-important. The consequences of such a businessman's calculating viewpoint is the loss of the idealist drive, of the natural instinct for the secrets of life relationships, of the ability to sacrifice and of the power of organic growth. Human qualities recede and the nature of labor leaves man no longer the possibility for the unfolding of personality. The reign of a purely economic thinking has as its consequence the destruction of personality and of common culture.[14]

Dr. Otto Conrad agreed. "His [the American's] soul is rationalized," he wrote; "it weighs everything by numbers and by the measure of money."[15] One of the characters in a Jakob Wassermann novel expressed the same conclusion much more pointedly: "There were [in America] things, things, things; for a hundred years there could be no talk of the spirit."[16]

And Robert Müller asserted that the materialism of American life placed an unmistakable stamp on the features of the American. "Life there [in America]," he wrote, "is forced, flat, and meager; in the big cities it is under more spiritual pressure than in our provincial villages [Krähwinkel]." And, he charged, "Social pressure is greater than anywhere else; the life of the spirit and of freely-reached opinions, of nerves, of the erotic, and of private affairs is more restricted and more solidary than anywhere else in the world." All of these things, he asserted, combined to produce the typical American:

> The American we conceive as neither blond nor blue-eyed nor brunette nor straight-haired, nor of a particular complexion; he is much more, as once was true of the Jews and of the Romans, an arrangement of features and a style which can be given that particular assessment. Actually men of all European and Asiatic origins are so much altered after they have worked awhile in American business enterprises that they could be taken for original, native-born Americans. . . . Accordingly, what we regard as the American physiognomy in the physical sense is the expression of an abstract power of personality. The powers of understanding are hypertrophied; the factual intelligence, the managerial

14Ibid., 238-239.
15"Amerikanismus und Ethik," Brunsviga Monatshefte, XVI (1929), No. 7/8, 320.
16Quoted, Kurt von Wistinghausen, "Amerika-Europa," Die Christengemeinschaft, V (1928), 122-123.

abilities, the stored-up energy which the individual produces in his labor, have left their stylistic marks upon his countenance.[17]

But the activism which Müller described seldom won respect. "Nature," wrote German railway magnate, Oskar Sommer, "gives us material and means to build houses of fifty-four stories. On the other hand nature seldom brings two-story men."[18] This was particularly true of Americans. Germans almost universally deplored the retarded mentality of Americans! Americans couldn't even talk, complained Dr. Paul Rohrbach; "they go to shows and watch silently; they go to dances and watch silently; they go for rides and kiss silently."[19] The use of the term "big children" for Americans, the recurrence of such phrases as "rationalized soul" and "spiritual leveling" have been mentioned above. "Doing" was accomplished at the cost of "thinking." "To be interested in purely intellectual matters," wrote a German school teacher on his return from America, "is, all things considered, usually least rewarding, not very well paid, and therefore not very common."[20]

Therefore, wrote another teacher, Carl Baumann, America was a land where "thinking" was subordinated to "doing":

> Americanism is a culture of the deed. It is the deed which alone creates things that are worthwhile. But it is a deed which creates only material values and these alone are considered worthwhile. . . . Thus America is the land of great accomplishment, of the deed, not of the thought.[21]

And Gustav Müller believed that this emphasis on the temporal and the temporary also extended to the intelligentsia:

> For the intelligentsia only the life of the moment counts.
> All values are reduced to the one dimension of the present.
> Life is a movie, the crown of life a snapshot of the moment.[22]

[17]"Der amerikanische Typus," *Germanisch-Romanische Monatsschrift*, XI (1923), 7-14.

[18]*Amerika will die Zeit festbinden*, 25.

[19]"Was heisst Amerikanismus?" *Deutsche Monatshefte*, V, subvol. II, 467-470 (November, 1929).

[20]"Schwager," a teacher in Arnstadt, "Amerikanismus von der positiven und negativen Seite," *Praxis der Berufschule*, VIII, No. 17, 341-343 (May 18, 1928).

[21]"Zum Wesen des Amerikanismus," *Zofingia: Centralblatt des Zofingvereins*, LXXI (1931), 220-237 at 232.

[22]"Die amerikanische Intelligentsia," *Zeitwende*, VI, 169-172 (August, 1930).

If, then, the American was purely materialistic, a man of limited mental horizons with a stultified soul, other opprobrious characteristics followed in the train of these. One was "sentimentality," an exaggeration of feelings which did not reflect genuine emotion. Erich von Salzmann, one of Germany's professional traveler-journalists of the period, found this "sentimentality" playing a mighty role both in business and politics:

> For him [the American] there is only one thing: business and again business. Simple, sober, practical, almost brutal is the American and yet feeling plays a giant role here. It sounds almost like a contradiction in itself to say this, but the feeling which is aroused among the masses by the great newspapers scarcely knows any limits once it is started and therefore goes far beyond what was intended.[23]

Johannes Buschmann agreed: "in spite of all business sobriety, rhetoric and sentimentality are the most effective means of influencing this people."[24] Richard Müller-Freienfels, the psychologist-psychiatrist, gave this judgment even sharper expression:

> If we attempt to characterize the emotional life of the Americans, we shall have to say that it is quick, excitable, undiscriminating, not very profound, and in a remarkable degree uncontrolled by the reason; that is, it is ultimately "impersonal," if we may take it that "personal" experience implies a certain depth and individuality, and also a certain correspondence between the emotional and the intellectual life. . . .
> Sensation and sentimentality are equally characteristic of the American soul. Intellectual control seems to be completely eliminated; the reason has very little contact with the emotional life, and moves on quite another plane. Men who are as cold as ice in matters of commerce produce sensational and sentimental films; hard business men listen to pious sermons, and frivolous women of fashion are subject to benevolent and childishly sentimental impulses. But there is no depth in these impulses and emotions; on the contrary, they change like the weather.[25]

To the newspapers as a source of this sentimentality, Buschmann added the magazines with their "tear-jerking" stories, and Dr. Paul Rohrbach placed on the list "leg-shows," movies, alcohol,

[23]"Sentimentality," *Vossische Zeitung*, February 18, 1921.
[24]"Amerika—das Tor zu neuen Wegen der Kultur?" *Zeitwende*, VII, No. 2, 154-171 (February, 1931) at 166.
[25]*Mysteries of the Soul* (New York, 1929), 265-266.

and sports.[26] But for many Germans American sentimentality was a sign of inherent moral weakness. Count Keyserling, answering the question why "Americans are so often mawkishly sentimental," found little difficulty; this, in his view, represented "the compensation of arid intellectualism by primitive emotionalism."[27] And Professor Alfred Forcke, an Orientalist, denying that American sentimentality reflected genuine emotion and asserting that American friendliness was only a surface manifestation, went on to proclaim that these things reflected the inherent effeminacy of American character:

> This softness is, however, not just superficial, but rather the sign of a soft, mollusk-like being. Most Americans have no backbone, no character. The clinging to principles, even to one's damage, seems foolish to them. They let themselves be driven by the stream and do only that which is advantageous to them, even if it doesn't accord with their views. If one cannot make his convictions count without danger, he keeps them to himself, or, in the worst case, he renounces them and publicly declares as his opinion that which in his heart he condemns.[28]

In similar vein Johannes Gaulke pronounced the American people "in its masses less capable of judgment than any other,"[29] and Friedrich Schönemann declared that they were "more easily led about by the nose" than all other peoples.[30]

American religiosity was also, in the view of some Germans, a sign of shallowness of character and dullness of life. "The triviality, the monotony, the shocking spiritual poverty of American life," wrote Arthur Holitscher, "find in two morning hours on a Sunday a brief salvation."[31] And Hans Zbinden found roughness and cruelty lurking behind the Puritan mask and religion serving the ends of the leveling process in American life.[32] Another *litterateur*, "Matzanel," declared that of all peoples there was none more unmythological, more a-metaphysical, more irreligious than the Yankees.[33]

[26]"Was heisst Amerikanismus?"—see *fn.* 19.

[27]*America Set Free*, 336.

[28]"Aus dem Land der grossen Kinder," II, Berlin *Tägliche Rundschau*, April 20, 1920.

[29]"Amerika, du hast es besser . . . ?" *Die Gegenwart*, LVII (1928), 11-17.

[30]*Die Kunst der Massenbeeinflussung*, 58.   [31]*Wiedersehn*, 79.

[32]*Zur geistigen Lage Amerikas*, 14-15.

[33]"Der deutsche Irrtum über Amerika," *Der freie Geist*, I, 17-21, 170-178 (January, 1927) at 171.

The adverse critical element has predominated in the list of American characteristics described above. There were, however, some American traits which Germans admired. But not infrequently they joined their praise of these to reservations and exceptions. Thus, they constantly stressed the optimism of Americans, but frequently attached to the reference the allegation that this was only a "keep-smiling" convention, or proclaimed with unconcealed *Schadenfreude* that it would be discarded when good luck ran out and the Americans "grew up."[34] On the other hand, many Germans regarded this optimism as a sign of strength, of the will to maintain one's self, of the confidence in one's own abilities. "Kopf hoch!"—"Head High!"—advised one guidebook of the period for prospective emigrants to America. There's no use for you to go over there unless you're a "fighter," ready to work to put yourself across.[35]

Optimism, of course, reflected also a pride in accomplishment, which was in turn the source of a highly developed, even aggressive nationalism. America had *created* out of nothing, noted Carl Baumann. "This was only possible because man believed in himself and trusted in God."[36] And Erwin Rosen (Carlé), who has his "American" proclaiming on every other page, "I am an American! And I am damned proud of it!" summed up the combination of optimism, activism, and nationalism in vivid words:

> Money was not their idol.
> Nothing is falser than to speak of the dollar land and dollar chasers. Their idol was the deed. Money was a pleasant consequence, but the deed, the active life was what was really important. It was as though the very air of the land inculcated in the new citizen those two characteristics which the American demanded of each man:
> Self-reliance!
> Accomplishment!
> One must believe in himself; one must accomplish something. These things the American regards as moral demands.

[34]Bonn used the term, "Sunshine campaign": "Optimism is manufactured, loudly proclaimed, and broadcast far and wide." But with the advent of the depression, the failure of the sunshine campaign, Bonn asserted that Americans were just beginning to conjure with the art of living. *The American Adventure*, 136, 222-223, 290, 302.

[35]Johannes Saalfeld, *Wie komme ich in den Vereinigten Staaten vorwärts?* 13-14.

[36]"Zum Wesen des Amerikanismus," [see *fn.* 21] 232.

Out of these concepts of man's role grew national pride and with it the feeling of belonging together as a nation. The American nation was born in that moment when the American ideal of mankind acquired firm features. The American nation has become a nation by virtue of its internal strength, not by the deeds of a general or the unifying accomplishment of a leading genius. So the American stands and falls as a man as well as a representative of his people with self-reliance, which is based upon work and accomplishment.

America, he summarized it, was different from all other nations—"First there was the man. Then came the nation."[37]

In similar words Colin Ross labeled the American a visionary:

The American with all his sober reckoning is a visionary. In all things, whether it be politics, religion, technics, or finance. Always he seeks for the largest. The biggest—that which he starts he must finish. In an idealism which seems to be childishly courageous he ignores thereby all limits and possibilities and—overcomes them. Thus came the skyscrapers and all the "skyscraperish" in this land.[38]

There was another overriding characteristic which Germans attributed to Americans. This was expressed in the term "bourgeois." In the subtitle of his *American Adventure* Moritz Bonn labeled the United States "a bourgeois civilization." Carl Baumann called the United States "the classic land of bourgeois culture" and asserted, "For the American his bourgeois idea-world is an absolute religion and he defends it with the fanaticism typical of all religious men."[39]

For Germans this concept carried both good and bad connotations. It was often symbolic of intellectual narrowness and lack of spirituality. In this connotation it was expressed by the term *Spiessbürger* for which there is no real English equivalent. Babbitt was, of course, the *Spiessbürger* par excellence. And German observers found Americans more "*spiessig*" than their German equivalents.[40] They regarded Americans as distinctly "conservative" in their attitude towards life—in realms of politics, economics, morals. Thus Annalise Schmidt, the author of a book-length sketch

[37]*Amerikaner*, 15-16.

[38]*Fahrten- und Abenteuerbuch*, 131.

[39]"Zum Wesen des Amerikanismus," [see *fn.* 21] 221, 224.

[40]E.g., R. Bremer, "Wie ich die amerikanischen Bürger sah," *Allgemeine Rundschau*, XXIII, 106-107 (February 13, 1926).

of American character, wrote, "People are very conservative over there. More than in any other land," and added, "The United States is the bourgeois land par excellence. The psyche of the bourgeois we in Germany have learned to know to the full—their rabbit-like [lack of] courage, their self-satisfaction, their fear of basic alterations in this best of all worlds."⁴¹ This conservatism was accompanied by a veneration of property. Property, declared Carl Baumann, was almost holy in America—it was the tangible evidence of the life work of each individual.⁴²

But Germans also admitted that American *Spiessbürger* were less likely than those at home to content themselves with their existing economic status. Kerr called the Yankee "the most earnestly daring man of today."⁴³ Albrecht Penck spoke of the "*Kampfnatur*," "the fighting nature" of the American.⁴⁴ And the quotations above in respect to American fantasy demonstrated the difference between a complacent sense of possession and a constant press forward towards something better.

Germans also noted the willingness of the American bourgeoisie to help one another in time of difficulty, to sacrifice possessions for charitable, religious, and educational causes. The American, said one observer, liked "to play God" by helping comrades in need.⁴⁵ "The American gives, when he gives, never little," reported another observer.⁴⁶

The above sketching of American characteristics by German observers is on the whole not a flattering one. For the majority of those who wrote "America books" and articles, the figure of the American was a *Schreckgespenst*—a symbol of what they most feared and hated. For the characteristics of the American revealed the end product of the process of "Americanization," which confronted all of Europe, but Germany perhaps most particularly.

3. *The Fear of the Misoneists*: "An America tumult has gripped Europe," wrote Joseph Draim in 1932.⁴⁷ "America has become

---

⁴¹*Der amerikanische Mensch*, 16-17, 34, 44.
⁴²"Zum Wesen des Amerikanismus," [see *fn*. 21] 233.
⁴³*Yankee-Land*, 41.
⁴⁴*U.S.-Amerika*, 16.
⁴⁵Baumann, "Zum Wesen des Amerikanismus," [see *fn*. 21] 224-225.
⁴⁶Bremer, "Wie ich die amerikanischen Bürger sah," [see *fn*. 40] 107.
⁴⁷"Der Amerikanismus," *Pharus*, XXIII (1932), No. 10, 237-241 at 237.

trump,"[48] declared Rudolf Kindermann in 1930. America, wrote Hermann Fackler in 1929, "imposes a transition in learning. It speaks in naive language of a new time; it tells us that we have entered into an age of the feverish transformation of our planet, which first finds its physical form in America while the spiritual change is left more to Europe. But Europe has not yet understood this."[49]

Hundreds of voices in Weimar Germany raised themselves in concern at what they regarded as an insidious physical and spiritual invasion from abroad: physical in that large quantities of American capital were entering into German business;[50] physical also in that new Ford plants made their appearance; but spiritual in that the shock of flamboyant advertising, the glare of lights and blare of obtrusive advertising accompanied the opening of the new Ford plants;[51] physical also in the visible evidence of the American movie in Germany,[52] and, perhaps even more disturbingly, the proclamation of a German straw hat day, that standardizing determinant of male modes which had so amused German visitors to American shores![53] And German girls in the big cities were even beginning to spit their chewing gum on the streets![54]

As noted above, none concerned himself more poignantly with the dangers of this invasion of "Americanism" than Adolf Halfeld:

> One still knows very little about America. Thus Americanism is at first only a symbol of the vague and naively worshipful conceptions which the average European of today possesses in respect to America—a legend for which, as has been said, the way is prepared by films and newspapers. . . . We speak of Americanization, of a new factuality, of rationalization and of managerial men (*Chauffeurmenschen*) with-

[48]"Was können wir von Amerika lernen?" *Volkswohl*, XXI (1930), No. 5, 175-183 at 175.

[49]"Amerikanische Geistigkeit," *Die Christengemeinschaft*, VI (1929), 219-20.

[50]Heinrich Müller, "Die Amerikanisierung Europas," *Allgemeine Rundschau*, XVII, 510-511 (October, 1920).

[51]Pastor Eilert, "Die amerikanische Gefahr," Berlin *Tägliche Rundschau*, June 24, 1928; see also description of opening of Ford plant in Cologne, *Kölnische Zeitung*, January 22, 1930.

[52]Buschmann, "Amerika—das Tor zu neuen Wegen der Kultur" [see *fn.* 24], 155.

[53]"Glossen," *Amerikanische Stimmen*, I (1925), No. 8, 19.

[54]Hans Christoph Kaergel, "Kleinigkeiten aus dem grossen Amerika," *Die Bergstadt*, XIV (1925/6), No. 4, 465-476 at 476.

out qualifications, as if thereby the spiritual needs of a cultured people were served. We underscore the observation that the American worker in many fields produces within a given time two or three times as much goods as the German worker and do not ask at the same time whether the American worker can also call his own three times as much enjoyment and beauty of life. We enthuse over American tempo and travel and stupidly seek to forget how productive Europe is in its leisure. What good are thirty story residential hotels if the men who must live in them are a thousand stories further from the sun and the spirit?[55]

This fear of the loss of Europe's "culture" was widespread. "He who hasn't yet felt with his inner being that which blows our way across the ocean," wrote Albert Lorenz, "sees it in the jazzing-up of Beethoven, the sentimental *Kitsch* flood of American films, the excerpts from American newspapers. We shook our heads, it all ran off us, it didn't concern us—we were secure. But the people; the masses?"[56] And Joseph Draim rhetorically questioned "America," "What good is all this [prosperity] to you if you lose your soul thereby?"[57] For art professor Fritz Behn this was already accomplished and about to be repeated: "The Americans have lost their souls and we are about to follow them in it." "America," he added, "is for us not an example but a warning."[58]

These expressions of fear showed also deeply injured pride:

Whether pleasant or not, the question arises: are we Europeans destined to be in the future nothing more than an outmoded culture, a travel attraction, an antique business, all of Europe in respect to America something like that which [until now] Spain or Greece has been for Europe?[59]

"Americanization," said a friend of Josef Hengesbosch, represented the feelings he would have if his daughter told him she was going to marry a foreigner. Possibly, added the speaker, he might be wrong, but the feelings would be there, and he would have the feeling that they were justified.[60]

Some observers, of course, pointed out that the flow of in-

[55]*Amerika und der Amerikanismus*, xiii-xiv.

[56]"Amerikanismus," *Volkserzieher*, 1928, Beilag, "Der Bücherfreund," 1.

[57]"Der Amerikanismus" [see *fn.* 47], 241.

[58]"Amerikanismus in Deutschland," *Süddeutsche Monatshefte*, XXVII, 672-674 (June, 1929).

[59]Prosinagg, *Das Antlitz Amerikas*, 275.

[60]"Amerikanismus und Kultur," *Gelbe Hefte*, IV (1928), 895-902 at 900.

fluence across the Atlantic was two-directional—that America was being Europeanized as Europe was being Americanized. Hans Zbinden, among others, complained that Europe was blindly copying some of the worst features of Americanization while energetic groups in the United States were seeking to moderate them.[61]

Even more widespread, however, than this criticism by the misoneists was the charge that the discussion of "Americanization" in Germany placed a foreign label on problems which were intrinsically domestic. Sociologist Charlotte Lütkens said that all of the talk sought to veil realities; it purposefully created false impressions; it was based on legends rather than fact:

> This America fashion is actually an "America" fashion. Under the covering names of America and Americanism a legend has been spread (naturally in [professedly] objective form, if possible with an exposition of statistics), which serves two social groupings and which the German middle class has gladly and unskeptically accepted because it rang true to certain favorite views and judgments concerning their own and the outside world. The "America" which this legend sees and describes is *a legend of the intellectuals and the businessmen.*[62]

Mrs. Lütkens, with quite apparent socialist malice, went on to suggest that each group had feared the effects of "Americanization" upon its existence as a class. The forward press of an industrial society, the rise of the masses, seemed to pose the probability of an expropriation of the intellectuals, the disappearance of their role in society. Hence, she suggested, the intellectuals had exaggerated into gigantic dimensions the standardizing and leveling features of life in the United States. Not that Mrs. Lütkens disagreed with these basic evaluations. She was quite willing to accept the fact that the United States had "shudder-producing" churches but enchanting railroad stations, that romance there was confined principally to the skylines of the cities, and that the spiritual-minded would find there no nourishment or inspiration. But, she stressed, what was involved was sociologically determined—the German intellectuals were exaggerating its menace to the homeland.

[61]*Zur geistigen Lage Amerikas*, 7-8.
[62]Die Amerikalegende," *Sozialistische Monatshefte*, XXXVIII (1932), 45-50 at 45.

Similarly, she stated, the German business enterprisers had used the "American legend" for two somewhat conflicting purposes—on the one side to join high production with labor complacency; on the other side to exploit the fear of leveling and standardization to retard pressure for rationalization and technical change. "Thus everyone," she concluded, "shoves under America that which is basically his own problem." This process, she added, writing in 1932, was now no longer so much the mode with the clear evidence of depression and economic crisis in America.[63]

Other critics followed similar lines. Richard Müller-Freienfels found Americanism essentially a product of European spiritual forms grown precipitately into weeds. The things Europeans hated in America existed at home but were moderated there by forms of life which were grounded in an older culture. "The Americanization of Europe," he wrote, "is not the external action of America on Europe; it is an internal transformation which is taking place in Europe also, and in all the other continents, which would have occurred even without the influence of America, but which has nevertheless been accelerated and intensified by the example and influence of America."[64]

In similar vein writer-critic Johannes Gaulke related disillusionment growing from successive journeys to America. In his first he had seen it as an ideal of freedom. But the "youthful enthusiasm" had passed, and he now regarded it as "inwardly and outwardly a coarsened version of the old world." In America, he asserted, "schematism" in life had reduced to insignificance the lingering effects of European romanticism and poetry.[65]

Even more strikingly, Robert Müller denied that Americans were a "race" or a "people." They were a "function of civilization." Americanization, he declared, was "the physical and spiritual expression of a particular status of civilization in which the whole culture of the world finds itself." Müller asserted that Americanization was actually proceeding more rapidly in the Orient than in Europe and that Americans, on their part, were taking up Asiatic cult and social forms. The future, he believed, would see the

[63]*Ibid.*

[64]" 'Amerikanismus' und europäische Kultur," *Der deutsche Gedanke,* IV (1927), 30-35; *Mysteries of the Soul,* 287-288.

[65]"Amerika, du hast es besser . . . ?" *Die Gegenwart,* LVI, 217-219 (October, 1927).

movement of both extremes into Europe and the creation of "an Americanoid world mestizo group."[66]

4. Voices in Defense: America the Hope of the Future: In the midst of this emotional maelstrom of Americaphobia, the voices of moderation and calm, the defenders of the American way of life were few. In a class by himself was, of course, the poet Alfred Kerr:

> Europe scolds. Strange how its people are still lured to become Yankees. How no one at all wants to go back to the old homeland.
> There must be a reason for it.[67]

> This book doesn't regard America under the viewpoint: "But Upton Sinclair!"
> (I don't regard Venice under the viewpoint: "But how dirty!")[68]

> The American of today is an outline-man. Full of hope, because he doesn't bog down in details. His innermost being is provisional: a desired narrowness.
> Yes, exclusion of that which has no purpose. Fabulous wonder, therefore the accomplishment. ("Swimming [forward] by will without the lead boots of thinking himself to pieces"—that's how I see him.)
> That he possesses only a technical civilization remains nonsense— I have disproved it.[69]

> One thing I know, filled with anger: in Europe one paints all the Yankees crazier than they are. It's a swindle just to make a joke. Also a swindle because of jealousy. Predominantly a swindle of the provincial bourgeoisie (*Krähwinkeltum*).[70]

> My countrymen don't have enough sense to do what is needed in the midst of misfortune. I believe the Germans are made of passion and political weakness. (Passion without sense and without accomplishment.)
> America has constructive passion; fruitful passion; creative passion; a working passion.[71]

[66]"Der amerikanische Typus," *Germanische-Romanische Monatsschrift*, XI (1923), 7-14. Richard Müller-Freienfels expressed the same view in *Mysteries of the Soul*, 235 ff.

[67]*Yankee-Land*, 8.　　　　[68]*Ibid.*
[69]*Ibid.*, 56.　　　　[70]*Ibid.*, 161.
[71]*Ibid.*, 201.

Less poetic but almost as defensive was Emil Müller-Sturm-heim. "One is so proud of the history of Europe," he wrote. "And has, however, so little reason for it! An unbroken chain of wars beginning in the Roman period and reaching up to modern times; wars, which never have the veil of an ethical and moral purpose and can be ascribed only to the thievery and greed of individual rulers."[72] The shining sun of European geniuses, he declared, was hidden not only from the masses of the people but from those who actually made the history of the European states.[73] America had, he declared, in two centuries created a wonderful state system which lacked only its Homer to defend it. The criticism of America for lack of history and tradition derived, he proclaimed, "from that same self-conceit which allows the European aristocrat, no matter how low he may stand in moral and spiritual accomplishment, to charge the citizen who can't produce his ancestors in evidence with inferiority and lack of significance."[74] "America," he proclaimed, has solved with genial intuition problems from which Europe still suffers today."[75] "The future of mankind," he concluded, "lies doubtless in binding together into a unity European culture and European methodical thinking with the American love of freedom and justice, with the American genial intuition."[76]

Much in the same tone Prof. Carl Brinkmann warned against the easy judgments of his contemporaries. To see America properly one must free himself from hostile preconceptions. When this was done, he said:

> The naive experience is exactly reversed. What impresses is the simplicity, calm, and happiness of a manner (*Habitus*) which seems to lighten life much more than all technique and apparatus. And now one should not seek to find an explanation [for this] along the comfortable lines of social analysis and say: Of course, that is the unburdened man of the colonial sphere with his unexhausted physical powers and the unexhausted opportunities of his economic and social mobility; that is the childishness of modern civiliza-tion-barbarians, who in part do not see and in part do not

[72]*Ohne Amerika geht es nicht*, 31. Some portions of these quotations appeared in Ch. VIII on culture, but have renewed significance here. Quotation with permission of Amalthea Verlag.

[73]*Ibid.*, 36.

[74]*Ibid.*, 40.

[75]*Ibid.*

[76]*Ibid.*, 41.

wish to see what is for us the earnest and tragic beauty of the fate of mankind and society.[77]

On the contrary, said Brinkmann, "The quiet [of their lives] gives this democratic and young people a characteristic of aristocracy and age."[78] When one saw the Americans at home, he added, the impression of weightiness was strengthened by "the manner of quiet self-possession, of the ability to wait, and of a peculiar reserve in respect to crude expressions and hasty gestures."[79]

And Brinkmann predicted a future of significance for America:

[these] are the elements of that which one might call the original democracy: the unquestioning acceptance of life among equals, not in some involved legal sense but rather in the sense of equality of kind, and the unquestioning acceptance of a religion which is nothing else than a repetition of this sense of equality, deriving from longing, from myth, from the end goals of action and a search for security. One must not let himself be deceived by the external, I might say statistical, lack of relationship between this giant land and giant people and those elements of spirituality which are separated from them in the European sense, above all artistic and intellectual originality. The greatest portion of all American *Kitsch* in these areas proves nothing more than the inferiority of that which has been taken over from Europe. The land without a Middle Ages had first of all to create the artistic work of its own existence, and where this exists pure and free of European borrowings, as in the architecture of the great cities and in technical accomplishments or in all those intellectual creations which, like this architecture, are not the result of criticism but of expression, one is surprised repeatedly not only by the mass of newness but also by the great self-will, which reminds one unexpectedly of the "primitive" cultures of the East and of other non-European parts of the world.[80]

Economics Professor Hermann Lufft also found his American experiences different from those of many of his contemporaries. He had found little of "Dollar Land America." He found men of good will anxious to help one another. He found men capable of excellent judgments of their fellows. He had learned, most of all,

[77]*Demokratie und Erziehung*, 10-11. Quotation with permission of S. Fischer Verlag.
[78]*Ibid.*, 12.
[79]*Ibid.*
[80]*Ibid.*, 102.

in America, that one gets further with good will than with hate and animosity. He had returned to see the notes of bitterness and doubt in Europe, of hatefulness toward children, of negation of life, of unproductive classes, of "alcoholization." America held up, he proclaimed, the ideal of a happy and prosperous working class. This was not the product of "fairy stories and cuckoo tales." "Compared with this unfortunate Europe," he concluded, "America is a dream. A dream which is reality. But we must also make this dream come true for our Germany."[81]

Erwin Carlé, the novelist, also proclaimed the great values of Americanization:

> For out of this land America good can come. Its fresh, healthful naturalness is made by God. Refreshing often, like a cool spring. Its joyful pleasure in the struggle and its strong assurance in daily life can well be an example and model for those confused [peoples] around her. Its splendid joy in labor may show the despairing the one, the good, the safe way. Its happiness may spring across to those who are sad.[82]

By far and away, however, the most commonly met defense of America was one which joined critical notes with the end conclusion: "but all of this is in Germany too much exaggerated; out of America comes good as well as evil." Many sections of this volume have reflected the significance of the "but." In the field of economics Germans were prepared to hear of American superiority. References to contributions in the cultural and religious fields were more skeptically received. The ideal of American democracy was often considered American self-deception. But reservations and doubts aside, many naturally critical observers still found in America some signs of hope for the future.

For Alfons Paquet, the poet, that hope was the ideal of peace, the fervent wish that America would return to ways of pacifism and that all peoples, everywhere, might find her a symbol of this hope.[83] For others the hope related to prohibition—that the American example of sobriety might have its effect in Europe![84]

[81]"Aus meinen amerikanischen Erfahrungen," *Deutsche Arbeit*, XI (1926), 24-26.

[82]*Amerikaner*, 91.

[83]"Vorschläge an Amerika," *Der neue Merkur*, VII, subvol. II (April-September, 1924), 578-588.

[84]See *fn.* 56, Chapter X.

But much more frequently the muted optimism of this group of observers was not expressed in terms of clearly definable objectives, but rather in terms of overall spirit—the hope that the initiative of America might be helpful to Europe and that, in turn, American excesses related to this initiative might be moderated. Dr. Waldemar Gurian, for example, called Americanism "a harmless matter." It was a sign of modern life and modern thinking. For Germans, he suggested, the radio portrayals of Dr. Eisenbart, the seventeenth century physician who combined medicine and showmanship, viewed a man much like contemporary Americans:

> that is the type of Americanized man of our days. A man who knows the stupidity of the masses but is not wicked if he exploits it since he uses that which helps his business. He is presently of such great positive significance that one can only welcome him. He destroys knotted-up, false traditions. He stirs up life which has become sluggish; he lightens existence in that he doesn't burden it with thought; in the place of the heavy problematic for which he is not mature enough, he sets the freshness of initiative.[85]

Richard Müller-Freienfels also provided a hopeful note. He could not, he said, be certain that the American type of mankind represented a decline:

> If, with Nietzsche, we regard the Greek type as the absolute ideal (a type which, for that matter, was only an ideal, not an exactly observed historical type), then *Homo americanus* as an individual, is a pitiful decline. As an individual he displays unmistakable signs of retrogression; neither in the faculties of artistic expression, nor in the profoundity of his religion and philosophy, nor in the harmonious cultivation of his intellectual powers, can he be compared with this ideal type. Yet we have a very different picture if we regard the new type not in individual isolation, but as a social whole. Then we are forced to admit that in respect of the domination of nature and the development of human power the new type is far superior to the classic Athenian or the men of the Renaissance.[86]

[85]"Vom Weltbild der Gegenwart: Kritische Betrachtungen," *Kölnische Zeitung*, January 27, 1929. Dr. Eisenbart (Johann Andreas, 1661-1727) was a physician of the city of Münden in Hannover whose reputation varied between that of a quack (because of the exhibitionist accompaniments of his medical work) and an innovator. During the 1920's he was the subject of a popular opera and a novel.

[86]*Mysteries of the Soul*, 290-291.

An effort to avoid Americanization was, suggested Müller-Freienfels, futile. It was the part of a future which "is in some degrees already present, and is daily drawing near." But the future need not represent a static condition—it would also lead forward to something different, possibly better. "The Americanization of the soul," he concluded, "will not be overcome from without, but only from within; it will be overcome only if it is 'uplifted,' sublimated in the Hegelian sense; only if the good in it is retained, that new forms of life may be created from it."[87]

Other critics echoed these mixtures of criticism and praise. Dr. Erwin Stranik, a correspondent for the *Tageblatt* and *Volkszeitung* in Berlin represented his mixed feelings by labeling the United States "the land of contrasts." To praise of American democracy which recognized no difference between a king and a U.S. citizen, Stranik joined sharp criticism of American universities, advertising, and business motifs. America provoked, he declared, both hatred and love.[88] In similar vein Arnold Scheibe found freedom for economic activity and progress in the United States "the largest and most generous conceivable in the whole world of today," but individualism in cultural development was seriously threatened.[89]

Prof. Josef Hengesbosch of the University of Frankfurt also evaluated American culture negatively; he had found, he said, nothing to contradict the critical assessments of Halfeld's book. But his concluding estimate of Americanism was far from completely negative:

> If, however, America seeks to speak to us of its economic order or methods of labor as culture or tries to force them upon us, then we must remind ourselves of our great handicraft tradition. With American democracy we can do nothing because we must begin with a very different set of historical circumstances. . . . But to keep life, at least publicly, pure according to the Sixth Commandment, in this we should copy America, just as its practical Christianity, its rightfully famous welfare activity, its tested sense of citizenship provide examples for the old world; these are the virtues, the advantages of a youthful, uncomplicated people called upon for leadership.[90]

[87]*Ibid.*, 291-292.

[88]"Das Land der Gegensätze," *Der getreue Eckart*, IX, No. 6, 428-432 (March, 1932).

[89]"Nordamerika in Rahmen der Weltgeschichte, seine Zukunft und seine begrenzenden Bedingungen," *Eiserne Blätter*, IX, No. 2, 32-33 (Jan. 9, 1927).

[90]"Amerikanismus und Kultur" [see *fn.* 60], 902.

American pragmatism, often the whipping-boy of German scholars, found also its defenders. Walter Fischer wrote, "Behind this [American pragmatism] lurks somehow the idealist respect for the questioning spirit as an old, Puritan heritage and most particularly the optimistic social faith in a development towards something better for the welfare of everyone."[91] And Julius Richter, professor of "Mission-Science" at the University of Berlin, regarded American pragmatism as a harbinger of the future. Although it varied in form, he suggested,

> A common element is the rejection of eternal, unalterable principles, of axiomatic truths, of natural rights, of the sense of duty to a supernatural being; common also is the maintenance of the fluidity of all thinking, of the necessity of ever new experimentation, of mistrust of all axiomatic preconceptions. Perhaps it is a healthy struggle against traditional but outlived ways of thinking. Perhaps this pragmatism, which first of all destroys the old idols, may lead to a new, immediate, realistic spiritual life. For the present one has the impression that this development is the true expression of the modern American will to life, as it rules over broad academic and youth circles—a rosy optimism which sees before it unlimited opportunities of development, an outspoken realism which wants proven realities and therefore trusts only the experiment, a preference for "exact science," which applies to all phases of life the "proven methods of the natural sciences," an almost emotional rejection of the whole spiritual world, of God, of ideals, of absolute values, [those things] in which former generations found their highest goals, an energetic will for the reconstruction of the life of the individual and society and, therefore, a passionate adherence to democracy and rejection of every authority. That which interests so much in this is that here [in America] is developing a modern view of the world which is the expression of the modern feeling of life and therefore has prospects of spreading itself broadly among other peoples.[92]

For another German observer America's prospective gift to Europe lay in the spirit of the frontier. To call Americans soulless was in his view nonsense. "Without a soul and a hot heart one does not erect such heaven-storming skyscrapers; one does not show such

---

[91]*Hauptfrage der Amerikakunde*, 21.

[92]"Religion, Kirche, und Philosophie in Nordamerika," in Fischer *et al.*, *Handbuch der Amerikakunde*, 319-320.

daring, such genius—and such youth." What Europe needed, he proclaimed, was a little dose of America; and what America needed was a little dose of Europe. The danger for both lay in the peril of copying those things which were least worthwhile.[93]

Perhaps it is appropriate to conclude this section on the defense of "Americanism" and "Americanization" with the words of two men who probably devoted the greatest efforts during the Weimar period to counteracting the fears of their fellow scholars. Friedrich Schönemann in concluding his *magnum opus* on the United States in 1932 pointed out that America had long ago embarked on the pathway to cultural development. The simplicity of American thinking, he said, was the product of a philosophical rejection of the European problematic, of a conscious choice of placing greater emphasis upon organization, upon the welfare of the masses, upon the fullness of modern life. But Schönemann believed that in America a "new humanism" was also developing which would be of value to Europe. "And Europe makes all the vital problems of the present much too easy when it characterizes everything bad and hateful as 'Americanism,' in order on its part to maintain itself in the arrogance (or ignorance) of a more or less self-contented and passive European cultural heritage." Europe and America, he complained, were both moving without goals. But he hoped that as the American spirit became more introspective, it would create a new synthesis of matter and spirit which would have a beneficial effect in Europe.[94]

And Kühnemann also concluded his observations on a hopeful note, although he believed that Germany's future would best be served by the preservation of its own peculiar traditions:

> For one thing is certain: the longings of men today. They want to create a realm of good will where all men are joined in joyful cooperation. They all want to bring an end to the terrible difficulties of these days. To work together we must know one another. Everything is to be considered desirable which helps nations to know one another at their best. It is not easy to know America, because it is in the midst of such powerful and rapid development and its countenance changes constantly. Every European should keep in mind one simple thought: there are no [valid] generalizations in respect to

[93]Pastor Eilert, "Die amerikanische Gefahr," Berlin *Tägliche Rundschau,* June 22, 23, 24, 1928.

[94]*Die Vereinigten Staaten,* II, 431-435.

America. What is today declared impossible is there tomorrow. What is not there today will be there tomorrow. Every prediction is proved faulty. It is not easy to know Germany because we differ greatly from the common patterns of Western life. We lose our identity when we seek to make ourselves over to conform to those patterns. We do not dare to be anything but Germans. As Germans we give our best service to mankind. . . . We [also] want the unity of mankind in the love of God.[95]

It can only be regretted that the stereotyped definitions of "Americanism" and "Americanization" continued to win broad acceptance in spite of the qualifications and reservations suggested by more objective scholars. Perhaps the democracy of Weimar might have been strengthened if more of the authors of the "America books" of that day had been able to create sympathetic views of the nation which was considered the prototype of democratic government. As it was, the terms "Americanism" and "Americanization" were too frequently symbols of the emotional malaise which contributed significantly to the failure of the Weimar Republic.

[95]*Amerikafahrt, 1932*, 66.

Chapter XII

THIRTY YEARS LATER: THE CONTINUING
SEARCH FOR INTERPRETATION

ost-mortem on Weimar: Its America Image Judged by Its Failure: Weimar Germany died over thirty years ago. Only a minority of Germans mourned its passing. The number of those who wept at the demise of democracy was exceeded by those who climbed on the bandwagon of an emotional Nazism, marched in or watched with throbbing heart the spectacles of the endless night parades, stood awed before the pageantry of the Nuremberg party rallies, joined in the jingoist cries of the great mass meetings, and unleashed the *innere Schweinehund* to justify excesses which reason condemned. Many of these were the same Germans who had written with disdain of American childishness and sensationalism, had detailed American lynch justice with horror, and had complained of American anti-semitism and racialism. Many of them were intellectuals who had criticized the aridity of American scholarship and the domination of thought by public opinion in the United States, but now stood by approvingly at Nazi book burnings and, indeed, immolated scholarship itself on the funeral pyre erected by an anti-intellectual neo-Romanticism.

Strangely enough, many of the defenders as well as the critics of Americanism found hope in the Hitler movement. Insofar as Americanism had been an inspiration, it was its spirit of initiative, its dynamism, its will to the future which was emulated. Democracy *per se* carried little appeal except as it reflected a sense of comradeship, of solidarity in meeting national problems, and for many Germans these were also reflected in the Nazi movement. A recent German book characterizes Nazi election methods as directly based upon American ones and labels the Third Reich "a super America."[1]

[1]Gerhard Herm, *Amerika erobert Europa* (Düsseldorf und Wien, 1964), 318-321.

This is, of course, more than a clever apology for an era of disgrace. It is an outright deception. Basically, Hitler turned the German mind back upon itself, sought to unleash the slumbering powers of a great state by appeals to its pride and its traditions. Hitler, the great simplifier, replaced the questioning of the intellect with the dynamic forces of defiance and hatred, sought for and got the unreserved trust and confidence of most of his people, that of the authors of ponderous tomes and sophisticated disquisitions, as well as that of the simple-minded peasant and the narrow-minded *Krähwinkeltum*, the petty bourgeoisie of the provincial villages. In time of crisis few German scholars displayed the civil courage which they had found lacking in the United States or the sense of judgment which they had missed on the American scene.

All of these circumstances, of course, highlight the profound lack of self-criticism which affected German scholarship of the Weimar era. German scholars were so imbued with the certainty of German cultural preeminence that they failed to pause to examine this assumption. They were so conscious of the literary, philosophical, and scientific achievements of the nineteenth century that they ignored the fact that these achievements would become a dying heritage unless current scholarship reshaped them to fit the mold of new days and new ways. How difficult it has been, sometimes impossible, to identify the little men who prated so proudly of German cultural achievements! They left behind nothing positive—only their criticism, only their negative contributions to the cause of scholarship.

The defects of the America books of the Weimar period have been detailed above. They were one clear sign of the decline of German scholarship. It may be objected that they were not meant to be scholarly studies, "just" travelogues. But few of these volumes warned of their limitations. Few of the professors, educators, or literary men who wrote them admitted their own inadequacy for the task of evaluating the whole scope of an alien civilization. The professional title and the doctorate lent an unwarranted weight of authority to their observations and commentaries on matters outside their realm of competence. But the most serious criticism of the America literature is that which relates to objectives and goals. German scholarship had spoken much of understanding, of empathy, of penetrating deeply into the spirit of the things being studied. But few German scholars really looked beneath the surface of things in America; few sought empathy with Americans. Confronted with that which was different, they drew back within themselves in shocked dismay and voiced horror not understanding. One sees Count Keyserling bestriding America (or for that matter, other parts of the world) and carefully preening his ego with assertions that reflected his inward links with his Latvian homeland and his aristocratic background. Or one sees Professor Alfred Forcke (and others of his breed) testily complaining of the American crudities he found and the pitiful remnants of what might have been a Germanic impulse to something better!

A great deal of that which was criticized was not specifically American. It was a part of modern life, of the growth of great cities, the building of factories, the expansion of mining, the extension of modern business ideals and practices. It was already present in Germany, much of it begun and developed entirely independently of American influence or example. Those who visited America seem often to have done little exploration at home. They were contrasting the actuality of America with a fictionalized Germany.

At this point, however, it is high time to admit that many of these defects were not and are not characteristic of German travel literature alone. They are too frequently reflected in books written by Americans on their experiences abroad—in Paris or in Berlin or lately in newer and stranger parts of the world. And the acidity of German judgments often reflected the unbridled character of American cultural self-criticism. Henry L. Mencken supplied many of the barbs hurled by German visitors. Edgar Ansel Mowrer portrayed the American civilization as a warning to Europe.[2] Other cultural critics found lesser but significant attention.

Moreover, as has been seen above, in spite of obvious misinterpretations, lacunae, even conscious distortions, there was also in the America literature of the Weimar period much of truth. In respect to every category of American life there were some accounts which were reasonable and understanding, in some cases unusually perceptive and penetrating. The pages of this book have sought to highlight these accounts, to select from them the passages which

[2]*This American World* (New York [c. 1928]) was translated by Annemarie Horschitz as *Amerika, Vorbild und Warnung* (Berlin [1928]).

best underscored the inner urges and most sharply delineated the outward forms of American life in that period. The patchwork quilt which could be constructed by this eclectic process would mirror in depth and color the fabric of American life.

But few Germans of that period sought to construct such a patchwork quilt. The evidence indicates that they chose as often the trivial as the significant when they read about America. On the other hand, the evidence also indicates that the emotional antipathy of the intellectuals often left the masses unmoved. The prosperity and sense of progress which they identified with Americanism were more appealing than the defense of the cultural heritage.

2. *Changing of the Scene: The Old Sages Give Way to New*: Weimar gave way to Hitler, and the Third Reich crumpled amidst the flames of Berlin and the pseudo-Wagnerian demise of the dictator. Germany came under Allied occupation, and each power accompanied its presence with an effort to promote the values to which it gave allegiance. The influence of the United States exceeded that of its western allies by virtue of its power, significance, and prestige. West Germany, a pawn in the Cold War, recovered materially and politically more rapidly than it would have otherwise because of the conflicts between the United States and the Soviet Union. Since 1949 it has increasingly exercised political autonomy and freedom of expression concerning the new world about it. In this period the United States has once again been an object of overwhelming interest and concern. A new generation of Germans has arisen to pass judgment on American civilization.

This generation has had many advantages which that of Weimar lacked. The process of political "reeducation" imposed upon West Germans after World War II carried with it a conscious effort to explain and justify American traditions. The translation of American novels and plays and of American histories and other works on the American way of life has gone on apace. The German reading public is offered in such popular book clubs as the Bertelsmann *Lesering* a broad selection of books written by Americans.[3]

[3]The *Bertelsmann Lesering Illustrierte* for October-December, 1965, lists over thirty-five translations of American authors for the choice of its readers, including Dale Carnegie, Ernest Hemingway, John Steinbeck, Sinclair Lewis, Thornton Wilder, and a considerable selection of newer authors.

American movies and American jazz are even more widely known than during the twenties and thirties. "America Houses" provide large collections of books on the United States, and Fulbright and Schmidt-Mundt lecturers and scholars seek to disseminate a fuller and deeper view of American civilization than was available during the Weimar period.[4] "America Institutes" and courses in American studies are more widespread and diverse than formerly. And, of course, Germans have seen close at hand many more Americans than they saw during the Weimar era.

But the production of travel literature and of new "America books" written by Germans still adds its dimensions to the German image of the United States. Surprisingly, the temper and tone of many of these volumes are much the same as those of the Weimar era. Americans may often look back to the twenties with some nostalgia. They are conscious of the disappearance of the complacency of that era, of the great onset since the Second World War of urbanism, of the tensions of the atomic age, of changes in social and ethical mores. They also have the impression that the days of political immaturity are past and that American civilization itself, in spite of television and "go-go," may have gained in cultural stature. It is, therefore, somewhat disconcerting to find the commentary of many German visitors following a line so similar to that of the earlier period.[5]

3. The New America Books: The America books of the Bonn era display the same broad variety of approaches, the same fluctuations between love and hate, the same variations of comprehensiveness, of perceptivity, and of understanding, which characterized those of Weimar. Some of those who wrote during the postwar era were of note during the Weimar period also. Friedrich Schönemann had given his allegiance to the Third Reich but had never completely relinquished his interest in and respect for the United States. During the Bonn era he republished a little handbook on

[4]A significant collection of these interpretative lectures in German is found in James B. Conant, *et al., Zwei Völker im Gespräch; aus der Vortragsarbeit der Amerika-Häuser in Deutschland* (Frankfurt a. M., 1961). Included are lectures in the fields of history, literature, and government.

[5]Thus Alfred Gong in choosing selections for his *Interview mit Amerika: 50 deutschsprachige Autoren in der neuen Welt* (München [c. 1962]) includes without differentiation selections from the Weimar and Bonn eras.

American studies which had first been printed in 1943 with appropriate anti-American bias but now appeared minus the criticisms and snide comments of the war years.[6] But Schönemann's new version met caustic criticism, and his long-worked-on project of a literary history of the United States remained incomplete at his death in 1956.[7]

Another prominent Americanist of the Weimar period, Walther Fischer, made notable contributions to the advancement of American studies during the Bonn era particularly through the founding of a periodical devoted to publication in this field.[8] Ernst Jäckh, who had in 1926 as the president of the German University for Politics (Hochschule für Politik) found the basis for a community of ideas between the United States and Germany, wrote in the postwar period as a "Swabian-American" that the time of "fulfillment" had come. America's democracy, rooted in spiritual conceptions, had also found, he felt, a firm and steadfast anchor in the new Germany.[9]

For some German writers the post-Hitler period brought the return to the homeland after lengthy but disillusioning residence in the United States. Heinrich Hauser, whose enthusiam for Chicago had been moderated by lengthy service as a gardener for the University of Chicago accompanied by "moonlighting" for Marshall Fields, returned to Germany to visit dying parents and to write with nostalgia of the last years of his stay in America in the rural splendor but hard and unprofitable life on his farm in Mississippi.[10] Alfred Auerbach reported that even a Swabian actor and dramatics teacher faced tough sledding and disillusionment in

[6]The wartime edition, *Die Vereinigten Staaten von Amerika* (*Kleine Auslandskunde*, Bd. 14/15. Berlin, 1943). The postwar edition, *Kleine Amerikakunde* (Bonn, 1950).

[7]See my article, "Friedrich Schönemann, German Americanist," *The Historian*, XXVI, No. 3, 381-404 (May, 1964), 403-404.

[8]See Horst Oppel, "Walther Fischer zum Gedächtnis," *Die neueren Sprachen*, X, n.s. (1961), 143-145. See also Fischer's article, "Die Amerikanistik im gegenwärtigen Universitätslehrplan und in den Prüfungsordnungen der deutschen Länder," *Neuphilologische Zeitschrift*, III (1951), 412-417. Fischer edited the *Jahrbuch für Amerikastudien* published in behalf of the German Society for American Studies from 1956 through 1959.

[9]*Amerika und wir, 1926-1951: amerikanisch-deutsches Ideen-Bündnis* (Stuttgart [1951]), 177-197.

[10]*Meine Farm am Mississippi* (Berlin [c. 1950]).

America.[11] And Herbert Weichmann, before Hitler a Prussian Minister of State, also found daily life in America monotonous and unhappy and, in spite of wartime devastation, returned to reestablish himself in the postwar life of Hamburg.[12]

But new Columbuses were numerous and their urge to publish their impressions as compelling as ever. The light and "chatty" accounts of experiences in America continued to find ready publication. Wilhelm Ehmann, the director of the Westphalian chapel choir, recorded brief impressions of the concert tour of his singing group. Ehmann found that the anticipation that his group would have to include "sweet tunes" to get a favorable reception was entirely false, that his American audiences listened with great appreciation and empathy.[13] Another postwar visitor, Karl Korn, the cultural editor of the *Frankfurter Allgemeine Zeitung*, suggested after his return from the United States that Faust had taken Mephistopheles to America, but warned that some of the influence of the demonic gentleman remained on the home scene and reported an upward trend in the United States in the appreciation of cultural matters, in better taste in furniture and clothing, in the significant influence of the public library.[14]

Bruno E. Werner, a well-known novelist and journalist, apologized for writing an "America book" after leading his readers through humorously related and ironically illustrated views of American life, with special reference to museums and theaters. Although he posed as his title the rhetorical question, "Can you forget Europe?" he shied modestly away from caustic criticism and denied any intention of passing judgments based on a three-months' visit.[15]

Another literary figure, Wolfgang Koeppen, a Munich writer several times honored by prizes for his literary achievements, returned from the customary pattern tour of the big cities, broken by sleeping cars and railroad diner meals, to report the prevailing sense of loneliness among Americans. His book, however, gives

[11]*Ein Schwabe studiert Amerika* (Stuttgart [1948]).

[12]*Alltag in USA* ([Hamburg, c. 1949]).

[13]*Alte Musik in der neuen Welt. Bericht und Gedanken über eine Konzertreise der Westfälischen Kantorei durch USA* (Darmstadt [1961]).

[14]*Faust ging nach Amerika* (Olten und Freiburg im Breisgau, 1958).

[15]*Kannst du Europa vergessen? Notizen von einer Amerikareise* (Stuttgart [1952]).

little indication that he had many conversations with Americans; the loneliness was probably as much his own as that of those whom he observed.[16] In contrast, a Swiss author, Paul Rothenhäusler, followed a similar route in his visit, but established enough contact with Americans to discover that one could not judge American food by the ordinary restaurant meal and that American girls could provide some intrinsic interest even for a cultured European.[17]

One of the new visitors began his travels with four dollars as his working capital and managed to see a good deal of America in spite of this shortness of funds.[18] This was, of course, accomplished by having an operating base on a tramp steamer, by luckily earning some money in the United States, and by engaging in the "bumming" adventures which had been frequently related during the Weimar era.

Several of the new visitors were quite careful to warn their readers of the limitations of their accounts. Hans Johann Reinowski, the chief editor of the Darmstädter *Echo*, prefaced his report with the comment, "America has been too long, too often, and too basically discovered, to allow reports on it still to claim originality."[19] And Carl Hermann Hager, one of eleven businessmen sponsored by the United States for a "study trip" dealing with American retail trade, set forth a variegated view of American business in his report on his travels, entitled *Amerika ist noch nicht entdeckt*, but ended his description of the five-weeks' journey with a double warning: the visitor is much too likely to see things with glasses of many colors, and "Only he can criticize who loves the object of his observations. Otherwise his gaze remains clouded and he sees only that which displeases him."[20] Hager concluded his book as its title proclaimed with the denial that he had yet "discovered America." More time and more observation would be required.[21]

No such reservations troubled the Frankfurt journalist, Harald

[16]*Amerikafahrt* (Stuttgart [c. 1959]).

[17]*Amerika für Anfänger* (Zürich [c. 1952]).

[18]Rudolf Jacobs, *Mit 4 Dollar nach USA* (Stuttgart [1947]).

[19]*Ein Mann aus Deutschland besucht Onkel Sam. Rückschau auf eine Amerikareise* (Darmstadt, 1958), 2-3.

[20]*Amerika ist noch nicht entdeckt* (Flensburg [1957]), 93-94.

[21]*Ibid.*, 96.

Ingensand, however. For him a hundred days in America left a
plethora of fixed judgments. In his foreword he pictures his book
defending its right to have been written against the imagined
criticisms of the more painfully researched "America books" reposing beside it on the shelves of the bookstore![22] But the American reader would not be so convinced as the author that his book
was successful in its literary engagement with its rivals! The volume is typical of those written by the pattern tourists, providing
sketchy views of "the hell" of New York, the stockyards of Chicago,
disappointing remnants of the Wild West and of Indian life, the
sights of Hollywood, Salt Lake City, and Houston. Americans, as
Ingensand saw them, are children who like strip-tease shows but
are still embarrassed in bed with their wives and, of course, can't
understand Goethe's Faust. Typical of Ingensand's "brilliant" performance is an eight-page character study of Americans which he
purportedly gave to his wife as they lay abed immediately after his
return. It was, of course, a sign of the intellectual character of
German women and the sense of "togetherness" between husband
and wife that she listened carefully and critically to this lengthy
exposition before she finally laid aside her glasses on the night
table![23]

Perhaps the closest present-day approximation of America's
erstwhile defender, Alfred Kerr, is Rudolf Hagelstange, who is
also a poet, although Hagelstange writes with less enthusiasm
and verve. Hagelstange describes his encounter on his flight across
the Atlantic with the foreign editor of a German newspaper who
was going to America "to see what's wrong over there," and adds,
as he observes the editor's sausage confiscated at customs, "poor
America" —it was destined to come off badly in that man's report!
Hagelstange provided some verses for his account, saw some of
the literary leaders in America, but remained in his own eyes
essentially an "on-looker."[24]

One of the most appealing of the new accounts is that of
Peter von Zahn, who spent two years in America as a correspondent
for the Northwest German Radio before returning to Germany to

[22]*Amerikaner sind auch Menschen* (Stuttgart, 1956), 7-9.

[23]A colleague suggests this also underscores the author's freedom from
American pragmatism!

[24]*How do you like America? Impressionen eines Zaungastes* (München
[c. 1957]).

continue his career as a television and radio reporter and journalist. Von Zahn gained what many German visitors did not—a deep
sense of empathy by virtue of direct and active involvement in
American life. His view of big cities (except for Chicago) was
considerably more understanding than that of most visitors. His
assessment of civilization in the United States stressed its variety
and internal contradictions: "First of all, life in America is stream-
lined. Secondly, life in America is everything else but stream-lined.
Thirdly, these two judgments are apparently mutually exclusive
and yet they are equally justified."[25]

Two of the postwar travel books stand above their companions
in the sharpness and vividness of their picture-sketches. The first
of these is *The Future is Already Here* (1952) by Robert Jungk, a
German journalist now resident in Vienna, who has dealt extensively with the theme of atomic warfare and its dangers. The title
of his book stresses his concept that America is the harbinger of a
future which is far from appealing.[26] Jungk sees with the clear
eye of the camera which reproduces the scenes displayed before it in
crisp detail but has no heart or understanding. Much of his
volume is highlighted by stark and dramatic descriptions of atomic
installations, a macabre sketch of the technique of artificial in-
semination of cattle (even animals are treated as though they were
machines), and bitter-clear portraits of mechanized industry and
business. But he rings all the old changes—America is totally
mechanized, over-sexed but loveless, without soul. America is the
symbol of the future, a flat, dreary, uninspiring future, and the
future is already here. Only at the end of his volume does Jungk

[25]*Fremde Freunde. Bericht aus der neuen Welt* (Hamburg [c. 1953]),
19-20. A similar volume might well have been mentioned here also, that of
Max Thurn, the former Austrian Minister of Finance, who was a member of
the Board of Directors of the World Bank in Washington, 1956-1959, *Amerika:
Hast du es wirklich besser. Mit 6 Zeichnungen von Ironismus* (Wien und
Stuttgart [1960]). Thurn stresses the friendliness, helpfulness, and idealism of
Americans as well as their shortcomings. But he doubts that the twentieth
century will be an American century as the nineteenth century was a British
one and cannot feel the security under the protection of American bombers
which he claims Europe felt under the cannon of the British battleships in
the nineteenth century. Suffice it to say that the last comment is a remarkable rendition of history on the part of an Austrian! (203)

[26]*Die Zukunft hat schon begonnen: Amerikas Allmacht und Ohnmacht*
(Stuttgart [1952]), translated by Marguerite Waldman as *Tomorrow is Already
Here* (New York, 1954).

suggest the existence of those in America who are taking thought for a better tomorrow—at the Princeton Institute for Advanced Studies.

Similar in the author's mastery of colorful and picturesque prose is A. E. Johann's (A. E. J. Wollschläger's) beautifully printed and illustrated volume, *Der grosse Traum Amerika. Sieben Reisen in die USA, 1926 bis 1965.*[27] "The great dream, America" which Wollschläger describes in comprehensive detail is the dream of a better and fuller life, which he finds only imperfectly fulfilled and threatened by retrogression rather than progress with the continuing trend towards urban life. Wollschläger loves America more than he loves Americans! He loves the natural beauties still unspoiled by civilization; he finds small towns and rural areas appealing; he preserves admiration for the spirit of enterprise and worries about the broad extension of governmental activities. He details with passion the sorrows of the Indians to whom America had "belonged" and sets forth vignettes of the problem of Negro civil rights, which grips the nation. He finds in some particular Americans and some isolated groups of Americans qualities which he greatly admires. But he remains clearly and firmly, in spite of all his visits and the impressive extensiveness of his travels, an outsider, an onlooker, an observer. Nor is he entirely free from the perhaps unconscious sense of superiority which has so falsely colored many German observations. What can his concluding observation that the future demands the combination of the great dream of America with the great dream of Europe mean unless it means that the cultural traditions of the mother continent must reform and reguide a new civilization which so clearly lacks them? But after World War II Americans have found it hard to believe in the superiority and humanizing quality of those traditions![28]

4. The New Quest for Interpretation: The critical tone also dominates the "America books" which combine observation with

[27] (Hamburg, 1965).

[28] Another colorful volume on America might also have been cited here, that of the novelist Hans Habe, *The Wounded Land. Journey through a Divided America* (New York [c. 1964]), which exemplifies the tremendous impact John F. Kennedy had on many Europeans and in this particular case on Habe himself, whose emotional shock at Kennedy's death is the major subject of the book.

analysis. Reasonably moderate and objective was one of the earlier volumes which set forth the observations and judgments of twenty journalists and other prominent leaders of German thought. Still employing the occupation period's nickname for Americans in its title, *Amis unter sich* (*Americans at home*), it provided varied views of education, love life, militarism, and religion, and capsule descriptions of some American cities. Notable was a relatively friendly view of American education and of cultural trends.[29]

Just a year after its publication followed the violent excoriation of American life by Leo L. Matthias, *Die Entdeckung Amerikas Anno 1953, oder das geordnete Chaos* (*The Discovery of America in the Year 1953, or the Organized Chaos*).[30] Matthias stemmed from the Weimar generation and had written during that period on Russia, Mexico, and the Orient. His volume on America gave no indication of the length or extent of his visit to the United States but did reflect extensive and careful search through the literature of American self-criticism. The result is something of a *tour de force* in destructive analysis. Well might the French translation of Matthias's book be labeled "an autopsy of the United States!"[31]

Matthias' central theme is that the United States represents the first society completely and solely organized on the principle of acquisitiveness. America's classlessness, he finds, is by no means an advantage. The absence of the concept of *rang*, of rank and its attendant prestige, deprives governmental officials, scholars, and cultural leaders of the social status which crowned their work in Europe. As a result the level of American achievement is virtually at rock bottom. In Matthias' view the United States lacks all elements of refinement and culture; its claim to democracy is pure fiction; its history is one of violence, aggressive warfare, and exploitation; the status of those on the lower end of the economic scale is degraded; religion was never genuine in America and has lost all significance; marriage and love life are warped; and the control of policy is in the hands of incompetents, since "the businessman is no statesman."[32]

Monstrous exaggerations and distortion of evidence dominate

29Edited by Kurt von Gleichen (Wiesbaden, 1952), 10-19, 148-167.
30 (Hamburg [c. 1953]).
31*Autopsie des États Unis,* trad. par Madeleine Gabelle (Paris [1955]).
32*Die Entdeckung Amerikas Anno 1953,* 321.

Matthias' account. The American worker, he assures his German readers, can, of course, buy a second-hand car; he *has* to, in fact, to get to his work; it is a necessity not a luxury. But he can no longer afford to purchase his own home.[33] Indeed, says Matthias, thirty-nine percent of the population lives in great poverty. This is evident in their diet, the quality of their homes and dwellings, and the condition of their health.[34] American foodstuffs are inedible and unnourishing; the American eats ice cream because he can't stand his own bread![35] The United States, he adds, has the highest percentage of mentally disturbed people in the world. Indeed, "It is probable," he concludes, "that the American nation possesses worse conditions of health than any other civilized nation on the earth."[36]

Racketeering dominates political life, Matthias continues, because everyone profits from it.[37] A sense of fear, he feels, had dominated the Ford production system, and then was carried over into the area of political life. The fear system of Ford had even served as a model for the techniques of totalitarian rulers.[38] Education has been "one of the greatest disappointments of America."[39] Matthias describes inadequate schools, censorious school boards, disillusioned and uninspiring teachers. Religion in America is also uninspired, moribund: "One could," suggests Matthias, "throw out of the civilized world all that which is described as Christianity in America without losing anything [of that which was originally conveyed by the term]."[40]

As for international policy, "The wars which America has conducted were for the short period of its history uncommonly numerous."[41] Most, he goes on to suggest, were offensive in character. In spite of the fact "that a portion of the American people possess a great antipathy to war, this has clearly never prevented another part of the population from conducting as many wars as they considered necessary."[42] But the absence of "rank" in

[33]*Ibid.*, 28.
[34]*Ibid.*, 38.
[35]*Ibid.*, 31-32.
[36]*Ibid.*, 32.
[37]*Ibid.*, 51.
[38]*Ibid.*, 54-56.
[39]*Ibid.*, 69.
[40]*Ibid.*, 115.
[41]*Ibid.*, 145.

[42]*Ibid.*, 145-151.

society forced military discipline like politics to turn to "the fear system of the Ford works." Personal relationships in the military remained cool, and American soldiers did poorly in the fighting: "America neither in the first nor second world war stood on the heights of war technique."[43]

And, most important of all, America has no claim to be a haven of freedom; personal rights there are given much less protection than in Europe. Violence and disregard of law are condoned. A sense of security is lacking—even among high governmental officials. For many the only way out is suicide, and Matthias details a number of examples.[44]

As for American women, they have failed in the cultural responsibilities which earlier rested upon them. In their search for equality they have de-sexed themselves. The consequence is a loss of personality. "The uncommon lack of interest which both sexes have for the personality of the other sex is accordingly institutionally anchored, and as long as the institutions remain unaltered [*e.g.* coeducation], all reforms which affect the relationship of the sexes will remain in vain."[45] The American wife lives "near" her husband not "with" him. Love has disappeared in the American world, and "at the same time, there is no land in which the sexual desire has found such a brutal expression as in America."[46]

Matthias, in the concluding statement of this lengthy volume of caustic "debunking," recognizes that his work will occasion anger and hatred. But, he says, if even five hundred of his readers recognize that there is an America-myth, just as there has also been a Russia-myth [Matthias had written earlier on the Soviet Union], his work will not have been in vain.[47]

Matthias need not have been worried. As has been seen, his volume was by no mean *sui generis*. Nor was it the last in the line of critical works. Two volumes of the 1960's reflected much of its tone of disillusion and disdain. One was somewhat more moderate than that of Matthias. The other outdid Matthias!

In his volume entitled *Wofür zu leben lohnt: Ketzereien eines Europäers* (*What makes life worthwhile: Heresies of a European*) [48]

[43]*Ibid.*, 162.
[44]*Ibid.*, 216-220.
[45]*Ibid.*, 243-244.
[46]*Ibid.*, 230-231, 239.
[47]*Ibid.*, 322.   [48] (Düsseldorf und Wien, 1963).

Joachim Besser, the editor-in-chief of the *Kölner Stadtanzeiger*, leads off on a much more moderate note. He stresses the strengths of the United States, its willingness for self-criticism, its concept of the state as servant of its citizens, its adoption of tolerance as a principle of life. The United States, he suggests, has accomplished a "quiet revolution" by which it has created more successfully than the Soviet Union a classless society. He even admits the existence of some cultural accomplishments.

But soon Besser is off on a critical bent—some of it justified—the critique of the deification of the private life of the individual; some of it, like that of the Weimar years and of Matthias, grossly exaggerated. In the latter class is his treatment of sex and love. He admits that in a nation of 180 million there may be seven to ten million Americans who experience love in the European sense.[49] Henry Miller is his authority for the complete absence of tastiness in American meals! And funerals he calls ceremonials accompanied by a complete absence of feeling. Advertising and racial prejudice receive the usual criticisms. Besser believes Europe and America are indeed growing closer together and that only by the complete union of Europe in a partnership including Great Britain can a relationship be developed in which Europe will be able to share with America a formative influence in the future—with the implication that cultural remnants would be thereby preserved.[50]

Far more comprehensive and much more caustic than Besser's book is the recent work of Gerhard Herm, *Amerika Erobert Europa* (*America Conquers Europe*).[51] Through a quasi-historical approach Herm, also a Cologne editor and writer, traces from the founding of the colonies to the present an ever-increasing tempo of influence by the United States on Europe. In the end Europe has, in his view, lost all individuality; it is nothing more than an American province.

The treatment of this theme is biting and bitter but also imaginative. Each period of American history finds the United States exporting a new product—"new times," freedom, good luck, revolution, totalitarianism, myth, "luxury state," "new order," illusion,

---

[49]*Ibid.*, 80.   [50]*Ibid.*, 189-217.

[51] (Düsseldorf und Wien, 1964). Herm had earlier written such works as "Ihr Rolls Royce ist vorgefahren, Mr. Rembrandt," and "Mephisto wohnt Madison Avenue." The author has not seen these publications, but the titles are revealing.

crisis, discontent, capitalism. The author's support for this succession of exports resembles prestidigitation as much as it does scholarship. Many aspects of the volume are historically inaccurate and deceptive, revealing a search for material designed to develop his central theme. Among the most dramatic "discoveries" of Herm are that the Civil War originated total warfare (Sherman's March); that an American adventuress was responsible for Bismarck's fall; that the depression was almost totally due to the United States; that American capital saved communism; and that America supplied the election methods by which Hitler came to set up the Third Reich, "a super America."[52]

Today, he says, Europe is so fully Americanized that every provincial town must have its own "strip-tease" show and automation rules there as it does across the Atlantic. Where it will all end he does not say, but like Besser he stresses the union of Europe in a super state capable of standing as a full partner of America. What policies this state should establish to escape the shadows of Americanism he does not suggest.

Fortunately, among the German views of America which shock, anger, horrify, and distress us, there are some which also impress us as sane and reasonable. Not that these are completely uncritical. Like Schönemann's study of the Weimar period, they combine criticism with reasonable appraisal and with the recognition that it ill-befits Europeans to regard America as a world apart, some fantasy which can be looked upon as utterly strange and alien and hostile to their future. The best studies of the United States of the recent past contain many similarities of structure, approach, and interpretation. They reflect a genuinely scholarly study of the object of their attention. They recognize the great difficulties involved in seeking generalizations in respect to a subject of such diversity and of so many contradictions. They stress the fluidity, the transitory nature of the *status quo* in America. They synthesize a broad sampling of personal observations and of innumerable conversations.

[52]Term used, *ibid.*, 321. Herm also spoke of the "Brauner Zirkus à l'americaine" and suggested Hitler had derived his "babykissing" ritual from America, 318-319. The comments on the Civil War as the origin of war against civilians, 138-139 [Herm conveniently forgets episodes of the Thirty Years' War or even earlier]; on Mary Esther Lee, "Pompadour aus den USA," 229-234; the saving of Communism, 307-311; the depression, 311 ff.

The author of the first of these bears a famous name—he is Golo Mann, the son of the famous novelist, Thomas Mann. As he says in his foreword, he is one of those writers who feels equally at home in Europe or America. Educated in Germany, he began his teaching career in France, but came in 1942 for a sixteen-year stay in the United States before returning to become one of Germany's best known and most productive scholars. His book on the United States, *Vom Geist Amerikas. Eine Einführung in amerikanischen Denken und Handeln im zwanzigsten Jahrhundert (On the American Spirit. An Introduction to American Thought and Action in the Twentieth Century)*[53] binds together Mann's original specialty, philosophy, with his later predominant interest in history. No German author has so perceptively, so clearly, so sympathetically summarized for a German audience the main course of American history and the intricacies of the more recent period. The contradictions of Wilsonianism and *Realpolitik* which have characterized American diplomacy are explained and in part defended. Mann's most serious criticism rests on America's China policy, where he suggests, with considerable conviction, that the American conception of the unlimited capabilities and influence of their country has led to many faulty decisions.[54] But Mann criticizes with the knowledge that the foreign policy of no country has been impeccable: "But he who wishes to live in a country with a perfect foreign policy must look for it on another star."[55] And he stresses the community of interests and of background of the United States and Europe:

> In the crisis confronting the Americans' optimistic faith in progress we in Europe need find no occasion for *Schadenfreude*. For . . . Europeans and Americans in the nineteenth century held basically the same beliefs. There is no real conceptual difference between the faith of Mazzini and Hugo [on the one side] and that of Woodrow Wilson [on the other]; [if a difference exists,] it lies in the fact that Wilson actually thought along more aristocratic, not to say pessimistic lines than they did. Furthermore, the great adventure of Americans is our own adventure. The question what Europe might have made out of such a beautiful continent as North America, had it possessed it, finds its own answer in the fact

[53]Zweite Auflage (Stuttgart, 1955).
[54]*Ibid.*, 153 ff.
[55]*Ibid.*, 168.

that Europe did begin everything there. We need America
not merely because it helps to balance power against power.
We need it because we ourselves are America. America's
misfortune would be our misfortune, America's catastrophe our own catastrophe. With all the brutal, vulgar,
hateful that she conceals, with all her harshly, grossly, rankly
growing life, the American democracy remains the greatest
accomplishment of the European genius for state-building
and is decisive for the fate of [that genius] itself. This, I
believe, is the more fundamental reason why Europeans and
Americans in spite of mutual antipathies find themselves
joined ever and again in the great political crises. They
know it—one would not outlive the other.[56]

It might be added that Mann by no means emphasized "the
brutal, vulgar, hateful" aspects of America which he mentioned in
this passage. Quite the contrary, he employed knowledge of philosophy to set forth one of the most reasonable and appreciative
expositions of the pragmatism of James and Dewey and of the
more metaphysical conceptions of Reinhold Niebuhr yet presented
to German readers.[57] Mann found "the spirit of America stronger,
simpler than the spirit of Germany or France."[58] Pragmatism, he
declared, became in America not a philosophy but a way of life,
devoted to the search for improvement and betterment. As he
expressed it in respect to Dewey:

And wherever Negroes and Whites in a section of Chicago
create and jointly administer welfare institutions so that
their section shall not decline and lose its value, wherever by
research and experiments peace shall be brought about between Mexican and native rowdies, wherever young gangsters
shall be educated to become citizens rather than being left
to rot in jail cells— there is John Dewey's spiritual heritage,
there is, in the broadest sense of the word, pragmatism in
action. Who would condemn such methodically activistic
humanitarianism?[59]

Mann went on, of course, to recognize that there were ridiculous
aspects of pragmatism derived from a naive over-valuation of its
potentialities. For this excessive optimism he found a corrective in
the pessimism of Niebuhr:

[56]Ibid., 172. Quotations with permission of W. Kohlhammer G.m.b.H.
[57]Ibid., 89-124.
[58]Ibid., 90.
[59]Ibid., 103.

The tragic presents no means of escape. On the other hand irony is something which can be conquered. Conquered by a surrender of illusions, by humility, by comparison [of one's self with others]. To see one's self with the eyes of others; to understand the others with their sorrows, fears, passions; to show mercy—charity. In this lies salvation.[60]

And, he adds, "Relatively weighed, Niebuhr's thinking is for Americans today more necessary and more beneficial than Dewey's."[61] By this, he was referring to the spiritual crisis which he saw confronting Americans in days when the optimism of the past would be increasingly more difficult to maintain.

Mann concluded this section on philosophy, which must have been quite shocking to many Germans accustomed to reading cliché castigations of American accomplishments in this field, with the description of a personal experience that was probably even more disturbing. The prevailing German conception of American university students as sport-conscious, superficial rationalists, was contradicted by Mann's description of a retreat in which students gathered together to discuss the subject, "Is religion essential?" As Mann described his experiences:

> With this question I at first had no idea what to do, as with the whole project.
> But soon the subject pleased me more and more. Never have I seen so many earnest and intelligent young people, girls and boys, together; unhampered [in expression] but [possessed] of natural tact; good-humored but not silly, and capable of expressing their thoughts in a truly admirable fashion. Here was nothing of hysteria, faith-healing, or hypocrisy, no sentimentality, no cynicism. Questions which one could not otherwise discuss in a larger circle were dealt with without shyness, with natural directness.[62]

Indeed, Mann was more impressed with the students than with the professors present. American students were, he concluded, not different from those he had known on the Boulevard Saint-Michel:

> They love their land and have reason to love it but are not [excessively] nationalist. They are curious, generous, travel conscious. They respect the European past almost more than their own and the European present almost more than it de-

60*Ibid.*, 113.
61*Ibid.*, 116.
62*Ibid.*, 124.

serves. They are fundamentally good-natured and still they seek betterment and also are self-critical. If all this is "Americanization," then let it come.[63]

All in all, therefore, Mann's book was a real boon to American studies in Germany. Of similar character, although not attaining the same stature, was the volume on the United States by Will Schaber, a writer resident in the United States since 1941. Unlike Golo Mann, Schaber has not returned to his native Germany. Although all his published works found outlets in Germany in his native language, he must be counted as a German-American and this has probably reduced the impact of his writing on his German readers.

His *USA: Koloss im Wandel. Ein Amerika Bericht* (*U.S.A.: Colossus in Transition, a Report on America*)[64] is, however, a comprehensive and colorfully presented overview of American civilization. Modest in tone, without claim to authoritative judgments, Schaber's volume highlights both strengths and weaknesses ("Tweedledum" and "Tweedledee" in politics; "Aspirin of the Soul" in respect to religion; "The Babble of the Ether," etc.). In his conclusions Schaber stresses the continuing formative character of American civilization: "America is even yet—or ever again—a world in new construction."[65] The technical aspect still predominates, he says, and will continue to do so. But social betterment—greater leisure and security against old age—accompanies this. And cultural beginnings have also been made. Europe forgets, he suggests, that Goethe was a thousand years away from Charlemagne, Shakespeare a half of that from Hastings:

America, still stands in the springtime period [of its history]. It is still all too stormily and breathlessly engrossed with the experiment of living to have time left over for contemplation. But it has begun to reflect upon itself and its mission.[66]

Signs of improvement, Schaber believes, are clearly evident in architecture and art, and these are independent of external schools.[67] Historiography and literature are showing greater maturity; the summer music festival in Tanglewood in the Berkshire

63*Ibid.*, 126.
64 (Darmstadt [c. 1958]).
65*Ibid.*, 347.
66*Ibid.*, 358.
67*Ibid.*, 359.

Hills of Massachusetts provides "an effective American counterpart of Salzburg and Edinburgh"; and the reading tastes of Americans may also be expected to mature.[68]

America, he concludes, retains great strength and undiminished potentiality:

> America resembles in the midpoint of the twentieth century a giant who stalks his land with mounting strength, but who is not yet fully conscious of his strength. He is stormy and impulsive, good-natured and generous, occasionally awkward and occasionally stubbornly offended like a boy who hungers for praise and recognition and believes that the outside world unfairly withholds these from him.[69]

America is confronted, he says, by the dangers of an ever increasing materialism and conformity, but "in spite of all inward and outward pressures is not yet motionless. It has retained its dynamic character."[70] And, Schaber adds, its future hinges more on the development and dispersion of its cultural life than on its placing an American on the moon.[71]

The third of these studies which may be classified as much more mature than their predecessors is the volume written by Herbert von Borch, the American representative of *Die Welt*, the Hamburg newspaper which holds an outstanding position within the press of West Germany. Originally entitled *Die unfertige Gesellschaft; Amerika, Wirchlichkeit und Utopie*, von Borch's volume has also found an American audience in its translation, *The Unfinished Society*.[72]

One can only echo the appraisal of the volume by Max Lerner in the preface—in spite of differences of opinion with the author, his work deserves high praise. Like Schaber and Mann he sees American society in the midst of a cultural transformation, one involving a crisis of the spirit. "The best minds in the country," he asserts, "know that the American dream has spent itself and that the nation must live without it."[73] The American faith in the infinite perfectability of man and society is, in other words, no longer possible. America must bid "farewell to Utopia."[74]

---

[68]*Ibid.*, 358-363.　　　　[69]*Ibid.*, 364.

[70]*Ibid.*, 368.　　　　[71]*Ibid.*, 369.

[72] (München [1960]); translation by Mary Ilford (New York, 1962).

[73]*Ibid.*, 12.

[74]Title of Chapter I. Quotations with permission of Hawthorn Books, Inc.

But von Borch is by no means solely critical. His book, he declares, shows *"that there exist so much capacity for self-redress, so many sources of strength in this as yet unfinished American society, that one surely need not despair about the future of this nation or of the West."*[75] Borch presents a thoughtful and perceptive description of "the permeable state," a government of loose and elastic form, subject to change with public opinion, thus avoiding the crisis and upheavals of European states.[76] He describes economic life as a "self-correcting capitalism."[77] He finds many problems: a "power elite" in government; the problem of automation in industry; the tendency of intellectuals to become excessively reconciled to things as they are; the "deification of society"—another phrasing for the problem of excessive conformity; continued racial difficulties; the "self-conscious Eros"; and the shortcomings of television. Borch's handling of these problems is considerably more restrained than that of many of his countrymen, although he also relies too heavily on the literature of cultural criticism. As an American reviewer pointed out: "The technique demonstrates how poorly these works survive export. Typically they represent a dissent from some common view, and when an American reads them, he knows what majority view is being attacked and why the author suggests a corrective. Von Borch uses them as if they represented the whole story."[78] The present author would only add that von Borch's guilt in this respect is a very mild one compared with that of Matthias or Besser!

A fourth assessment of American civilization falls short of real significance because of its author's prejudices. This is the book by Helmut Schoeck, *USA: Motive und Strukturen* (*U. S. A.: Motives and Structures*).[79] Schoeck, presently a Professor of Sociology at Emory University, came to the United States in 1950. The author frankly admitted at the time of writing that his principal measurement of America was his own experience. Some portions of his portrayal of his adopted country are quite sound and reasonable—he does seek to counter myths of America's "lack of his-

[75]*Ibid.*, 27. Italics in original.

[76]*Ibid.*, 38-76.

[77]*Ibid.*, 76-106.

[78]George E. Probst, "After Visions, Values," *Saturday Review of Literature*, XLVI, 834 (January 5, 1963).

[79] (Stuttgart [c. 1958]).

tory," "lack of soul," and of its menace to the personality of the individual. But he writes from the standpoint of an extreme conservatism which leads to continual denunciation of all American intellectuals as "left-standing radicals,"[80] to bitter tirades against the centralizing tendencies unloosed by the Supreme Court's racial decisions,[81] and to severe indictments of the egalitarianism underlying the American system of public education.[82] Schoeck's arguments have some cogency in places. Presented in English as a part of the continuing debate about current policy, they would be justifiable. But presented in German in a book designed to interpret the United States to a foreign audience, they are not. The professor who indicts his colleagues *en bloc* belies the scientific approach which he is supposed to represent. He who criticizes the concept of equal opportunity for high school education ought at least to present the viewpoint of his opponents when he is dealing with a foreign audience to which this is unfamiliar. Schoeck with seven years' residence in the United States speaks with much more self-confidence than the present author could if he sought to explain American "motives" and "structures." Like too many of his countrymen's writings, Schoeck's book tells us more about the author than it does about the U. S. A.!

There have been other German studies worthy of attention. Richard Sallet has published a sketch of the United States which falls somewhat short of his hope of providing for his countrymen an interpretation of America which would be a counterpart of Madame Necker's much earlier interpretation of Germany, which he believed had created real understanding of Germany in America. But his volume, although not marked by genius, is sober, moderate, and factual, and certainly a useful contribution to the advancement of American studies.[83]

80*Ibid.*, Ch. 5, 166 ff. and 192.

81*Ibid.*, 36-50. He is glad that there are those men in the United States who defend states rights by a constant challenge of "the bureaucratic orders of the federal ministeries."

82*Ibid.*, 166-171.

83*Die Vereinigten Staaten von Amerika. Land-Leute-Leben* (Darmstadt [c. 1956]). In much the same class as Sallet's book may be placed the volume by Robert Lohan, *Amerika, Du Hast es Besser. Die Vereinigten Staaten wie sie sind und wie sie geworden sind* (New York [c. 1946]). Lohan's treatment is objective but sketchy and the New York publication probably reduced the circulation of the book in Germany.

Munich economist Christian Egbert Weber has provided a careful and intensive study of industrial relationships in the United States.[84] Undergirding his assessment of American economic life with a search for its philosophical bases, Weber concludes that America has indeed found "quite satisfying" solutions of the social problems which capitalism carries with it; from a religious basis it has moved to emphasize the primacy of economic factors without totally losing that religious basis. Its political and economic "ethos" is different from that of central Europe—assumed is, of course, the conclusion that it is not possible for Europe to "Americanize" herself.[85]

Another view of American economic life, the use of public opinion surveys and their relationship to advertising, forms the central concern of Carl Hundhausen's book, deceptively entitled *Amerika, 1950-1960. Kontinentale Nation und Weltmacht (America, 1950-1960. Continental Nation and World Power).*[86]

Undoubtedly, the field of American Studies has won greater prestige in recent years. The publication of the periodical, *Jahrbuch für Amerikastudien* and its *Beihefte* (supplements) has provided an outlet for scholarly work in this field. The volumes reflect an increasing interest in and more discriminating study of American history and literature. It is unfortunate that one of the most prolific of the new historians of the United States, Hellmuth Günther Dahms, mars his scholarship with a "neo-revisionist" approach in which he seeks to underscore the malevolent war-mongering of Franklin D. Roosevelt.[87] Other German historians, notably Erich Angermann of the America Institute at the University of Munich, Waldemar Besson of the University of Erlangen, and Günter Moltmann of the University of Hamburg, have written more moderately and soberly on the recent era.[88] In the field of political science

[84]*Wirtschaft und Gesellschaft in den Vereinigten Staaten von Amerika* (Berlin [c. 1961]).

[85]*Ibid.*, 243-255.

[86] (Essen, 1950).

[87]*Geschichte der Vereinigten Staaten von Amerika* (München, 1953); *Roosevelt und der Krieg; die Vorgeschichte von Pearl Harbor* (München [1958]).

[88]Angermann, "Die Vereinigten Staaten von Amerika," in *Weltgeschichte der Gegenwart*, herausgegeben von Felix von Schroeder, Band I, *Die Staaten* (Bern und München, 1962), 385-405; Besson, *Von Roosevelt bis Kennedy. Grundzüge der amerikanischen Aussenpolitik, 1933-1963* (Frankfurt a. M. [c.

the scholarly work of Ernst Fraenkel has provided much more sophisticated views of the American governmental system than were available during the Weimar period.[89]

But the work of the specialists in American Studies continues to confront obstacles in the German academic world. Apparently it is not a clearly defined field in either history or literature. And the number of German specialists in American history or literature is vastly exceeded by the number of American specialists in German history and literature. Perhaps when American Studies reach a status of greater maturity within the German universities, the production of ill-considered and superficial America books will decline. At least they would have to confront better informed and more critical reviewers.

1964]); Moltmann, *Amerikas Deutschlandpolitik im zweiten Weltkrieg (Beihefte zum Jahrbuch für Amerikastudien*, III, Heidelberg, 1958). Obviously this listing makes no pretense of mentioning all of the noteworthy books on American history by contemporary German historians.

[89]*Amerika im Spiegel des deutschen politischen Denkens.* (already cited); *Das amerikanische Regierungssystem. Eine politologische Analyse.* (Köln und Opladen, 1960). Another recent scholarly volume deserves mention, although its purpose is to present the other side of the coin—the history of the American image of Germany. This is Christine M. Totten's *Deutschland—Soll und Haben. Amerikas Deutschlandbild* (München, 1964). In her carefully researched study Miss Totten reflects an impressive depth of knowledge in respect to American cultural achievements.

Chapter XIII

POLISHING THE AMERICAN IMAGE

he Machine in the Garden: New Variations on an Old Theme: The cultural criticism of the United States which has been so prominent in the America books of Germany has, of course, also been significant in those of other European countries. In Great Britain Francis Williams warns in would-be kindly and moderate fashion against *The American Invasion*,[1] and Denis W. Brogan presents restrained criticism in his *American Aspects*.[2] In France André Siegfried has spoken of the "mégalomanie de la technique" in America, the eclipsing of culture by technics and gadgets, the reduction of the role of the individual, the decline of the humanities.[3] The "bad press" devoted to America is virtually universal and it does have its effect—witness the frequent notes of surprise at the contrast between American realities and that which they had anticipated in the essays of foreign viewers collected by Franz M. Joseph, *As Others See Us: the United States through Foreign Eyes*.[4]

[1] ([London, 1962]). *E.g.*, 11, "The American Eagle is a friendly bird. It does not wish to swoop upon the little lambs. It desires only to help them to be good. . . .

"To complain of the world-wide advance of American power is silly. Such an advance is inevitable in the current nature of the world. . . .

"But need alliance involve occupation? Must we become Americans to save Western civilization?" And, 13, "This is an intelligence report on an invasion. No doubt the invasion is benevolent. But that does not make it less threatening. There are few things so menacing as wholesale benevolence."

[2] (New York, 1964).

[3] From Jacques Freymond, "America in European Eyes," in *America Through Foreign Eyes* (*The Annals of the American Academy of Political and Social Science*, CCXCV, September, 1954), 36. The last section of the bibliography indicates a number of recent surveys of foreign views of the United States which amply detail the prevailing critical assessment.

[4] (Princeton, New Jersey, 1959).

Much of this European criticism is, of course, strongly supported by that of domestic origin. H. L. Mencken has been re-
placed by even more biting critics, and once again these provide
much grist for the mills of European observers. As noted above,
Joachim Besser made extensive use of Henry Miller's devastating
examination of contemporary United States, *The Air-Conditioned
Nightmare*. Gerhard Herm was familiar with James G. Burnham's
Managerial Revolution, Ernest Dichter's *The Strategy of Desire*,
John K. Galbraith's *The Affluent Society*, William H. Whyte's *The
Organization Man*, Norbert Wiener's *The Human Use of Human
Beings: Cybernetics and Society*, David Reisman's *The Lonely
Crowd*, and Albert K. Cohen's *Delinquent Boys: the Culture of
the Gang*.[5] Herbert von Borch and Leo Matthias both made use
of Philip Wylie's *Generation of Vipers*, and von Borch also knows
the works of Vance Packard. Rather puzzling because Germans
have been much intrigued by American Freudianism is the fact
that no German writer seems yet to have exploited Richard La-
Piere's *The Freudian Ethic*[6] which would add new facets to their
interpretation of this theme. Undoubtedly, this will still come.

European commentators usually make use of studies of this
sort quite uncritically and superficially. It is the catchword concept which is of utility—Wylie's "momism," Whyte's "organization
man," Galbraith's "affluent society," Dichter's "motivational research," Wiener's "cybernetics," etc. Wylie's book was written in
the heat of anti-German passion, and its denunciation of Hitler's
Reich is virulent indeed. To use his "momism" and ignore the
rest of what he says is misleading as well as superficial. Most of
the other volumes could be applied *mutatis mutandis* to the German scene as well as to the United States. Few Germans seem to
have studied carefully Max Lerner's *America as a Civilization*,
although it has been published in German. The writer has yet
to find a reference to Thomas Griffith's *The Waist-High Culture*[7]

[5]The author is aware of the fact that not all of these belong to the
literature of cultural dissent, but, as suggested below, they are used in that
sense by Herm.

[6] (New York [c. 1959]). A number of other recent volumes are probably
destined for support of foreign criticism also, *e.g.*, Lawrence Lipton, *The Holy
Barbarians* (New York [c. 1959]); Norman Lobsenz, *In Anybody Happy? A
Study of the American Search for Pleasure* (New York, 1962); and Marya
Mannes, *More in Anger* (New York [c. 1958]).

[7] (New York [c. 1959]).

which links with his view of his own country the extensive experiences abroad of a thinking American journalist. Even worse, few of the German authors of "America books" seem to pay attention to those written by their own countrymen, past and present. Far too few German interpreters of America really uphold by their own publications the high standards of culture which they claim for Europe and particularly for their own country.

American cultural self-criticism is, of course, one of the great traditions of this country. The philosophical undergirding of much of it has been described in Leo Marx's recent work, *The Machine in the Garden: Technology and the Pastoral Idea in America.*[8] It is typical of the blasts of passionate hostility unloosed by those who are disturbed from the quiet of peace and reflection by the hustle and bustle of modern life. It contains, as another recent writer has suggested, a note of wistful nostalgia, a longing for a return to "better times."[9]

The foreign critic writes largely from the same motivation as the domestic. But he gains the additional advantage of categorizing his fears and concerns as exterior to his homeland. The domestic critic at least faces his problems honestly and sincerely; the foreign critic creates the fiction that these problems are theirs only because they have been imposed from abroad.

2. *The Vanity of Cultural Criticism*: Much of this cultural criticism both domestic and foreign reveals a high degree of personal vanity. The egomania of Henry Miller is apparent in everything he writes. He seeks to set himself apart, away from, above the environment from which he sprang. Some of his defenders say he cudgels America with love in his heart, his purpose that of reform. The present writer sees in his books only self-love, self-praise, self-deification—he is the god who does no wrong although he whores, uses obscene language, ignores all niceties and felicities of feelings and emotions. He is not really so much a figure of present day literature as a throwback to the German literature of *Sturm und Drang*.

Philip Wylie's famous book leaves us with the view of a latter-

---

8 (New York, 1964).

9Robert L. Duffus, *Nostalgia U.S.A.; or, If you don't like the 1960's, Why don't you go back where you came from* (New York, 1963).

day prophet who seeks to raise the benighted masses to the supreme level of personal wisdom he has found by self-exploration. Although he lacks Count Keyserling's aristocratic background, he could change places with that diffuse philosopher with little difficulty.

Moreover, these volumes and those of other domestic cultural critics have a sensationalist element which contradicts their professed standards. They sound alarums; they jangle; they create headlines. In this they signal the fact that these critics, in spite of their criticism, are indeed a part of the scene they criticize, of it, not above it. Their writings fit into the pattern of excitement, of the exploitation in vivid language of malaise and uncertainty, which is certainly one of the weaknesses of contemporary culture. This is not to say that none of these works is valid or of value. But too frequently they result in hyperbolic criticisms of existing cultural weaknesses without providing a vital inspiration for improvement.

The same reproach may be laid even more strongly at the door of contemporary German critics. Accounts like those of Matthias and of Herm represent a denegation of scholarship which positively lowers the standards of German culture! The superficial and supercilious travel account underscores the falsity of its author's claim to represent century-long traditions of cultural achievement. Undoubtedly, the time has arrived when Americans should be able to provide the answers to criticism. They may well declare, as does Thomas Griffith, for example:

> The splendors of Europe are largely survivals. If one levels off what has been done in America in his own generation, and sets against it what has been achieved in Europe—in architecture, art, music or theater—I do not think that Americans need be uncomfortable with the comparison. . . .
> All this goes through my head when I hear The European Speech [patronizing America from the Olympian heights of European culture]. And when I hear that patronizing appendix to it, that Europe is Greece and America Rome—that wise old Europe, with its serene and moderate wisdom, must now guide that powerful but clumsy adolescent, strong but insensitive America—I am prepared to accept the comparison if it is made exact; that is, if Europe is really ready to compare itself with the fallen Greece of slaves and school teachers in the era of Roman greatness, rather than with the creative earlier Greece of Pericles. On these terms, I am not sure

that Europe would welcome the comparison and we need not insist upon it.[10]

3. *The Improvement of Cultural Communication*: At the end, then, of a very minute and detailed examination of one era of cultural communication, the Weimar period, and of a somewhat more sketchy look at the recent period, it may be possible to arrive at some practical suggestions to improve the American image abroad. This is a matter of great concern, for in spite of the growing ease of transportation and communication, it is obvious that one nation still derives its "image" of another in a haphazard and random fashion that perpetuates cliché superficialities and misconceptions. For the United States this communication of its image abroad is of serious moment. Certainly the creation of an informed and sympathetic public view of this country and its policies and procedures is intimately connected with a more successful utilization of its power and influence in world politics. Some improvement could be obtained with a relatively modest expenditure of funds. These funds might well be devoted to the following purposes:

1. An organized effort to improve the "image" of America seen by travelers from abroad. One might legitimately doubt from the examination of its contents whether the whole genre of travel literature is worthy of the attention given it by publishers and the public. But doubts of its fundamental utility will not bring its disappearance from the scene. On the other hand, it might properly be recognized that many travelers from abroad do come to this country with the conscious object of studying its civilization. Their efforts are too frequently subject to the shortcomings attached to any process of self-education and to lack of language proficiency. Their study leaves gaps in observation, analysis, and understanding.

The federal government might well consider a project by which it would contract with chosen universities and travel agencies for a real study tour to be characterized by a full sampling of geographical sections, social classes and occupations, educational and religious institutions, cultural and recreational activities. This should be accompanied by lectures and discussions led by *competent* specialists in American studies. If these specialists are unilingual, translations of their statements should be provided. It

[10]*The Waist-High Culture*, 140-141.

will, of course, be objected that this smacks of propaganda methods, but the procedures of such a tour could provide a clear contradiction of this charge, and it must, once again, be emphasized that the traveler who proceeds on his own very seldom obtains the more discriminating views which he could acquire with skillful guidance.

2. Even more significant would be the provision of increased opportunity for the serious student of this country to come for an extended and meaningful stay. In particular, this should be provided for the opinion-forming segments of foreign countries—educators and religious leaders, journalists and other professional people, and politicians. The provisions for exchange professorships ought to be extended. Larger numbers of public school teachers and religious leaders should be added. It should not be too difficult to make provision for subsidized temporary employment in the United States of journalists or free-lance writers with an established record of publication. Efforts should be made to provide for the temporary residence of professional people or businessmen who indicate a serious intention of studying the life of their counterparts in this country. And visits for politicians should make possible a more extended stay than the guided tours conducted by the State Department.

Obviously, not every individual who came under such arrangements would return to his homeland to praise the United States. Many would probably be too much a part of an alien cultural pattern to make the adjustments necessary to gain a sympathetic understanding. Language barriers would still remain. And some personalities stubbornly resist the intrusion of points of view which contradict their own! But it is clear from the examination of the "America books" written in Germany that the best appraisals of life in this country have been written by those whose stay here involved a period of months or years rather than weeks, who came under an arrangement which made them temporarily part of the life of the nation rather than transient aliens, and which provided them broad opportunities for acquaintance with and friendship for Americans. It would not require very much imagination to extend very greatly the opportunities for such views of our country.

3. It is worth some effort to provide for American students and professors going abroad a current analysis of the recent writings about America in the country which they will visit. The author is

not maligning his colleagues when he suggests that few Fulbright or Schmidt-Mundt professors have really been aware of the scope of literature on the United States published in the country to which they were assigned. Although seven years of study and research have been devoted to the present volume, its coverage of the contemporary period remains quite incomplete, but surely the Fulbright professor who reads this volume prior to going to Germany will be better prepared to explain the strengths and weaknesses of American life and to suggest to Germans the more appropriate works relating to the subject. Similar studies relating to other countries are needed. The "sample" studies, such as Franz M. Joseph's *As Others See Us: the United States through Foreign Eyes* and James Burnham's *What Europe Thinks of America* do not at all meet this need. A scholar teaching American studies abroad should have a knowledge in depth of the works on the United States written in the country where he will be teaching. Unfortunately, many of the scholars best equipped by their experience and research to lecture on American studies abroad do not have the language capabilities of obtaining this knowledge. It would not be amiss and it would not be propaganda or thought-control for the government to make available précis of recent writings.

4. It is also worth some effort and expense to subsidize the translation of those works which provide affirmation, or at least a reasonably balanced study, of American accomplishments. The literature of cultural dissent is quickly translated. It finds a ready market abroad. The translation of more sober and serious studies is often long delayed. The assumption that everyone seriously interested in the United States will study English is a faulty one. The "America Houses" abroad would have a much greater impact on the thinking of those who visited them if they provided a larger sampling of literature in translation. In particular, because this is one of the most critical areas in our national image, it would be of value to facilitate the translation of those works dealing with the accomplishments of this country in the cultural sphere. Judgment should not be left to critics who proclaim that the United States has no art, music, or literature worthy of the name nor to the pervading influence of exported jazz and Hollywood movies. This is a matter of concern to all Americans, for the warmth, the depth, the nuances of light as well as of shadow, which are a part

of our own feelings about our country are too often lost in the transmission of its image overseas.

5. Finally, it would serve not only to improve the American image abroad but also to render due recognition for strivings against great academic obstacles if the United States were to provide in each of the great countries of the world a prize or prizes for those professors who have made distinctive contributions to the advancement of the field of American studies. Although Schönemann and Hylla received recognition for their work from individual American universities, none of the men who gave their lives to the effort to find a niche in the German academic system for this new discipline of *Amerikakunde* received official recognition or support from America. Perhaps it might be more appropriate to seek funds for such a purpose from private sources, but the prestige conferred by such a prize would add weight to the work of those who view this country more soberly, considerately, and sympathetically.

Undoubtedly there are many other ways in which the transmission of the American cultural image could be improved. A larger measure of responsibility on the part of our own cultural critics, a realization on their part of the need to suggest the limitations and scope of their criticism, would be helpful. The efforts being launched to advance the position of the humanities and those directed to the improvement of the beauty of our cities and highways are positive measures. Even more important than all of these, however, will be the strivings of individual teachers, professors, artists, musicians, and actors to provide an exemplification of their role in life which will be a living memorial of continued creativity, a recognition that the proper task of cultural leaders is to inspire their contemporaries to greater accomplishment rather than to carp at the existing weaknesses of society. The professor who leads his students further along the road of self-examination and reflection, the artist who creates new beauty in visual form, the musician whose composition lifts his contemporaries above the drabness of their daily lives, the literary genius who touches the heart of man whether he be sophisticated or simple—all of these contribute more to the advancement of society than does the cynical critic. And this is true not only on the domestic scene but also abroad. For in this world increasingly linked by the marvelous advances which have been made in transportation and communication, it becomes also increasingly important to raise the levels of international understanding and sympathy, to underscore the positive accomplishments of our neighbors rather than their defects, to encourage mutual respect among those of varying cultural heritages, to bring about international cooperation in raising the level of cultural accomplishment everywhere.

The present study has underscored the great difficulties confronted by those who seek to understand the cultural traditions and accomplishments of other nations. The culture of a modern, civilized state is highly complex. It does not lend itself to description by easy generalizations. Efforts to summarize and characterize result too frequently in the trite and the cliché. Years of study of the geography, history, politics, economics, and literature of an alien civilization provide some keys to understanding. But even these are in themselves insufficient—above and beyond lies the requisite quality of empathy, of one's ability to project oneself into thought patterns and emotional responses differing from his own. Too few travelers, too few scholars, too few statesmen today recognize the enormity of the task of bridging the gaps which lie between the great powers of the world. Perhaps this is the greatest educational problem confronting mankind. It is, of course, not a new one, but the science, the technology, the military capabilities of today make it impossible to treat it with the self-satisfied complacency which has existed in the past. Its solution requires the expansion and intensification of the existing dialogues between scholars of nations seeking mutual understanding.

BIBLIOGRAPHY

PART ONE: THE AMERICA LITERATURE OF THE WEIMAR PERIOD

1. Books:

Abel, Othenio. *Amerikafahrt. Eindrücke, Beobachtungen und Studien eines Naturforschers auf einer Reise nach Nordamerika und Westindien.* Jena: G. Fischer, 1926.

Aeroboe, Friedrich. *Wirtschaft und Kultur in den Vereinigten Staaten von Nord-Amerika.* Berlin: Parey, 1930.

Angermann, Adolar. *The Ways of the Americans. Lesebuch zur amerikanische Wesenskunde für Oberklassen.* Bielefeld: Velhagen & Klasing, 1932.

Anon. *Erlebnisse und Betrachtungen eines Deutsch-amerikaners.* Dresden: C. Reissner, 1929.

Anon. *Im Schatten amerikanischer Demokratie und Freiheit.* Charlottenburg: Raben Verlag [1918].

Barthelme, Georg. *Aus meinem amerikanischen Skizzenbuch.* Köln: J. G. Schmitz, 1918.

Baumann, Felix, *Aus dunklen Häuser Amerikas. Chicago, die Stadt der Verworfenen. Sittengeschichte aus den Vereinigten Staaten.* Stuttgart: W. Digel, 1920.

Bernstorff, Johann Heinrich. *Deutschland und Amerika. Erinnerungen aus dem fünf-jährigen Kriege.* Berlin: Ullstein, 1920.

Bloch, Chajim [Hayim]. *Das jüdische Amerika. Wahrnehmungen und Betrachtungen.* Wien-Brigittenau: Verlag "Das Leben," 1926.

Böhler, Eugen und Dr. Hans Wehberg. *Der Wirtschaftskrieg. Die Massnahmen und Bestrebungen des feindlichen Auslands zur Bekämpfung des deutschen Handels und zur Förderung des eigenen Wirtschaftslebens. Fünfte Abteilung, Vereinigten Staaten von Amerika.* Jena: Gustav Fischer, 1919.

Bonn, Moritz J. *Amerika als Feind (Die Staaten und der Krieg,* hrsgbn. von Palatinus, Heft 1). München und Berlin: Georg Muller [1917?].

——————. *Amerika und sein Problem.* München: Meyer & Jessen, 1925.

——————. *Geld und Geist. Vom Wesen und Werden der amerikanischen Welt.* Berlin: S. Fischer [1927].

——————. *Die Kultur der Vereinigten Staaten von Amerika.* Berlin: Volksverband der Bücherfreunde, 1930. [tr. by Mabel Brailsford. *The American Adventure; a Study of Bourgeois Civilization.* New York: The John Day Company [c. 1934]].

——————. *Musste es sein?* 3. völlig umgearbeitete und stark erweiterte ausg. von "Amerika als Feind." (*Fehler und Forderungen. Schriftenfolge zur*

Neugestaltung deutscher Politik. Hrsgbn. von Palatinus, 7. Heft) München: G. Müller, 1919.

——————. *"Prosperity"! Wunderglaube und Wirklichkeit im amerikanischen Wirtschaftsleben.* Berlin: S. Fischer, 1931. [tr. by Winifred Ray. *The Crisis of Capitalism in America.* New York: The John Day Company [c. 1932].]

——————. *Was will Wilson?* (*Fehler und Forderungen. Schriftenfolge zur Neugestaltung deutscher Politik.* Hrsg. von Palatinus, 6. Heft). München: Georg Müller [n.d.–1918?].

Borchardt, Julian. *Demokratie und Freiheit. Eine Untersuchung über das parlamentarische System und seine Wirkungen in den westlichen Kultur-staaten, I, Amerikanische Freiheit.* Berlin: Buch und Zeitschriftenverlag. G. Sturm, 1918.

Bornhausen, Karl. *Der christliche Aktivismus Nordamerikas in der Gegenwart.* Giessen: A. Töpelmann, 1925.

Bratter, Carl Adolf. *Amerika, von Washington bis Wilson.* Berlin: Ullstein, 1917.

——————. *Amerikanische Industriemagnaten.* Berlin: Ullstein [c. 1927].

——————. *Die Vereinigten Staaten von Amerika; ihre Entstehung und Entwicklung.* Berlin: Ullstein [c. 1928].

Brinkmann, Carl. *Democratie und Erziehung in Amerika.* Berlin: S. Fischer Verlag, 1927.

——————. *Geschichte der Vereinigten Staaten.* Leipzig: B. G. Teubner, 1924.

Büchler, Eduard. *Rund um die Erde. Erlebtes aus Amerika, Japan, Korea, China, Indien und Arabien.* Bern: A. Francke a.g. [c. 1921].

Carlé, Erwin [ps. Erwin Rosen]. *Amerikaner.* Leipzig-Gaschwitz: Dürr & Weber, m. b. H., 1930.

——————. *Der deutsche Lausbub in Amerika; Erinnerungen und Eindrücke von Erwin Rosen.* 3 vols. Stuttgart: R. Lutz [c. 1911-1913].

Cohnstaedt, Wilhelm. *Amerikanische Demokratie und ihre Lehren.* Frankfurt: Frankfurter Societätsdruckerei, 1919.

Cramer, Hugo. *Als Junglehrer nach U.S.A. Erlebnisse eines Ehepaares.* Leipzig?: Rektor Hugo Cramer, 1932.

Daenell, Ernst Robert. *Geschichte der Vereinigten Staaten von Amerika.* 1st Ed., Leipzig: Teubner, 1907. 3rd Ed., Leipzig: Teubner, 1923.

Darmstädter, Paul. *Die Vereinigten Staaten von Amerika; ihre Politische, Wirt-schaftliche und Soziale Entwicklung.* Leipzig: Quelle & Meyer, 1909.

Descovich, Emo. *Unsere Technik und Amerika.* 15 aufl. Stuttgart: Dieck & Co., 1927.

Dessauer, Friedrich. *Auslandsrätsel. Nordamerikanische und spanische Reise-briefe.* München: J. Kösel & F. Pustet, 1922.

Deutscher Gewerkschaftsbund. *Amerikareise deutscher Gewerkschaftsführer.* Berlin: Verlagsgesellschaft des Allgemeinen Deutschen Gewerkschafts-bundes, 1926.

Devaranne, Theodor. *Amerika, du hasts nicht besser! Reisebriefe aus Amerika.* Heidelberg: Evangelischer Verlag, 1929.

Dietrich, Bruno. *U.S.A. Das heutige Gesicht.* Breslau: Ferd. Hirt, 1926.

Dorfmann, Jakob. *Im Lande der Rekordzahlen. Amerikanische Reiseskizzen.* Berlin: Verlag für Literatur und Politik, 1927.

Dovifat, Emil. *Der amerikanische Journalismus. Mit einer Darstellung der journalistischen Berufsbildung.* Stuttgart: Deutsche Verlags-anstalt, 1927.

Dubreuil, H[yacinthe]. *Arbeiter in USA.* Mit einem Vorwort von Dr. Ernst Michel. Leipzig: Bibliographisches Institut [1930].

Eberhardt, Fritz, ed. *Amerika-Literatur. Die wichtigsten seit 1900 in deutscher Sprache erschienenen Werke über Amerika.* Leipzig: Koehler & Volckmar 1926.

Erkelenz, Anton. *Amerika von Heute. Briefe von einer Reise.* Berlin-Charlottenburg: Weltgeist-Bücher, 1927.

Escher, Hermann. *Aus dem amerikanischen Bibliothekwesen. Beobachtungen und Studien.* Tübingen: Mohr, 1923.

Eulenberg, Herbert. *Amerikanus. Amerikanische Lichtbilder.* Wien: Thrysos-Verlag, 1924.

Ey, Karl—see Meyer, Karl H.

Faber, Kurt. *Rund um die Erde. Irrfahrten und Abenteuer eines Grünhorns.* Berlin: Globus Verlag, 1924.

Faldix, Arno Guido. *Henry Ford als Wirtschaftspolitiker.* München: F. A. Pfeiffer, 1925.

Feiler, Arthur. *Amerika-Europa. Erfahrungen einer Reise.* Frankfurt a. M.: Societäts Verlag, 1926 (tr. by Margaret L. Goldsmith, *America seen through German Eyes.* New York: New Republic, 1928.).

Feuchtinger, Stadtdirektor, Ulm, a. D. and Dr. Ing. Neumann, *Bericht über eine Studienreise in den Vereinigten Staaten von Nordamerika.* Charlottenburg: Studiengesellschaft für Automobilstrassenbau, 1925.

Fischer, Walther Paul. *Amerikanische Prosa. Vom Bürgerkrieg bis auf die Gegenwart (1863-1922).* Leipzig: B. G. Teubner, 1926.

——————, with A. Haushofer, E. Hylla, H. Levy, L. Müller, H. Mutschmann, J. Richter, and M. Schoch. *Handbuch der Amerikakunde.* Frankfurt a. M.: Moritz Diesterweg, 1931.

——————. *Hauptfrage der Amerikakunde. Studien und Aufsätze.* Bielefeld: Velhagen & Klasing, 1928.

Francé, Raoul Heinrich. *Lebender Braunkohlenwald. Eine Reise durch die heutige Urwelt.* Stuttgart: Kosmos, Gesellschaft der Naturfreunde, 1932.

Francé-Harrar, Annie. *Florida. Das Land des Überflusses.* Berlin-Schöneberg: Peter J. Oestergaard [c. 1931].

Francke, Kuno. *Deutsche Arbeit in Amerika. Erinnerungen von . . .* Leipzig: F. Meiner, 1930.

Frenssen, Gustav. *Briefe aus Amerika.* Berlin: G. Grote'sche Verlag, 1923.

Friederici, Georg. *Das puritanische Neu-England. Ein Beitrag zur Entwicklungsgeschichte der nordamerikanischen Union (Studien über Amerika und Spanien* hrsg. von Karl Sapper, Arthur Franz, Adalbert Hämel, völkerkundlich-historische Reihe, 1. Heft). Halle an der Saale: Max Niemeyer, 1924.

Gagern, Friedrich von. *Das Grenzerbuch. Von Pfadfindern, Häuptlingen und Lederstrümpfen.* 2.aufl. Berlin: P. Parey, 1927.

Giehrl, Hermann von. *Das amerikanische Expeditionskorps in Europa 1917/18.* Berlin: E. S. Mittler & Sohn, 1922.

Glaser, Curt. *Amerika baut auf.* Berlin: Bruno Cassirer, 1932.

Gley, Werner. *Die Grossstädte Nordamerikas und die Ursachen ihrer Entwicklung.* Frankfurt a. M.: Gebr. Knauer, 1927.

Goldberger, Ludwig Max. *Das Land der unbegrenzten Möglichkeiten. Beobachtungen über das Wirtschaftsleben der Vereinigten Staaten von Amerika.* Leipzig: F. Fontane & Co., 1903.

Goldschmidt, Alfons. *Die dritte Eroberung Amerikas. Bericht von einer Pan-Amerikareise.* Berlin: Rowohlt, 1929.

Goldschmidt, Bernhard. *Von New York bis Frisco. Ein deutsches Reisetagebuch.* Berlin: Dietrich Reimer, 1925.

Gontard, Paul C. von. *West vom Mississippi. Bilder aus den unpolierten Breiten des heutigen Nordamerika.* Berlin: G. Stilke, 1928.

Goslar, Hans. *Amerika, 1922.* Berlin-Wilmersdorf: Hermann Paetel, 1922.

Gottl-Ottlilienfeld, Friedrich von. *Fordismus: Ueber Industrie und technische Vernunft.* Jena: Gustav Fischer, 1926.

Haebler, Konrad. *Geschichte Amerikas.* Leipzig: Bibliographisches Institut, 1923.

Halfeld, Adolf. *Amerika und der Amerikanismus.* Jena: Diederichs, 1927.

Hassert, Kurt. *Die Vereinigten Staaten von Amerika als politische und wirtschaftliche Weltmacht geographisch betrachtet.* Tübingen: J. C. B. Mohr, 1922.

Hauser, Heinrich. *Feldwege nach Chicago.* Berlin: S. Fischer, 1931.

Hausmann, Manfred. *Kleine Liebe zu Amerika. Ein junger Mann schlendert durch die Staaten.* 7.-11. Aufl. Berlin: S. Fischer Verlag, 1931.

Hawk, C. B. *Im Schatten amerikanischer Demokratie und Freiheit.* Chemnitz: Raben Verlag, 1918.

Hedin, Alma. *Arbeitsfreude. Was wir von Amerika lernen können.* Leipzig: F. A. Brockhaus, 1921.

Hegemann, Werner. *Amerikanische Architektur und Stadtbaukunst. Ein Überblick über den heutigen Stand der amerikanischen Baukunst in ihrer Beziehung zum Staedtebau* (1. Band von "Der Städtebau."). Berlin: E. Wasmuth, 1927. 2. Aufl.

Hellmann, Siegmund. *Deutschland und Amerika.* (Nach einem Vortrag). München: Duncker & Humblot, 1917.

Hensel, Rudolf. *Die neue Welt. Ein Amerikabuch.* Dresden: Hegner, 1929.

Hirsch, Julius. *Das amerikanische Wirtschaftswunder.* Berlin: S. Fischer, 1926.

Hitler, Adolf. *Hitlers zweites Buch; ein Dokument aus dem Jahr 1928.* Eingeleitet und kommentiert von Gerhard L. Weinberg mit einem Geleitwort von Hans Rothfels. Stuttgart: Deutsche Verlags-Anstalt, 1961 (tr. by Salvator Athanasio. *Hitler's Secret Book.* New York: Grove Press [c. 1961].).

Holitscher, Arthur. *Amerika Heute und Morgen. Reiseerlebnisse.* 11. Aufl. Berlin: S. Fischer, 1919.

——————. *Amerika. Leben, Arbeit, und Dichtung.* Berlin: Verlag der neuen Gesellschaft, 1923.

——————. *Das amerikanische Gesicht.* Berlin: S. Fisher, 1916.

——————. *Wiedersehn mit Amerika. Die Verwandlung der U. S. A.* Berlin: S. Fischer, 1930.

Hollweg, Karl. *Columbusfahrt. Politische, wirtschaftliche und soziale Entdecker-betrachtungen auf einer Amerikareise.* Berlin: E. S. Mittler & Sohn, 1925.

Hoppé, Emil Otto. *Romantic America, picturesque United States.* New York: B. Westermann Co., Inc. [1927]. (tr. of *Die Vereinigten Staaten. Das romantische Amerika. Baukunst, Landschaft, und Volksleben.* Berlin: Atlantis Verlag, 1927. German edition not available.)

Hylla, Erich. *Die Schule der Demokratie; ein Aufriss des Bildungswesens der Vereinigten Staaten.* Langensalza: J. Beltz [1928].

Jacobi, Marie. *Im Dollarland. Reisen und Erlebnisse einer deutschen Schul-meisterin.* Bremen: Lloyd-Buchhandlung, 1928.

Jäckh, Ernst. *Amerika und wir. Amerikanisch-deutsches Ideenbündnis.* Stuttgart: Deutsche Verlags-anstalt, 1929.

Johann, Alfred Ernst—see Wollschläger, Alfred Ernst Johann.

Jungmann, Erich. *Meine zweite Amerikafahrt, 1932.* (Vortrag im Deutschen Rotary-Club Liegnitz am 11. April 1933). Liegnitz [n. p., n. d.].

Karlweis, Marta—see Wassermann, Marta

Keller, Adolf. *Dynamis; Formen und Kräfte des amerikanischen Protestantis-mus.* Tübingen: Mohr, 1922.

Kende, Oskar. *Die Vereinigten Staaten von Amerika. Landeskundlich-wirt-schaftsgeographische Übersicht.* Hamburg: Hanseatische Verlagsanstalt, 1927.

Kerr, Alfred. *New York und London. Stätten des Geschicks. Zwanzig Kapitel nach dem Weltkrieg.* 8. und 9. Aufl. Berlin: S. Fischer, 1929.

——————. *Yankee-Land. Eine Reise.* Berlin: R. Mosse, 1925.

Key, Helmer. *Amerikareise (En Amerikaresa).* übers. von Fr. Stieve. 2 aufl. München: Drei Masken-Verlag, 1922.

Keyserling, Graf Hermann. *Amerika: der Aufgang einer neuen Welt.* Stuttgart: Deutsche Verlagsanstalt, 1931 (translated from *America Set Free.* New York and London: Harpers, 1929).

——————. *Mensch und Erde (Der Leuchter, Weltanschauung und Lebens-gestaltung,* Achtes Buch). Darmstadt: Otto Reichl Verlag, 1927.

——————. *Das Spektrum Europas.* Heidelberg: Niels Kampmann Verlag [c. 1929].

——————. *The Travel Diary of a Philosopher.* 2 vols. Tr. J. Holroyd Reece. New York: Harcourt, Brace & Co. [c. 1925].

——————. *The World in the Making [Die neuentstehende Welt].* Tr. Maurice Samuel. New York: Harcourt, Brace & Co. [c. 1927].

Keyserling Archiv, herausgeber. *Graf Hermann Keyserling. Ein Gedächtnis-buch.* Innsbruck: Margarete Friedrich Rohrer, 1948.

Kimpen, Emil. *Die Ausbreitungspolitik der Vereinigten Staaten von Amerika.* Stuttgart: Deutsche Verlags-anstalt, 1923.

Kircheiss, Carl. *Meine Weltumsegelung mit dem Fischkutter Hamburg.* Leipzig: Hase & Koehler Verlag, 1942 [Originally published 1928].

Kisch, Egon Erwin. *. . . beehrt sich darzubieten: Paradies-Amerika.* Berlin: Erich Reiss, 1930.

Kleinschmitt, Edmund. *Durch Werkstätten und Gassen dreier Erdteile. Das soziale Bild von Amerika, Ostasien, und Australien.* Hamburg: Hansea-tische Verlagsanstalt, 1928.

Knapp, Paul. *Fahrten und Erlebnisse in Amerika.* Königsberg: Evangelischer Jungmännerbund Ostpreussen E. V. [1931].

Kollbrunner, Oskar. *Treibholz. Irrgänge eines Amerikafahrers.* Frauenfeld: Huber & Co., 1926.

Köttgen, Carl. *Das wirtschaftliche Amerika.* Berlin: V. D. I. Verlag, 1925.

Krüger, Fritz-Konrad. *Gesichtspunkte, Methoden, Ziele einer wissenschaftlicher Amerikakunde. Antrittsvorlesungen.* Berlin: Julius Springer, 1927.

Kühne, Georg. *Von Mensch und Motor, Farm und Wolkenkratzer. Reiseskizzen eines deutschen Ingenieurs.* Leipzig: J. C. Hinrichs, 1926.

Kühnelt, Richard. *Gold und bunte Menschen. Amerikanische Abenteuer.* Wien: Österreichische Bundesverlag, 1929.

Kühnemann, Eugen. *Amerikafahrt, 1932.* Breslau: Korn Verlag, 1933.

————. *Charles W. Eliot, President of Harvard University (May 19, 1869-May 19, 1909).* Boston: Houghton Mifflin, 1909.

————. *Deutschland, Amerika und der Krieg.* Chicago: A. Kroch & Co., 1915.

————. *Deutschland und Amerika: Briefe an einen deutsch-amerikanischen Freund.* München: Beck, 1918.

————. *Georg Washington, sein Leben und Werk.* Bremen: G. A. von Halem, 1932.

————. *Mit unbefangener Stirn. Mein Lebensbuch.* Heilbronn: Eugen Salzer, 1937.

Küppersbosch, Marta. *Das Alkoholverbot in Amerika. Die nationale Prohibition in den Vereinigten Staaten von Amerika und ihre volkswirtschaftliche Bedeutung.* München: Duncker & Humblot, 1923.

Kuh, G. *Das wahre Amerika (Flugschriften für Österreich-Ungarns Erwachen, 36. Heft).* Wien: E. Strache, 1918.

Lamprecht, Karl. *Americana: Reiseeindrücke, Betrachtungen, Geschichtliche Gesamtansicht.* Freiburg i. Br.: H. Heyfelder, 1906.

Langewiesche, Wolfgang. *Das amerikanische Abenteuer. Deutscher Werkstudent In U.S.A.* Stuttgart: J. Engelhorns Nachf., 1933.

Lassen, John [pseudonym, original not found]. *Das andere Amerika. Bilder, Skizzen, und Reiseschilderungen.* Deutsch von Stefan J. Klein. Leipzig-Lindenau: Freidenker Verlag, 1924.

Laurent, Vivi. *Vivis Reise. Ein Jahr als Dienstmädchen in Amerika; das Abenteuer einer schwedischen Studentin.* Übersetzt von Nora Feichtinger. 2 vols. Gotha: L. Klotz, 1925-26.

Leitich, Ann Tizia. *Amerika, du hast es besser.* Wien: Steyrermühl, 1926.

Lenel, Otto. *Das amerikanische Regierungssystem. Rede.* Berlin: W. de Gruyter & Co., 1922.

Lettenbaur, J. A. *Jenseits der Alten Welt. Eine neue Amerika-betrachtung.* Leipzig: S. Hirzel, 1919.

Lewisohn, Ludwig. *Up Stream; an American Chronicle.* New York: Boni & Liveright [c. 1922]. Translated by Thea Wolf as *Gegen den Strom. Eine amerikanische Chronik.* Frankfurt a. M.: Frankfurter Societäts-druckerei, 1924.

Liefmann, Robert. *Die kommunistischen Gemeinden in Nordamerika.* Jena: G. Fischer, 1922.

Linn, Fritz. *Die staatsrechtliche Stellung der Präsidenten der Vereinigten Staaten von Amerika.* Bonn: Karl Schroeder, 1928.

Lothar, C. L. (pseudonym "Persius"). *Der Meteor. Charakterbilder und Streiflichter aus der nordamerikanischen Welt.* Magdeburg: Zacharias, 1928.

Lovestone, Jay. *Weshalb Amerika Europa erobern will (Internationale Zeit- und Streitfragen, I).* Hamburg: C. Hoym Nachf., 1925.

Luckner, Felix Graf von. *Seeteufel erobert Amerika.* Leipzig: Koehler & Amelang, 1928.

Luckwaldt, Friedrich. *Geschichte der Vereinigten Staaten von Amerika.* 2 bde. Berlin: W. de Gruyter & Co., 1920.

Lütkens, Charlotte. *Staat und Gesellschaft in Amerika. Zur Soziologie des amerikanischen Kapitalismus.* Tübingen: Mohr, 1929.

Lufft, Herman. *Samuel Gompers, Arbeiterschaft und Volksgemeinschaft in den Vereinigten Staaten von Amerika.* Berlin: R. Hobbing, 1928.

Medinger, Wilhelm. *Vier Reden auf das Kongress der Inter-parlamentarischen Union 1925. Amerikanische Eindrücke.* Prag: Deutsche Völkerbundliga in der Tschechoslowakischen Republik, 1927.

Mendelsohn, Erich. *Amerika. Bilderbuch eines Architekten.* Berlin: R. Mosse Buchverlag, 1928.

Meyer, Eduard. *Die Vereinigten Staaten von Amerika; Geschichte, Kultur, Verfassung und Politik.* Frankfurt a .M.: H. Keller, 1920.

Meyer, Gustav Wilhelm. *Die Amerikanisierung Europas. Kritische Beobachtungen und Betrachtungen.* Bodenbach: Technischer Verlag, 1920.

Meyer, Karl H. (pseudonym Karl Ey). *Mit 100 Mark nach U.S.A. Ein deutsches Schicksal in Amerika.* Berlin: A. Scherl [1930].

Monsky, Max. *Tagebuchblätter während seiner Amerikareise.* Wien: Österreichische Volksmission, 1925.

Montgelas, Albrecht, Graf von. *Abraham Lincoln, Präsident der Vereinigten Staaten von Nordamerika.* Wien und Leipzig: K. König [c. 1925].

Moog, Otto. *Drüben steht Amerika. Gedanken nach einer Ingenieurreise durch die Vereinigten Staaten.* 4. Aufl. Braunschweig: G. Westermann, 1928.

Müller, Alfred. *Meine Reise nach Amerika. Vortrag.* Berlin-Charlottenburg: Zementverlag, 1926.

Müller, Wilhelm. *Amerikanisches Volksbildungswesen.* Jena: Eugen Diederichs, 1910.

——————. *Die Deutschamerikaner und der Krieg.* Wiesbaden: Heinrich Staadt, 1921.

——————. *Das religiöse Leben in Amerika.* Jena: E. Diederichs, 1911.

Müller-Freienfels, Richard. *Mysteries of the Soul.* New York: Alfred A. Knopf, 1929.

Müller-Sturmheim, Emil (actually Emil Müller). *Ohne Amerika geht es nicht.* Wien: Amalthea-Verlag, 1930.

Münsterberg, Hugo. *Aus Deutsch-Amerika.* Berlin: Ernst Mittler und Sohn, 1909.

——————. *The Americans.* Tr. E. B. Holt. New York: McClure, Phillips & Co., 1907.

Neutra, Richard J. *Wie baut Amerika?* Stuttgart: Julius Hoffmann, 1927.

Oehlke, Waldemar. *In Ostasien und Nordamerika als Deutscher Professor. Reisebericht 1920-1926.* Darmstadt: Ernst Hoffman & Co., 1927.

Oeri, Albert. *Europäische Briefe über Amerika.* Basel: Buchdruckerei zum Basler Berichthaus, 1930.

Omaha, Jack [pseudonym]. *Wilde Fahrten im wilden Westen. Mit Gaunern, Gauklern, und Rothäuten unterwegs.* Hamburg: W. Nölting, 1927.

Oncken, Hermann. *Deutschlands Weltkrieg und die Deutsch-amerikaner. Ein Gruss des Vaterlandes über den Ozean (Der deutsche Krieg, VI),* Stuttgart-Berlin: Deutsche Verlags-Anstalt, 1914.

Otto, Heinz. *Mein "Bummelleben" in Amerika. Die Beichte eines Toren.* Hamburg: Weltbund-Verlag, 1925.

Paquet, Alfons. *Amerika. Hymnen, Gedichte.* Leipzig: Verlag Die Wölfe (O. Klemm), 1924.

Penck, Albrecht. *U.S.-Amerika. Gedanken und Erinnerungen eines Austauschprofessors.* Stuttgart: J. Engelhorns Nachf., 1917.

Persius—see Lothar, C. L.

Pfannmüller, Donatus. *So sah ich Amerika. Reise von Fulda nach Chicago.* Essen: Fredebeul & Koenen, 1931.

Pfyffer von Altishofen, Siegfried. *Mit dem "Swiss-Mission" in Amerika. Tagebuch.* Zürich: Polygraph. Institut, 1920.

Pollak, Heinrich. *Die Gewerkschaftsbewegung in den Vereinigten Staaten.* Jena: Gustav Fischer, 1927.

Ponten, Josef. *Besinnliche Fahrten im Wilden Westen.* Leipzig: Reclam, 1937.

Prosinagg, Ernest. *Das Antlitz Amerikas. Drei Jahre diplomatischer Mission in den U.S.A.* Wien: Amalthea Verlag, 1931.

Reichwein, Adolf. *Blitzlicht über Amerika.* Jena: Urania, 1930.

Rein, Adolf. *Die drei grossen Amerikaner; Hamilton, Jefferson, Washington. Auszüge aus ihren Werken, ausgewählt und eingeleitet von . . . Übersertzt von Helga Rein.* Berlin: R. Hobbing, 1923.

————————. *Die europäische Ausbreitung über die Erde.* Wildpark-Potsdam: Akademische Verlagsgesellschaft [c. 1931].

————————. *Der Kampf Westeuropas um Nordamerika im 15. und 16. Jahrhundert.* Stuttgart-Gotha: F. A. Perthes, 1925.

Richter, Kurt. *Reisebilder aus Amerika. Jugendwohlfahrt in den Vereinigten Staaten* (Veröffentlichungen des Preussischen Ministeriums für Volkswohlfahrt aus dem Gebiete der Jugendpflege, der Jugendbewegung, und der Leibesübung). Berlin: R. v. Decker, 1929.

Riebensahm, Paul. *Der Zug nach U.S.A. Gedanken nach einer Amerikareise, 1924.* Berlin: Julius Springer, 1925.

Roda Roda—see Rosenfeld, Sandor Friedrich

Rohrbach, Paul. *Amerika und wir. Reisebetrachtungen.* Berlin: Buchenau & Reichert, 1926.

Rosen, Erwin—see Carlé, Erwin

Rosenfeld, Sandor Friedrich (pseudonym Roda Roda). *Ein Frühling in Amerika.* München: G. Langes, 1924.

Ross, Colin. *Fahrten- und Abenteuerbuch.* Berlin: Verlag der Büchergilde Gutenberg, 1930.

_____. *Unser Amerika; der deutsche Anteil an den Vereinigten Staaten.* Leipzig: F. A. Brockhaus, 1936.

_____. *Die Welt auf der Waage; der Querschnitt von 20 Jahren Weltreise.* Leipzig: F. A. Brockhaus, 1929 (English, *The World in the Balance; an Analysis of World-problems after Twenty Years' Travel about the World.* London: G. Routledge & Sons. ltd., 1930.).

Rundt, Arthur. *Amerika ist anders.* Berlin-Charlottenburg: Volksverband der Bücherfreunde, 1926.

Saalfeld, Johannes. *Wie komme ich in den Vereinigten Staaten vorwärts? Winke und Ratschläge für Auswanderer nach die Vereinigten Staaten von Amerika unter besondere Berücksichtigung der Kopfarbeiter und nicht Handwerker.* Dresden: Gutzmannsche. Buchdr., 1926.

Salomon, Alice. *Kultur im Werden. Amerikanische Reiseeindrücke.* Berlin: Ullstein, 1924.

Salten, Felix. *5 Minuten Amerika.* Wien: Paul Zsolnay, 1931.

Sasse, Hermann. *Amerikanisches Kirchentum.* Berlin: Wichern-Verlag, 1927.

Schäfer, Dietrich. *Die Vereinigten Staaten als Weltmacht. Eine geschichtliche Betrachtung zur Beleuchtung der Gegenwart.* Berlin: G. Grote, 1917.

Scheffauer, Herman George. *Blood Money; Woodrow Wilson and the Nobel Peace Prize.* Hamburg: Overseas Publishing Co. [1921].

_____. *Das geistige Amerika von Heute.* Berlin: Ullstein, 1925.

_____. *The German Prison-House; How to Convert it into a Torture-Chamber and a Charnel; Suggestions to President Wilson.* Leipzig: T. Weicher, 1920.

_____. *Das Land Gottes. Das Gesicht des neuen Amerikas.* übersetzt von Tony Noah. Hannover: R. Steegemann, 1923.

Scheller-Steinwartz, Robert R. von. *Amerika und wir. Ein Wink am Scheideweg.* München: Duncker & Humblot, 1919.

Schmidt, Annalise. *Der amerikanische Mensch. Vom Wesen Amerikas und des Amerikaners.* Berlin: Deutsche Verlagsgesellschaft für Politik und Geschichte, 1920.

Schoch, Alfred Diehl and R. Kron. *The Little Yankee. A Handbook of Idiomatic American English, Treating of the Daily Life, Customs, and Institutions of the United States.* Freiburg: J. Bielefeld, 1927.

Schönemann, Friedrich. *American Humor.* hrsg. von . . . Bielefeld & Leipzig: Velhagen & Klasing [1934].

_____. *Amerikakunde. Eine zeitgemässe Forderung.* Bremen: Angelsachsen-Verlag, 1921.

_____. *Amerika und der Nationalsozialismus. (Schriften der Deutschen Hochschule für Politik,* hrsg. v. Paul Meier-Benneckenstein) Berlin: Junker & Dünnhaupt, 1934.

_____. *Demokratie und Aussenpolitik der USA.* Berlin: Junker & Dünnhaupt, 1939.

_____. *England gegen Amerika, eine geschichtlich-kritische Betrachtung (Schriften des Deutschen Instituts für aussenpolitische Forschung,* Heft 34). Berlin: Junker & Dünnhaupt, 1940.

_____. *Geschichte der Vereinigten Staaten von Nordamerika* (part of

Geschichte Amerikas ausser Kanada, Die grosse Weltgeschichte, **Band** 15). Leipzig: Verlag Bibliographisches Institut [c. 1942].

————————. *Kleine Amerikakunde*. Bonn: Athenäum Verlag, 1950.

————————, Adolf Halfeld, *et al. Kultur in USA. Die Wirklichkeit eines Massenwahns*. Berlin: Junker & Dünnhaupt, 1943.

————————. *Die Kunst der Massenbeeinflussung in den Vereinigten Staaten von Amerika*. Stuttgart: Deutsche Verlags-Anstalt, 1924.

————————. *Mark Twain als literarische Persönlichkeit*. Jena: Fromann, 1925.

————————. *Die Vereinigten Staaten von Amerika*. 2 bde. Stuttgart: Deutsche Verlags-Anstalt, 1932.

————————. *Die Vereinigten Staaten von Amerika in Handbuch der Kulturgeschichte* hrsg. von Heinz Kindermann, Abteilung 2, Heft 3 (Lieferungen 25, 29, 43, pp. 127-204) of *Die Kulturen Grossbritaniens, der Vereinigten Staaten, Skandinaviens und der Niederlande*. Potsdam: Akademische Verlagsgesellschaft Athenaion [c. 1934].

————————. *Die Vereinigten Staaten von Amerika (Kleine Auslandskunde*, Bd. 14/15). Berlin: Junker & Dünnhaupt, 1943.

Schulthess, L. *Durch den amerikanischen Kontinent*. Augsburg: H. R. Sauerländer, 1920.

Schulze, Alfred. *Griechenland und Amerika. Plaudereien über Reiseeindrücke aus der alten und neuen Welt*. Dresden: W. Jess, 1928.

Schurch, Ernst. *Aus der neuen Welt. Mit der schweizerischen Pressemission in Amerika*. Bern: A. Francke, 1919.

Sommer, Oskar. *Amerika will die Zeit festbinden*. Berlin: C. Schmalfeldt, 1927.

Sonnenschein, Adolf. *Eindrücke eines Verwaltungsbeamten von den Vereinigten Staaten. Vortrag (Weltwirtschaftliche Gesellschaft* zu Münster i. W., Heft 13). Leipzig: Quelle & Meyer, 1927.

Souchy, Augustin. *Schreckenherrschaft in Amerika*. Berlin: Verlag "Der Syndikalist," 1927.

Spiegel, Käthe. *Kulturgeschichtliche Grundlagen der amerikanischen Revolution*. München und Berlin: R. Oldenbourg, 1931.

Spoerri, William T. *The Old World and the New. A Synopsis of Current European views on American Civilization (Schweizer Anglistische Arbeiten*, 3. Bd.). Zürich-Leipzig: Max Niehans Verlag, 1936.

Spohr, Karl. *Der Auswanderer in Amerika. Vorteile und Nachteile*. Paderborn: Bonifacius-Druckerei, 1930.

Steiner, Lajos. *Unter Palmen, Bohrtürmen, Wolkenkratzern. Eindrücke aus Nord- und Latein-Amerika*. Stuttgart: Strecker & Schröder, 1931.

Stolper, Ernst. *Werkstudent im Wilden Westen. Aus dem Tagebuch eines jungen Deutschen*. Leipzig: P. List [c. 1933].

Tänzler, Fritz. *Aus dem Arbeitsleben Amerikas. Arbeitsverhältnisse, Arbeitsmethoden und Sozialpolitik in den Vereinigten Staaten von Amerika*. Berlin: Reimar Hobbing, 1927.

Tischert, Hans. *Es Interessiert Europa (Amerikanische Reiseeindrücke)*. 2 aufl. Berlin-Wilmersdorf: Hans Tischert, 1928.

Toller, Ernst. *Quer durch. Reisebilder und Reden*. Berlin: G. Kiepenheuer, 1930.

Venzmer, Gerhard. *New York ohne Schminke*. vi. bis viii. vollständig neuges- taltete Auflage der "New Yorker Spaziergänge." Hamburg: Weltbundver- lag [1930].

Vershofen, Wilhelm. *Rhein und Hudson. 11 Grotesken*. Wiesbaden: Walther Gericke, 1929.

Voegelin, Erich. *Über die Form des amerikanischen Geistes*. Tübingen: J. C. B. Mohr, 1928.

Voss, Ernst. *Vier Jahrzehnte in Amerika. Gesammelte Reden und Aufsätze*. Hrsg. v. Otto E. Lessing. Stuttgart: Deutsche Verlags-Anstalt, 1929.

Vossler, Otto. *Die amerikanischen Revolutionsideal in ihrem Verhältnis zu den europäischen untersucht an Thomas Jefferson* (Beiheft 17 der *Historischen Zeitschrift*). München und Berlin: R. Oldenbourg, 1929.

Walther, Andreas. *Soziologie und Sozialwissenschaften in Amerika und ihre Bedeutung für die Pädagogik*. Karlsruhe: G. Braun, 1927.

Wassermann, Marta (pseudonym Marta Karlweis). *Eine Frau reist durch Amerika*. Mit einer Vorbemerkung von Jakob Wassermann. Berlin: S. Fischer, 1928.

Weiser, Franz. *Im Lande des Sternenbanners*. Regensburg: Habbel, 1933.

Werdermann, Hermann. *Das religiöse Angesicht Amerikas; Einzeleindrücke und Charakterzüge*. Gütersloh: C. Bertelsmann, 1926.

Westermann, Franz. *Amerika, wie ich es sah. Reiseskizzen eines Ingenieurs*. Halberstadt: H. Meyer, 1925.

Winckler, Ferdinand Oskar von. *Der Yankee-Spiegel. Wir Deutschen und Bru- der Jonathan*. Berlin: Brunnen Verlag K. Winckler, 1926.

Winkler, Magda. *Sketches of American Life*. Stettin: Dunker Bell, 1929.

Witte, Irene M. *Taylor, Gilbreth, Ford. Gegenwartsfragen der amerikanischen und europäischen Arbeitswissenschaft*. München und Berlin: R. Olden- bourg, 1924.

Wollschläger, Alfred Ernst Johann (pseudonym A. E. Johann). *Untergang am Überfluss*. Berlin: Ullstein, 1932.

Zbinden, Hans. *Zur geistigen Lage Amerikas*. München: G. Hirth Verlag, 1932.

Zurbruchen, Rosa. *Kreuz und quer durch Nordamerika. In den Jahren 1915- 1919*. 2 aufl. Bern: P. Haupt, 1923.

2. *Periodicals*: (Note, the following list indicates periodicals consulted. The titles of articles are given only when they are of particular significance to the theme of the book. The order of listing follows that in the *Bibliographie der deutschen Zeitschriftenliteratur*, which provides major bibliographical assistance in this area.)

Abend-Gymnasium (F. Kellermann, "Amerikakunde im Abendgymnasium," I (1928), No. 4, 23-8.)

Amerika-Post; a Messenger of Good Will between the United States and Ger- many (Hamburg).

Anglia, Zeitschrift für englische Philologie.

Anthropos.

Arbeit, Zeitschrift für Gewerkschaftspolitik, Berlin. (Fritz Naphthali, "Bericht deutscher Gewerkschaftsführer," 1926, 363-7.)

Deutsche Arbeit, Köln. (Hermann Lufft, "Aus meinen amerikanischen Erfahrung-
en," XI (1926), 24-28.)

Arbeitsnachweis in Deutschland. Zeitschrift des Verbands deutscher Arbeits-
nachweise.

Archiv für angewandte Soziologie, Berlin.

Archiv für Sozialwissenschaft und Sozialpolitik. (Charlotte Lütkens, "Bureaukratie und Parteimaschine in den Vereinigten Staaten," LX (1928), 280-
301; by same author, "Europäer und Amerikaner über Amerika," LXII
(1929), 615-30.)

Weltwirtschaftliches Archiv. (A. Salz, "Das Land ohne Mittelalter," XXIII
(1926), 90-117.)

Atlantis. (Werner Hegemann, "Ehe und Familie im Land der Wolkenkratzer,"
1932, 748.)

Neue Bahnen. Illustrierte Monatsheft für Erziehung und Unterricht. (Reinhold Lehmann, "Hemmungen und Hoffnungen im Erziehungswesen der
Vereinigten Staaten," XXXII (1921), 164-6; 189-93.)

Bausteine. Monatsblatt für die innere Mission.

Schweizerische Bauzeitung. (A. J. Bühler, "Reiseeindrücke aus den Vereinigten
Staaten," XCVII (1931), 198-204, 215-220, 253, 263, 290, 300, 329-32.)

Rheinischer Beobachter. Potsdam.

Die Bergstadt. Breslau. (Hans Christoph Kaergel, "Kleinigkeiten aus dem
grossen Amerika," XIV (1926), 465-476.)

Betrieb und Organisation. Stuttgart. (F. Neuhaus, "Reiseeindrücke in dem
amerikanischen Besuch bei Henry Ford," 1924, 27.)

Eiserne Blätter. Berlin.

Historisch-politische Blätter für das katholische Deutschland. (Later, *Gelbe
Hefte.*)

Volkswirtschaftliche Blätter.

Brunsviga. Monatshefte.

Börsenblatt für den deutschen Buchhandel.

Freie deustche Bühne (later, *Das blaue Heft*). Berlin.

Centralblatt des Zofingvereins [Zofingia].

Christengemeinschaft.

Daheim. (Dr. Julie Langen, "Heimleben der berufstätigen Frau in Amerika,"
LXII (1925), subvol. I, No. 6.)

Dawes-Weg (Dawes-Way) Berlin. (Justizrat Dr. Waldschmidt, "Traveling Impressions gathered in the United States of America," (English edition) I
(1925), Nr. 3/4/5, 31-35.)

Das freie Deutschland. Berlin.

Evangelisches Deutschland. Kirchliche Rundschau. Berlin. (Missionsdirektor
Steinweg, "Nordamerikanische Reiseeindrücke," VI (1929), 38.)

Deutschlands Erneuerung.

Die evangelische Diaspora. Leipzig. (Carl Schneider, "Von Amerika und der
Amerikanismus," X, No. 3 (August, 1928), 116-131.)

Das Literarische Echo (later *Die Literatur*).

Der getreue Eckart. Wien. (Erwin Stranik, "Land der Gegensätze," IX (1932),
428-32; "Sekten, Glaubensgemeinschaften und Geschäftsreligionen in
Amerika," IX (1932), 745-8; "Kleinstadtleben in Amerika," X (1933), 64-8.)

Die Erzeihung. Leipzig.

Schweizerisches Erziehungs-Rundschau. Zürich.

Das neue Europa. Zürich. (Victor Kienböck, "Was kann Europa von Amerika lernen?" 1926, No. 1/2, 19; No. 3/4, 23-8.)

Faust. Eine Monatsschrift für Kunst, Literatur und Musik. (Robert Müller, "Der amerikanische Typus," I (1922-3), No. 10, 7-14.)

Fortschritt des Medizins.

Form, die Zeitschrift für gestaltende Arbeit. Bonn.

Die Frau. Köln. (Alice Salomon, "Soziale Ausbildung," XXXIII, 398-407 (1926); Dorothee von Velsen, "Eindrücke aus Amerika," XXXVII (1930), 385-95; Marie Baum, "Amerikana," XXXIX (1932), 544-9, 626-33.)

Freie Welt. Eine Halbmonatsschrift für deutsche Kultur. Reichenberg.

Die Freude. Monatshefte für deutsche Innerlichkeit. Egerstorf.

Die Furche. Berlin. (W. Kolfhaus, "Wie ich Amerika sah," XVI (1930), 103-10.)

Gartenlaube. (H. G. Scheffauer, "Amerikakunde," 1922, 454.)

Der deutsche Gedanke. (Ch. Boeck, "Amerikanische Gefahr," III (1926), 283-286; Richard Müller-Freienfels, "Amerikanismus und europäische Kultur," IV (1927), 30-35.)

Gegenwart. (C. A. Bratter, "Amerika von Heute und Morgen," LI (1922), 339; Georg Hartmann, "Meine Amerikafahrt," LII (1923), 105; Johann Gaulke, "Amerika, du hast es besser . . . ?" LVII (1928), 11-17.)

Der freie Geist.

Die neue Generation.

Die Gewerkschaft. Berlin. (A. Siemsen, "Soziologische Beobachtungen eines jungen Arbeiters in USA," XXXII (1928), 1189.)

Gewerkschaftsarchiv.

Die rote Gewerkschaftsinternationale.

Glocke.

Goetheanum. (R. Boos, "Amerikanismus als Aufgabe," X (1931), 194.)

Die Grenzboten. Berlin. (Friedrich Schönemann, "Amerikakunde," LXXX (1921), subvol. II, 189; "Deutschamerikanertum," LXXX (1921), subvol. IV, 7.)

Handelswacht, deutsche Zeitschrift des deutsch-nationalen Handlungsgehilfen Verbandes. (A. E. Günther, "Amerika—eine neue aber keine junge Nation," XXXVIII (1931), 100.)

Literarischer Handweiser. (Friedrich Schönemann, "Der Amerikanismus in deutscher Auffassung," LXIV (1927), 161-165; by same author, "Das Amerika von Heute," LXVII (1931), 454-460.)

Heimat. Badische Zeitung für Volkskunde. Karlsruhe. (Karl Raab, "Amerikanismus. Historische-psychologische Studie," IV (1928), 131-5.)

Heimdall.

Die Hilfe. (Wilhelm Vershofen, "Student-Reise in den Vereinigten Staaten," 1924, 313, 363, 423; Anton Erkelenz, "Quer durch das amerikanische Festland," 1925, 365.)

Hochland. Monatsschrift für alle Gebiete des Wissens/der Literatur und Kunst. München. (Eugen Rosenstock, "Der Kreuzzug des Sternenbanners," XVI, Vol. I (Nov., 1918), 113-22; Friedrich Dessauer, "Nordamerikanische Reisebriefe," XIX, Vol. I (1921), 138-44, 330-45, 446-69; Hugo Graf von

Lerchenfeld-Köfering, "Meine Reise durch die Vereinigten Staaten," XXI, Vol. I, (1923), 25-34, 163-71, 278-87, 397-414.)

Hochschule und Ausland.

Neue Jahrbücher für Wissenschaft und Jubendbildung. (Walther Fischer, "Amerikakunde und die deutsche Schule," V (1929), 54-64.)

Allgemeine evangelische-lutheranische Kirchenzeitung.

Reformierte Kirchenzeitung. (W. Kolfhaus, "Strömungen im Geistesleben der Vereinigten Staaten," LXXIX (1929), 297-300, 307-9, 313-15; "Das andere Amerika," 377-80.)

Koralle. Berlin.

Korrespondenzblatt des allgemeinen deutschen Gewerkschaftbundes.

Deutsches Philologenblatt (früher *Korrespondenzblatt für das akademische gebildete Lehrerstand*). (Sebald Schwarz, "Die Schulfahrt des Zentralinstituts nach Nordamerika," 1928, 556; by same author, "Was ist für uns in Amerika zu lernen," 1928, 630-3.)

Kunst und Künstler. (Ludwig Hilberseimer und Udo Rukser, "Amerikanische Architektur," XVIII (1920), 537-45; Edmund Schüler, "Der Wolkenkratzer," XXIII (1924), 228-39; Carl Georg Heise, "Amerikanische Museen," XXIII (1924), 219, 333-47; Walter Curt Behrendt, "Aus dem Tagebuch einer Amerikareise," XXIV (1925), 18-23, 61-6, 97-9; George Grosz, "Briefe aus Amerika," XXXI (1932), 273-8, 317-22, 433-43.)

Der Kunstwanderer. (Hermann Voss, "Amerikanische Eindrücke," X, 417-19 (June, 1928).)

Deutsche Lehrerinnenzeitung. (Emmy Beckmann, "Schule und Erziehung der Vereinigten Staaten anknüpfend an den Kongress des Frauenweltbundes in Washington," XLII (1925), 169-72; by same author, "Briefe aus Amerika," XLIX (1932), Nrs. 30-36.)

Leipziger Lehrerzeitung. (Reinhold Lehmann, "Ein Katechismus der Moral für amerikanische Kinder," XXVII (1920), 179-81; by same author, "Die weltliche Schule in den Vereinigten Staaten," XXVIII (1921), 165.)

Der neue Merkur. (Alfons Paquet, "Vorschläge an Amerika," VII, Part II (1924), 578-88.)

Schweizerische Militär-Zeitung. (A. Stutz, "Bei den amerikanischen Besatzungstruppen in Koblenz," LXVII (1923), 153.)

Deutsche Monatshefte. (Gerhard Venzmer, "Yankee-Psychologie," III (1926), 47-54; Paul Rohrbach, "Was heisst Amerikanismus?" V (1929), Part II, 467-470.)

Schweizerische Monatshefte für Politik und Kultur. (P. Lang, "Amerika von Europa aus gesehen," X (1931), 511-518; by same author, "Amerika im eigenen Spiegel," XI (1932), 76-82.)

Schlesische Monatshefte. (Eugen Kühnemann, "4 Schlesier über Amerika," IV (1927), 502-507.)

Sozialistische Monatshefte. (Adolf Hepner, "Deutschlands Amerika-kenntnis," XXV (1919), 342; M. Carssen, "Amerikanerin," XXXIV (1928), 619-622; Ernst Untermann, "Der junge Geist in Amerika," XXXVII (1931), 350-354; Charlotte Lütkens, "Das amerikanische Zweikammersystem," XXXVII (1931), 536-542, 654-659; P. F. Schmidt, "Untergang des amerikanischen

Genies," XXXVII (1931), 770-774; Charlotte Lütkens, "Amerika-legende," XXXVIII (1932), 45-50.)

Süddeutsche Monatshefte. (Adolf Keller, "Aktivismus und Fundamentalismus in Amerika," XXVI (1928), 673; Friedrich Schönemann, "Strömungen amerikanisches Lebens," XXVII (1929), 655-659; Toni Harten-Hoencke, "Amerikanisches Frauenleben," XXVII (1929), 660-664; Fritz Behn, "Amerikanismus in Deutschland," XXVII (1929), 672-674.)

Germanisch-romanische Monatsschrift. (Karl Brunner, "Amerikanische Lyrik der Gegenwart," XI (1923), 33-45; Friedrich Schönemann, "Amerikanischer Humor," VIII (1920), 152-164; 216-217.)

Deutsches Musikjahrbuch. (Siegfried Wagner, "Meine Amerikafahrt," 1925, 276.

Breslauer Nachrichten. ("P.K.," "Erinnerungen an Eugen Kühnemann, gest. 1946," II (1950), Nr. 18, 14.)

Der Neubau. Berlin. (Adolf Rading, "Reise nach die Vereinigten Staaten," VII (1925), 29-33; 57-60.)

Petermann's Mitteilungen aus Justus Perthes' geographische Anstalt. (H. Lehmann-Haupt, "Amerikas '50 Bücher,'" LXXV (1929), Part II, 239-244; J. Riepl, "Die amerikanische Jugend und das heutige Problem der Liebe und Ehe," LXXV (1929), Part II, 81-117.)

Pharus. Katholische Monatsschrift für Orientierung in der gesamten Pädagogik. (Joseph Draim, "Der Amerikanismus," XXIII (1932), Part II, 237-241.)

Deutsche Politik. (Gustav Erenyi, "Die amerikanische Gefahr," V (1920), Part III, 397-403; Friedrich Schönemann, "Die Reaktion in den Vereinigten Staaten," VI (1921), Part I, 442-448; by same author, "Der Sozialismus in den Vereinigten Staaten," VI (1921), Part II, 735-740.)

Praxis der Berufschule. Leipzig. (Schwager, Arnstadt, "Amerikanismus von der positiven und negativen Seite," 1928, 341.)

Soziale Praxis. (Friedrich Lembke, "Einige Reisebetrachtungen im trocknen Amerika," XXXVII (1928), 259-261.)

Europäische Revue. Leipzig.

Allgemeine Rundschau. München. (Heinrich Müller, "Amerikanisierung Europas," XVII (1920), 570-571; O. Kunze, "Amerika und Europa," XIX (1922), 616-618; A. Timpe, "Deutsche Kultur in Nordamerika," XXII (1925), 75-77; A. Bremer, "Wie ich die amerikanische Bürger sah," XXIII (1926), 106-107.)

Deutsche Rundschau. (H. G. Scheffauer, "Amerikanische Literatur der Gegenwart," CLXXXVI, 215-222 (February, 1921); by same author, "Whitman in Whitmans Land," CCI (July-December, 1924), 255-262; Hans Christoph, "Meine Entdeckung Amerikas," CCI (July-December, 1924), 312-325; Albrecht Haushofer, "Amerika-Europa," CCX, 181-188 (February, 1927); Paul Fechter, "Der amerikanische Raum," CCXIX, 47-59 (April, 1929); Friedrich Schönemann, "Amerikanische Literatur von Heute," CCXX, 67-72 (July, 1929); Theodor Lüddecke, "Amerikanismus als Schlagwort und als Tatsache," CCXXI, 214-221 (March, 1930).)

Neue Rundschau. Berlin. (Carl Brinkmann, "Geistiges aus Amerika," XXVII, subvol. II (1926), 24-52; Moritz J. Bonn, "Amerikanische Prosperität," XXXVIII (1927), 561-585; Carl Brinkmann, "Kameradschaft und Religion in Amerika," XXXVIII (1927), 53-62; P. Eichler, "Eindrücke von einer Amerikareise," XXXVIII (1927), No. 4, 253-260; No. 5, 1-9; Arthur Holitscher, "Wiedersehen mit Amerika," XLI (1930), No. 1, 71-106; No. 2, 188-222; No. 3, 350-370; H. A. Joachim, "Romane aus Amerika," XLI (1930), No. 9, 396-409; Moritz J. Bonn, "Sinn und Bedeutung der amerikanischen Krise," XLII (1931), 145-159.)

Spannung. Die A. E. G. Umschau. (Felix Deutsch, "Meine Eindrücke in Amerika," I (1927-8), 129-133, 168-172.)

Die neueren Sprachen. (Otto Dorner, "Vom Bildungswesen der Vereinigten Staaten," XXVII (1929), 617-642; Walther Fischer, "Ein Querschnitt durch die Kultur der Gegenwart in den Vereinigten Staaten," L (1942), 77-92; 97-109; Horst Oppel, "Walther Fischer zum Gedächtnis," X n.s. (1961), 143-145.)

Die Standarte. Magdeburg. (Helmuth Wohltat, "Ein Reisebrief aus den Vereinigten Staaten," IV (1929), 1105-1108; Anon., "Literatur über U.S.A.," V (1930), 617-619.)

Deutsche Stimmen. Berlin.

Stimmen der Zeit. (Jakob Overmans, "Beobachtungen in Nordamerika," CXVI (1929), 269-277; by same author, "Amerikanisierung des Geistes," CXVIII (1929), 161-173.)

Studierstube. (Rev. F. Braun, "Neue Briefe aus Amerika," XVIII (1920), 238-240; 320-327; 376-382; 425-432; XIX (1921), 29-32; 57-63; 93-96; XX (1922), 125-128; 223-224; by same author, "Juda in Amerika," XX (1922), 77-78.)

Das Tagebuch. Berlin. (C. Z. Klötzel, "Oh U.S.A.!" VIII (1927), Part I, 86-89.)

Der Türmer. (Toni Harten-Hoencke, "Deutschamerikaner und wir," XXIII (1921), 104-106; Friedrich Schönemann, "Amerikanische Pionierromane," XXVI (1924), 625; Toni Harten-Hoencke, "Amerikanismus als Schlagwort," XXXI (1929), 308-312; K. C. Bertling, "Deutschland und Amerika im Spiegel des deutschen Amerika-Instituts in Berlin," XXII (1930), 338-344.)

Urania. Jena. (Charlotte Lütkens, "Im Schlagschatten des amerikanischen Wirtschaftswunders," 1928/29, 249-52, 279-81.)

Velhagen und Klasings Monatshefte. (Fritz Giese, "Das tanzende Amerika," XLI (1927), Part II, 544-8.)

Volk und Rasse. München. (Hermann Lufft, "Weiss und Schwarz in der Bevölkerungsbewegung der Vereinigten Staaten," III (1928), 1-4.)

Der Volksehzieher. (Albert Lorentz, "Amerikanismus . . ." 1928, Beilag, "Der Bücherfreund," Blatt 1.)

Deutsches Volkstum. (E. Kalkschmidt, "Das Land Gottes," 1926, 12-17; by same author, "Amerikanisierung Europas," 1926, 590-8; Wilhelm Stapel, "Haben wir etwas gegen Amerika," 1929, 301; Günther, "Amerikanismus und die Amerikanisierten," 1929, 419-26.)

Volkswohl. Wien. (A. Bruck, "Überwindung des Amerikanismus— eine katholische Bildungsaufgabe," XXI (1930), 90-9; Rudolf Kindermann, "Was können wir von Amerika lernen," XXI (1930), 175-83.)

Christliche Welt. (Adolf Keller, "Europa und das amerikanische Protestantismus," XXXVII (1923), 684; 743; Karl Bornhausen, "Fundamentalismus," XXXVII (1923), 746; by same author, "Faszismus und Fundamentalismus," XXXVIII (1924), 235-43; Heinrich Frick, "Amerikanische Eindrücke," XXXIX (1925), 1188; XL (1926), 25, 80, 217, 434, 529-33, 691, 799, 853, 897; H. Schmimmelpfeng, "Amerikanische Jugend, Theologie und Mission," XLII (1928), 219-25; Theodor Devaranne, "Lords Day—Fords Day—Amerikanische Gottesdienste," XLIII (1929), 1154-8.)

Weltwirtschaft. (Otto H. Goebel, "Reiseeindrücke eines Volkswirtes aus Amerika," XVI (1928), 77.)

Wirtschaftsdienst. Hamburg. (Entire volume, XIV, 1929, devoted to U.S.)

Wissen und Leben. Zürich. (1926—*Neue Schweizerische Rundschau*) (R. Weer, "Amerikanerinnen," XIX (1926), 154-69; Rolf Hildebrand, "Feminismus in Amerika," XXI (1928), 55-62; H. Keyserling, "Spektrum Amerikas," XXIII, 567-78.)

Die Woche. (J. Delmont, "Going West, Der Weg der Pioniere," 1928, 1353; by same author, "Cowboys im Winter," 1929, 111.)

Welt-Echo. (C. A. Bratter, "Unser demokratische Vorbild," V (1919), Nr. 17, 4-5.)

Klinische Wochenschrift. (O. Gans, "Amerikanische Reiseeindrücke," VI n.f. (1927), 1957-60.)

Deutsche Medizinische Wochenschrift. (F. Grünbaum, "Reiseeindrücke in Nordamerika," LVI (1930), 2100, 2145, 2185.)

Münchner medizinische Wochenschrift. (Friedrich Müller, "Amerikanische Reiseeindrücke," LXXIV (1927), 1421-4, 1458-63, 1508-12.)

Medizinische Wochenschrift. Wien. (Ernst? Herz, "Ein paar Tage quer durch amerikanische Spitäler," LXXX (1930), 1686.)

Münchener tierärztliche Wochenschrift. (N. Lagerlöf, "Eine Studienreise nach Nordamerika," 1931, 555-59, 579.)

Die neue Zeit. Wochenschrift der deutschen Sozialdemokratie.

Zeiten und Völker. Stuttgart. (A. Holitscher, "Amerika und die Zukunft," XV (1919), No. 17, Beilag, 3; A. Hepner, "Deutschlands Amerikakenntnis," XVI (1920), 187.)

Zeitschrift für französische und englische Unterricht. (K. Arns, "Moderne amerikanische Dichter," XXIV (1925), 139-45; Paul Schulz, "Eindrücke von meiner Reise nach die Vereinigten Staaten im Sommer, 1926," XXVII (1928), 208-18; Walter Damus, "Der Amerikaner und seine Literatur," XXIX (1930), 110-20, 198-209; by same author, "Amerikabücher," XXIX (1930), 501-7; Walter Leitzmann, "Erfahrung auf einer Amerikareise," XXIX (1930), 625-31.)

Zeitschrift für Geopolitik. (G. Ludwig, "Wohnung und Bauen in den Vereinigten Staaten Amerikas," I (1924), 636-44; F. Termer, "Literarischer Bericht aus der amerikanischen Welt," I (1924), 661, 733-6, 822.)

Zeitschrift für Politik. (A. Haas, "Amerikanismus," XIII (1924), 1-40; Charles E. Stangeland, "Geist und Zukunft der amerikanischen Verfassung," XIII (1924), 41-64; Friedrich Schönemann, "Erziehung zum Staat in Amerika," XIX (1929), 34-45.)

Zeitschrift für pädagogische Psychologie. (G. Buetz, "Amerikanismus," XXI (1920), 25-32.)

Zeitschrift für die gesamte Staatswissenschaft.

Neuphilologische Zeitschrift. (Walther Fischer, "Die Amerikanistik im gegenwärtigen Universitätslehrplan und in den Prüfungsordnungen der deutschen Länder," III (1951), 412-417.)

Illustrierte Zeitung. Leipzig. (Friedrich Schönemann, "Was der Amerikaner liest," 1924, Nr. 4126; by the same author, "Köpfe der Literatur Amerikas von Heute," 1929, Nr. 4385.)

Zeitwende. München. (Gustav E. Müller, "Die amerikanische Intelligentsia," VI, 169-72 (August, 1930); Johannes Buschmann, "Amerika—das Tor zu neuen Wegen der Kultur?" VII, 154-172 (February, 1931); Gustav E. Müller, "Der 'neue Humanismus' in USA," VII, 250-257 (March, 1931); Hans Tietze, "Das amerikanische Kulturproblem," VIII, 181-189 (September, 1932); Ch. F. Weiser, "Amerikanische Hochschule und deutsche Bildung," VI, 481-498 (December, 1930).)

3. Newspapers consulted:

Berlin: *Berliner Tageblatt*
    Berliner Börsenzeitung
    Deutsche Allgemeine Zeitung
    Neue Preussische Zeitung
    Der Tag
    Tägliche Rundschau
    Vorwärts
    Vossische Zeitung
Bremen: *Bremer Nachrichten*
    Weser Zeitung
Frankfurt: *Frankfurter Zeitung*
Hamburg: *Hamburger Fremdenblatt*
Köln: *Kölnische Zeitung*
    Kölnische Volkszeitung
Munich: *Münchner Neueste Nachrichten*
Zürich: *Neue Zürcher Zeitung*

PART TWO: THE AMERICA LITERATURE OF THE BONN ERA

Angermann, Erich. "Die Vereinigten Staaten von Amerika," in *Weltgeschichte der Gegenwart* herausgegeben von Felix von Schroeder, Band I, *Die Staaten,* 358-405. Bern und München: Francke Verlag, 1962.

Auerbach, Alfred. *Ein Schwabe studiert Amerika.* Stuttgart: Behrendt-Verlag [1948].

Besser, Joachim. *Wofür zu leben lohnt. Ketzereien eines Europäers.* Düsseldorf, Wien: Econ Verlag, 1963.

Besson, Waldemar. *Von Roosevelt bis Kennedy. Grundzüge der amerikanischen Aussenpolitik, 1933-1963.* Frankfurt a. M.: Fischer Bücherei [c. 1964].

Boesch, Hans Heinrich. *Die Vereinigten Staaten von Amerika.* (Kleine K & F-Reihe für Auswanderer und Kaufleute, hrsggbn. in Verbindung mit dem Bundesamt für Industrie, Gewerbe und Arbeit, Sektion für Arbeitskraft und Auswanderung, 8.) Bern: Kümmerly & Frey [c. 1949].

Borch, Herbert von. *Die unfertige Gesellschaft; Amerika: Wirklichkeit und Utopie.* München: R. Piper [1960]; tr. Mary Ilford. *The Unfinished Society.* New York: Hawthorn Books, 1962.

Born, Franz. *So wurde Nord-Amerika; die Geschichte eines Kontinents.* Mit einem Beitrag von Walter Krickeberg. Berlin: Felguth Verlag, 1948.

Conant, James B., *et al. Zwei Völker im Gespräch; aus der Vortragsarbeit der Amerika-Häuser in Deutschland.* [Frankfurt am Main] Europäische Verlagsanstalt [1961].

Dahms, Hellmuth Günther. *Geschichte der Vereinigten Staaten von Amerika.* München: R. Oldenbourg, 1953.

——————. *Roosevelt und der Krieg; die Vorgeschichte von Pearl Harbor.* München: R. Oldenbourg [1958].

Dessauer, Friedrich. *Kontrapunkte eines Forscherlebens. Erinnerungen; amerikanische Reisebriefe.* Frankfurt am Main: Josef Knecht, 1962.

Ehmann, Wilhelm. *Alte Musik in der neuen Welt. Berichte und Gedanken über eine Konzertreise der Westfälischen Kantorei durch die USA.* Darmstadt: Tonkunst Verlag [1961].

Fraenkel, Ernst. *Amerika im Spiegel des deutschen politischen Denkens. Aeuserungen deutscher Staatsmänner und Staatsdenker über Staat und Gesellschaft in den Vereinigten Staaten von Amerika.* Köln und Opladen: Westdeutscher Verlag [c. 1959].

——————. *Das amerikanische Regierungssystem. Eine politologische Analyse.* Köln und Opladen: Westdeutscher Verlag, 1960.

Gleichen, Kurt von, ed. *Amis unter sich* [von] *Udo Bintz* [et al.]. Wiesbaden: Limes Verlag, 1952.

Gong, Alfred, ed. *Interview mit Amerika; 50 deutschsprachige Autoren in der neuen Welt.* [München] Nymphenburger Verlagshandlung [c. 1962].

Habe, Hans. *The Wounded Land. Journey Through a Divided America.* New York: Coward-MacCann, Inc. [c. 1964].

Hagelstange, Rudolf. *How do you like America? Impressionen eines Zaungastes.* München: R. Piper [c. 1957].

Hager, Carl Hermann. *Amerika ist noch nicht entdeckt.* 2. Aufl. Flensburg: Holsatia-Verlag [1957].

Hauser, Heinrich. *Meine Farm am Mississippi.* Berlin: Safari Verlag [c. 1950].

Herm, Gerhard. *Amerika erobert Europa.* Düsseldorf und Wien: Econ Verlag, 1964.

Hundhausen, Carl. *Amerika, 1950-1960, kontinentale Nation und Weltmacht.* Essen: Girardet, 1950.

Ingensand, Harald. *Amerikaner sind auch Menschen.* Stuttgart: Steingrüben Verlag [1956].

Jacobs, Rudolf. *Mit 4 Dollar nach USA .* Stuttgart: E. Rottacker [1947].

Jäckh, Ernst. *Amerika und wir, 1926-1951: amerikanisch-deutsches Ideen-Bündnis.* Stuttgart: Deutsche Verlags-anstalt [1951].

Jungk, Robert. *Die Zukunft hat schon begonnen; Amerikas Allmacht und Ohnmacht.* Stuttgart: Scherz & Govert [1952], tr. Marguerite Waldman. *Tomorrow is Already Here.* New York: Simon and Schuster, 1954.

Koeppen, Wolfgang. *Amerikafahrt.* 2. Aufl. Stuttgart: H. Goverts [c. 1959].

Korn, Karl. *Faust ging nach Amerika.* Olten und Freiburg i. Br.: Walter-Verlag [1958].

Kraus, Louise. *Zweimal erlebtes Amerika.* Luxembourg [Editions du Centre], 1956.

Leverkühn, Paul. *Geschichte der Vereinigten Staaten von Amerika.* Hamburg: C. Wegner, 1947.

Lohan, Robert. *Amerika, Du Hast es Besser. Die Vereinigten Staaten wie sie sind und wie sie geworden sind.* New York: Frederick Ungar [c. 1946].

Mann, Golo. *Vom Geist Amerikas; eine Einführung in amerikanisches Denken und Handeln im zwanzigsten Jahrhundert.* 2. Aufl. Stuttgart: Kohlhammer [1955].

Matthias, Leo L. *Die Entdeckung Amerikas Anno 1953; oder, Das geordnete Chaos.* Hamburg: Rowohlt [c. 1953].

Moltmann, Günter. *Amerikas Deutschlandpolitik im zweiten Weltkrieg (Beihefte zum Jahrbuch für Amerikastudien, III).* Heidelberg: Carl Winter Universitätsverlag, 1958.

Reinowski, Hans Johann. *Ein Mann aus Deutschland besucht Onkel Sam; Rückschau auf eine Amerikareise.* Darmstadt: F. Schneekluth [1958].

Rottenhäusler, Paul. *Amerika für Anfänger [Ein heiteres Reisebuch].* Zürich: Fritz & Wasmuth [c. 1952].

Sallet, Richard. *Die Vereinigten Staaten von Amerika: Land, Leute, Leben.* Darmstadt: C. Röhrig [1956].

Schaber, Will. *USA, Koloss im Wandel; ein Amerika-Bericht.* Darmstadt: C. W. Leske [1958].

Schoeck, Helmut. *USA; Motive und Strukturen.* Stuttgart: Deutsche Verlags-Anstalt [c. 1958].

Schütz, Edward. *Nordamerika; Eindrücke und Beobachtungen zweier Reisen.* Luzern: Offizielles Verkehrsbureau, 1953.

Thurn [-Valsassina], Max. *Amerika, hast du es wirklich besser. Mit 6 Zeichnungen von Ironismus.* [Wien] G. Prachner [1960].

Weber, Christian Egbert. *Wirtschaft und Gesellschaft in den Vereinigten Staaten von Amerika.* Berlin: Duncker & Humblot [1961].

Weichmann, Herbert. *Alltag in USA.* [Hamburg] E. Hausewedell [c. 1949].

Werner, Bruno Erich. *Kannst du Europa vergessen? Notizen von einer Amerikareise.* Stuttgart: Deutsche Verlags-Anstalt [1953].

Wollschläger, A. E. J. [Alfred E. Johann]. *Der grosse Traum Amerika. Sieben Reise in die USA, 1926 bis 1965.* Hamburg: Mosaik Verlag, 1965.

Zahn, Peter von. *Fremde Freunde; Bericht aus der neuen Welt.* [Hamburg] Hoffmann und Campe [c. 1953].

PART THREE: OTHER WORKS CITED

Beck, Earl R. *The Death of the Prussian Republic: a Study in Reich-Prussian Relations, 1932-1934* (Florida State University *Studies*, XXXI). Tallahassee: Florida State University, 1959.

Berg, Peter. *Deutschland und Amerika, 1918-1929. Über das deutsche Amerikabild der zwanziger Jahre (Historische Studien* herausgegeben von Wilhelm Berges *et al.*, Heft 385). Lübeck und Hamburg: Matthiesen Verlag, 1963.

Brogan, Denis W. *American Aspects.* New York: Harper & Row, 1964.

Bruckberger, Raymond L. *Image of America.* Tr. C. G. Paulding and Virgilia Peterson. New York: The Viking Press, 1959.

Burnham, James, ed. *What Europe Thinks of America.* New York: John Day Co. [1953].

Chester, Edward W. *Europe Views America: a Critical Evaluation.* Washington: Public Affairs Press [1962].

Cohen, Albert K. *Delinquent Boys: The Culture of the Gang.* Glencoe, Ill.: Free Press [1955].

Colby, Vineta, ed. *American Culture in the Sixties* (*The Reference Shelf*, Volume 36, No. 1). New York: the H. W. Wilson Company, 1964.

Cronon, Edmund David. *Black Moses. The story of Marcus Garvey and the Universal Negro Improvement Association.* Madison: the University of Wisconsin Press, 1955.

Dichter, Ernest. *The Strategy of Desire.* Garden City, New York: Doubleday, 1960.

Duffus, Robert L. *Nostalgia U.S.A.; or, If you don't like the 1960's, why don't you go back where you came from.* New York: Norton [1963].

Fiedler, Leslie A. *Waiting for the End.* New York: Stein and Day [1964].

Galbraith, John K. *The Affluent Society.* Boston: Houghton Mifflin, 1958.

Griffith, Thomas. *The Waist-High Culture.* New York: Harpers [c. 1959].

Henningsen, Jürgen. *Die neue Richtung in der Weimarer Zeit.* Stuttgart: E. Klett [c. 1960].

Huebener, Theodore. *The Schools of West Germany: a Study of German Elementary and Secondary Schools.* New York: New York University Press, 1962.

Joseph, Franz M. *As Others See Us. The United States Through Foreign Eyes.* Princeton, New Jersey: Princeton University Press, 1959.

Knoles, George Harmon. *The Jazz Age Revisited. British Criticism of American Civilization During the 1920's* (Stanford University Publications, University Series, History, Economics, and Political Science, Volume XI). Stanford, California: Stanford University Press [c. 1955].

Lambert, Richard D., ed. *America Through Foreign Eyes* (*The Annals of the American Academy of Political and Social Science*, CCXCV). Philadelphia: the American Academy . . . , 1954.

LaPiere, Richard. *The Freudian Ethic.* New York: Duell, Sloan and Pierce [c. 1959].

Lerner, Max. *America as a Civilization; Life and Thought in the United States Today.* New York: Simon and Schuster, 1957.

Lipton, Lawrence. *The Holy Barbarians.* New York: Julian Messner, Inc. [c. 1959].

Lobsenz, Norman M. *Is Anybody Happy? A Study of the American Search for Pleasure.* New York: Doubleday & Co., Inc., 1962.

Mannes, Marya. *More in Anger.* New York: Lippincott [c. 1958].

Marx, Leo. *The Machine in the Garden. Technology and the Pastoral Idea in America.* New York: Oxford University, 1964.

Miller, Henry. *The Air-Conditioned Nightmare*. [New York] New Directions [1945].

Mowrer, Edgar A. *This American World*. New York: J. H. Sears & Company, Inc. [c. 1928]; tr. Annemarie Horschitz, *Amerika, Vorbild und Warnung*. Berlin: E. Rowohlt [1928].

Paul, Eden and Cedar. *Mental Healers: Franz Anton Mesmer, Mary Baker Eddy, Sigmund Freud*. Garden City, New York: Garden City Publishers [c. 1932].

Riesman, David. *The Lonely Crowd: A Study of the Changing American Character*. New Haven: Yale University, 1950.

Samuel, R. H. and R. Hinton Thomas. *Education and Society in Modern Germany*. London: Routledge and K. Paul, 1949.

Skard, Sigmund. *The American Myth and the European Mind. American Studies in Europe, 1776-1960*. Philadelphia: The University of Pennsylvania Press [c. 1961].

——————. *American Studies in Europe. Their History and Present Organization*. 2 vols. Philadelphia: University of Pennsylvania Press [c. 1958].

Smith, Henry Nash. *Virgin Land: the American West as Symbol and Myth*. Cambridge, Mass.: Harvard University Press, 1950.

Totten, Christine M. *Deutschland—Soll und Haben, Amerikas Deutschlandbild*. München: Rütter & Loening Verlag, 1964.

Waters, Ethel. *His Eye is On the Sparrow*. Garden City, New York: Doubleday, 1951.

Wechsberg, Joseph. "Winnetou of Der Wild West," *Saturday Review*, XL, No. 42, 52, 60-61 (October 20, 1962). Also appeared in *The American West*, I, No. 3 (Summer, 1964), 32-39.

Wedge, Bryant M. *Visitors to the United States and How They See Us*. Princeton, New Jersey: Van Nostrand [1965].

Whittick, Arnold, *Eric Mendelsohn*. New York: F. W. Dodge, 1956.

Whyte, William H. *The Organization Man*. New York: Simon and Schuster, 1956.

Wiener, Norbert. *The Human Use of Human Beings; Cybernetics and Society*. New York: Doubleday [1954].

Williams, Francis. *The American Invasion*. [London] A. Blond [1962].

Wylie, Philip. *Generation of Vipers*. New York: Farrar [c. 1942].

LIST OF GERMAN AMERICANISTS AND OTHER COMMENTATORS MENTIONED IN THE TEXT

Abel, Othenio (1875-1946)—paleontologist and paleobiologist; Universities of Göttingen and Vienna.

Aeroboe, Friedrich (1865-1946)—economist, Universities of Breslau and Berlin; rector, University of Berlin.

Angermann, Adolar—identification uncertain; a Pastor Angermann was head of Evangelical Church archives in Merseburg.

*Angermann, Erich (1927-   )—Professor of English and American Studies and History, Munich, Cologne.

*Auerbach, Alfred (1873-   )—actor, publicist, drama teacher in Dr. Hoch's conservatory, Frankfurt a. M.

Barthelme, Georg—German newspaperman interned in the United States during World War I.

Baum, Marie (1874-   )—member of German National Assembly and Reichstag; instructor at University of Heidelberg; expert on family welfare matters.

Baumann, Carl A. (1888-   )—secondary school teacher with special interests in medieval history and pedagogy; lived in Braunschweig.

Baumann, E. C. Felix (1868- ?)—German-American journalist and writer; sensationalist accounts of the seamy side of life in the United States.

Beckmann, Emmy (1880-   )—teacher and school supervisor; wrote on women's affairs.

Behn, Fritz (1878-   )—professor of sculpture; art academies at Munich and Vienna; extensive travel.

Behrendt, Walter C. (1884-   )—adviser in the Ministry of Public Welfare in Berlin; interested in city planning, architecture, building arts.

Bernstorff, Johann Heinrich (1862-1939)—wartime ambassador to the United States; later member of the Reichstag.

*Besser, Joachim (1913-   )—journalist; chief reporter, *Die Welt*; later chief editor, *Kölner Stadt-Anzeiger*.

Bloch, Chajim (1881-   )—Viennese writer on Jewish theological and religious subjects.

Böhler, Eugene (1893-   )—professor of economics and finance at the technical university in Zürich.

*Boesch, Hans Heinrich (1911-   )—professor of geography at University of Zürich; chairman of geographical institute.

*Indicates post World War II commentator

311

Bonn, Moritz J. (1873-   )—professor of economics, commercial colleges in Munich and Berlin (later Rektor in latter), also University of California, Institute of Politics, Williamstown, Massachusetts, London School of Economics.

*Borch, Herbert von (1909-   )—journalist; foreign feature columnist of *Frankfurter Allgemeine Zeitung*; Washington correspondent of *Die Welt*.

Borchardt, Julian (1868-1932)—writer and translator interested in history, politics, public economy.

*Born, Franz (1912-   )—writer and editorial director with Felguth Verlag in Berlin.

Bornhausen, Karl E. (1882-1940)—professor of theology with special reference to America; Universities of Marburg and Breslau.

Bratter, Carl Adolf (1861-   )—journalist; editor of New York *Staatszeitung*, 1885-1901; later editor with Ullstein Publishing House in Berlin.

Bremer, A.—unidentified.

Brinkmann, Carl (1885-1954)—professor of political science, Heidelberg, Berlin, Tübingen; writings in fields of history, economics, and sociology as well as political science.

Büchler, Edward—Swiss student.

Bühler, A. J.—unidentified.

Buschmann, Johannes—unidentified.

Carlé, Erwin (1876-1923)—free-lance writer; pseudonym, Erwin Rosen.

Christoph, Hans—engineer.

Cohnstaedt, Wilhelm (1880-   )—editor of *Frankfurter Zeitung*; member of directorate of German Democratic Party.

Conrad, Otto (1880-   )—free-lance writer; for a short time student adviser in Berlin; interested in religion, psychology, ethics.

Cramer, Hugo (1892-1961)—teacher and principal of a German high school (*Mittelschulrektor*) in Niedersfeld über Bestwig.

Daenell, Ernst Robert (1876-1921)—professor of history, Chicago, Columbia, Leipzig, Kiel, Münster.

*Dahms, Hellmuth Günther (1918-   )—historian; teacher in upper school, Bebenhausen bei Tübingen; earlier journalist and editorial activities.

Damus, Walter—educator (city school director and chairman of West Prussian history union??).

Darmstädter, Paul (1873-1934)—professor, history and foreign studies, Göttingen.

Descovich, Emo—engineer.

Dessauer, Friedrich (1881-1963)—highly respected professor of experimental physics, Freiburg and Frankfurt.

Deutsch, Felix (1858-1928)—director of German General Electric Corporation.

Devaranne, Theodor—pastor of Evangelical Church who served as "missions inspector" (public relations agent for foreign missions).

Dibelius, Otto (1880-1967)—German Evangelical Church supervisor, later Bishop of Berlin.

Dietrich, Bruno (1886-1946)—professor of economic geography at Commercial College (*Hochschule für Welthandel*) in Vienna.

Dorfmann, Jakob—unidentified.

Dorner, Otto—teacher at Essen.

Dovifat, Emil (1890-   )—professor of journalism at University of Berlin.

Draim, Joseph—unidentified.

Eberhardt, Fritz—educator.

*Ehmann, Wilhelm (1905-   )—director, Westphalian state school for church music.

Eichler, P.—unidentified.

Elven, F. W.—journalist; American correspondent for *Münchener Neueste Nachrichten.*

Erkelenz, Anton (1878-1945)—newspaper editor and chairman of German Democratic Party, 1921-1930.

Escher, Hermann (1857-1938)—director of central library (*Zentralbibiolthek*) in Zürich.

Eulenberg, Herbert (1876-1949)—free-lance writer and dramatist.

Ey, Karl—see Meyer, Karl H.

Faber, Kurt (1883-1929)—traveler, publicist, correspondent of *Berliner Lokalanzeiger.*

Fackler, Hermann—unidentified.

Faldix, Arno Guido (1882-   )—chairman of the economic office and docent of academic course in Düsseldorf.

Feiler, Arthur (1879-1942)—leading economic editor, *Frankfurter Zeitung*, 1913-1931. Instructor, later professor, economics, Frankfurt, Königsberg, New School for Social Research, New York City.

Feuchtinger, ...?   —former city manager, Ulm.

Fischer, Walther (1889-1961)—professor of English philology, Giessen, Marburg.

Forcke, Alfred (1867-1944)—professor, Chinese language and culture, Hamburg.

*Fraenkel, Ernst (1898-   )—professor, political science, Berlin.

Francé-Harrar, Annie (1886-   )—professor of physical biology (*Bodenbiologie*) and free-lance writer; wife of Rudolf Francé.

Francé (originally Franzé), Rudolf (Raoul) Heinrich (1874-1943)—professor of biology, director of biological institute of the German micrological society in Munich; free-lance writer seeking to link biology and *Weltanschauung.*

Francke, Kuno (1855-1930)—professor, cultural history, and curator of Germanic Museum, Harvard University.

Frenssen, Gustav (1863-1945)—Lutheran pastor turned free-lance writer, poet.

Frick, Heinrich (1893-1952)—professor of systematic theology and director of Museum of Religion, University of Marburg.

Friederici, Georg C. E. (1866-1947)—military attaché in Washington (1894-1895), who later studied and became expert free-lance writer in fields of anthropology, geography, and history.

Friedrich, J.—German university student.

Gagern, Friedrich Heinrich von (1882-1947)—free-lance writer specializing in stories of hunting and adventure.

Gans, Oscar (1888-   )—medical doctor and professor, Frankfurt am Main.

Gaulke, Johannes (1869-193?)—free-lance writer and critic.

Giehrl, Hermann von—unidentified.

Giese, Wilhelm Oskar *Fritz* (1890-1935)—professor, psychology, Halle and Technical University at Stuttgart; founder of "psychotechnical laboratory."

Glaser, Curt (1879-   )—professor of art and custodian of State Museum of Art, Berlin.

*Gleichen, Kurt von—journalist.

Gley, Werner (1902-   )—instructor, Frankfurt, cultural geography, the development of cities.

Goebel, Otto H. (1872-1955)—professor, national economics, Technical University in Hannover.

Goldberger, Ludwig Max (1848-1913)—banker and economist; member of Prussian and Reich economic councils for preparation of commercial policies.

Goldschmidt, Alfons (1879-   )—professor, political science, Berlin.

Goldschmidt, Bernhard (1884-   )—director, Commercial bank in Hamburg, Th. Goldschmidt A. G. in Essen.

*Gong, Alfred (1920-   )—lyricist, in United States since 1951.

Gontard, Paul C. v.—identification uncertain—general director of German Weapons and Munitions factory??

Goslar, Hans—government inspector (Regierungsinspektor), Prussian State Ministry.

Gottl-Ottlilienfeld, Friedrich von (1868-1958)—professor of economics and business management; director of Political Science-Statistical Seminar, Berlin.

Grosz, George (1893-1959)—painter and artist.

Grünbaum, Fritz—medical doctor.

Günther, A. E. [Alfred? (1885-   )—writer and editor, *Dresdner Neueste Nachrichten;* chief editor, Reclam Publishing Company, Leipzig].

Gurian, Waldemar (1902-1954)—sociologist, historian, political scientist; editor *Kölnische Volkszeitung,* 1923-4; free-lance writer; professor, politics, Notre Dame, 1937-54.

Gurlitt, Hildebrand (1895-   )—professor of architecture, Technical University of Dresden; director of art museum, Hamburg.

Haebler, Konrad (1857-1946)—director of State Library in Berlin; historian.

*Hagelstange, Rudolf (1912-   )—writer, poet; holder of several literary prizes.

*Hager, Carl Hermann (1890-   )—head of union of retail businesses, Hamburg.

Halfeld, Adolf Friedrich (1898-   )—political scientist and journalist; later on editorial staff of *Hamburger Fremdenblatt.*

Harten-Hoencke, Toni (1872- ?)—first Mrs. Schönemann; also novelist, lyricist, essayist.

Hartmann, Georg (1865- ?)—specialist on colonial problems, geography, social questions; former administrative officer of South-West Africa Company.

Hassert, Kurt (1868-1947)—professor of geography, Technical University of Dresden; extensive travels.

Hauser, Heinrich (1901-1955)—doctor who became free-lance writer, settled in Chicago, then in Mississippi; returned to Germany after World War II.

Hausmann, Manfred (1898-   )—free-lance writer (best-seller class); editor of *Weser Zeitung* (post World War II, *Weser Kurier*).

Hawk, C. B.—pseudonym; unidentified.

Hedin, Alma (1876- ?)—sister of famous explorer, Sven Hedin; interested in social welfare matters.

Hegemann, Werner (1881-)—architect; publisher of periodical on city building.

Heinecken, Otto (1868-193?)—teacher and free-lance writer from Hamburg.

Heinig, Kurt (1886-)—journalist; until 1933 on editorial staff of *Vorwärts*; member of Reichstag.

Heise, Carl G. (1890-)—art historian; director of museum at Lübeck; art adviser for *Frankfurter Zeitung*; after World War II director of art gallery in Hamburg.

Hellmann, Siegmund (1872-1942)—professor of medieval history, Leipzig.

Hengesbosch, Josef—unidentified.

Hensel, Rudolf—unidentified.

Hepner, Adolf—unidentified.

*Herm, Gerhard (1931-)—journalist, editor, dramatist (radio plays).

Herz, Ernst (1900-)—medical doctor, professor of psychiatry and neurology, Frankfurt, Columbia, Yeshiva.

Hilberseimer, Ludwig—unidentified.

Hirsch, Julius (1882-1961)—former State Secretary in Reich Economic Ministry; after 1933, Professor and Director of Business Administration Center, New School for Social Research, New York City.

Hitler, Adolf (1889-1945)—the Nazi *Führer* never visited the United States, but his "second book" is almost an "America book"!

Holitscher, Arthur (1869-1939)—free-lance writer; world traveler.

Hollweg, Carl (1867-1932)—vice-admiral; director of naval academy; battleship commander, writer on naval matters.

Hoppé, Emil Otto—photographer.

Huldschiner, Gottfried—electrical engineer.

*Hundhausen, Carl (1878-)—businessman and temporary, later honorary, professor of advertising and public relations at Technical University in Aachen.

Hylla, Erich (1887-)—professor of international pedagogy, Frankfurt a. M., Columbia, Halle.

*Ingensand, Harald—journalist, Frankfurt a. M.

Jacobi, Marie (1906-)—schoolmistress in advanced school for girls (*Frauenoberschule der Ursulinen*) in Carlowitz near Dresden; after World War II member of Bundestag.

*Jacobs, Rudolf (1913-)—novelist, essayist, writer of travel books, Hamburg.

Jäckh, Ernst (1875-1959)—professor, German and Romance languages, philosophy of history, economics, oriental studies; President of German University for Politics (*Hochschule für Politik*), Berlin; to United States after Hitler; Columbia University—political science.

Johann, Alfred E.—see Wollschläger, A. E. J.

*Jungk, Robert (1913-)—journalist and publicist; foreign correspondent of Swiss newspapers in London, Paris, Washington; naturalized American citizen but "home" appears to be Vienna.

Jungmann, Erich—medical doctor.

Kaergel, Hans Christoph (1889-1946)—free-lance writer; leader of Saxon dramatic league.

Kalkschmidt, Eugen (1874-)—free-lance writer, especially on city growth.

Karlweis, Marta—see Wassermann, Marta.

Kauder, G.—theater critic.

Keller, Adolf (1872-   )—Swiss preacher and theology professor, Zürich.

Kende, Oscar (1881-1945)—professor, geography, Advanced Federal Technical School (*Bundesoberrealschule*), Vienna.

Kerr, Alfred (1867-1948)—free-lance writer and poet after studies in Germanic language, philosophy, history.

Key, Helmer (1864-1939)—Swedish traveler, writer, representative of *Svenske Dagbladet*.

Keyserling, Graf Hermann (1880-1946)—philosopher; director of "School of Wisdom" in Darmstadt.

Kienböck, Victor (1873-1956)—Austrian Minister of Finance and President of Austrian National Bank.

Kimpen, Emil (1880-   )—historian and private teacher, Godesberg.

Kindermann, Rudolf (1897-1933)—journalist and school official, Vienna.

Kircheiss, Carl Theodor (1887-1953)—naval officer, world traveler, writer; most famous exploit sailing around world on fish cutter "Hamburg," 1926-7.

Kisch, Egon Erwin (1885-1948)—free-lance writer; novelist; light essays on historical and adventurous themes.

Kleinschmitt, Edmund (1897-   )—free-lance writer, specialty economics.

Knapp, Paul—leader of youth group of Evangelical church in Königsberg.

Koellreutter, Otto (1883-   )—expert on constitutional law, Jena, Munich.

*Koeppen, Wolfgang (1906-   )—writer specializing in travel literature.

Köttgen, Carl Arn (1871-   )—engineer and managing director with Siemens-Schuckert works in Berlin; vice-chairman of the *Reichskuratorium für Wirtschaftlichkeit*, a government agency promoting business and industry.

Kolfhaus, W.—pastor in Vlotho.

Kollbrunner, Oscar-Swiss writer, adventurer.

*Korn, Karl (1908-   )—journalist; publisher and editor of cultural and literary sections of *Frankfurter Allgemeine Zeitung*.

*Kraus, Louise—writer from Luxembourg.

Krüger, Fritz-Konrad (1889-   )—professor, American studies, Hamburg.

Kühne, Georg (1880-1941)—engineer; professor at Technical University in Munich.

Kühnelt, Richard (1877-1930)—Viennese writer and translator.

Kühnemann, Eugen (1868-1950)—professor, philosophy and German language.

Küppersbosch, Marta—expert on prohibition.

Kuh, Georg—unidentified.

Kunwald, Ernst (1868-1939)—director of Berlin Philharmonic Orchestra and of symphony orchestras elsewhere, including Königsberg and Cincinnati, 1912-1917 (accused of engaging in enemy propaganda there).

Lagerlöf, V.—veterinary doctor.

Lang, Paul (1894-   )—professor, German, English, history, Cantonal Commercial High School, Zürich.

Langen, Julie—unidentified.

Langewiesche, Wolfgang (1907-   )—a work-student in America; sociology; later journalist with *Kölnische Zeitung*; turned from academic pursuits to small plane flying, became free-lance writer on aeronautics and research pilot for Kollsman Aircraft Instruments—series of books on private piloting.

Lassen, John—pseudonym; unidentified.

Laurent, Vivi—Swedish maid.

Lehmann, Reinhold—school teacher.

Leitich, Ann Tizia (1897-   )—Viennese novelist and essayist; correspondent for newspapers in United States.

Lembke, Friedrich (1869-195?)—professor, economics and welfare, Berlin.

Lenel, Otto (1849-1935)—professor of Roman and German civil law, Kiel, Marburg, Strassburg, Freiburg.

Lerchenfeld-Köfering, Hugo, Graf von und zu (1871-1944)— Bavarian Minister-President, 1921-2; German ambassador in Vienna and Brussels.

Lettenbauer, J. A. (-d. 1935)—German consul-general in New York, Chicago, Cape Colony, Batavia.

*Leverkühn, Paul (1893-195?)—lawyer, historian.

Lewisohn, Ludwig (1883-1955)—German-American novelist.

Leyen, Friedrich von der (1873-   )—professor, philology, Munich, Cologne, Yale, Harvard, Stanford.

Liefmann, W. Robert (1874-   )—professor, economics and finance, Giessen, Freiburg.

Lietzmann, Walter (1880-1959)—professor, mathematics and natural science, Göttingen.

Linn, Fritz—unidentified.

Litz, ? —engineer.

Löbe, Paul (1875-   )—publisher, vice president of Weimar National Assembly; president of Reichstag, 1920-1932.

*Lohan, Robert C.—unidentified.

Lorenz, Albert—identification uncertain, possibly (1885-   )—Austrian medical doctor specializing in orthopedics.

Lothar, C. L. (1864- ?)—sea-captain and free-lance writer and journalist with Berliner Tageblatt; pseudonym, "Persius."

Luckner, Graf Felix von (1881-1966)—sea-captain, explorer, adventurer; retained honorary citizenship of several American cities in spite of Nazi condemnation.

Luckwaldt, Friedrich K. (1875-   )—professor, modern history, Technical University in Danzig.

Ludwig, G.—unidentified.

Lütkens, Charlotte (1896-   )—international secretary, Social Democratic Party, 1920-2; foreign correspondent, Frankfurter Zeitung; instructor in sociology, London, 1937-1950; husband a career diplomat.

Lufft, Hermann (1880-   )—writer, specialty, economics; overseas correspondent for a number of newspapers; in the United States, 1914-1924.

Manes, Alfred (1877-   )—professor, insurance science, commercial college at Frankfurt a. M.

*Mann, Golo (1909-   )—professor, history, Claremont College, Münster, Westphalia, Stuttgart; son of Thomas Mann.

Mann, Klaus (1906-1949)—editor, free-lance writer, American reporter, brother of Golo Mann.

*Matthias, Leo L. (1893-   )—writer; travel literature.

Medinger, Wilhelm (1878-1934)—leader of German Society of Arts and Sciences in Czechoslovakia; member of Czech *Senat.*

Mendelsohn, Erich (1887-1953)—one of most famous of modern German architects.

Merleker, Hartmuth (1894-   )—journalist and editor, Ullstein Publishing House; chief editor, *BZ am Mittag;* post-World War II with *Die Zeit,* Hamburg.

Meyer, Eduard (1855-1930)—professor, ancient history, Leipzig, Halle, Berlin, Harvard.

Meyer, Gustav Wilhelm—unidentified.

Meyer, Karl H. (1892-1956)—free-lance writer, adventurer, translator; pseudonym, Karl Ey.

Monsky, Max—member of Austrian mission to United States, 1925.

Montgelas, Albrecht, Graf (1887-1958)—journalist, San Francisco *Examiner,* Chicago *Examiner,* Berlin *Vossische Zeitung;* free-lance writing.

Moog, Otto—engineer; manager *(Betriebsleiter)* of German machine works.

Müller, Alfred—director of a cement plant.

Müller, Emil (1889-   )—writer; political scientist; Vienna; pseudonym, Emil Müller-Sturmheim.

Müller, Friedrich (1891-   )—medical doctor and professor of internal medicine, Hamburg, Columbia University.

Müller, Heinrich (1887-   )—engineer and economist; writer dealing with economic matters, Offenbach a. M.

Müller, Robert—associated with academy of sculpturing arts in Dresden.

Müller, Wilhelm (1845- ?)—German-American writer; former school superintendent; extensive publications on United States published in Germany.

Müller-Freienfels, Richard (1882-1948)—psychologist, psychiatrist; instructor, Berlin Commercial College; after World War II at Humboldt University and Teachers' Institute in Weilburg.

Müller-Sturmheim, Emil—see Müller, Emil.

Münsterberg, Hugo (1863-1916)—German-American professor, psychology, Freiburg, Harvard; active in field of German-American relations.

Mund, Arthur—unidentified.

Naphthali, Fritz (1888-   )—journalist with specialty in economics and trade matters, Berlin *Morgenpost, Vossische Zeitung, Frankfurter Zeitung;* research center for economics and politics founded 1926.

Neubauer, Alfred (1891-   )—director, Daimler-Benz corporation, Stuttgart.

Neuhaus, F.—unidentified.

Neumann, Erwin—professor, engineering, Technical University of Braunschweig.

Neutra, Richard J. (1892-   )—German-American architect; disciple of Frank Lloyd Wright.

Oberhauser, Franz Fritz (1894-193?)—writer of short stories and sketches; correspondent for Dutch newspapers.

Oehlke, Waldemar (1879-1949)—professor, German literature, Peking, Tokyo, Cornell, Göttingen.

Oeri, Albert (1875-1950)—Swiss journalist; editor of *Basler Nachrichten;* member of Nationalrat.

Oestreich, Paul (1878-1959)—secondary schoolmaster in Berlin; founded League of Radical School Reformers, edited *Die neue Erziehung.*

Omaha, Jack—pseudonym; unidentified.

Oncken, Hermann (1869-1945)—professor, history, Berlin, Chicago, Giessen, Heidelberg, Munich.

Oppel, Siegfried von—unidentified.

Otto, Heinz—see Heinecken, Otto.

Overmans, Jakob (1874-1945)—priest, professor of theology, Tokyo, Frankfurt a. M.; editor *Stimmen der Zeit.*

Paquet, Alfons (1881-1944)—traveler, free-lance writer; poet. Leader of German Quakerism.

Penck, Albrecht (1858-1945)—professor, geography, Munich, Vienna, Berlin (Director of Institute for Oceanography and Geographical Institute), Yale, Columbia.

Persius—see Lothar, C. L.

Pfannmüller, Donatus (1873-193?)—Franciscan brother, Fulda; writer of short stories, religious novels, travel books.

Pfeffer, A.—editor of Münchener *Allgemeine Rundschau.*

Pfyffer von Altishofen, Siegfried—member of Swiss "Mission" to United States, 1920.

Pollak, Heinrich—unidentified.

Ponten, Josef (1883-1940)—free-lance writer, poet, traveler, Munich.

Prosinagg, Ernst (1886-   )—Austrian writer, governmental official.

Quidde, Ludwig (1858-1941)—historian, statesman; member of Bavarian Landtag, Weimar National Assembly; active pacifist, holder of Nobel Peace Prize, 1928.

Rading, Adolf—unidentified; Breslau.

Reichwein, Adolf—principal, *Volkshochschule,* Jena?

Rein, Gustav Adolf (1885-   )—professor, historian, Hamburg; *Rektor* of University, 1934.

*Reinowski, Hans Joachim (1900-   )—publisher and chief editor, *Darmstädter Echo.*

Richter, Julius (1862-1940)—professor of "mission science," Berlin.

Richter, Kurt—Youth Welfare Minister, Prussia.

Riebensahm, Paul (1890-   )—engineer; professor, technical aspects of handling materials in machine works, Technical University of Berlin.

Roda Roda—see Rosenfeld, Sandor Friedrich

Rohrbach, Paul (1869-1956)—writer specializing in theological and colonial questions; 1903-6, imperial commissioner for settlement work in South-West Africa.

Rosen, Erwin—see Carlé, Erwin.

Rosenfeld, Sandor Friedrich (1872-1945)—officer in Austro-Hungarian army, turned free-lance writer, dramatist; short stories in *Simplicissimus* and *Die Jugend*; satire; pseudonym, Roda Roda.

Ross, Colin (1885-1946)—world traveler; free-lance writer and journalist; lengthy list of travel accounts.

*Rothenhäusler, Paul—unidentified Swiss writer.

Rühle, E.—electrical engineer, Berlin.

Rukser, Udo—unidentified.

Rundt, Arthur (1881-)—writer, journalist with *Berliner Börsen-Courier, Neue Freie Presse, Prager Tageblatt, Basler National Zeitung.*

Sachs, Willy—Royal Swedish Consul, partner in firm of Fichtel & Sachs, Schweinfurt.

*Sallet, Richard (1900-)—unidentified.

Salomon, Alice (1872-1948)—feminist; founder of Woman's School for sociology (*Soziale Frauenschule*) and of Academy for Woman's Social and Pedagogical Work (*Akademie für Sozialistische und Pädagogische Frauenarbeit*); vice-president of Woman's International Union.

Salten, Felix (1869-1945)—Austrian writer and dramatist best known for "Bambi" stories.

Salz, Arthur (1881-)—professor, national economics, Heidelberg, later Ohio State University.

Salzmann, Erich von (1876-)—writer; representative of Ullstein Verlag; specialty, travel and politics.

Sasse, Hermann (1895-)—professor, theology and church history, Erlangen.

*Schaber, Will (1905-)—writer, journalist; since 1941, division head of British Information Services in New York.

Schäfer, Dietrich (1845-1929)—professor, medieval, German, and colonial history, Jena, Breslau, Tübingen, Heidelberg, Berlin.

Scheffauer, Hermann Georg (1878-1927)—American-born writer, journalist, resident in Germany after World War I.

Scheibe, Arnold—unidentified.

Scheller-Steinwartz, Robert R. von (1865-1921)—diplomat; service in embassies in London, Washington, Bucharest, Christiania.

Scher, Peter (1884-1956)—writer; specialty, humor; editor with *Simplicissimus.*

Schlosser, M. E.—member of academy of science, Munich.

Schmidt, Annalise—writer; subjects America, Bolshevism, young children.

Schneider, Carl (1900-)—professor, religion and cultural history, Wittenberg, Herder Institute in Riga, Leipzig.

Schoch, Alfred D.—unidentified.

Schoch, Magdeline—university teacher, Hamburg, law.

*Schoeck, Helmut (1922-)—Austrian-born, German educated professor, sociology, Fairmount State College, Emory.

Schönemann, Friedrich (1886-1956)—professor, American studies, Wesleyan, Harvard, Giessen, Berlin.

Schotthöfer, Fritz—unidentified.

Schüler, Edmund—unidentified.

Schulthess, Louis—unidentified.

Schulz, Paul—teacher, otherwise unidentified.

Schulze, Alfred (1861-1949)—director, university library, Marburg; philologist.

Schulze-Gaevernitz, Gerhart von (1864-1943)—professor, political economy, Freiburg i. Br.

Schürch, Ernst (1875-1961?)—city official, Berne, Switzerland; chief editor of Swiss newspaper.

*Schütz, Edward (1902-)—director of city tourist office, Lucerne, Switzerland; publicist.

Schwarz, G. Sebald (1866-1934)—school teacher and administrator, Dortmund, Lübeck.

Sender, Tony (1888-1964)—writer; Socialist member of Reichstag; after World War II representative of American Federation of Labor to Economic and Social Council of United Nations.

Siemsen, August (1884-)—"young German worker."

Skal, Georg von (1854- ?)—writer; publisher of *Trans-Atlantische Korrespondenz*; editorial staff of New York *Staatszeitung*; foreign correspondent of *Hamburger Fremdenblatt*; author of one of better pre-World War I studies on United States.

Sollmann, Wilhelm (1881-1951)—editor; Social Democratic member of Reichstag; Reich Minister of Interior.

Sommer, Oskar (1903-)—businessman; directorate for railroads.

Sonnenschein, Adolf (1886-)—governmental official, Prussian State Ministry; regional president (*Regierungs-präsident*), Osnabrück.

Souchy, Augustin—syndicalist writer.

Spiegel, Käthe—specialist in cultural history.

Spoerri, William T.—Swiss scholar.

Spohr, Karl—Monsignor; from 1923-1929, Rektor of Leo House and Secretary of Raphael-Verein in New York, an agency for German immigrants.

Steiner, Lajos—unidentified writer, Berlin.

Steinweg, Carl (1860- ?)—gymnasial professor, literature and art, Erfurt.

Stolper, Ernst—work student.

Stranik, Erwin F. (1898-)—Viennese writer, political theory, art criticism, travel; Austrian correspondent of *Berliner Tageblatt* and *Berliner Volkszeitung*.

Swarzenski, Georg (1876-)—professor of art history, director of city art institute, Frankfurt a. M.

Tänzler, Fritz (1869- ?)—lawyer, business-manager of Union of German Employers; writer on subjects of labor-management relations.

*Thurn [-Valsossina], Max (1910-)—former Austrian Minister of Finance and member of Board of Directors, World Bank, Washington, 1956-1959.

Timpe, Anton Aloys (1882-1959)—professor, mathematics, Technical University, Berlin.

Tischert, Hans (1904-)—writer, journalist; specialty, travel, industry, economics; after World War II, chief editor *Europa Pressedienst, Motor Echo, Kraftverkehr und Werkschaft*.

Toller, Ernst H. (1893-1939)—writer, dramatist; active in Bavarian Socialist Revolution after World War I.

Tönnies, Ferdinand (1855-1936)—professor, national economics and statistics, Kiel; also works in sociology, politics.

Tyrnauer, Alfred R. (1897-1958?)—journalist; associate foreign editor, International News Service; American correspondent of Ullstein News Service, *Vossische Zeitung, Neue Freie Presse*.

Untermann, E.—unidentified.

Velsen, Dorothee V. (1883-)—writer; chiefly biography and politics.

Venzmer, Gerhard (1893-)—medical doctor and writer; work with I. G. Farben, Kosmos Publishing company; travel, health books.

Vershofen, Wilhelm (1878-1960)—professor, economics, Commercial Colleges in Nuremberg and Erlangen.

Voegelin, Erich (1901-   )—professor, political science, history, philosophy, Vienna, Louisiana State, Munich.

Voss, Hermann (1884-   )—art historian; custodian of state museum in Berlin, later museums in Wiesbaden and Dresden.

Vossler, Otto (1902-   )—professor, historian, Leipzig, Frankfurt a. M.

Wagner, Siegfried (1869-1930)—son of composer; manager for *Bayreuther Festspiele*; himself director and composer.

Waldschmidt, Walter—judicial counselor in Berlin.

Wallfisch-Roulin, Paul (1881-   )—writer on business management, public speaking, reading techniques; translator.

Walther, Andreas (1879-1960)—professor, sociology, Göttingen, Hamburg.

Wassermann, Marta (1889-1965)—writer; first wife of Austrian poet, Jakob Wasserman; also psychoanalyst.

*Weber, Christian Egbert—economist at Munich; long residence in United States.

*Weichmann, Herbert (1896-   )—Prussian Minister of State during Weimar period; 1933-1948, outside of Germany; 1942-1948 in United States; 1948, returned to become President of Court of Accounts, later finance senator in Hamburg.

Weiser, Franz Xavier (1901-   )—Viennese Catholic priest; writer of youth literature, history, biography, travel.

Welsel, Albrecht—one-time police chief.

Werdermann, Hermann (1888-1954)—professor, theology, Hannover Pedagogical Academy, Eden Seminary in St. Louis.

*Werner, Bruno Erich (1896-   )—novelist, travel writer; literary editor with *Die Neue Zeitung* in Munich; president of German literary (P.E.N.) center; cultural attaché in Washington.

Werner, Josef—unidentified.

Westermann, Franz—engineer.

Winckler, Ferdinand Oskar von—unidentified.

Winkler, Magda—unidentified.

Witte, Irene M. (1894-   )—writer and translator; specialty, industry and industrial organization.

Wohltat, Helmuth—Ministerial Director in Reich and Prussian Economics Ministries; significant career in World War II.

Wollschläger, A. E. J. (1901-   )—writer, journalist, editor, Ullstein Publishing House in Berlin; travel literature; pseudonym, A. E. Johann.

Wynekin, L.—"cook"

*Zahn, Peter von (1913-   )—television and radio producer; columnist for *Die Welt* Hamburg; American correspondent of Northwest German Radio.

Zbinden, Hans (1893-   )—professor, cultural sociology and criticism, Berne, Wisconsin.

Zucker, Paul (1889-   )—professor, architecture, art history, Lessinghochschule, Berlin; New School for Social Research, New York City.

Zurbruchen, Rosa—unidentified Swiss writer.

INDEX

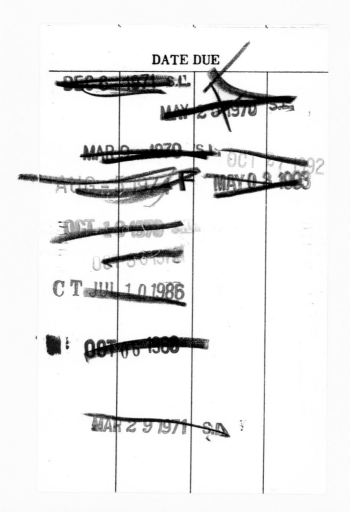